PandoraHearts

Mochizuki

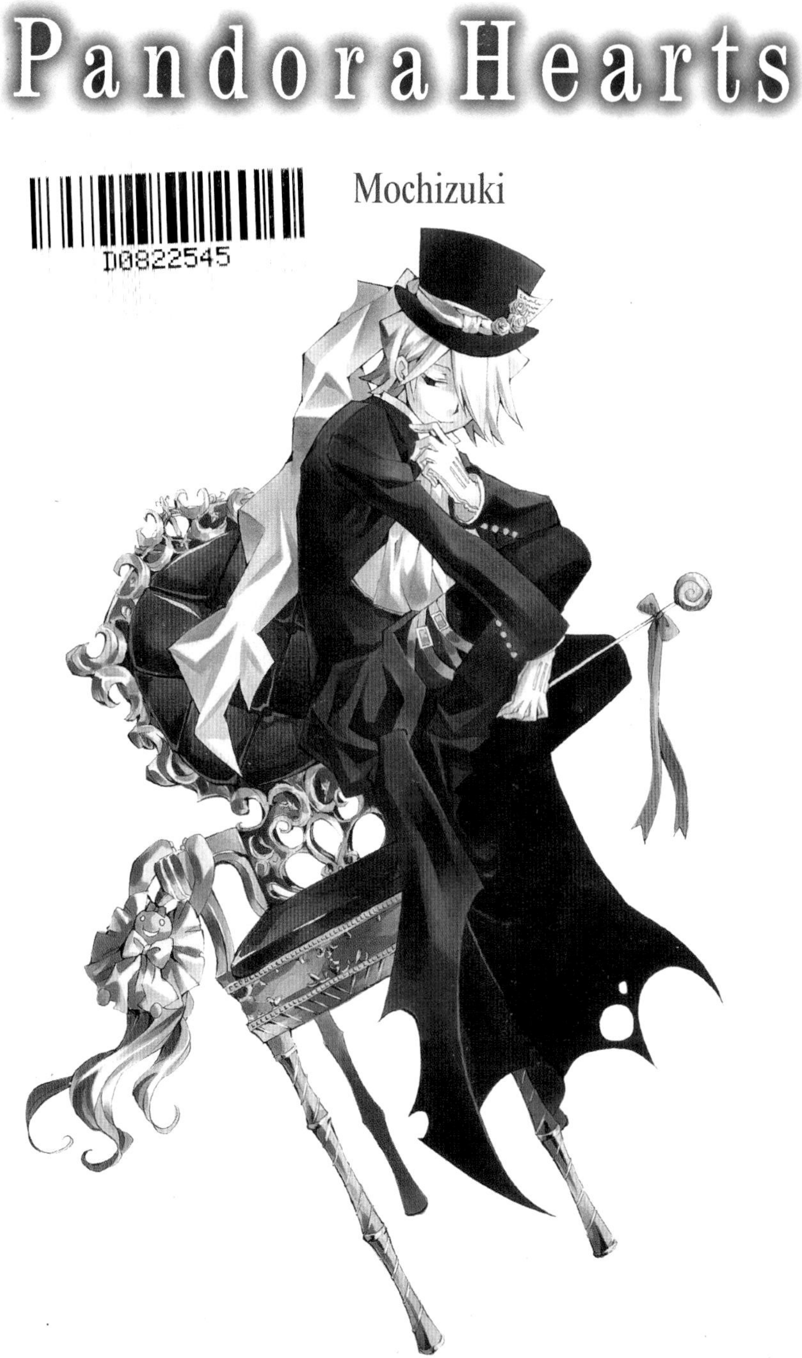

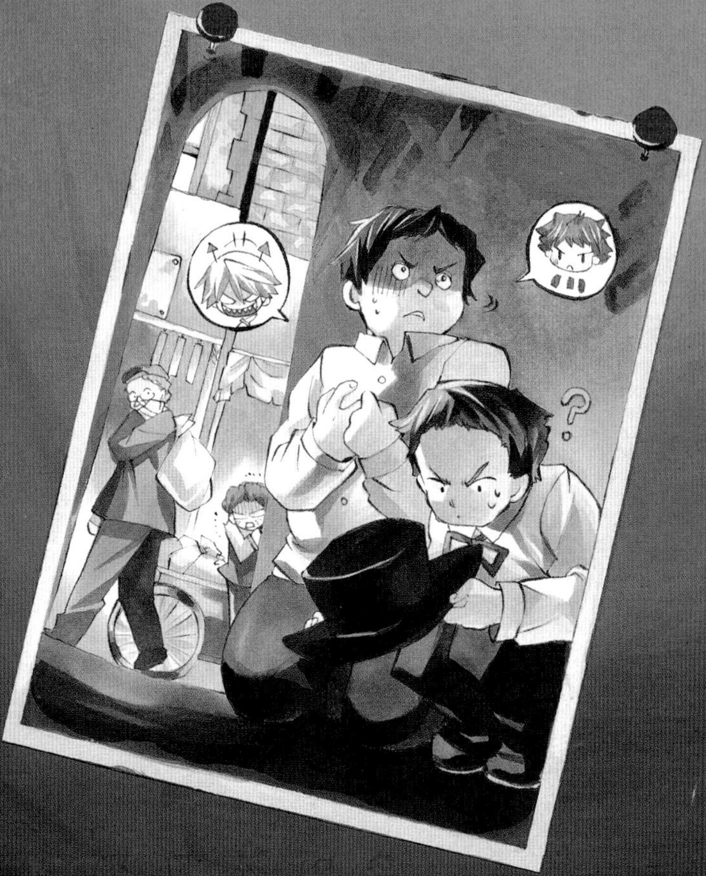

CONTENTS

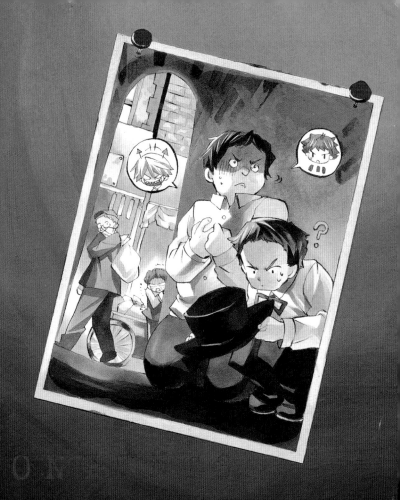

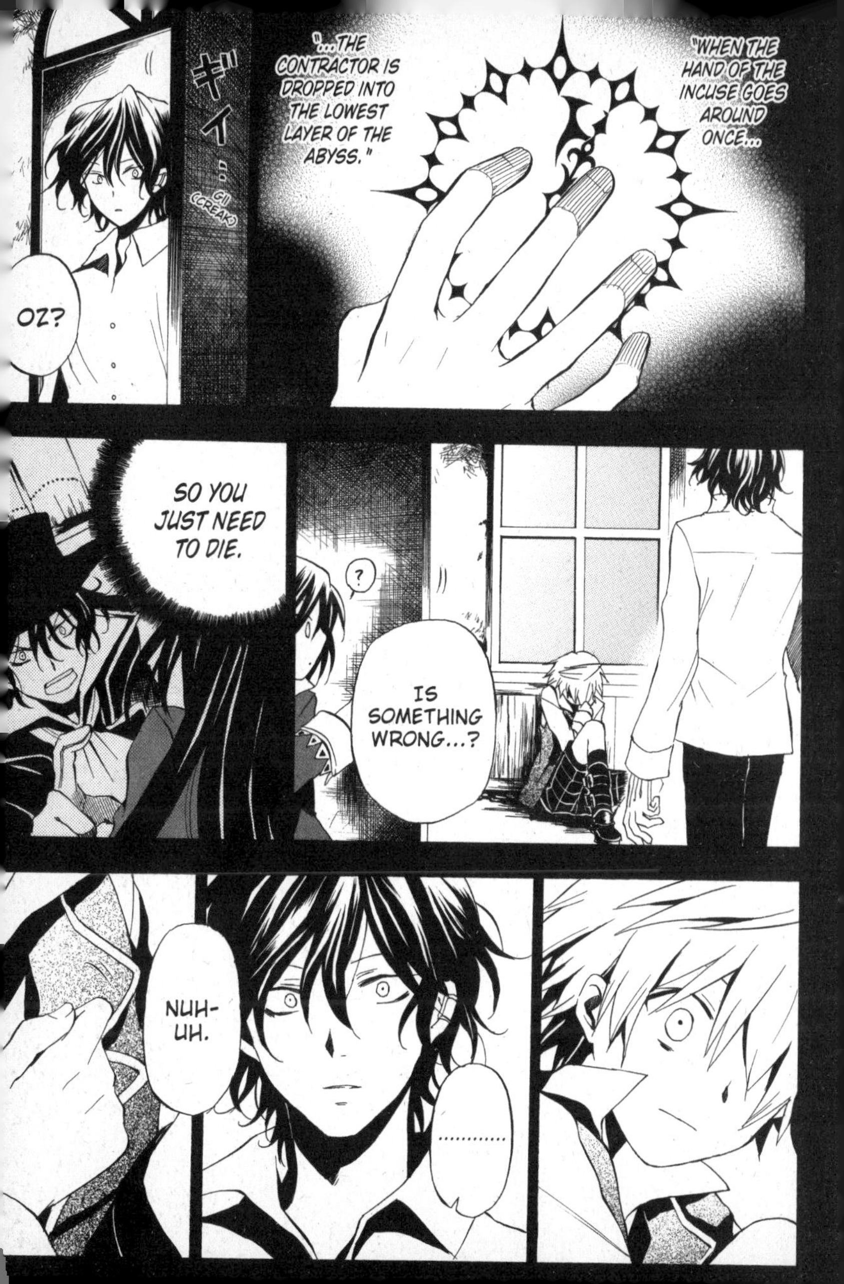
"WHEN THE HAND OF THE INCUSE GOES AROUND ONCE...
"...THE CONTRACTOR IS DROPPED INTO THE LOWEST LAYER OF THE ABYSS."
ギイ...
GII (CREAK)
OZ?
?
IS SOMETHING WRONG...?
SO YOU JUST NEED TO DIE.
....
NUH-UH.

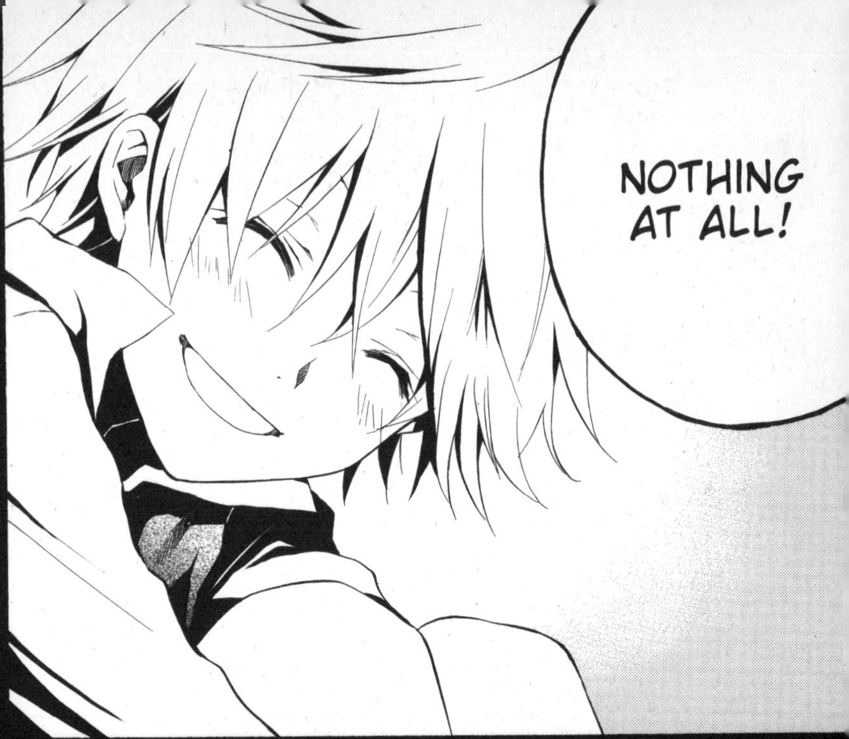
NOTHING AT ALL!

Retrace:X Malediction

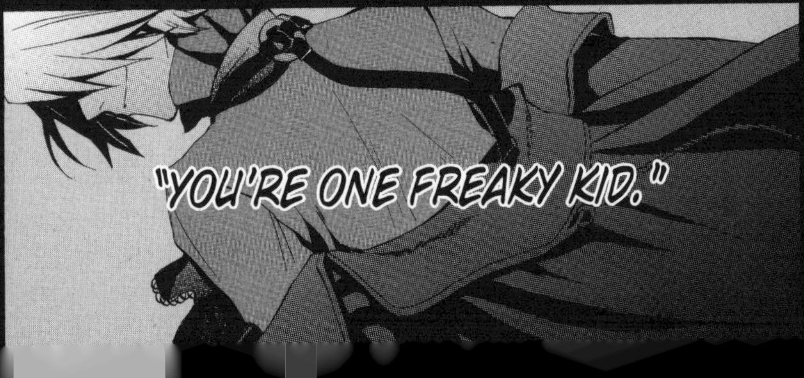
"YOU'RE ONE FREAKY KID."

AAH, THAT'S ...

?

WHAT IS THIS?

HIRA (GLITTER)
JIIN.....

WELL, A CUTE GIRL IN BLUE HAD THEM WITH HER—?

JURU (DROOL)

SMELLS GOOD...

....

KUN (SNIFF)
KUN

KASA (RUSTLE)

?

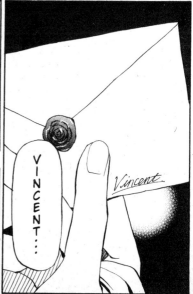

V I N C E N T ...

Vincent.

!

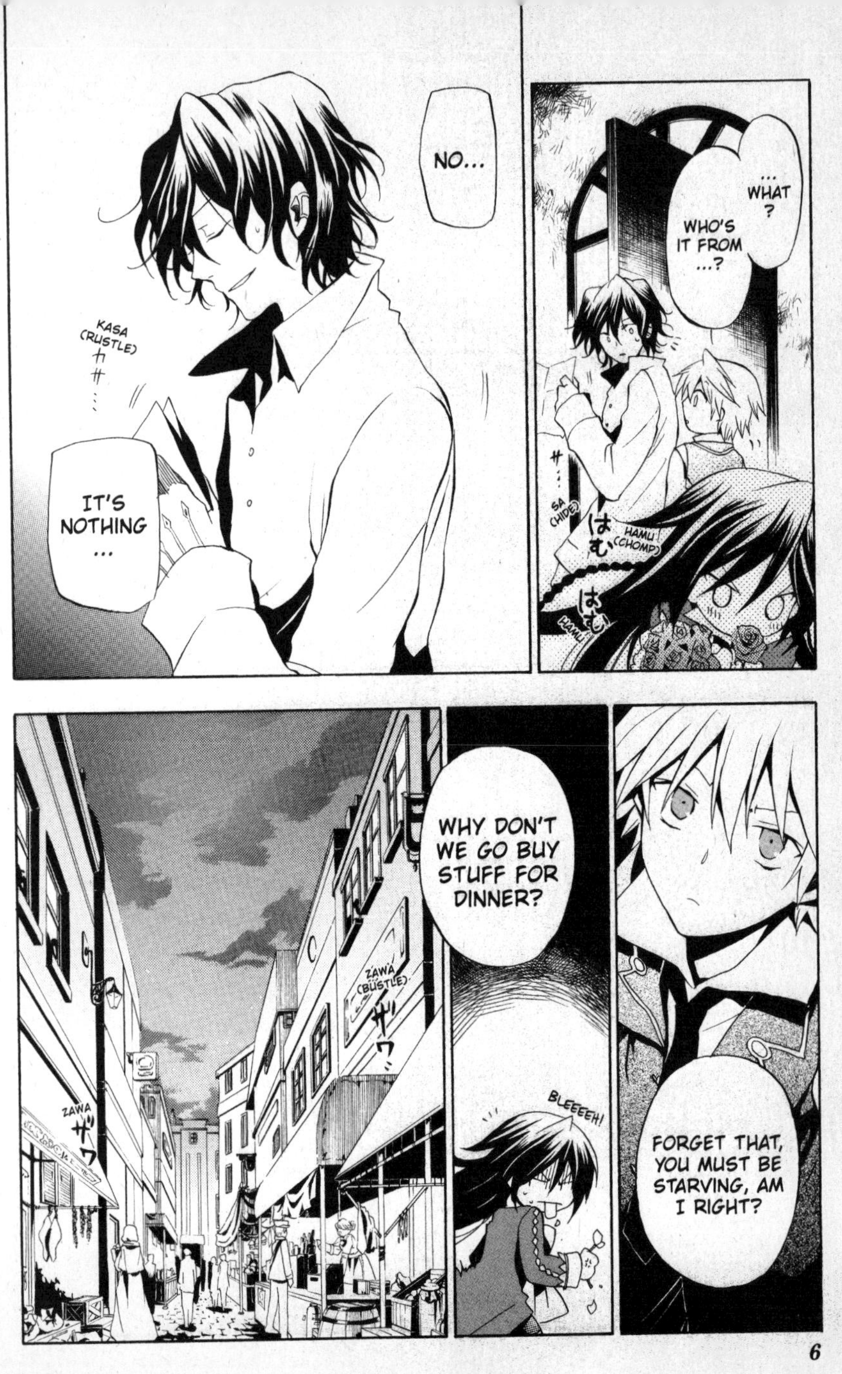
... WHAT ?
WHO'S IT FROM ...?
SA (HIDE)
HAMU (CHOMP)
はむ
HAMU
はむ
NO...
KASA (RUSTLE)
IT'S NOTHING ...
FORGET THAT, YOU MUST BE STARVING, AM I RIGHT?
WHY DON'T WE GO BUY STUFF FOR DINNER?
BLEEEEH!
ZAWA (BUSTLE)
ザワ
ZAWA
ザワ

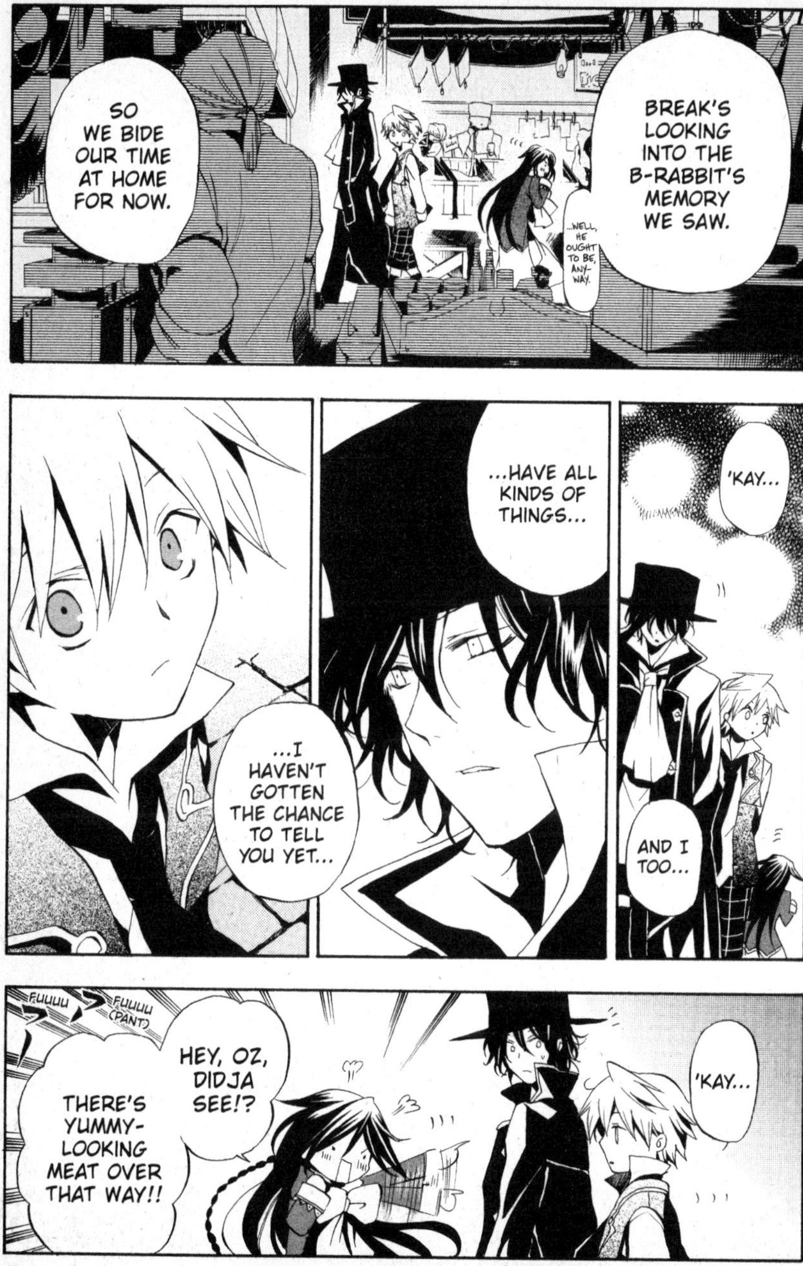

BREAK'S LOOKING INTO THE B-RABBIT'S MEMORY WE SAW.
...WELL, HE OUGHT TO BE, ANYWAY.
SO WE BIDE OUR TIME AT HOME FOR NOW.
'KAY...
AND I TOO...
...HAVE ALL KINDS OF THINGS...
...I HAVEN'T GOTTEN THE CHANCE TO TELL YOU YET...
'KAY...
HEY, OZ, DIDJA SEE!?
THERE'S YUMMY-LOOKING MEAT OVER THAT WAY!!
F.UUUU F.UUUU (PANT)

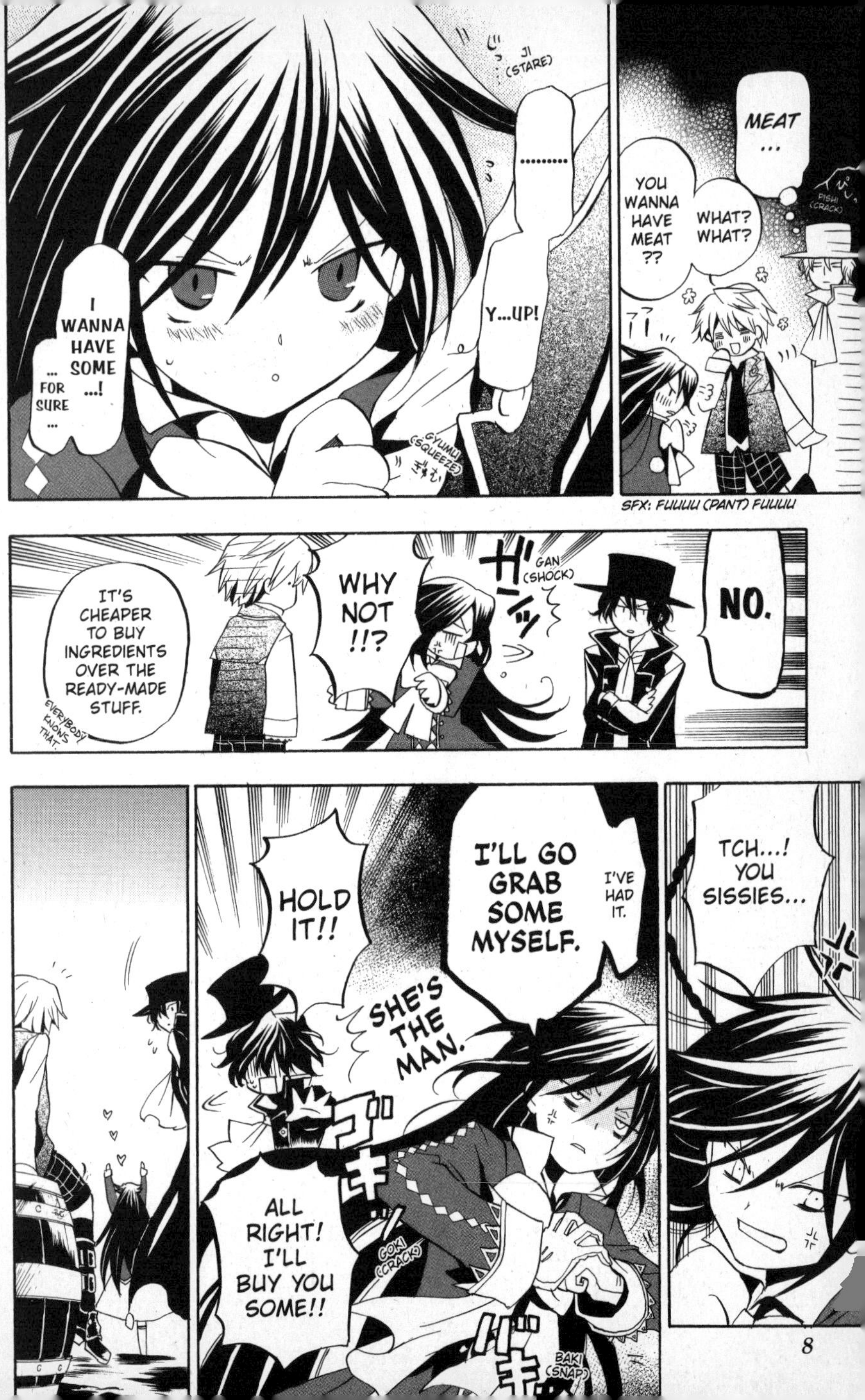
MEAT ...
PISHI (CRACK)
WHAT? WHAT?
YOU WANNA HAVE MEAT ??
SFX: FUUUU (PANT) FUUUU
JI (STARE)
....
Y...UP!
I WANNA HAVE SOME ...!
... FOR SURE ...
GYUMU (SQUEEZE)
NO.
GAN (SHOCK)
WHY NOT !!?
IT'S CHEAPER TO BUY INGREDIENTS OVER THE READY-MADE STUFF.
EVERYBODY KNOWS THAT.
TCH...! YOU SISSIES...
I'VE HAD IT.
I'LL GO GRAB SOME MYSELF.
HOLD IT!!
SHE'S THE MAN.
GOKI (CRACK)
ALL RIGHT! I'LL BUY YOU SOME!!
BAKI (SNAP)

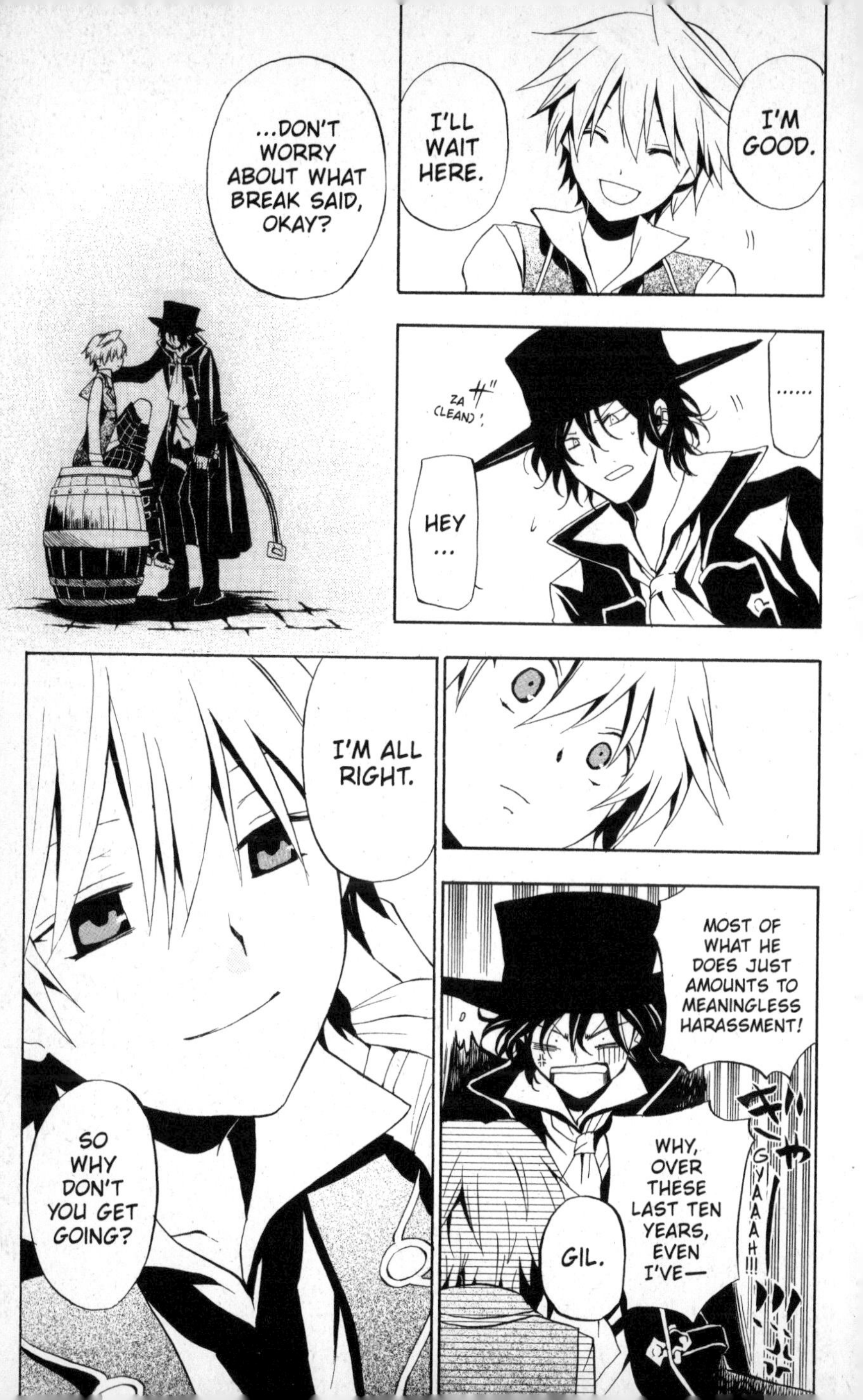
I'M GOOD.
I'LL WAIT HERE.
...DON'T WORRY ABOUT WHAT BREAK SAID, OKAY?
......
ZA CLEAND
HEY ...
MOST OF WHAT HE DOES JUST AMOUNTS TO MEANINGLESS HARASSMENT!
WHY, OVER THESE LAST TEN YEARS, EVEN I'VE—
GYAAAH!!!
GIL.
I'M ALL RIGHT.
SO WHY DON'T YOU GET GOING?

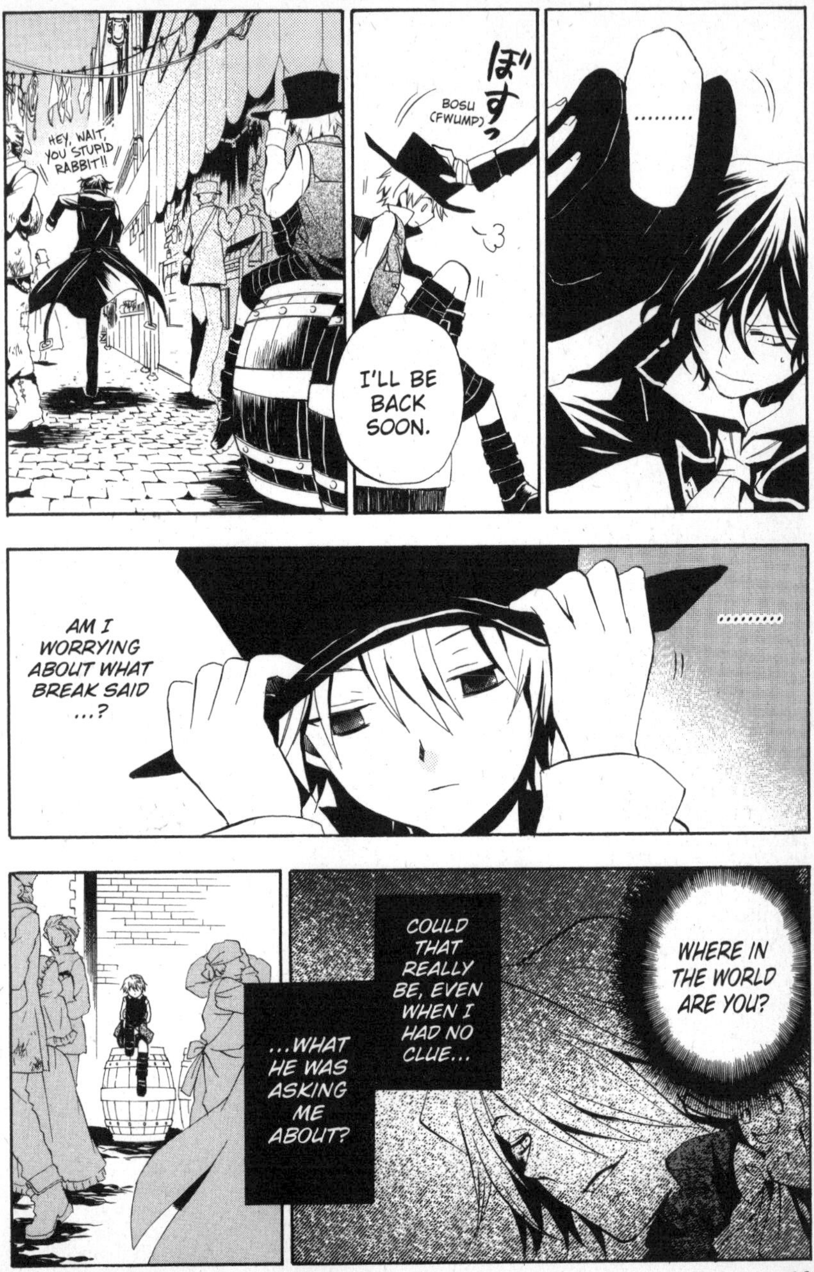
....
ぼすっ
BOSU (FWUMP)
I'LL BE BACK SOON.
HEY, WAIT, YOU STUPID RABBIT!!
....
AM I WORRYING ABOUT WHAT BREAK SAID ...?
WHERE IN THE WORLD ARE YOU?
COULD THAT REALLY BE, EVEN WHEN I HAD NO CLUE...
...WHAT HE WAS ASKING ME ABOUT?

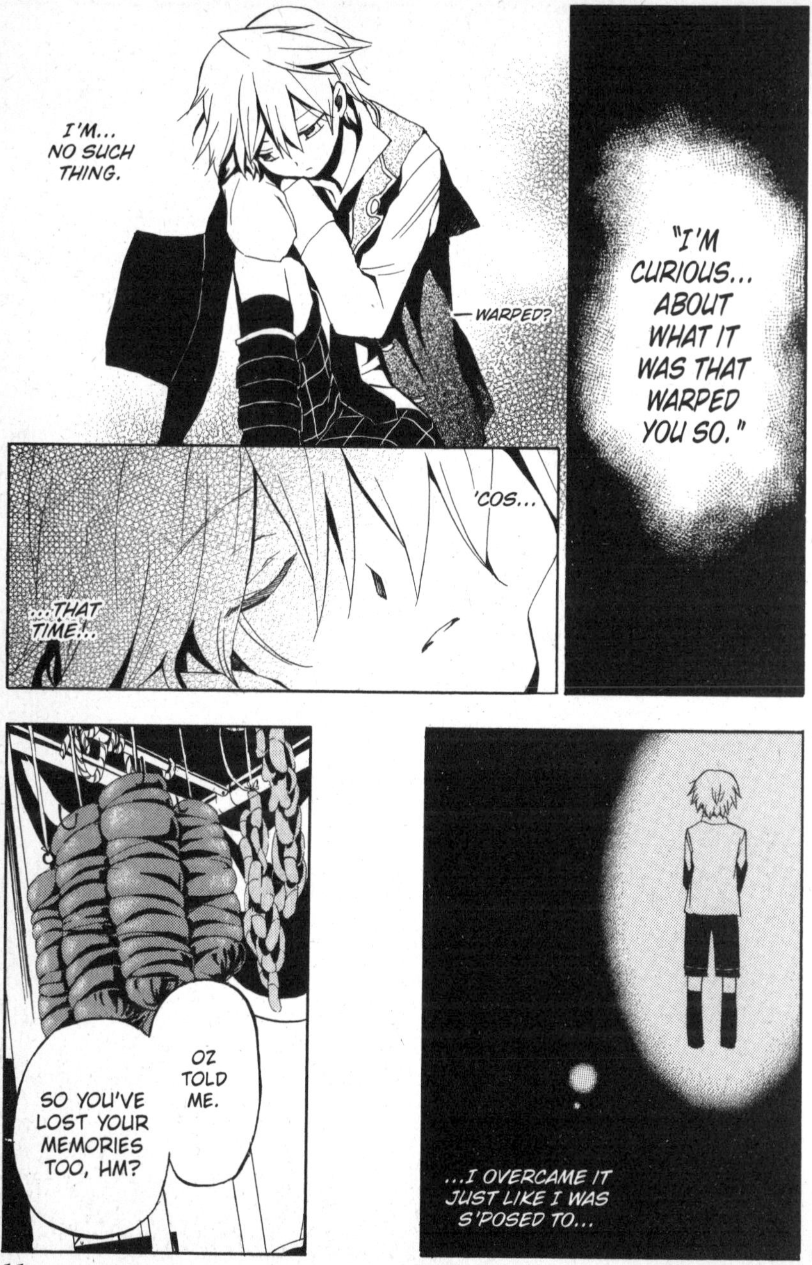
"I'M CURIOUS... ABOUT WHAT IT WAS THAT WARPED YOU SO."
—WARPED?
I'M... NO SUCH THING.
'COS...
...THAT TIME...
...I OVERCAME IT JUST LIKE I WAS S'POSED TO...
OZ TOLD ME.
SO YOU'VE LOST YOUR MEMORIES TOO, HM?

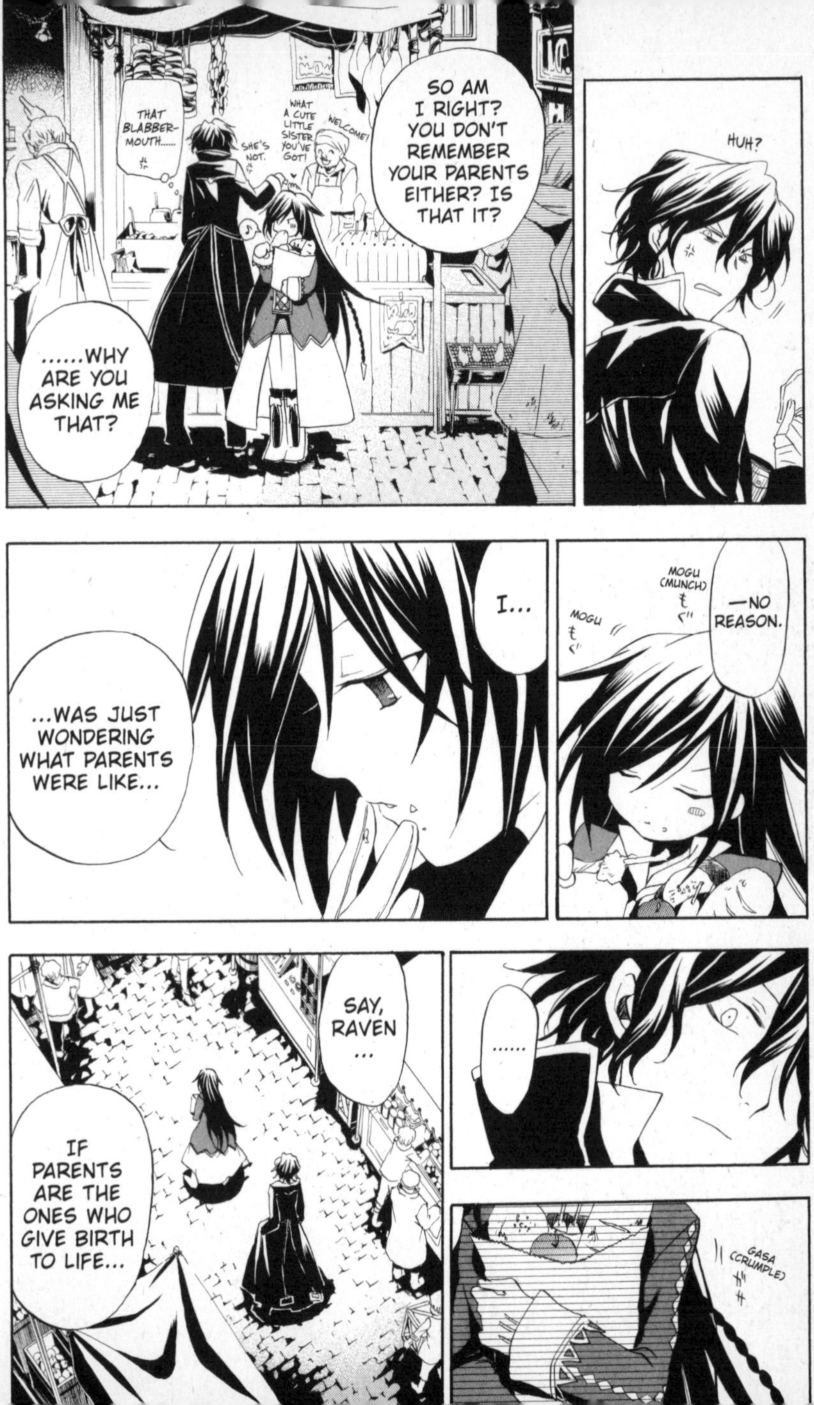
HUH?
SO AM I RIGHT? YOU DON'T REMEMBER YOUR PARENTS EITHER? IS THAT IT?
WELCOME!
WHAT A CUTE LITTLE SISTER YOU'VE GOT!
SHE'S NOT.
THAT BLABBER-MOUTH......
......WHY ARE YOU ASKING ME THAT?
—NO REASON.
MOGU (MUNCH)
MOGU
I...
...WAS JUST WONDERING WHAT PARENTS WERE LIKE...
......
GASA (CRUMPLE)
SAY, RAVEN ...
IF PARENTS ARE THE ONES WHO GIVE BIRTH TO LIFE...

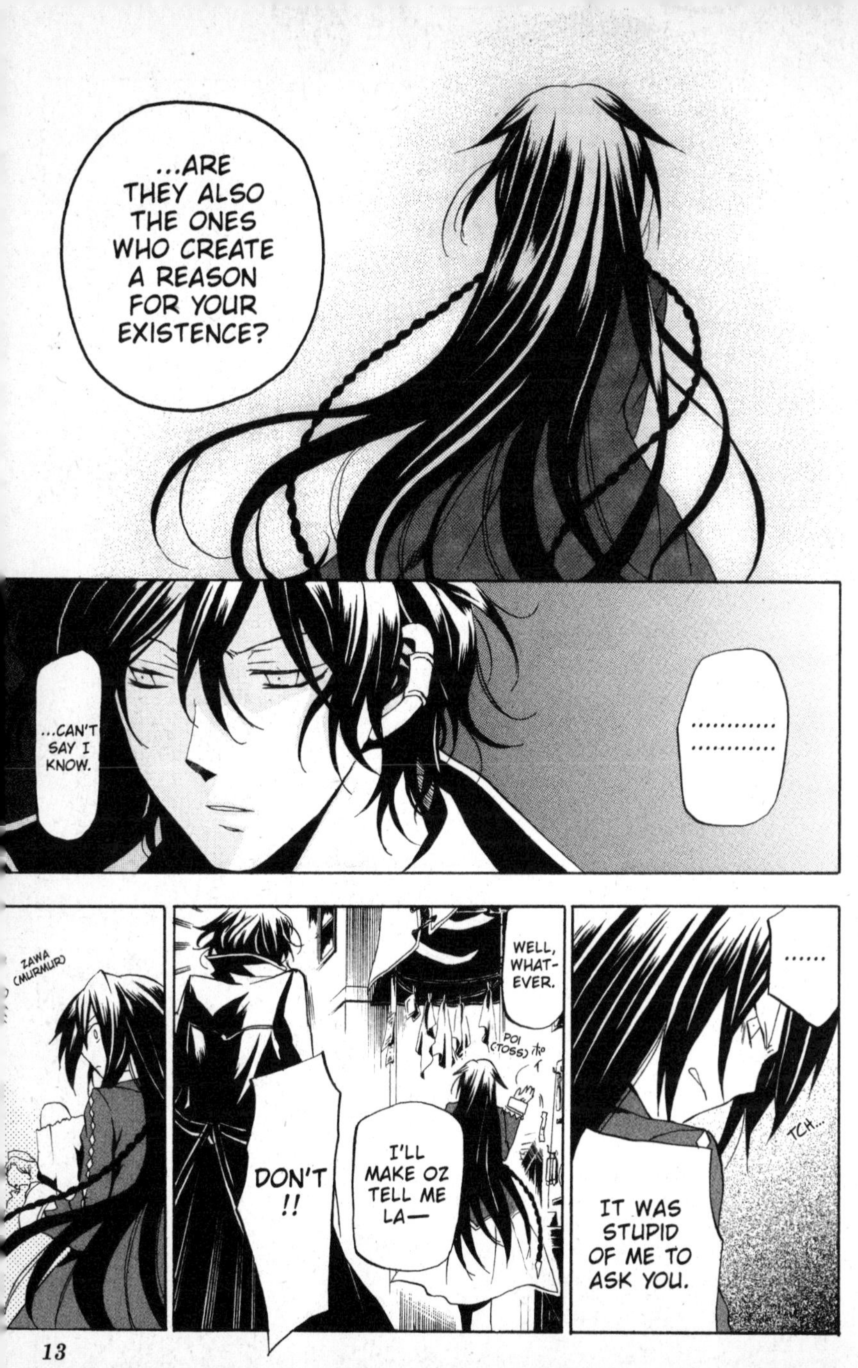
...ARE THEY ALSO THE ONES WHO CREATE A REASON FOR YOUR EXISTENCE?
....
...CAN'T SAY I KNOW.
......
TCH...
IT WAS STUPID OF ME TO ASK YOU.
WELL, WHATEVER.
POI (TOSS) ポイ
I'LL MAKE OZ TELL ME LA—
DON'T !!
ZAWA (MURMUR)

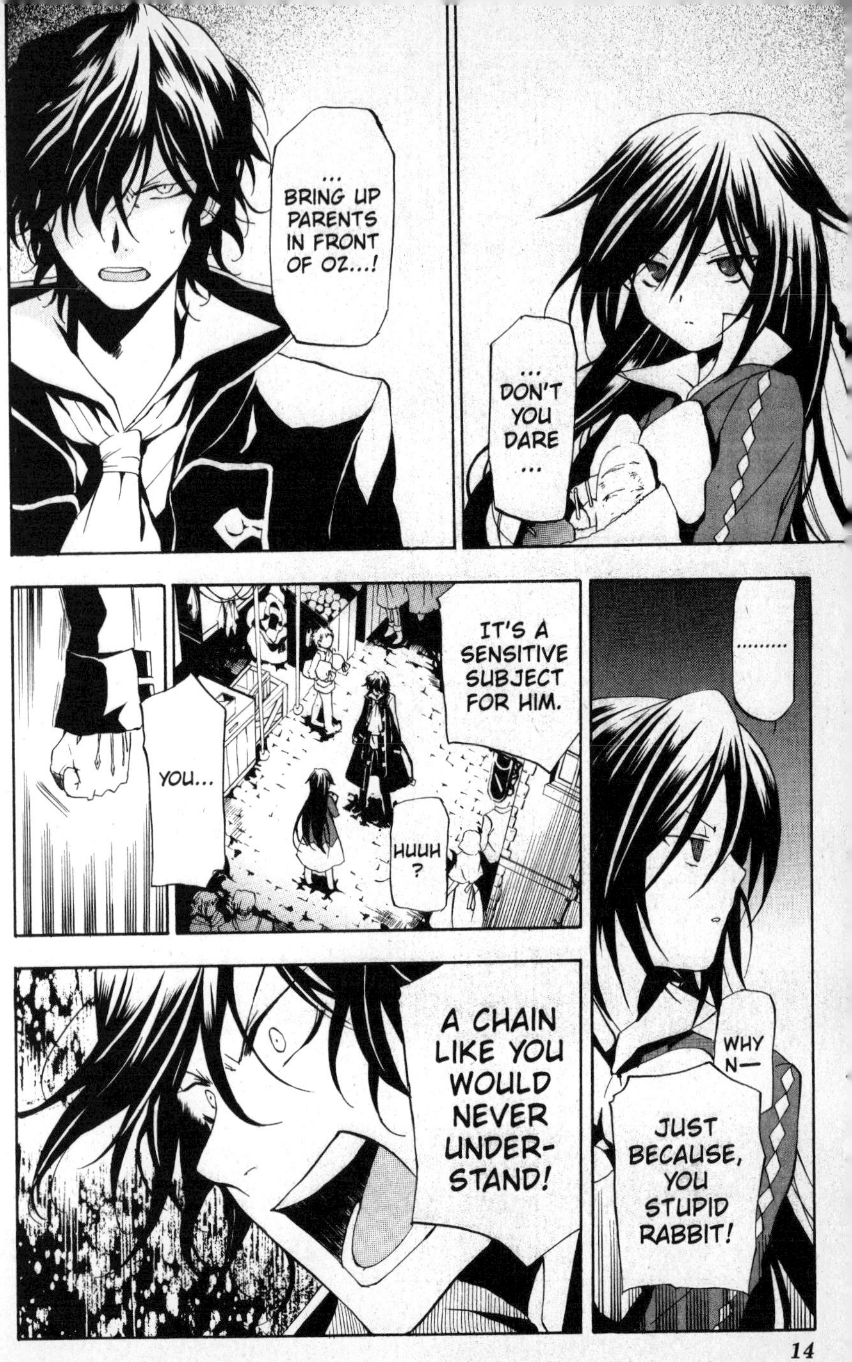

... DON'T YOU DARE ...
... BRING UP PARENTS IN FRONT OF OZ...!
....
WHY N—
JUST BECAUSE, YOU STUPID RABBIT!
IT'S A SENSITIVE SUBJECT FOR HIM.
HUUH ?
YOU...
A CHAIN LIKE YOU WOULD NEVER UNDER-STAND!

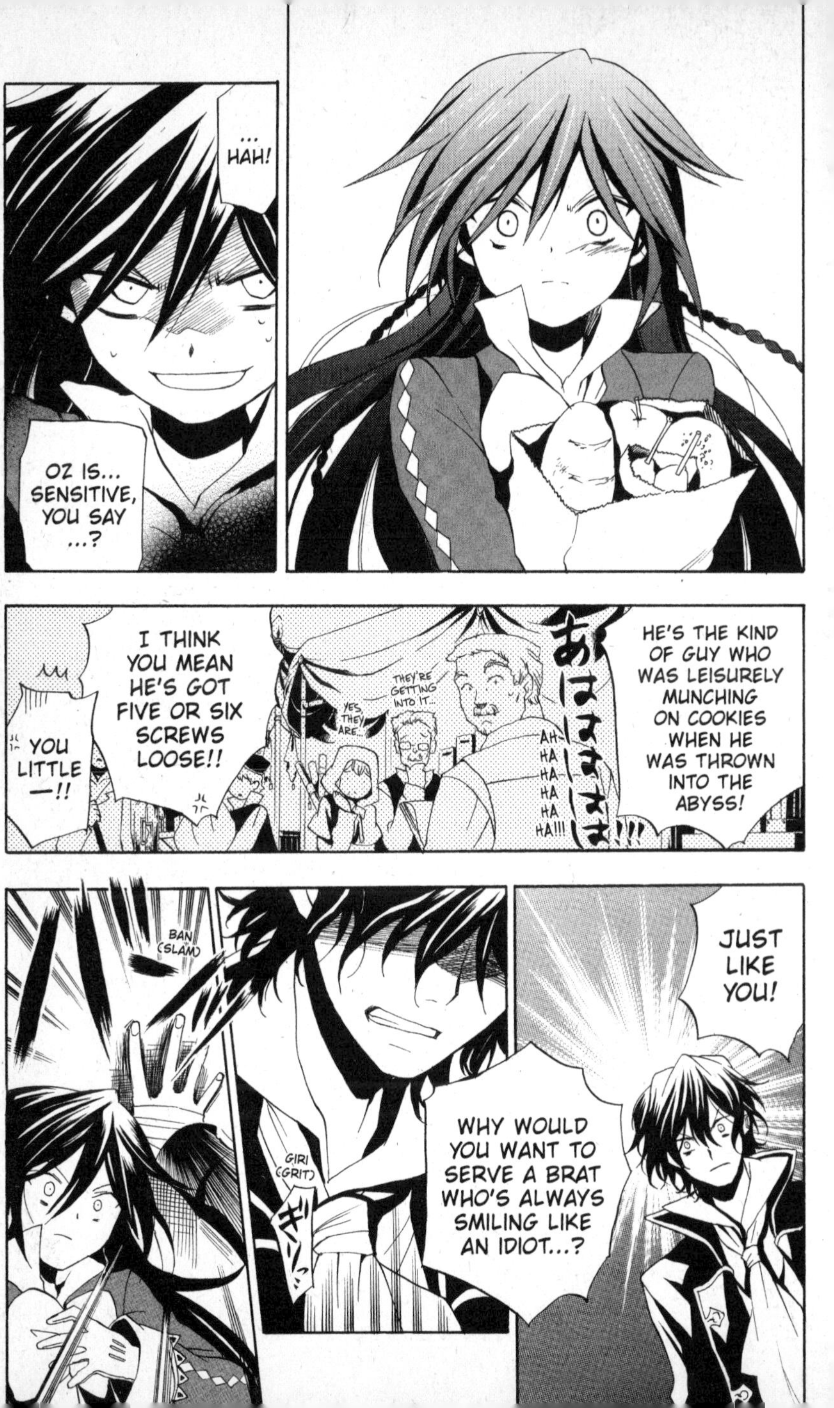
...HAH!
OZ IS... SENSITIVE, YOU SAY ...?
HE'S THE KIND OF GUY WHO WAS LEISURELY MUNCHING ON COOKIES WHEN HE WAS THROWN INTO THE ABYSS!
あははは
AH-HA HA HA HA HA HA!!!
THEY'RE GETTING INTO IT...
YES THEY ARE.
I THINK YOU MEAN HE'S GOT FIVE OR SIX SCREWS LOOSE!!
YOU LITTLE—!!
JUST LIKE YOU!
WHY WOULD YOU WANT TO SERVE A BRAT WHO'S ALWAYS SMILING LIKE AN IDIOT...?
GIRI (GRIT)
BAN (SLAM)

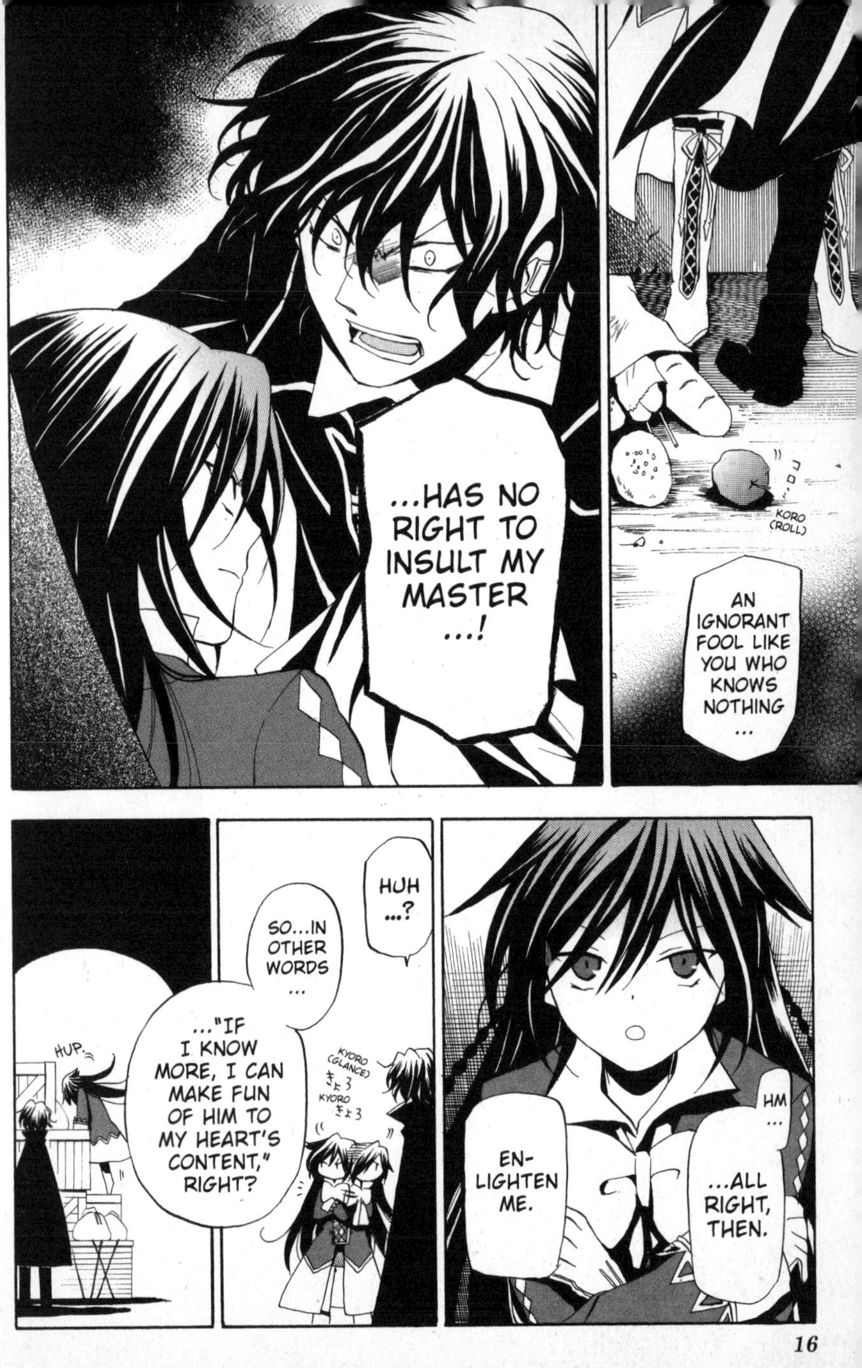
KORO (ROLL)
AN IGNORANT FOOL LIKE YOU WHO KNOWS NOTHING...
...HAS NO RIGHT TO INSULT MY MASTER...!
HM...
...ALL RIGHT, THEN.
EN-LIGHTEN ME.
HUH...?
SO...IN OTHER WORDS...
KYORO (GLANCE)
KYORO
..."IF I KNOW MORE, I CAN MAKE FUN OF HIM TO MY HEART'S CONTENT," RIGHT?
HUP.

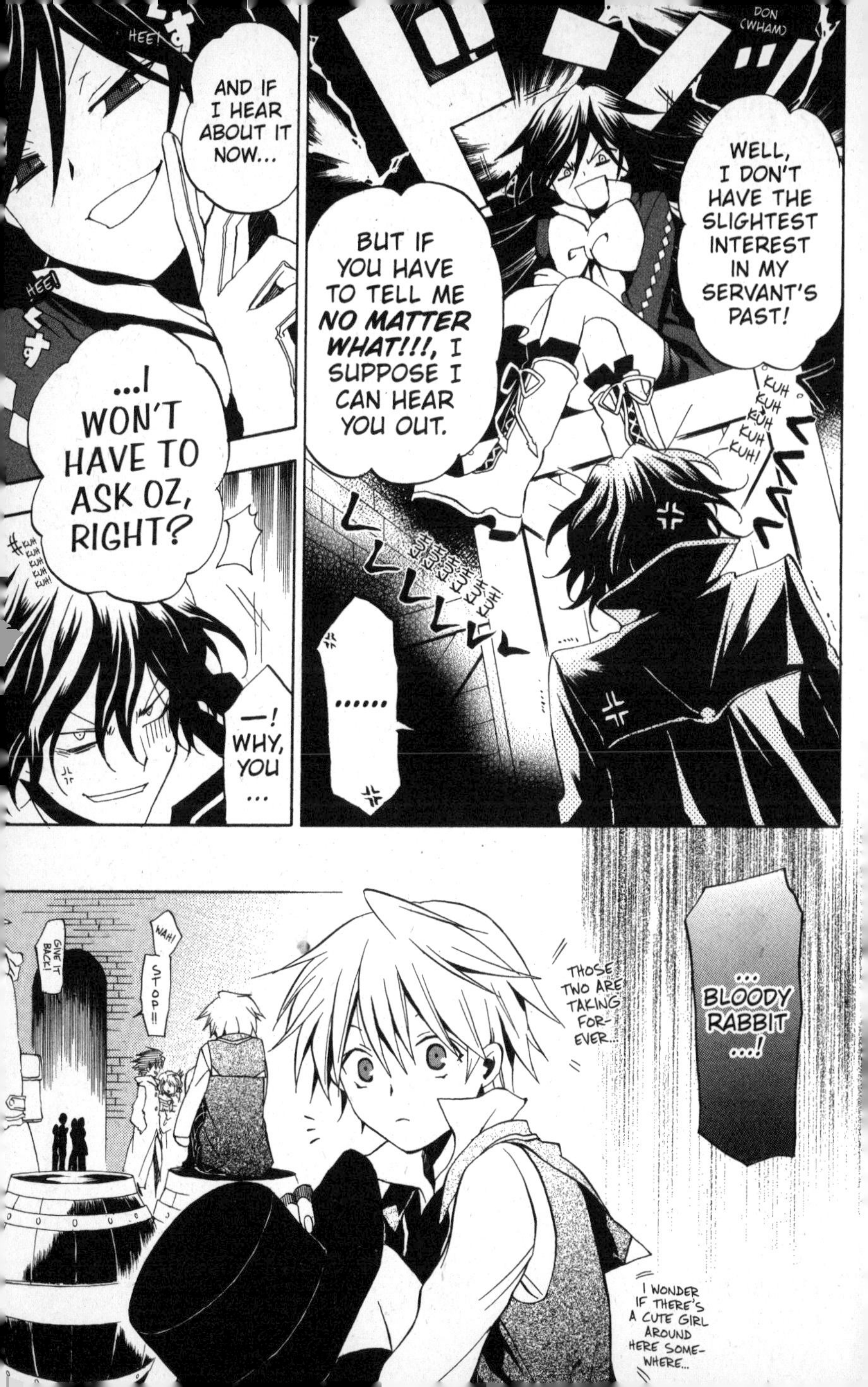
DON (WHAM)
WELL, I DON'T HAVE THE SLIGHTEST INTEREST IN MY SERVANT'S PAST!
BUT IF YOU HAVE TO TELL ME *NO MATTER WHAT!!!*, I SUPPOSE I CAN HEAR YOU OUT.
KUH KUH KUH KUH KUH!
KUH KUH KUH KUH KUH!
......
....
HEE!
AND IF I HEAR ABOUT IT NOW...
HEE!
...I WON'T HAVE TO ASK OZ, RIGHT?
KUH KUH KUH KUH KUH!
—! WHY, YOU...
...BLOODY RABBIT...!
THOSE TWO ARE TAKING FOR-EVER...
I WONDER IF THERE'S A CUTE GIRL AROUND HERE SOME-WHERE...
WAH!
STOP!!
GIVE IT BACK!

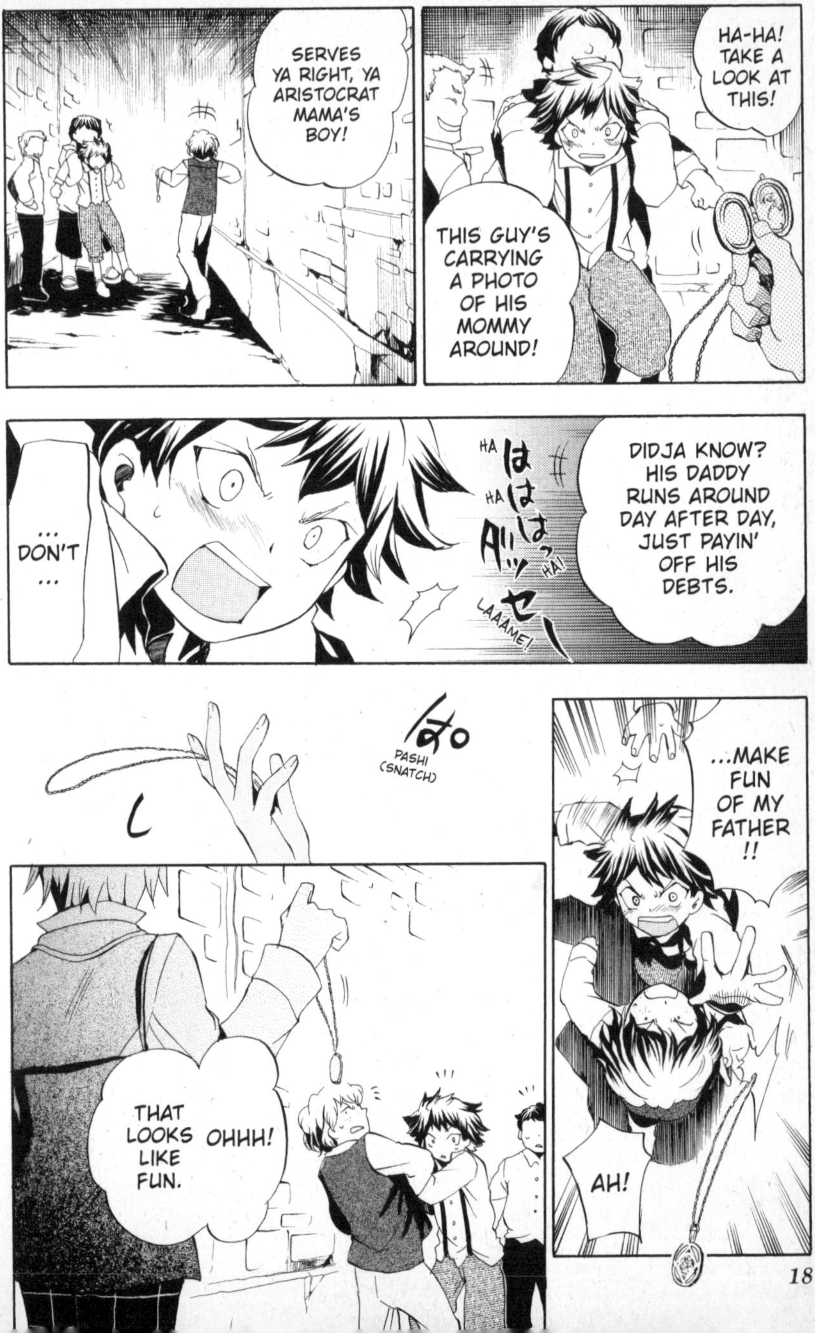
HA-HA! TAKE A LOOK AT THIS!
THIS GUY'S CARRYING A PHOTO OF HIS MOMMY AROUND!
SERVES YA RIGHT, YA ARISTOCRAT MAMA'S BOY!
DIDJA KNOW? HIS DADDY RUNS AROUND DAY AFTER DAY, JUST PAYIN' OFF HIS DEBTS.
HA HA HA!
LAAAME!
... DON'T ...
...MAKE FUN OF MY FATHER!!
AH!
PASHI (SNATCH)
OHHH!
THAT LOOKS LIKE FUN.

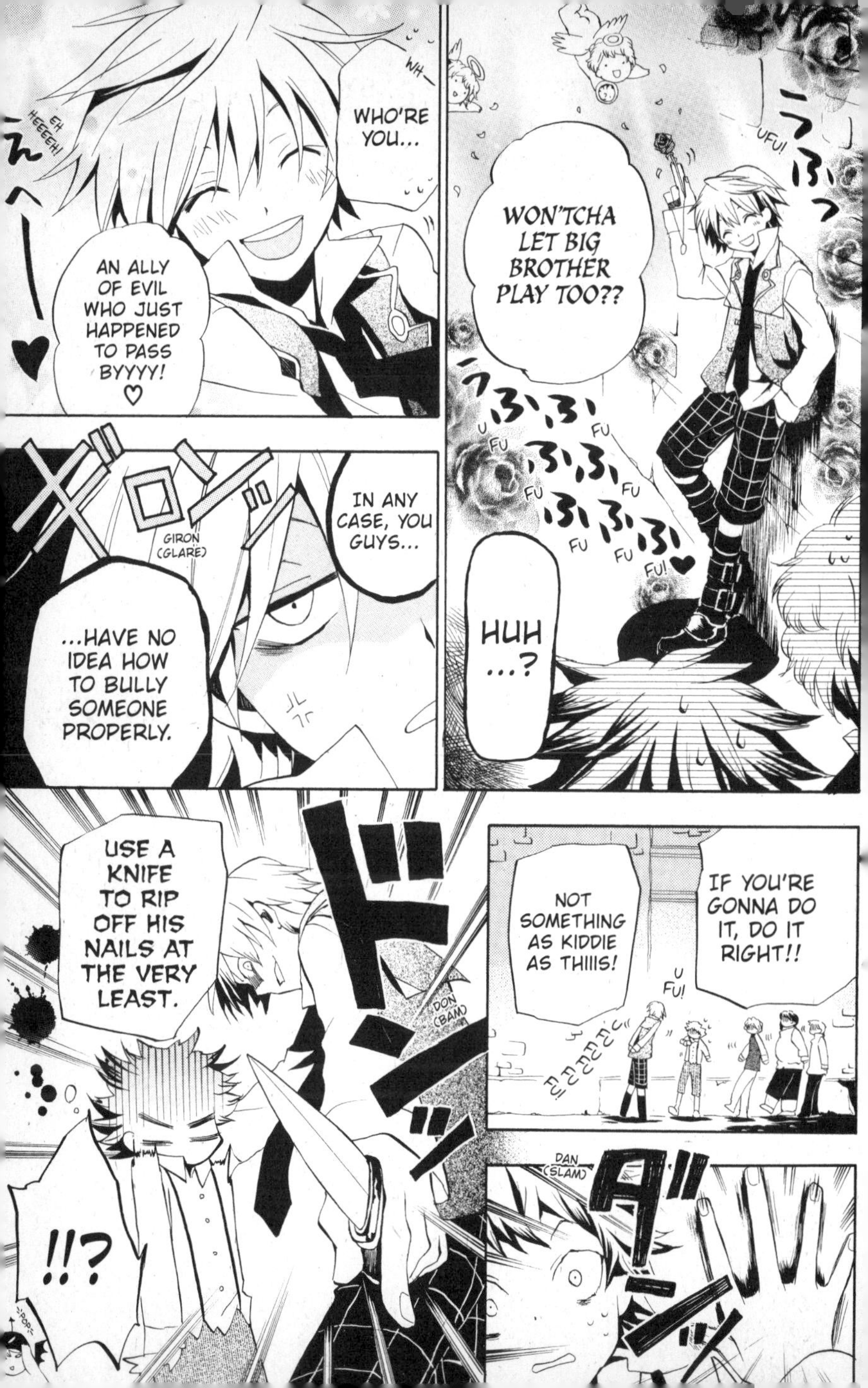
UFU!
WON'TCHA LET BIG BROTHER PLAY TOO??
U FU FU FU FU FU FU FU FU!♥
HUH ...?
WH—
WHO'RE YOU...
EH HEEEEH!
AN ALLY OF EVIL WHO JUST HAPPENED TO PASS BYYYY! ♡
GIRON (GLARE)
IN ANY CASE, YOU GUYS...
...HAVE NO IDEA HOW TO BULLY SOMEONE PROPERLY.
IF YOU'RE GONNA DO IT, DO IT RIGHT!!
NOT SOMETHING AS KIDDIE AS THIIIS!
U FU!
DAN (SLAM)
USE A KNIFE TO RIP OFF HIS NAILS AT THE VERY LEAST.
DON (BAM)
!!?
POP

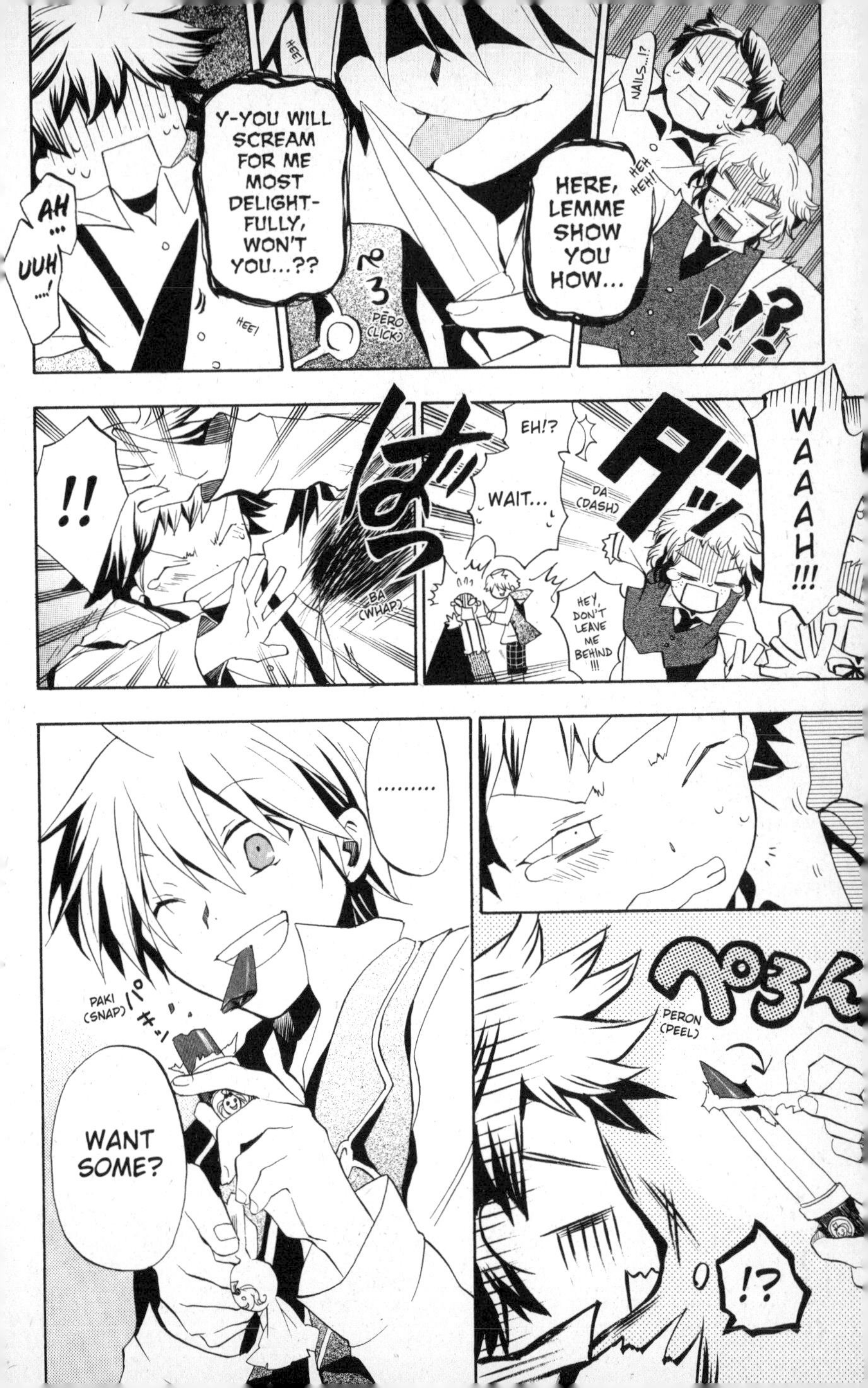
NAILS...!?
HEH HEH!!
HERE, LEMME SHOW YOU HOW...
!!?
HEE!
Y-YOU WILL SCREAM FOR ME MOST DELIGHT-FULLY, WON'T YOU...??
PERO (LICK)
HEE!
AH... UUH...!
WAAAAH!!!
DA (DASH)
EH!?
WAIT...
HEY, DON'T LEAVE ME BEHIND!!!
BA (WHAP)
!!
PERON (PEEL)
!?
....
PAKI (SNAP)
WANT SOME?

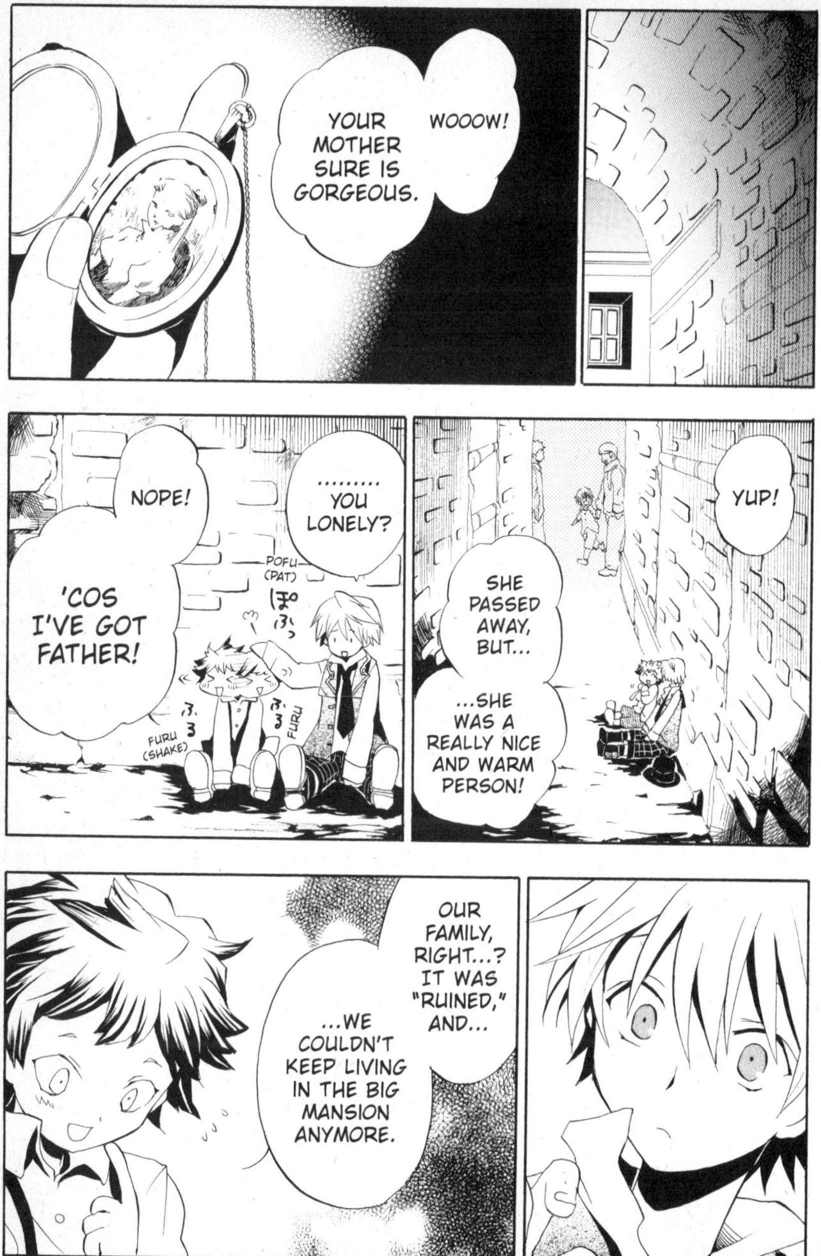
WOOOW!
YOUR MOTHER SURE IS GORGEOUS.
YUP!
SHE PASSED AWAY, BUT...
...SHE WAS A REALLY NICE AND WARM PERSON!
.... YOU LONELY?
NOPE!
'COS I'VE GOT FATHER!
ぽふっ POFU (PAT)
ふる FURU
ふる FURU (SHAKE)
OUR FAMILY, RIGHT...? IT WAS "RUINED," AND...
...WE COULDN'T KEEP LIVING IN THE BIG MANSION ANYMORE.

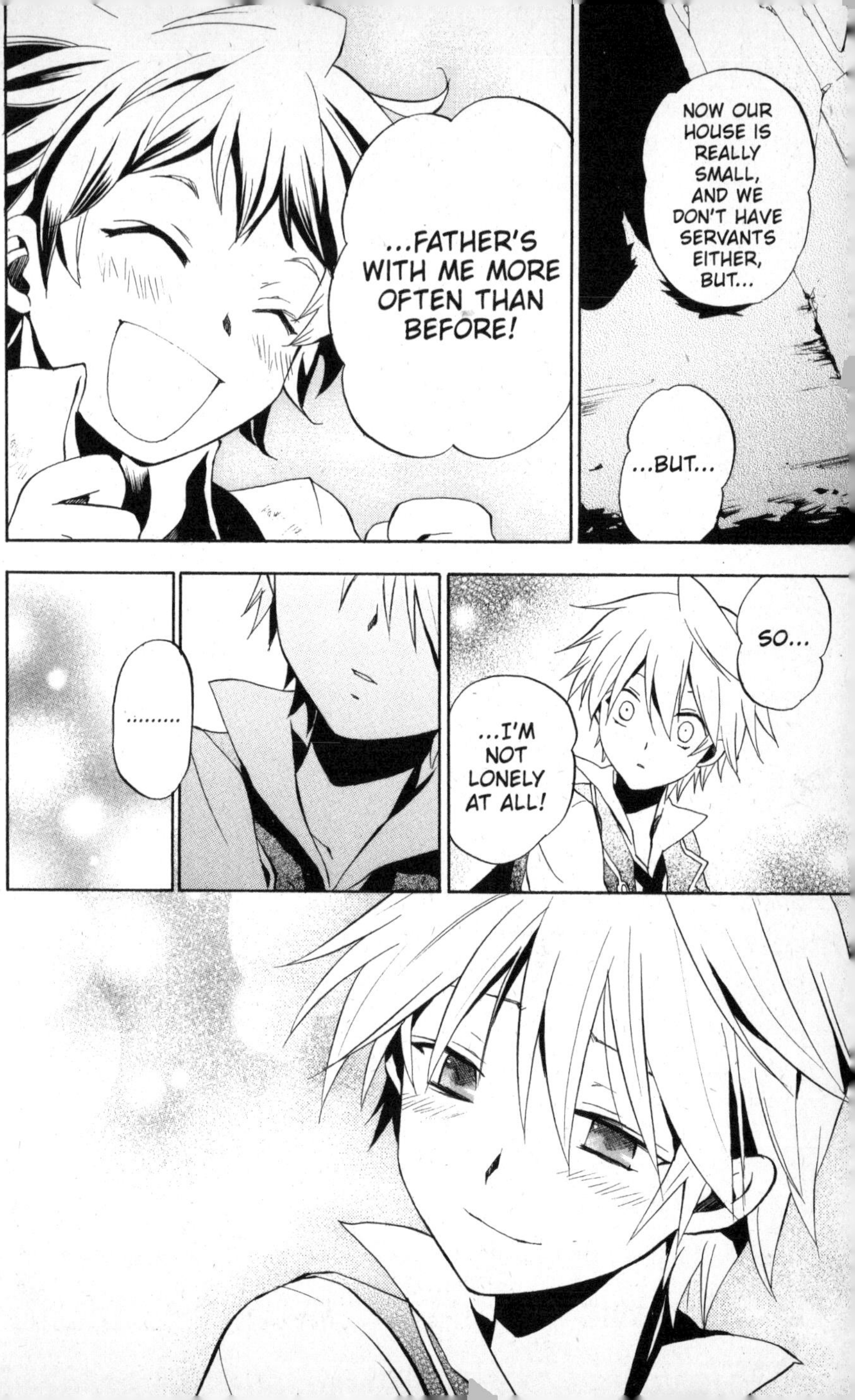
NOW OUR HOUSE IS REALLY SMALL, AND WE DON'T HAVE SERVANTS EITHER, BUT...
...BUT...
...FATHER'S WITH ME MORE OFTEN THAN BEFORE!
SO...
...I'M NOT LONELY AT ALL!
....

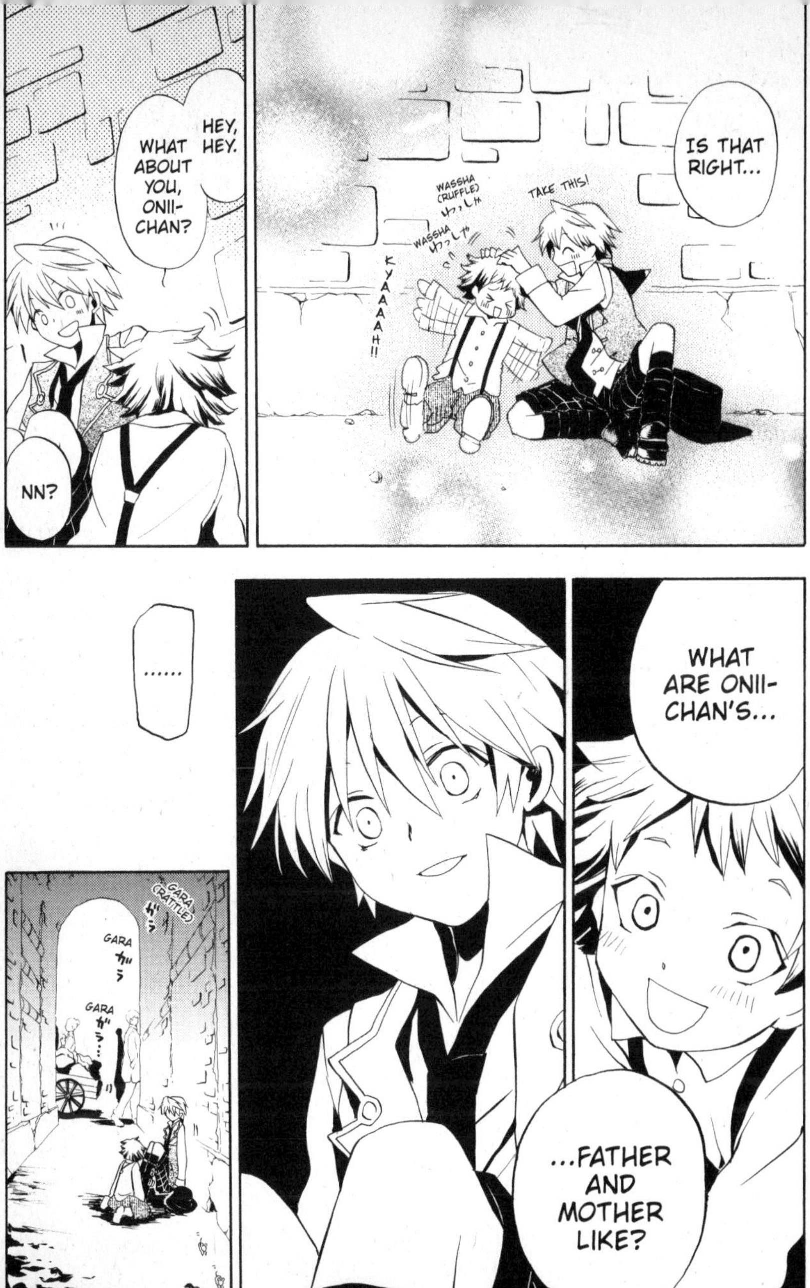
IS THAT RIGHT...
TAKE THIS!
WASSHA (RUFFLE)
WASSHA
KYAAAAAH!!
HEY, HEY. WHAT ABOUT YOU, ONII-CHAN?
NN?
WHAT ARE ONII-CHAN'S...
...FATHER AND MOTHER LIKE?
......
GARA (RATTLE)
GARA
GARA...

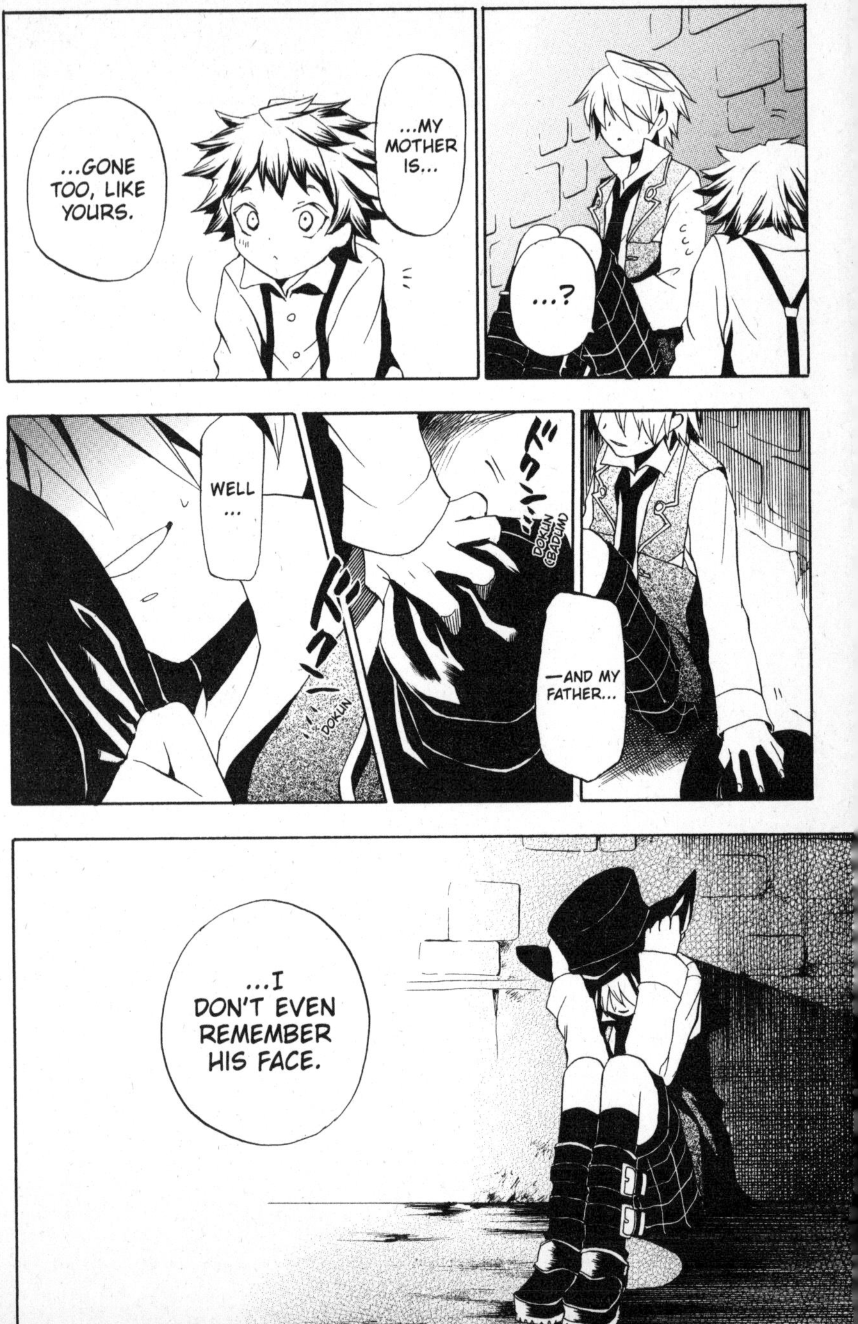
...?
...MY MOTHER IS...
...GONE TOO, LIKE YOURS.
—AND MY FATHER...
DOKUN (BADUMP)
WELL ...
DOKUN
...I DON'T EVEN REMEMBER HIS FACE.

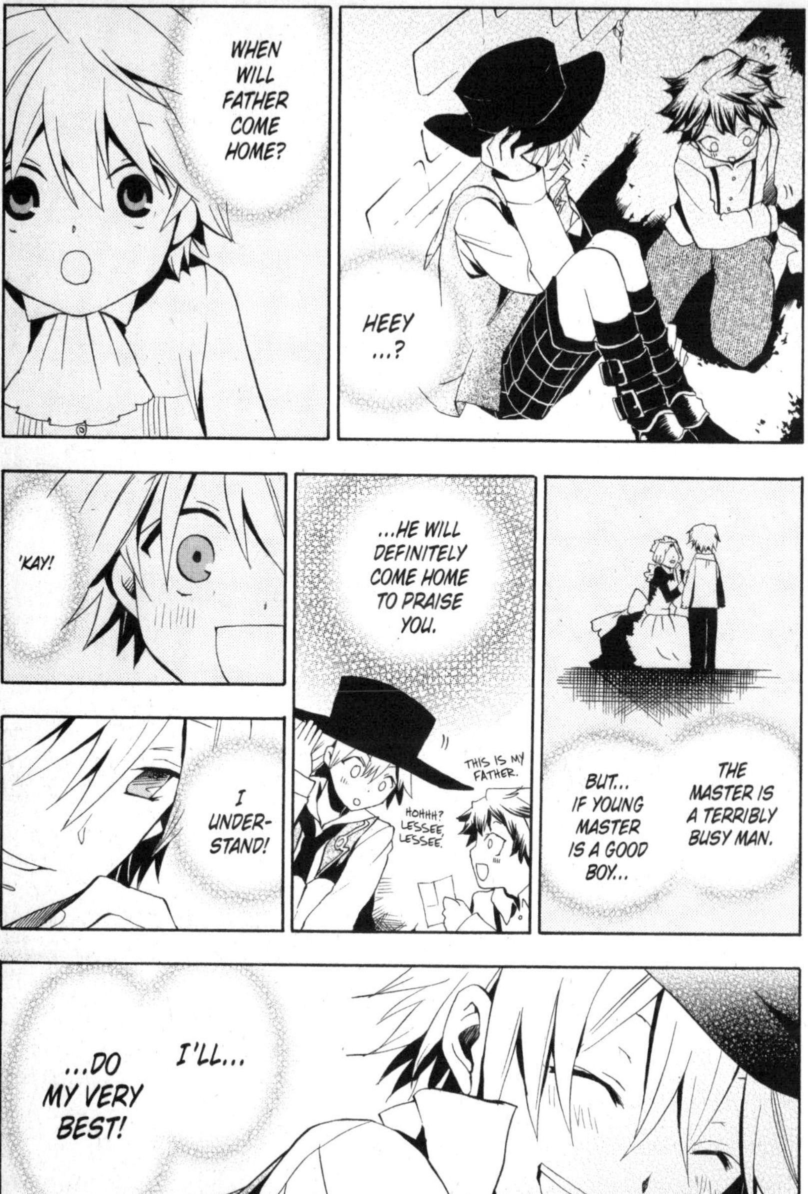
HEEY ...?
WHEN WILL FATHER COME HOME?
THE MASTER IS A TERRIBLY BUSY MAN.
BUT... IF YOUNG MASTER IS A GOOD BOY...
...HE WILL DEFINITELY COME HOME TO PRAISE YOU.
THIS IS MY FATHER.
HOHHH? LESSEE, LESSEE.
'KAY!
I UNDER-STAND!
I'LL...
...DO MY VERY BEST!

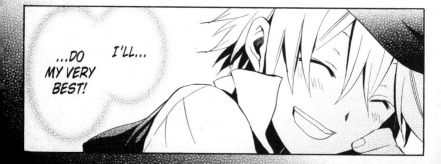

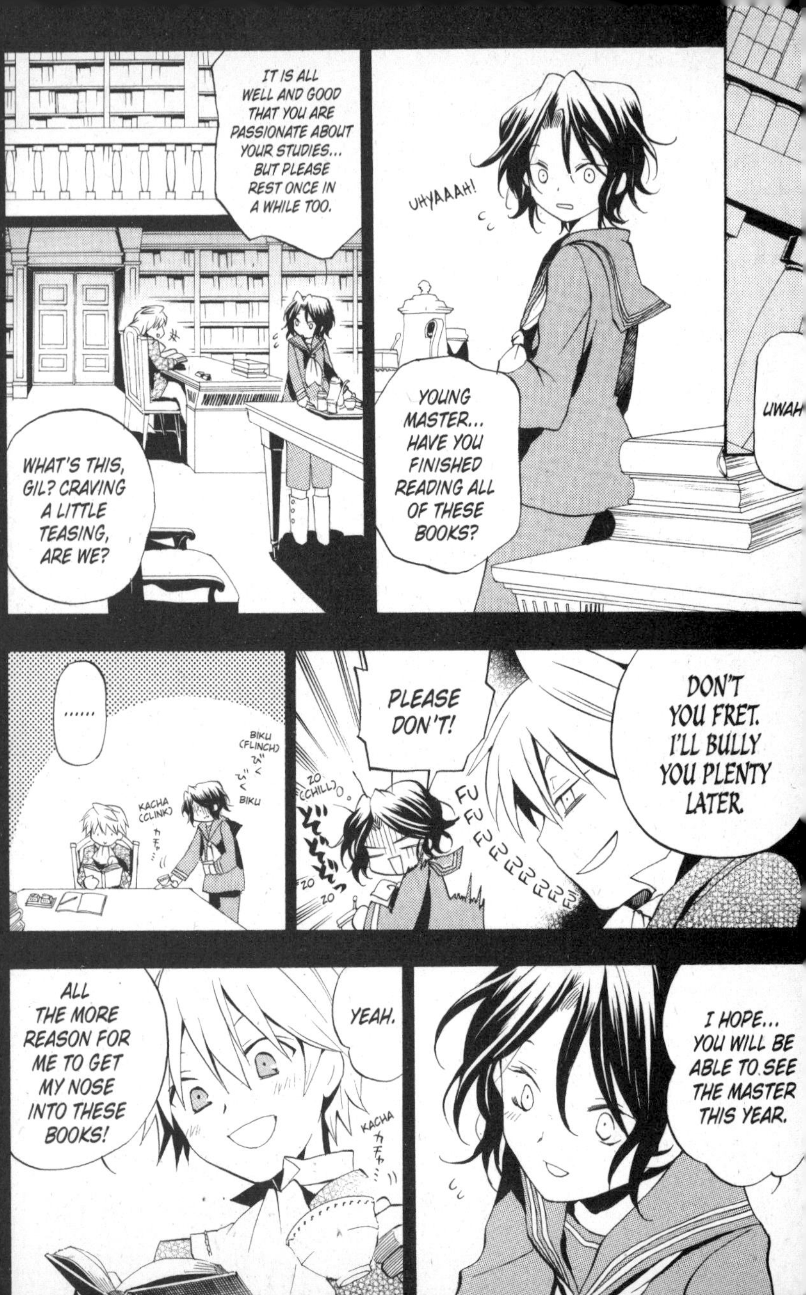
UWAH
UHYAAAH!
YOUNG MASTER... HAVE YOU FINISHED READING ALL OF THESE BOOKS?
IT IS ALL WELL AND GOOD THAT YOU ARE PASSIONATE ABOUT YOUR STUDIES... BUT PLEASE REST ONCE IN A WHILE TOO.
WHAT'S THIS, GIL? CRAVING A LITTLE TEASING, ARE WE?
DON'T YOU FRET. I'LL BULLY YOU PLENTY LATER.
PLEASE DON'T!
FU FU FU
ZO (CHILL)
ZO
ZO
BIKU (FLINCH)
BIKU
KACHA (CLINK)
......
I HOPE... YOU WILL BE ABLE TO SEE THE MASTER THIS YEAR.
YEAH.
ALL THE MORE REASON FOR ME TO GET MY NOSE INTO THESE BOOKS!
KACHA

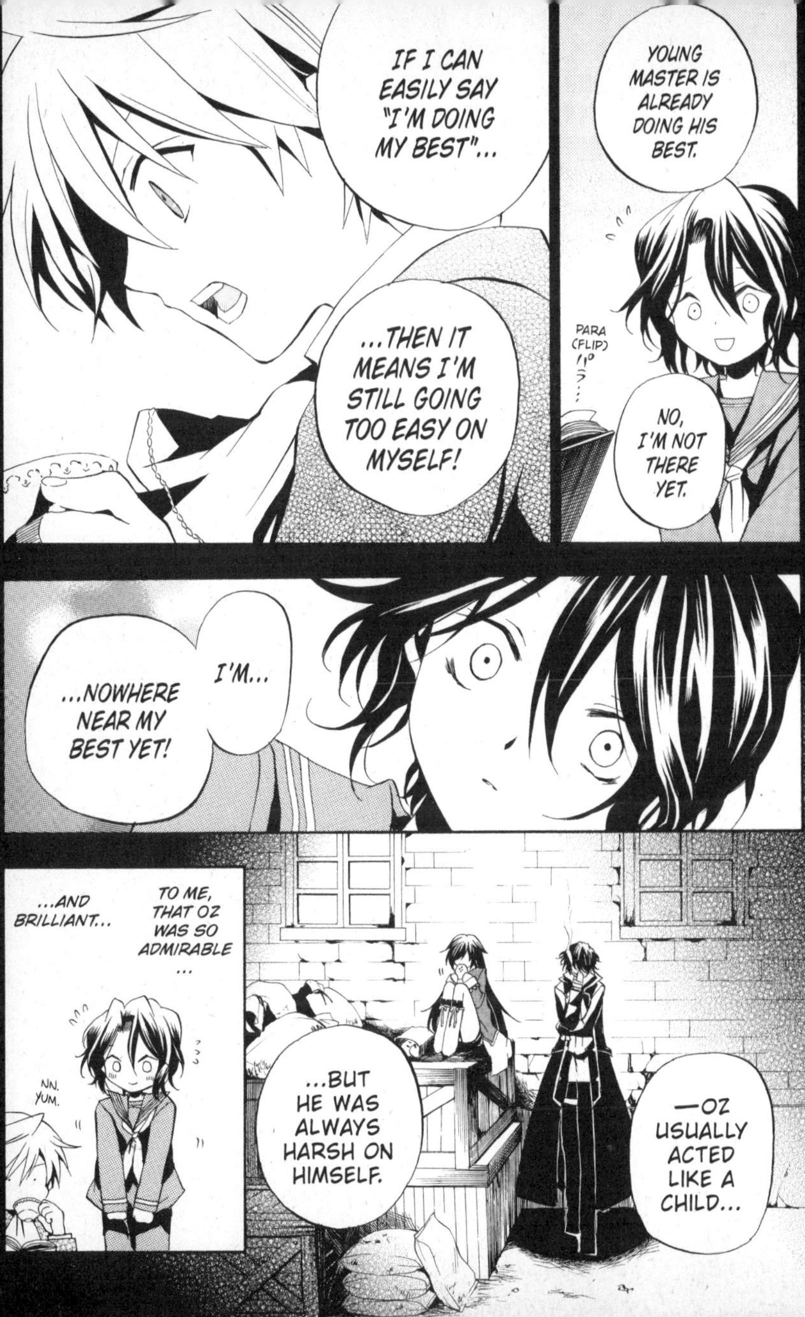
YOUNG MASTER IS ALREADY DOING HIS BEST.
PARA (FLIP)
NO, I'M NOT THERE YET.
IF I CAN EASILY SAY "I'M DOING MY BEST"...
...THEN IT MEANS I'M STILL GOING TOO EASY ON MYSELF!
I'M...
...NOWHERE NEAR MY BEST YET!
—OZ USUALLY ACTED LIKE A CHILD...
...BUT HE WAS ALWAYS HARSH ON HIMSELF.
TO ME, THAT OZ WAS SO ADMIRABLE ...
...AND BRILLIANT...
NN. YUM.

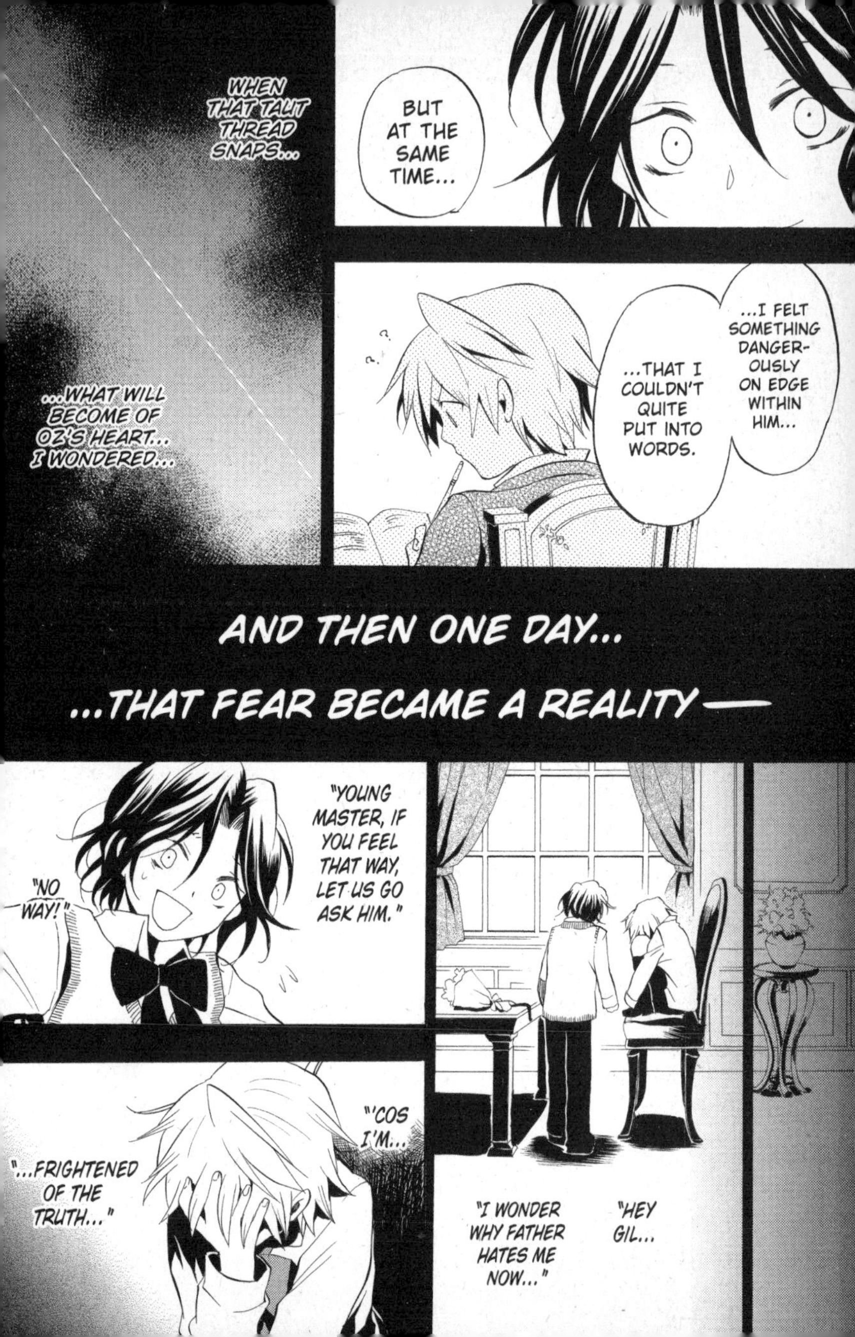
BUT AT THE SAME TIME...
...I FELT SOMETHING DANGER-OUSLY ON EDGE WITHIN HIM...
...THAT I COULDN'T QUITE PUT INTO WORDS.
WHEN THAT TAUT THREAD SNAPS...
...WHAT WILL BECOME OF OZ'S HEART... I WONDERED...
AND THEN ONE DAY...
...THAT FEAR BECAME A REALITY—
"HEY GIL...
"I WONDER WHY FATHER HATES ME NOW..."
"YOUNG MASTER, IF YOU FEEL THAT WAY, LET US GO ASK HIM."
"NO WAY!"
"'COS I'M...
"...FRIGHTENED OF THE TRUTH..."

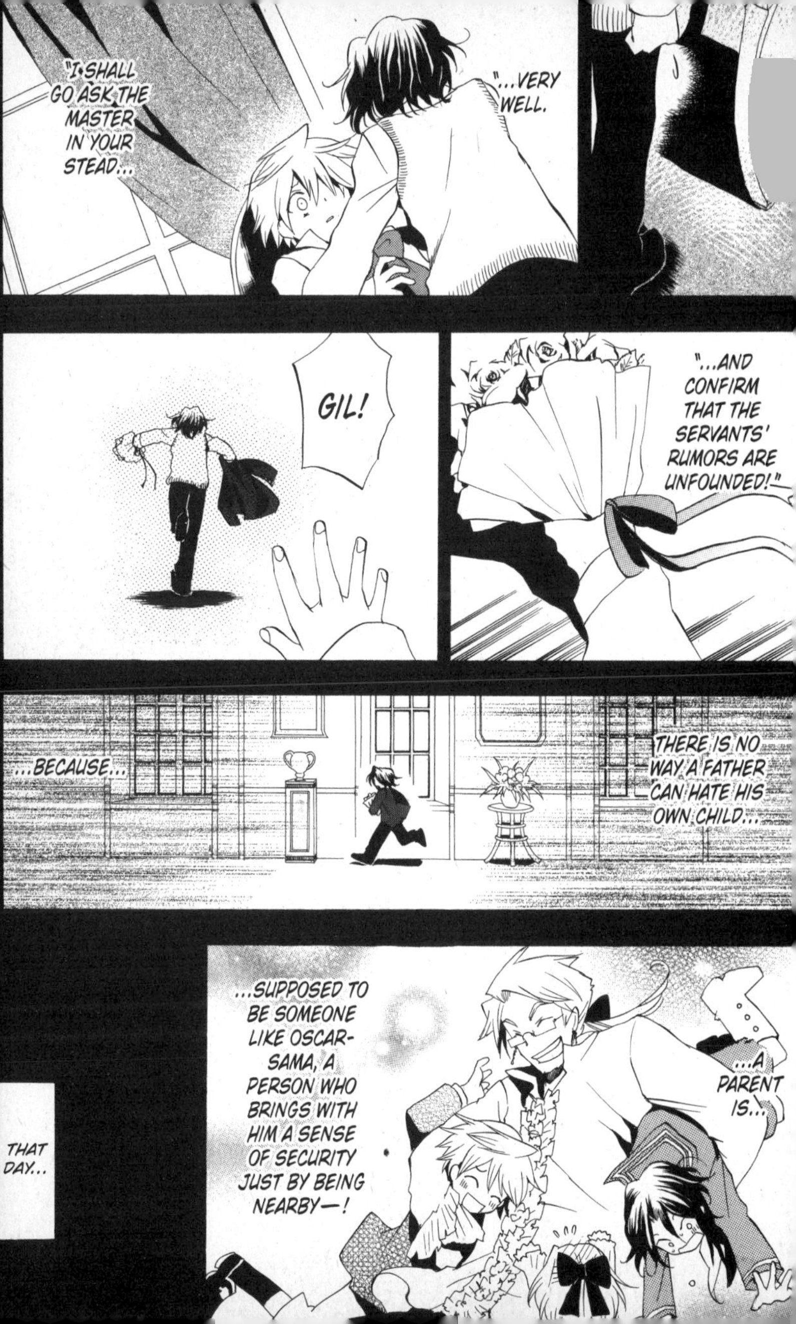
"I SHALL GO ASK THE MASTER IN YOUR STEAD...
"...VERY WELL.
"...AND CONFIRM THAT THE SERVANTS' RUMORS ARE UNFOUNDED!"
GIL!
...BECAUSE...
THERE IS NO WAY A FATHER CAN HATE HIS OWN CHILD...
...A PARENT IS...
...SUPPOSED TO BE SOMEONE LIKE OSCAR-SAMA, A PERSON WHO BRINGS WITH HIM A SENSE OF SECURITY JUST BY BEING NEARBY—!
THAT DAY...

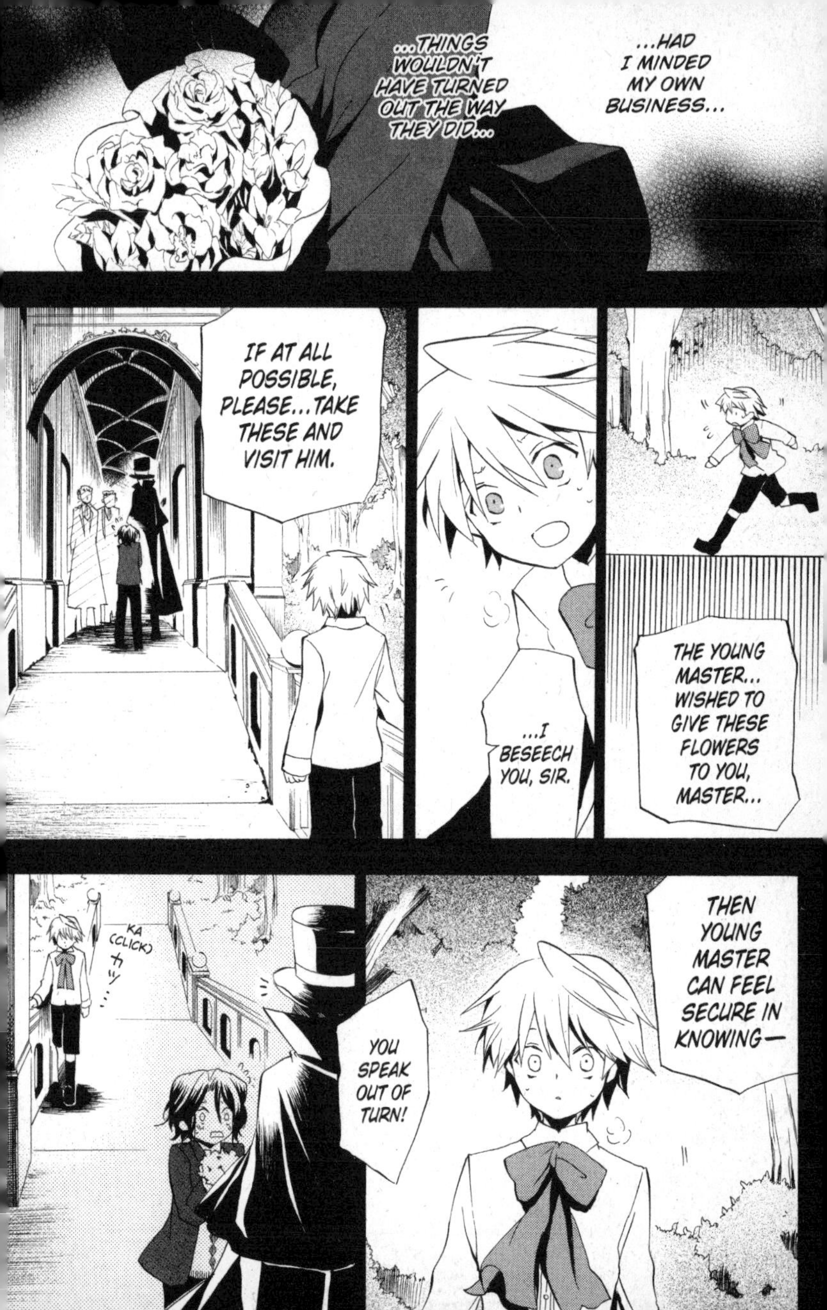
...HAD I MINDED MY OWN BUSINESS...
...THINGS WOULDN'T HAVE TURNED OUT THE WAY THEY DID...
THE YOUNG MASTER... WISHED TO GIVE THESE FLOWERS TO YOU, MASTER...
...I BESEECH YOU, SIR.
IF AT ALL POSSIBLE, PLEASE...TAKE THESE AND VISIT HIM.
THEN YOUNG MASTER CAN FEEL SECURE IN KNOWING—
YOU SPEAK OUT OF TURN!
KA (CLICK)
カッ...

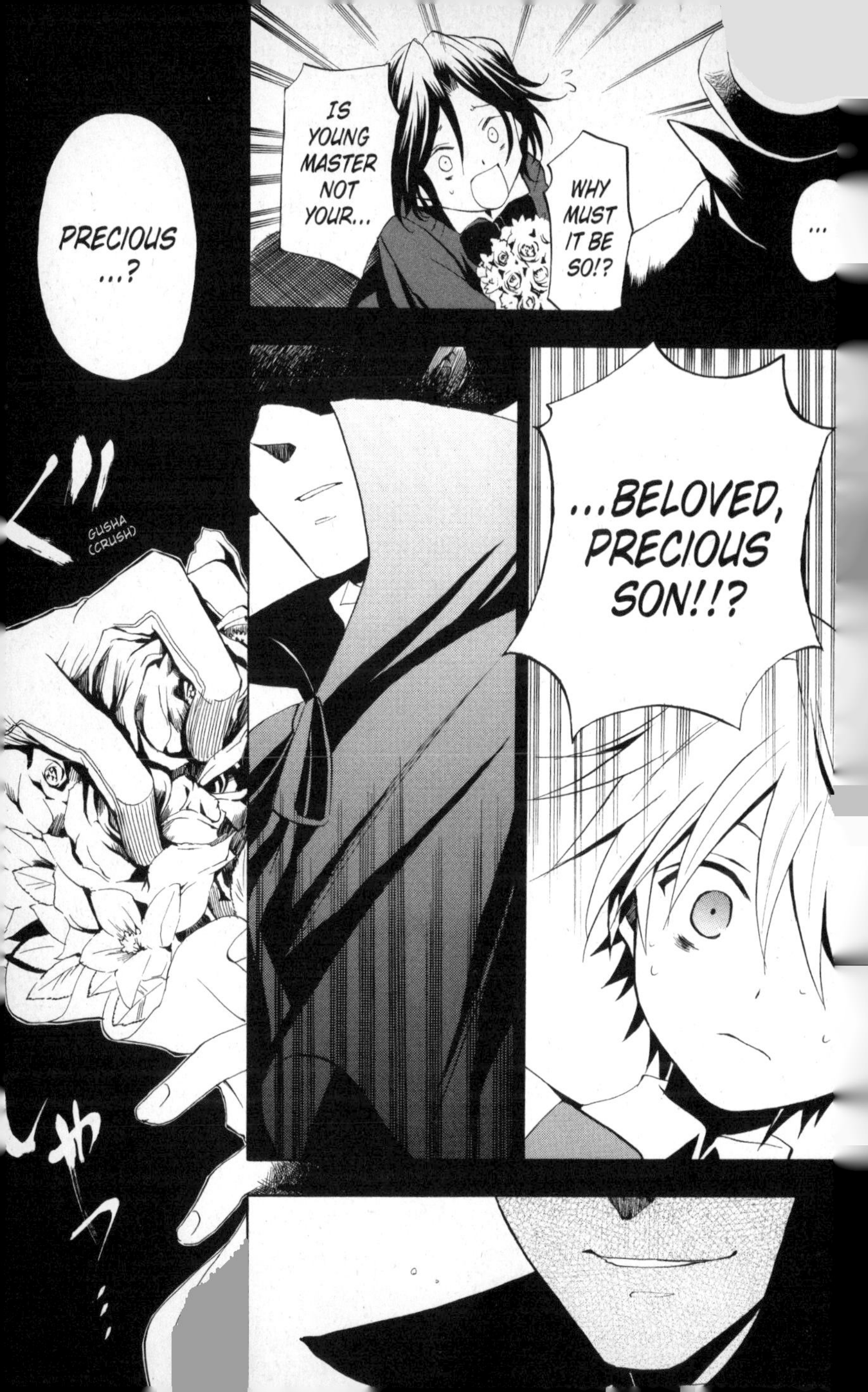
...
WHY MUST IT BE SO!?
IS YOUNG MASTER NOT YOUR...
...BELOVED, PRECIOUS SON!!?
PRECIOUS ...?
GUSHA (CRUSH)

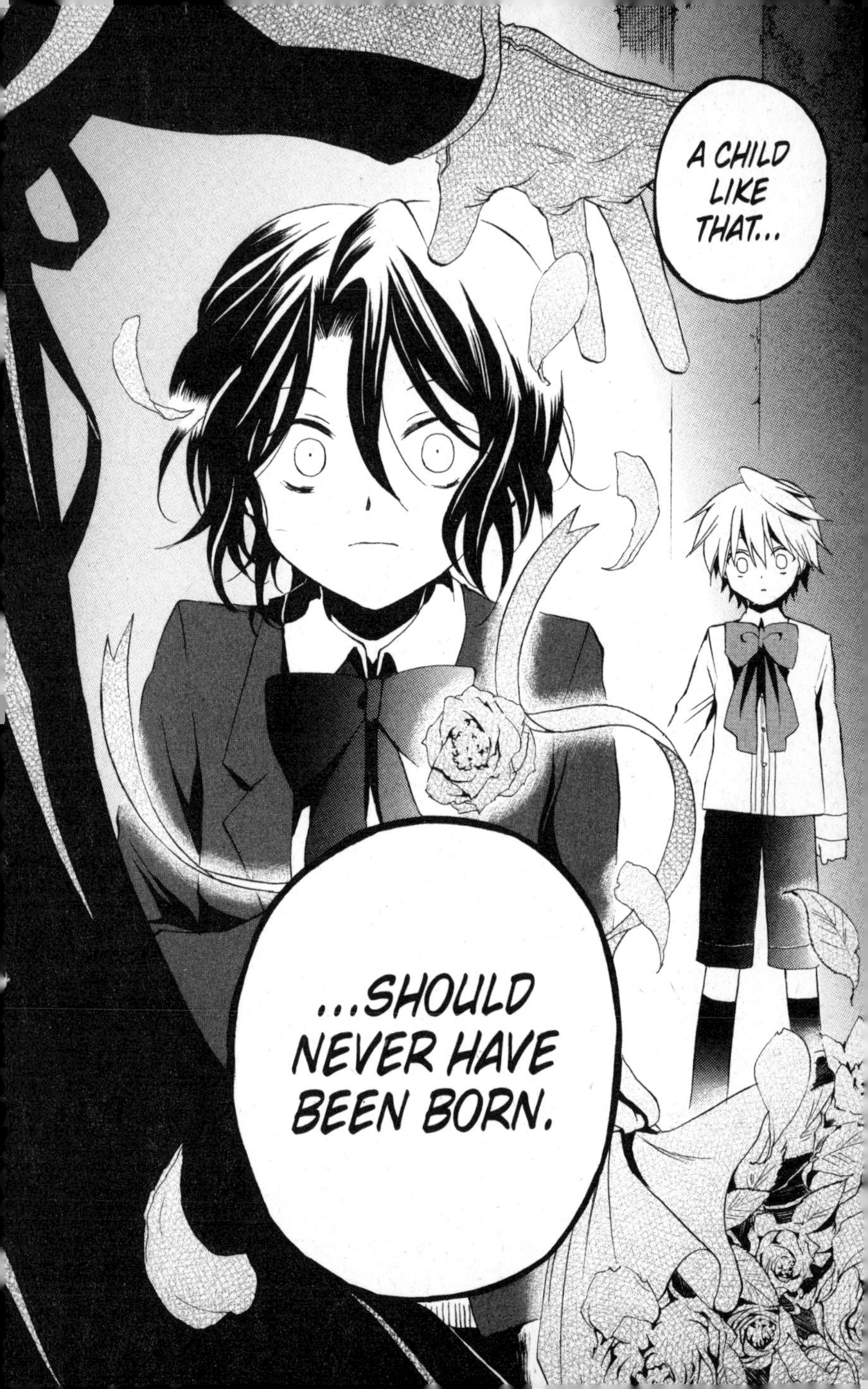
A CHILD LIKE THAT...
...SHOULD NEVER HAVE BEEN BORN.

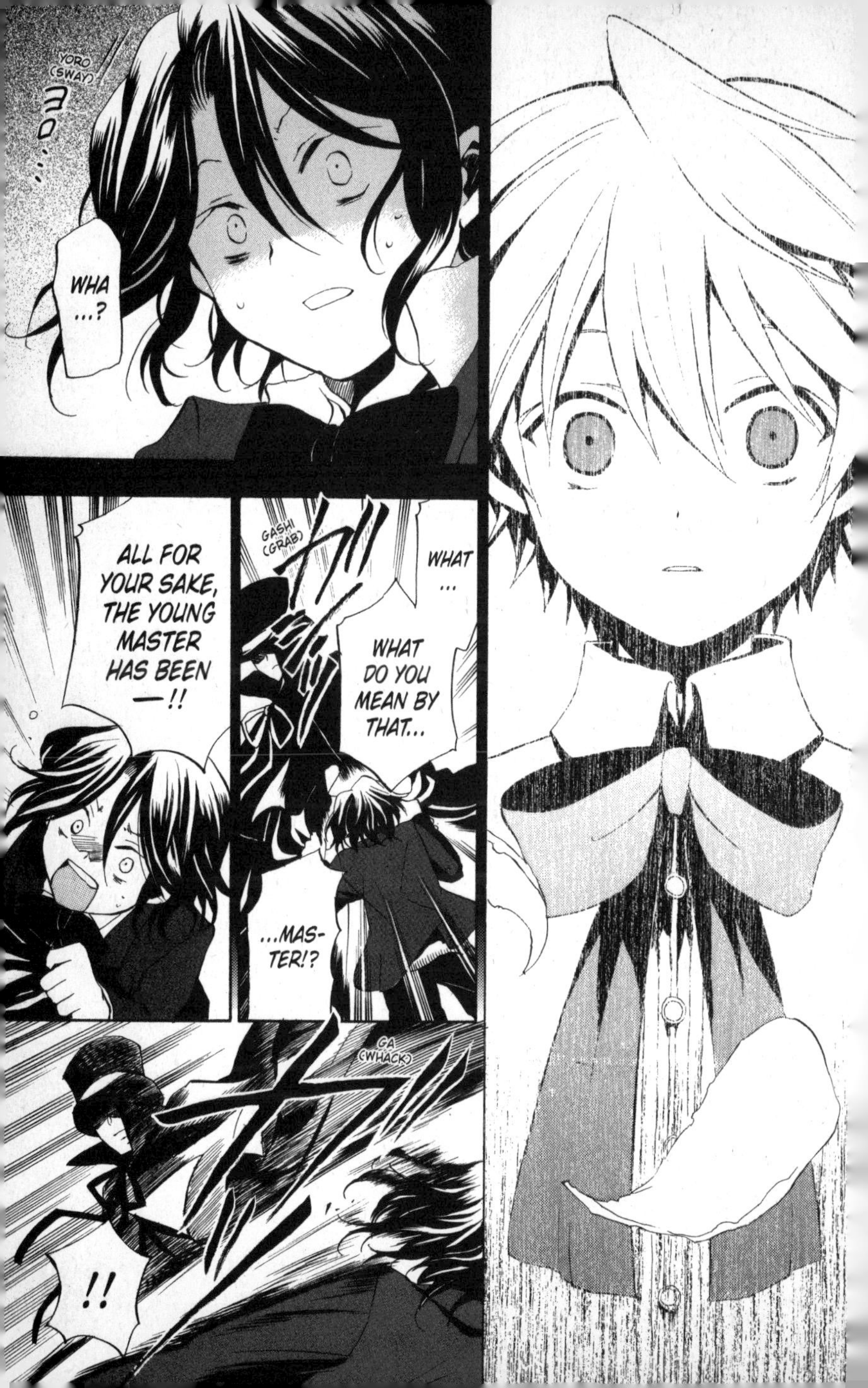
YORO (SWAY)
ヨロ…
WHA ...?
GASHI (GRAB)
WHAT ...
WHAT DO YOU MEAN BY THAT...
...MAS-TER!?
ALL FOR YOUR SAKE, THE YOUNG MASTER HAS BEEN —!!
GA (WHACK)
!!

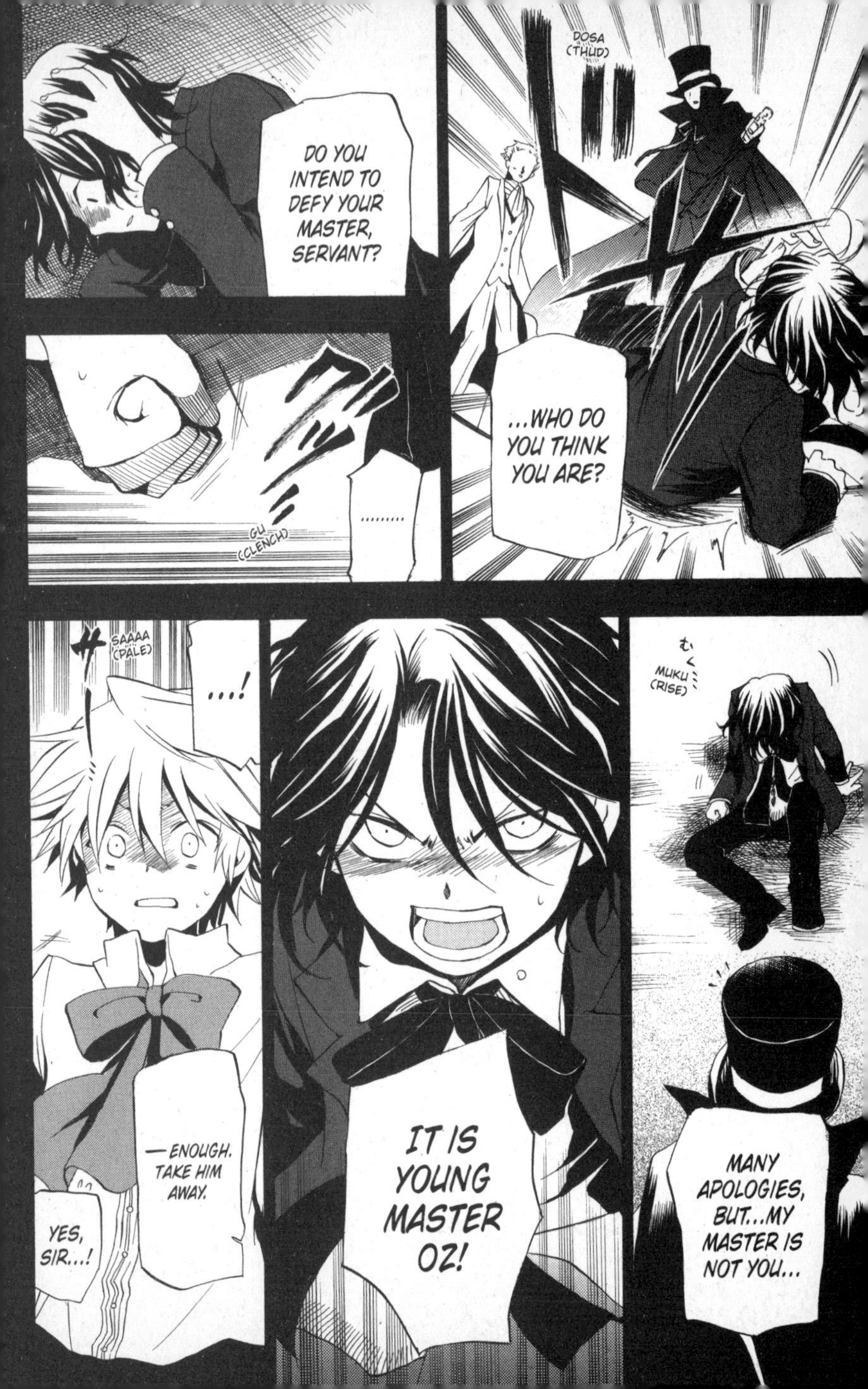
DOSA (THUD)
...WHO DO YOU THINK YOU ARE?
DO YOU INTEND TO DEFY YOUR MASTER, SERVANT?
GU (CLENCH)
....
むく
MUKU (RISE)
MANY APOLOGIES, BUT...MY MASTER IS NOT YOU...
IT IS YOUNG MASTER OZ!
SAAAA (PALE)
...!
—ENOUGH. TAKE HIM AWAY.
YES, SIR...!

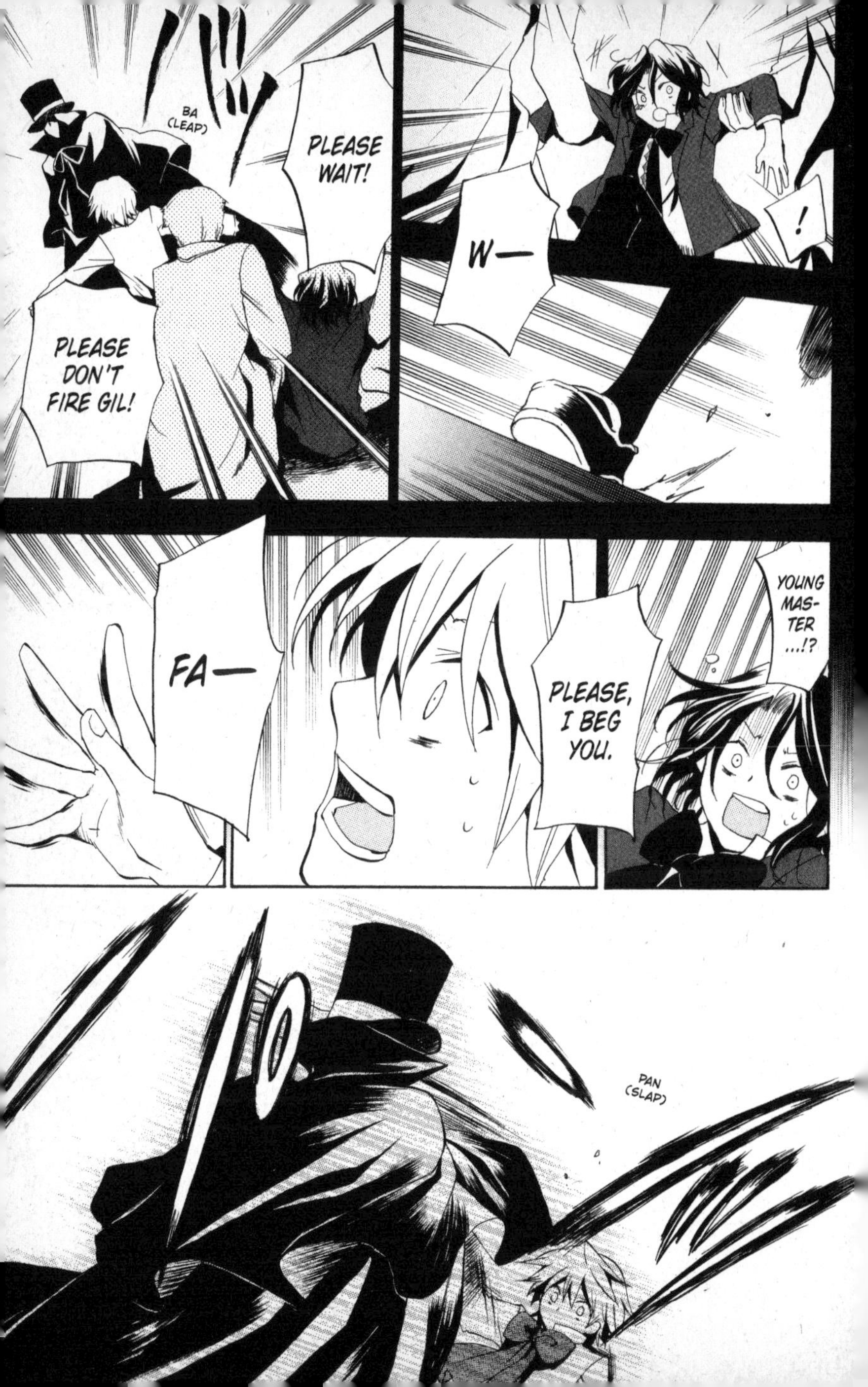
!
W—
PLEASE WAIT!
BA (LEAP)
PLEASE DON'T FIRE GIL!
YOUNG MASTER...!?
PLEASE, I BEG YOU.
FA—
PAN (SLAP)

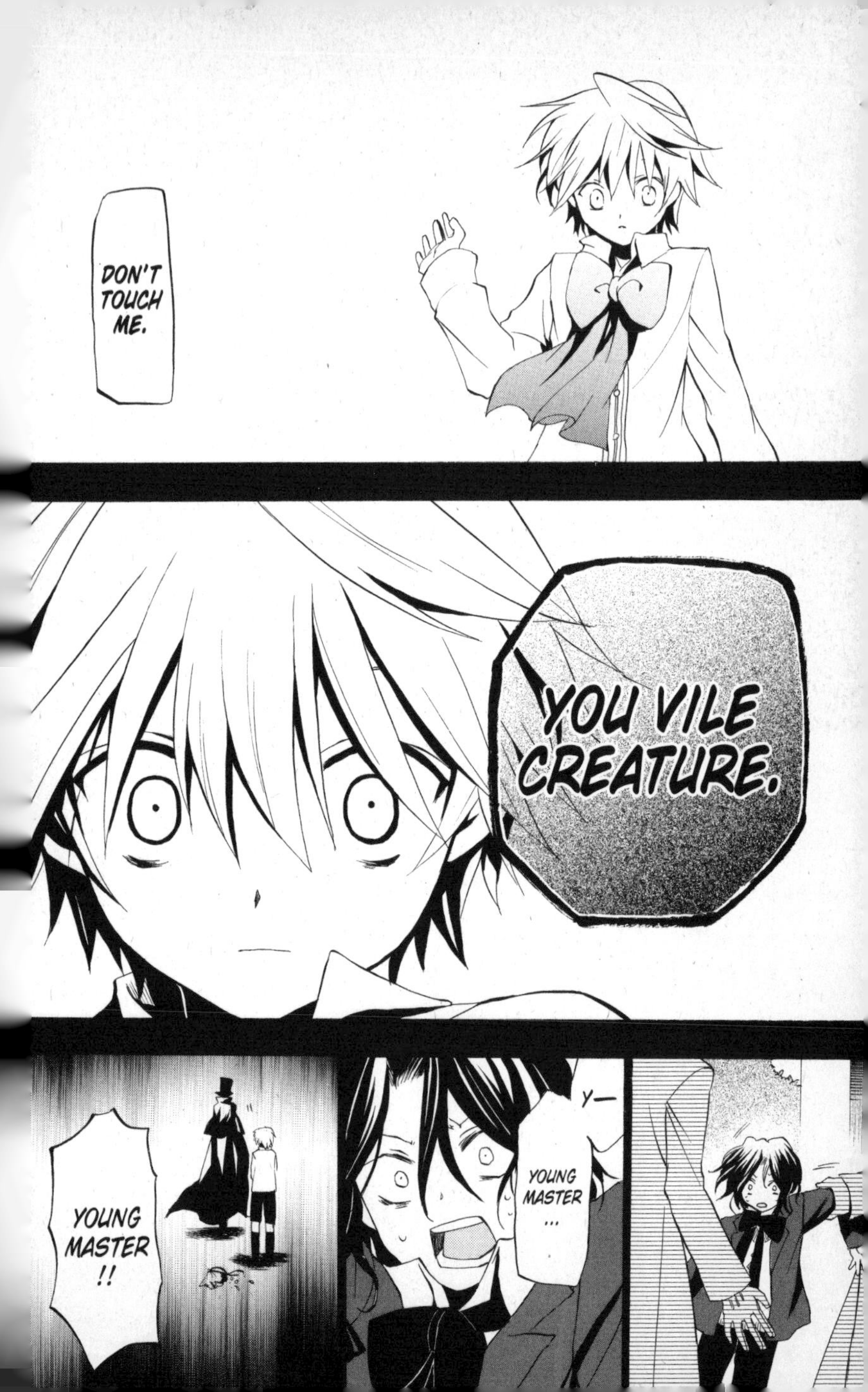
DON'T TOUCH ME.
YOU VILE CREATURE.
Y—
YOUNG MASTER ...
YOUNG MASTER !!

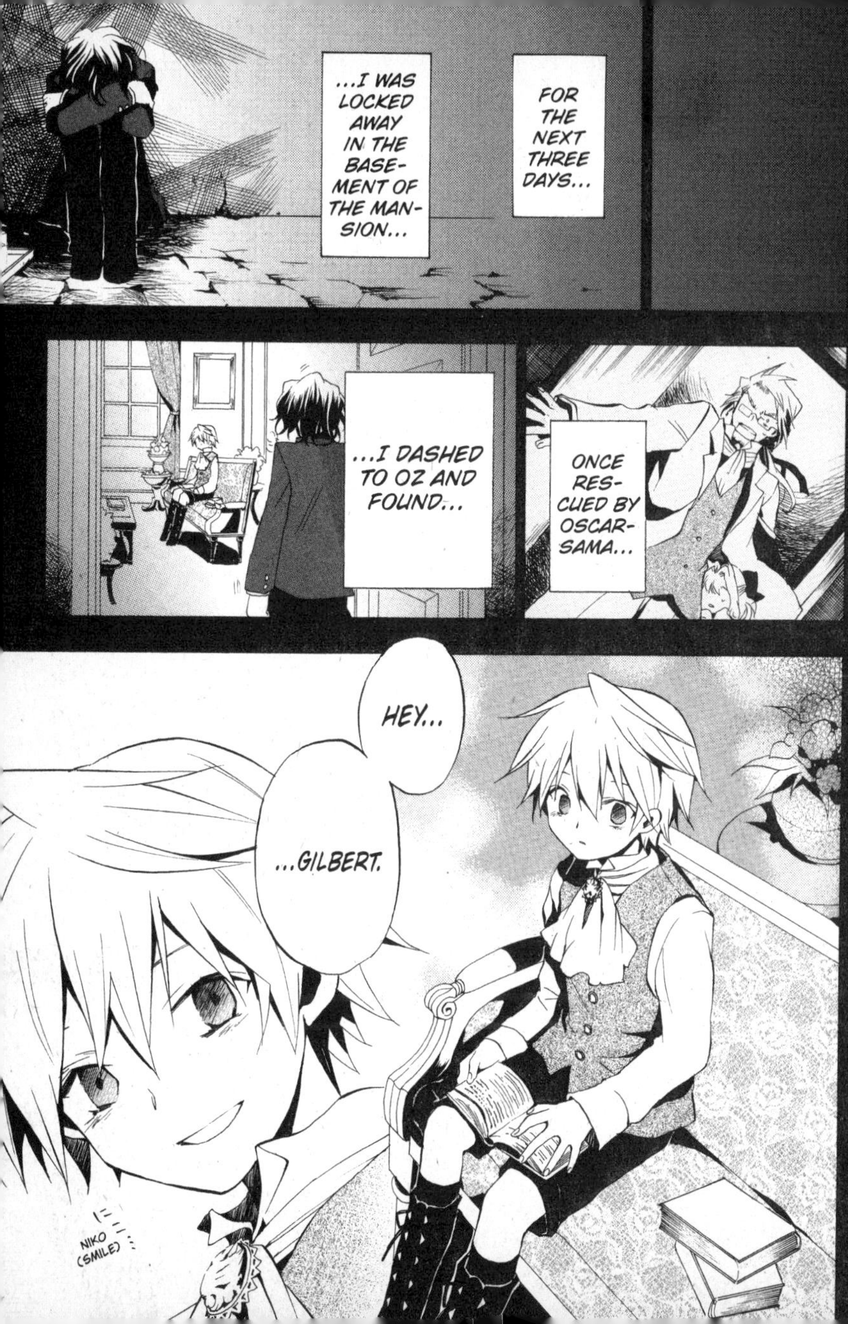
FOR THE NEXT THREE DAYS...
...I WAS LOCKED AWAY IN THE BASEMENT OF THE MANSION...
ONCE RESCUED BY OSCAR-SAMA...
...I DASHED TO OZ AND FOUND...
HEY...
...GILBERT.
NIKO (SMILE)

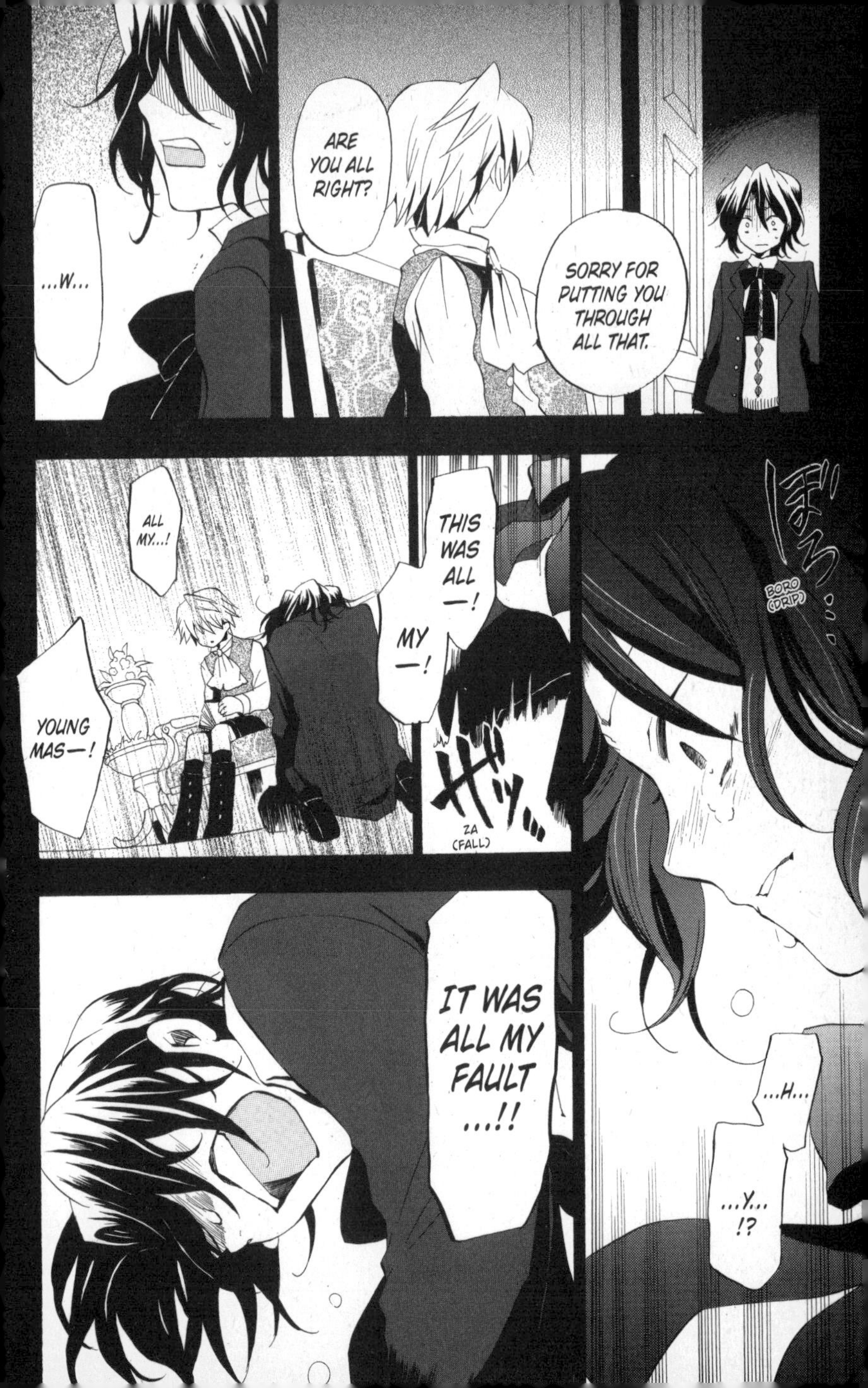
SORRY FOR PUTTING YOU THROUGH ALL THAT.
ARE YOU ALL RIGHT?
...W...
ぼろ
BORO (DRIP)
...H...
...Y... !?
THIS WAS ALL—!
MY—!
ザッ
ZA (FALL)
ALL MY...!
YOUNG MAS—!
IT WAS ALL MY FAULT ...!!

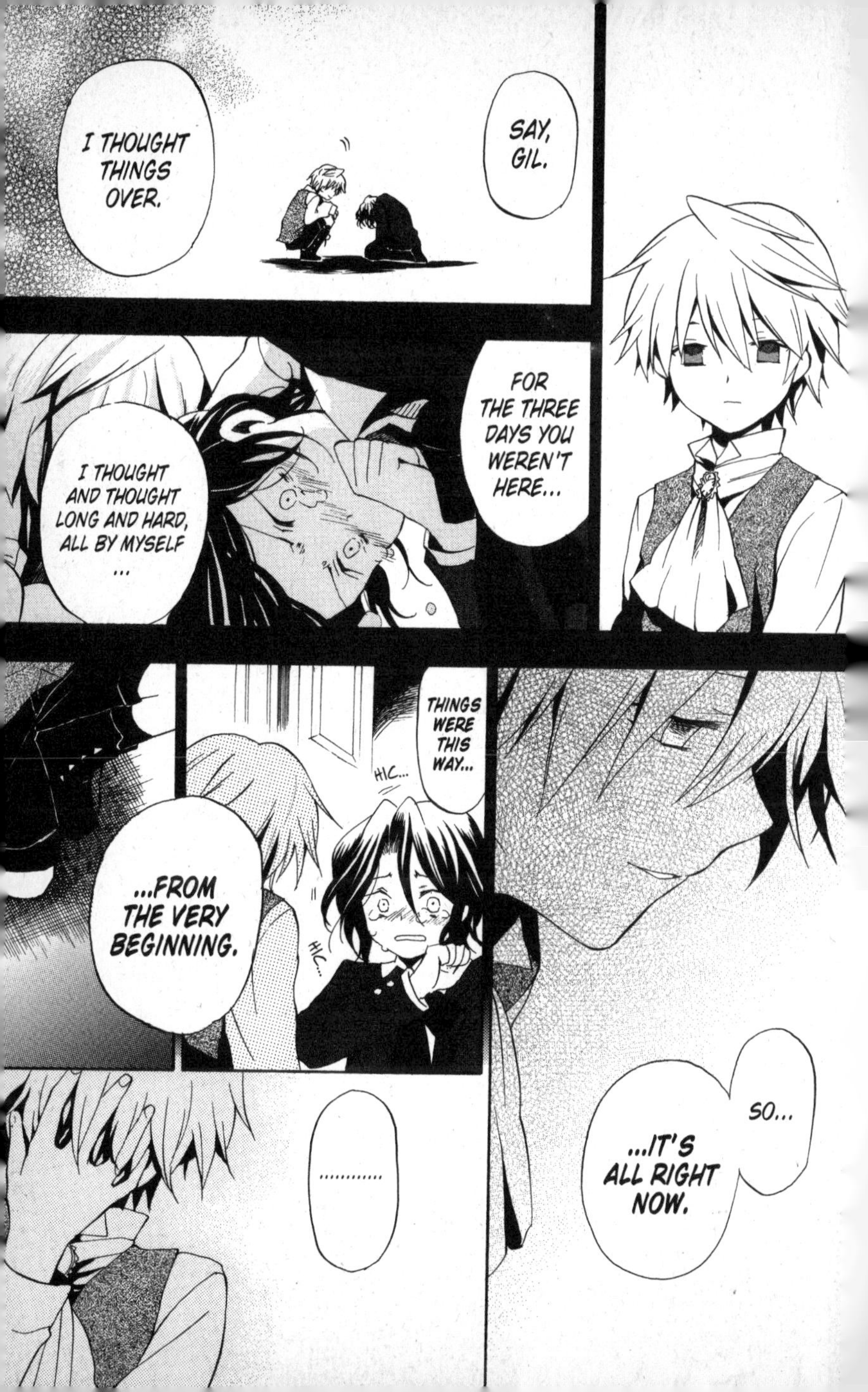
SAY, GIL.
I THOUGHT THINGS OVER.
FOR THE THREE DAYS YOU WEREN'T HERE...
I THOUGHT AND THOUGHT LONG AND HARD, ALL BY MYSELF ...
SO...
...IT'S ALL RIGHT NOW.
THINGS WERE THIS WAY...
HIC...
...FROM THE VERY BEGINNING.
HIC...
....

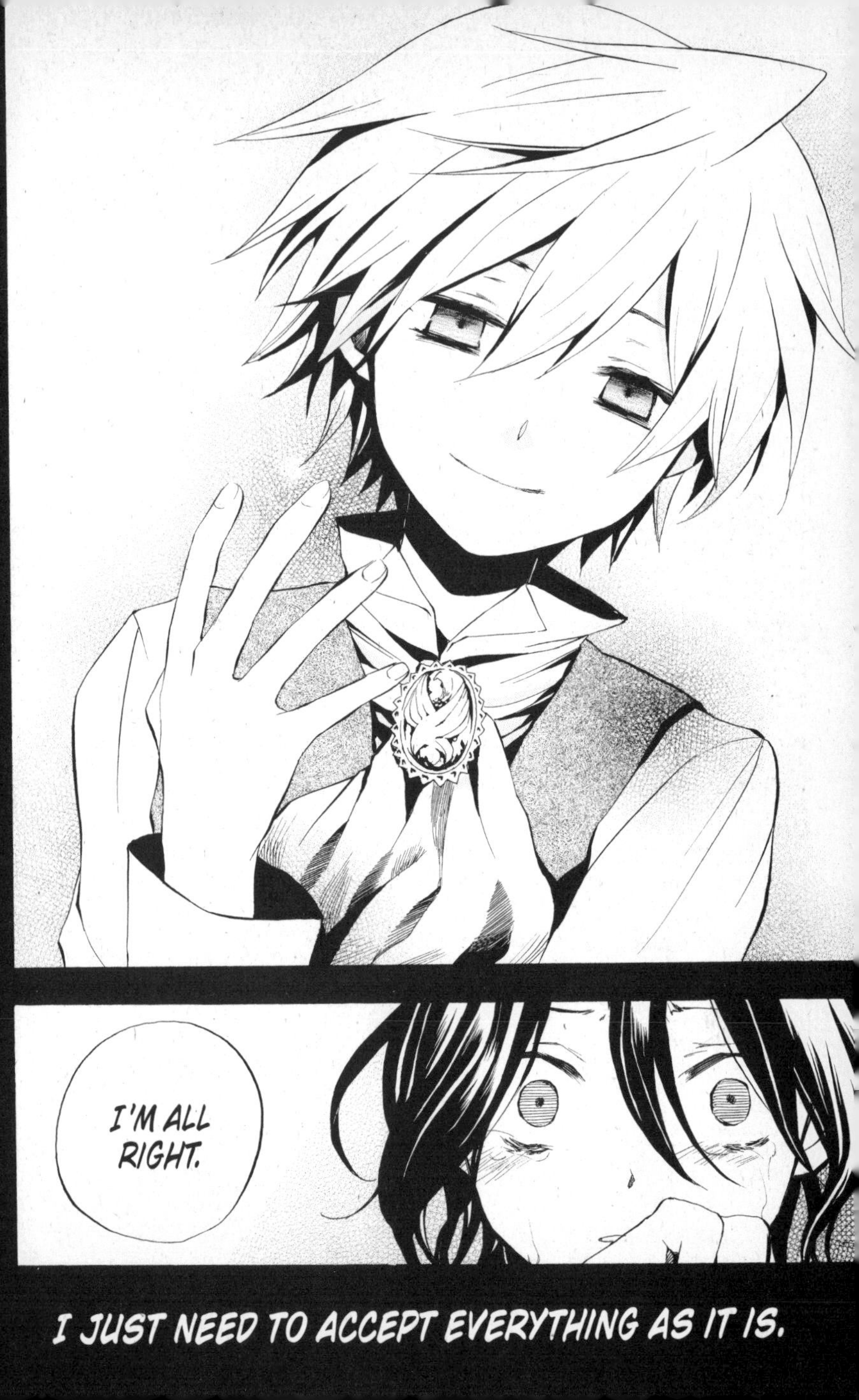
I'M ALL RIGHT.
I JUST NEED TO ACCEPT EVERYTHING AS IT IS.

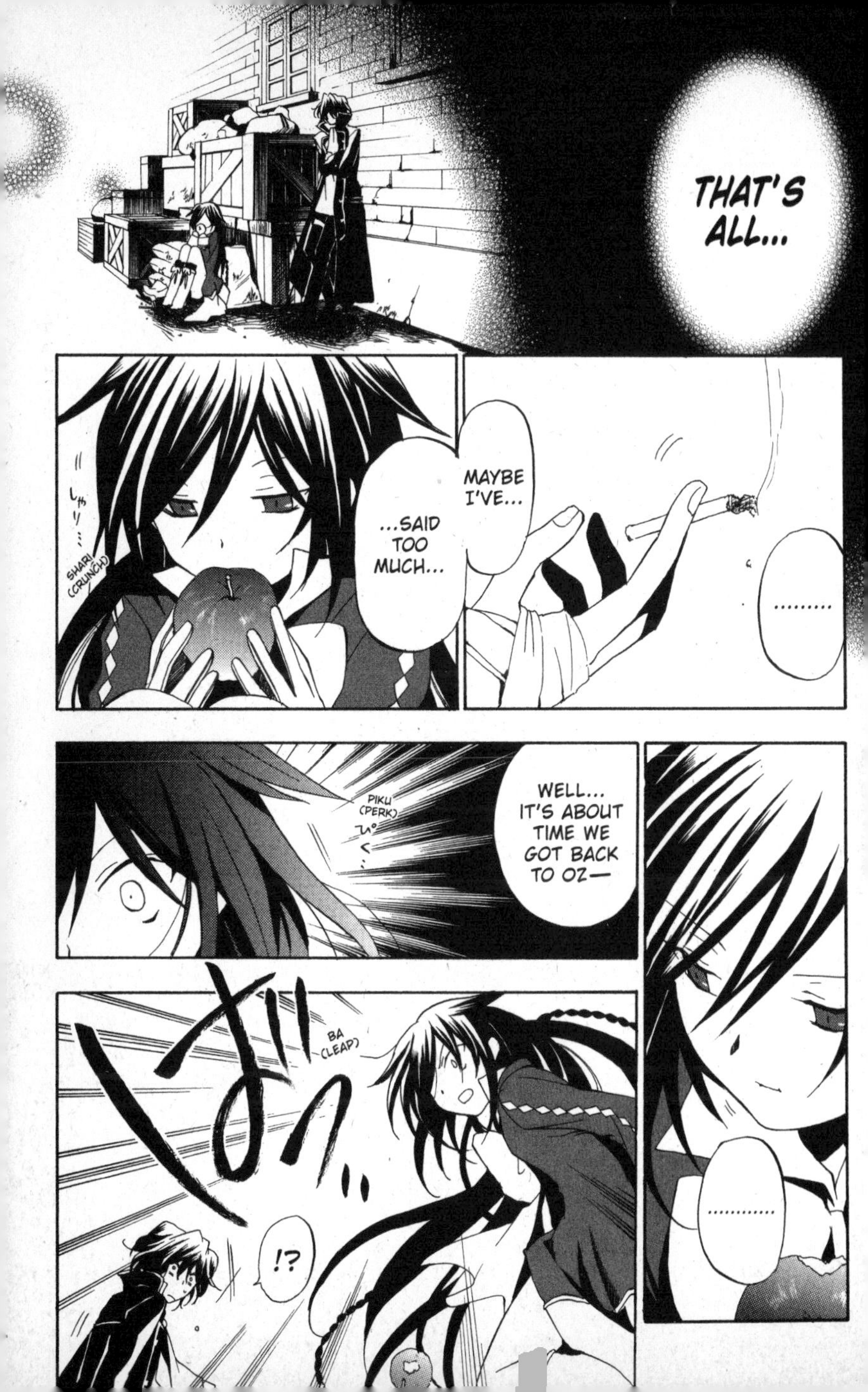
THAT'S ALL...
....
SHARI (CRUNCH)
MAYBE I'VE...
...SAID TOO MUCH...
....
WELL... IT'S ABOUT TIME WE GOT BACK TO OZ—
PIKU (PERK)
BA (LEAP)
!?

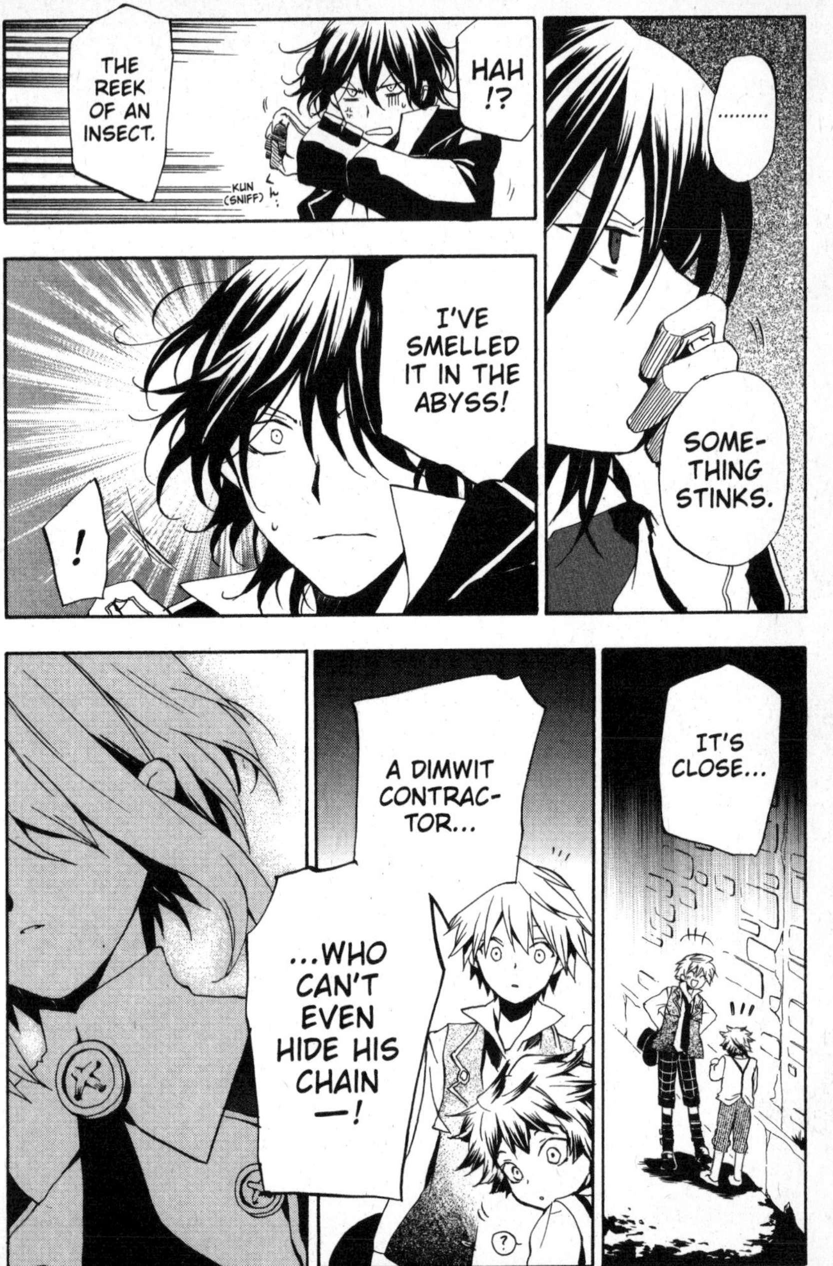

....
SOME-THING STINKS.
HAH!?
THE REEK OF AN INSECT.
KUN (SNIFF)
I'VE SMELLED IT IN THE ABYSS!
!
IT'S CLOSE...
A DIMWIT CONTRAC-TOR...
...WHO CAN'T EVEN HIDE HIS CHAIN—!
?

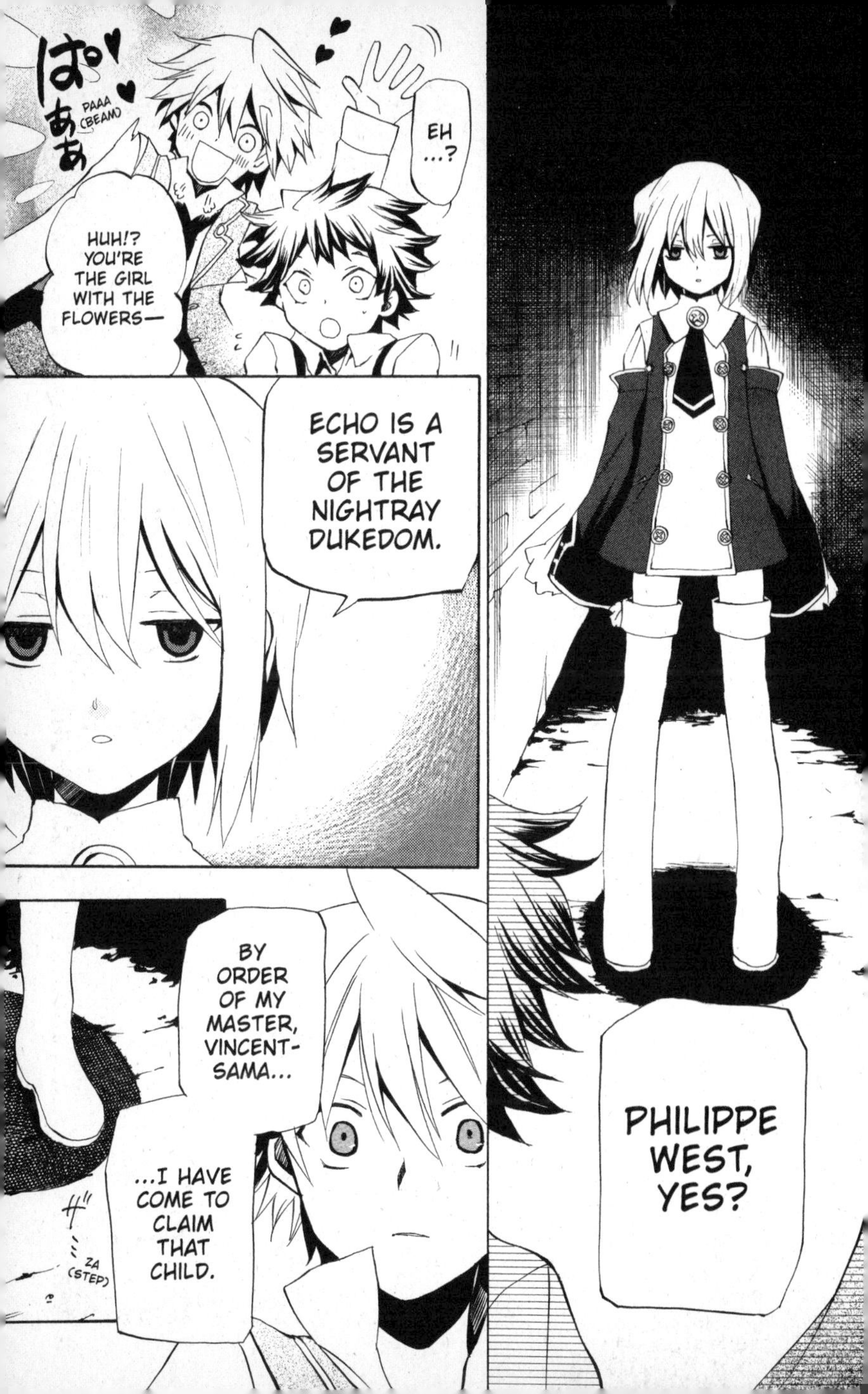
PHILIPPE WEST, YES?
EH ...?
HUH!? YOU'RE THE GIRL WITH THE FLOWERS—
ぱあ
PAAA (BEAM)
ECHO IS A SERVANT OF THE NIGHTRAY DUKEDOM.
BY ORDER OF MY MASTER, VINCENT-SAMA...
...I HAVE COME TO CLAIM THAT CHILD.
ザ
ZA (STEP)

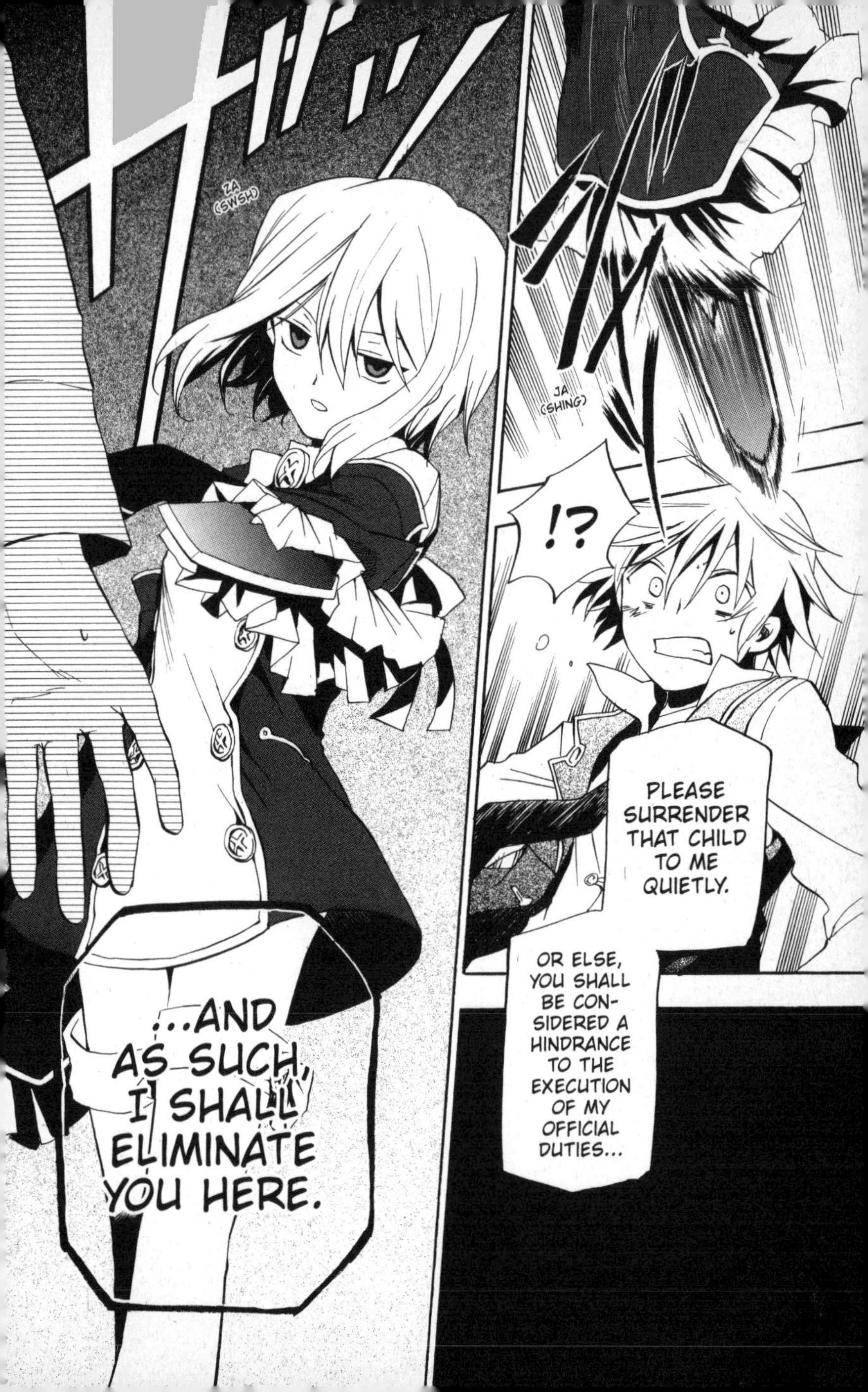
JA (SHING)
!?
PLEASE SURRENDER THAT CHILD TO ME QUIETLY.
OR ELSE, YOU SHALL BE CONSIDERED A HINDRANCE TO THE EXECUTION OF MY OFFICIAL DUTIES...
ZA (SWSH)
...AND AS SUCH, I SHALL ELIMINATE YOU HERE.

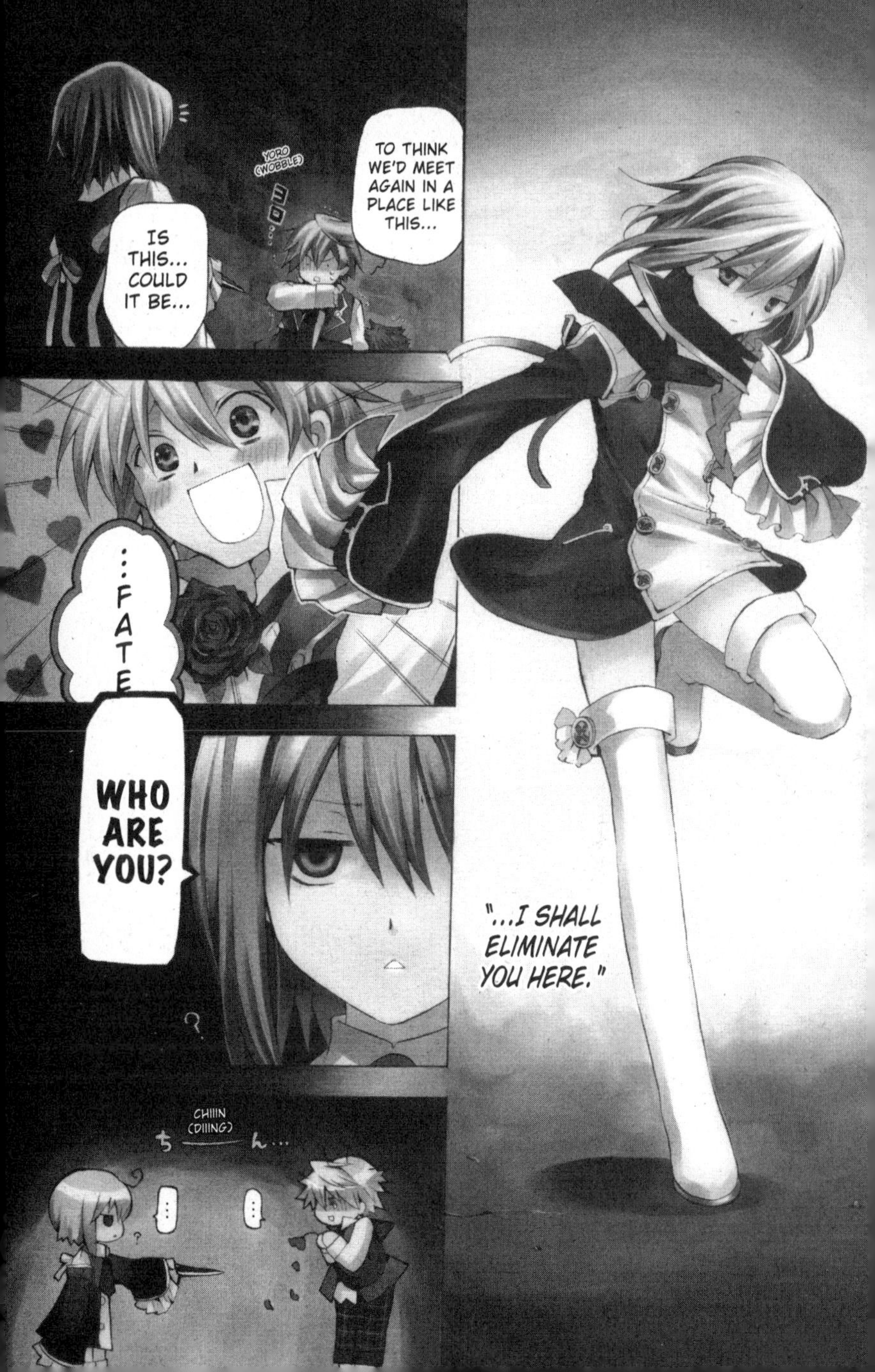
"...I SHALL ELIMINATE YOU HERE."
TO THINK WE'D MEET AGAIN IN A PLACE LIKE THIS...
YORO (WOBBLE)
IS THIS... COULD IT BE...
...FATE
WHO ARE YOU?
CHIIN (DIIING)
...
...

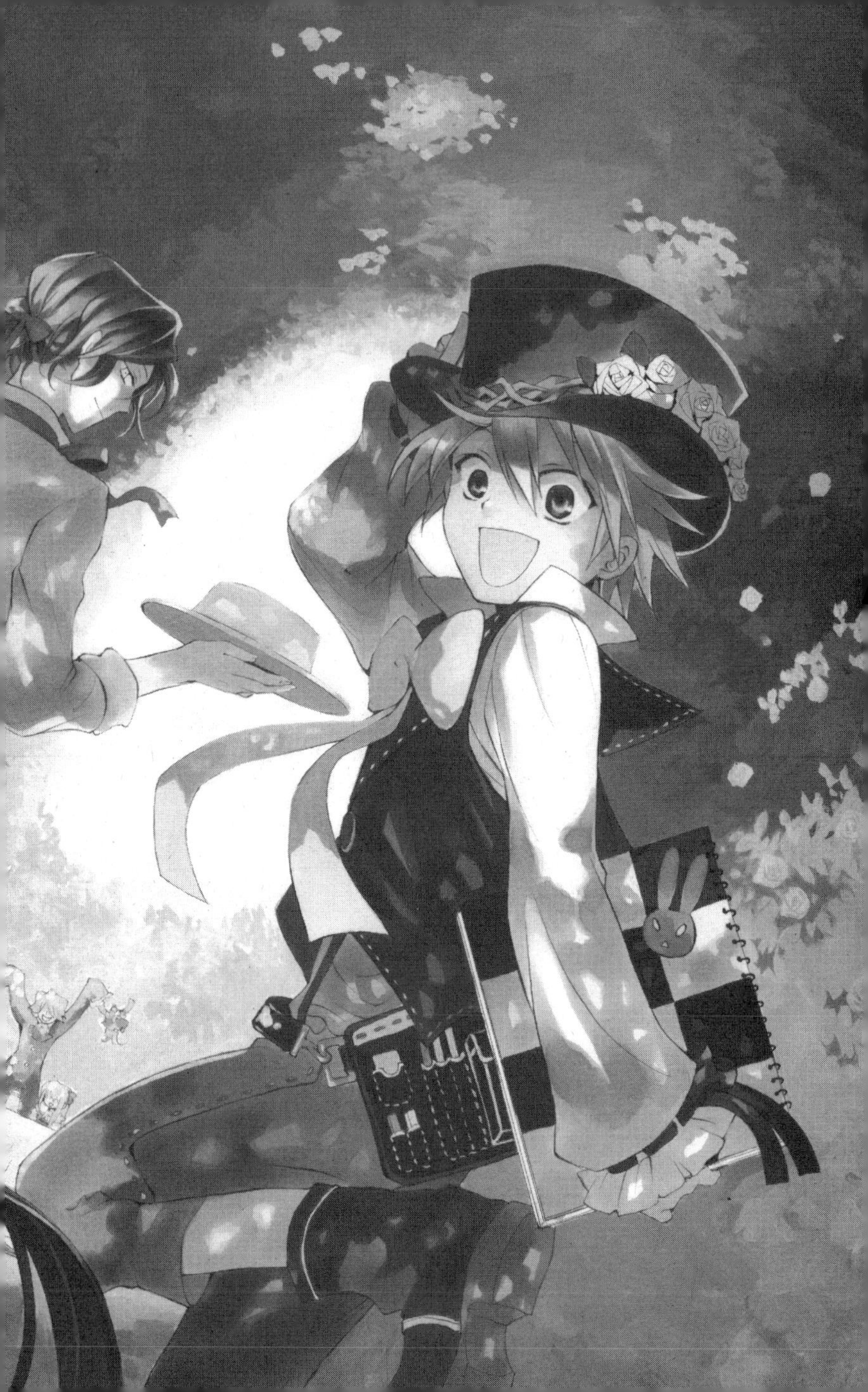

Retrace:XI Grim

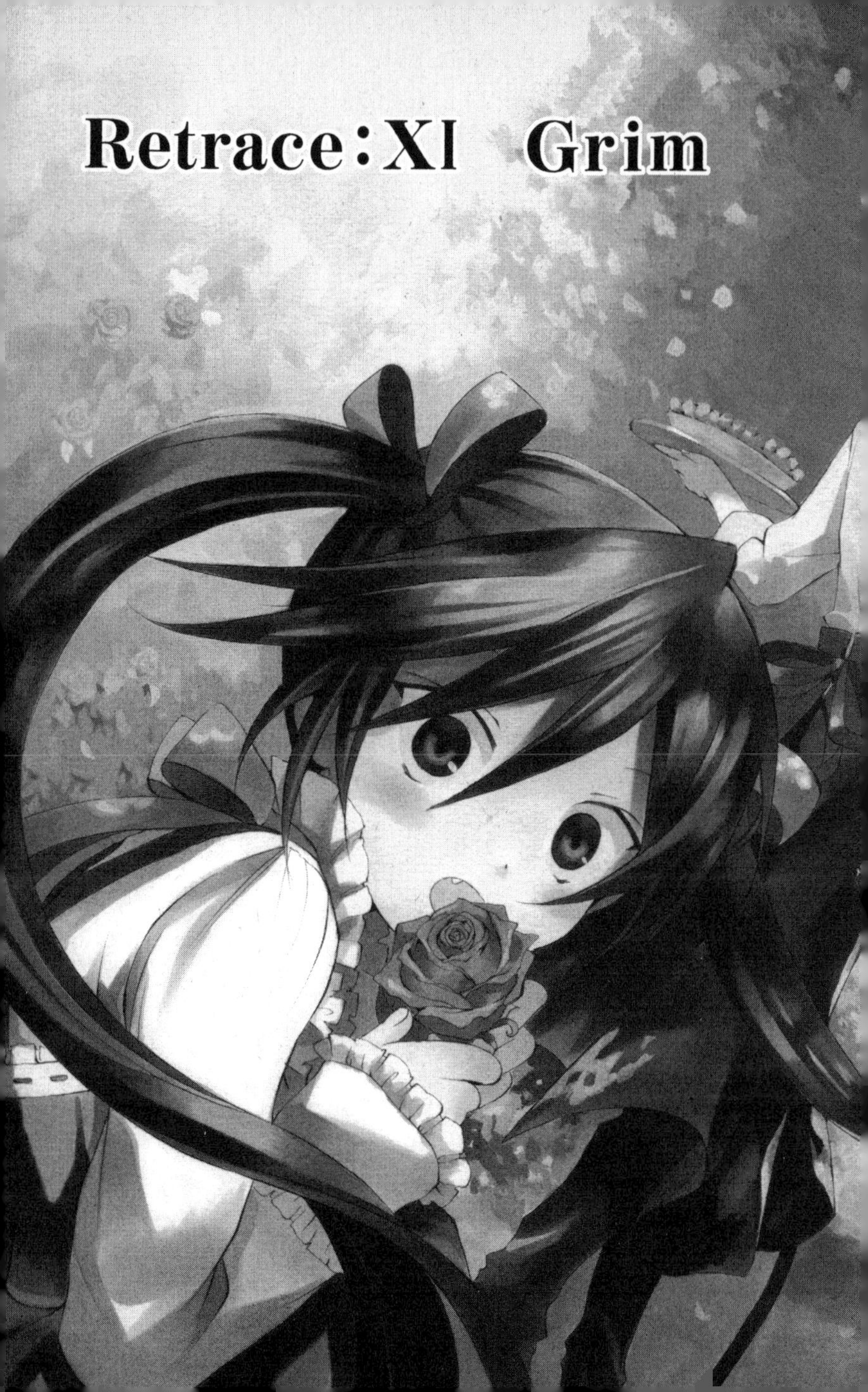

EXTRA PAGE

LET'S CHANGE THE LINES!!!

TITLE

"IF IT HADN'T BEEN THAT KIND OF SCENE, I THINK GIL WOULD'VE SAID THIS INSTEAD."

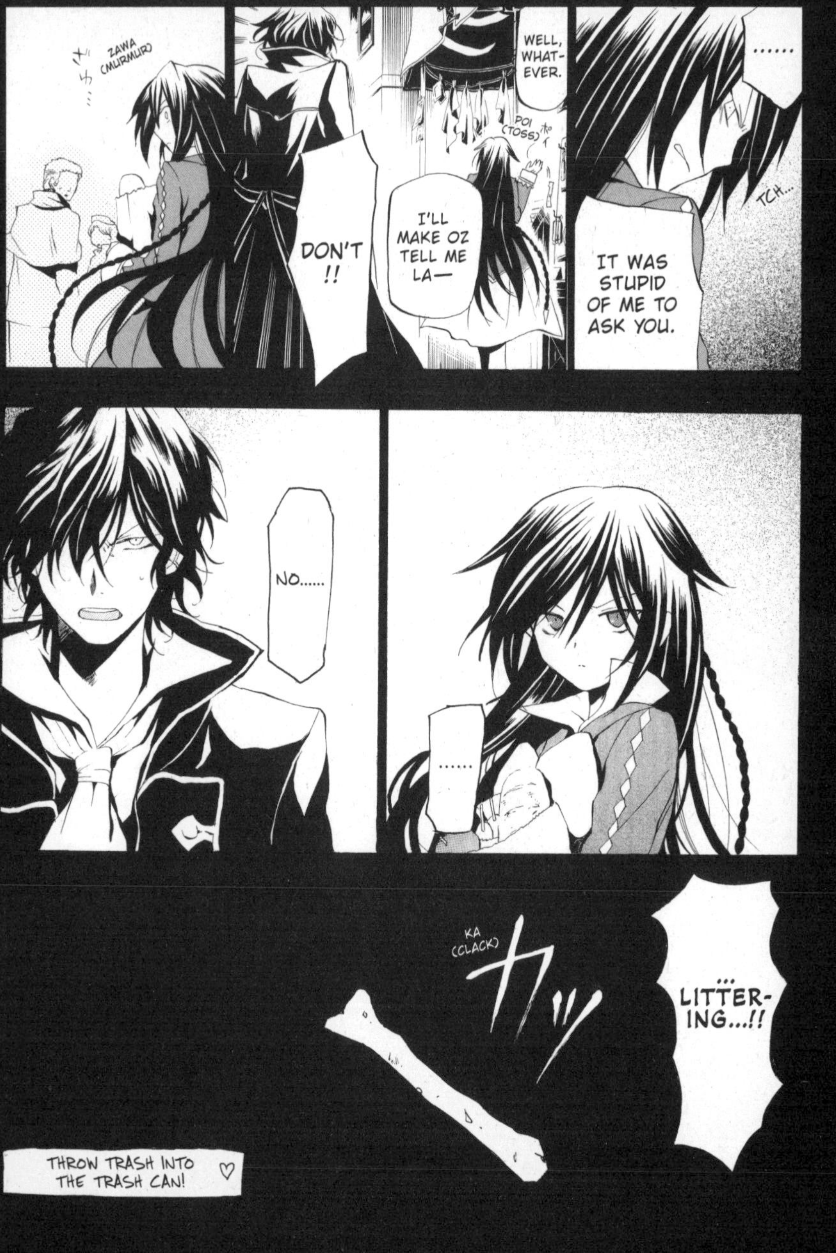
......
TCH...
IT WAS STUPID OF ME TO ASK YOU.
WELL, WHAT-EVER.
POI (TOSS)
I'LL MAKE OZ TELL ME LA—
DON'T !!
ZAWA (MURMUR)
......
NO......
KA (CLACK)
...LITTER-ING...!!
THROW TRASH INTO THE TRASH CAN! ♡

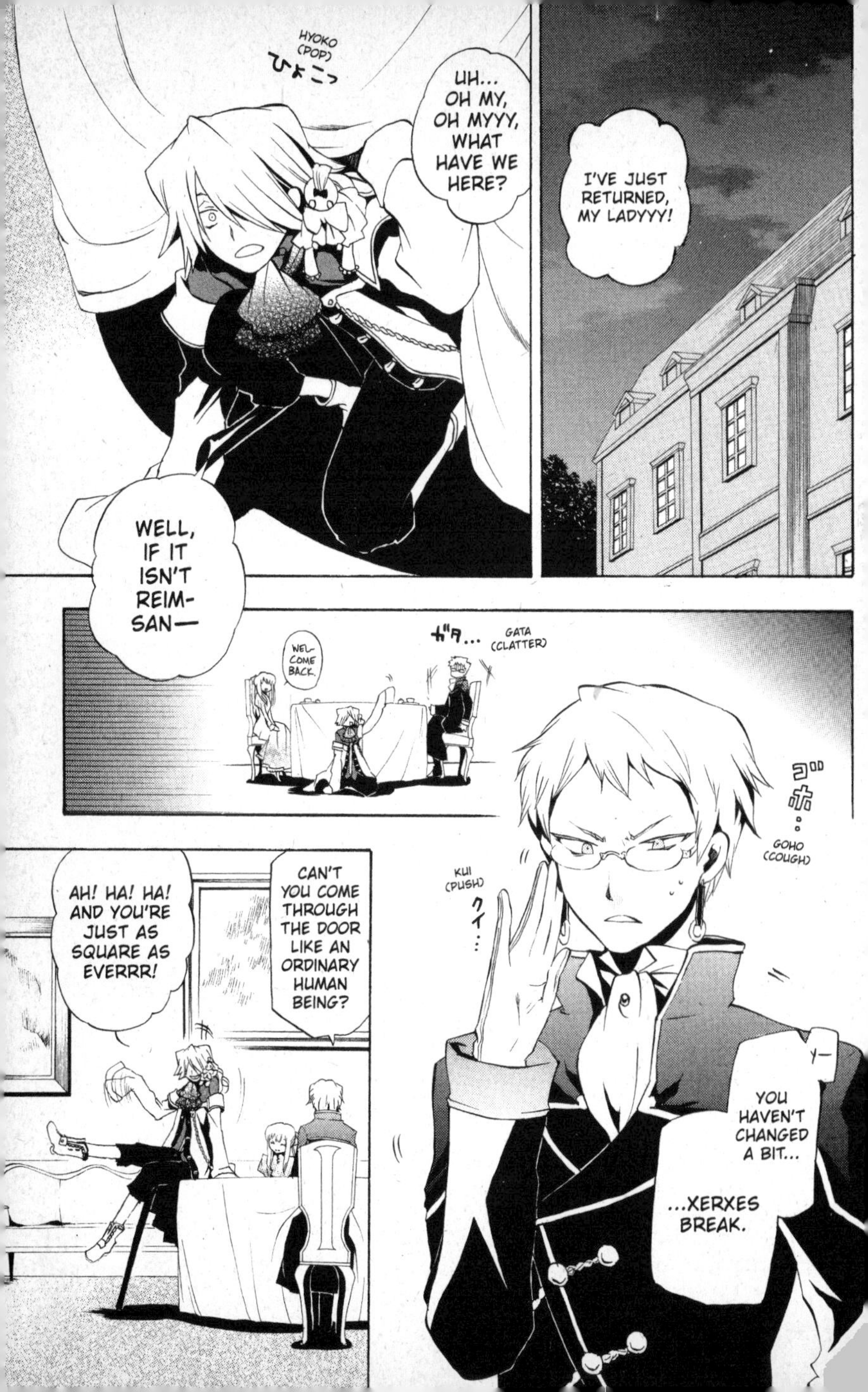
I'VE JUST RETURNED, MY LADYYY!
HYOKO (POP)
ひょこっ
UH... OH MY, OH MYYY, WHAT HAVE WE HERE?
WELL, IF IT ISN'T REIM-SAN—
ガタ...
GATA (CLATTER)
WEL-COME BACK.
ゴホ..
GOHO (COUGH)
KUI (PUSH)
クイ...
YOU HAVEN'T CHANGED A BIT...
...XERXES BREAK.
CAN'T YOU COME THROUGH THE DOOR LIKE AN ORDINARY HUMAN BEING?
AH! HA! HA! AND YOU'RE JUST AS SQUARE AS EVERRR!

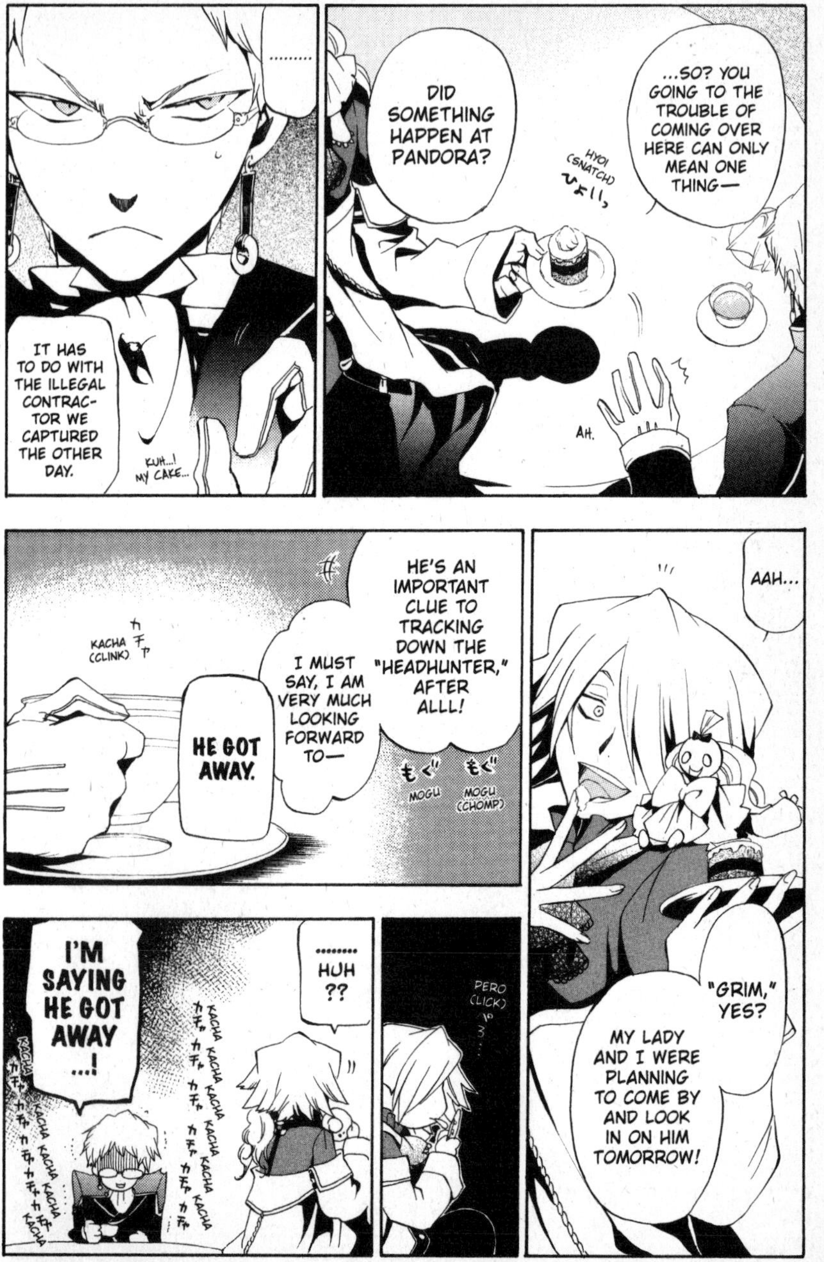

...SO? YOU GOING TO THE TROUBLE OF COMING OVER HERE CAN ONLY MEAN ONE THING—
DID SOMETHING HAPPEN AT PANDORA?
HYOI (SNATCH) ひょい
AH.
....
IT HAS TO DO WITH THE ILLEGAL CONTRAC-TOR WE CAPTURED THE OTHER DAY.
KUH...! MY CAKE...
AAH...
"GRIM," YES?
MY LADY AND I WERE PLANNING TO COME BY AND LOOK IN ON HIM TOMORROW!
HE'S AN IMPORTANT CLUE TO TRACKING DOWN THE "HEADHUNTER," AFTER ALLL!
I MUST SAY, I AM VERY MUCH LOOKING FORWARD TO—
もぐ MOGU
もぐ MOGU (CHOMP)
KACHA (CLINK) カチャ
HE GOT AWAY.
PERO (CLICK)
.... HUH ??
I'M SAYING HE GOT AWAY ...!
KACHA KACHA KACHA KACHA KACHA
KACHA KACHA KACHA KACHA

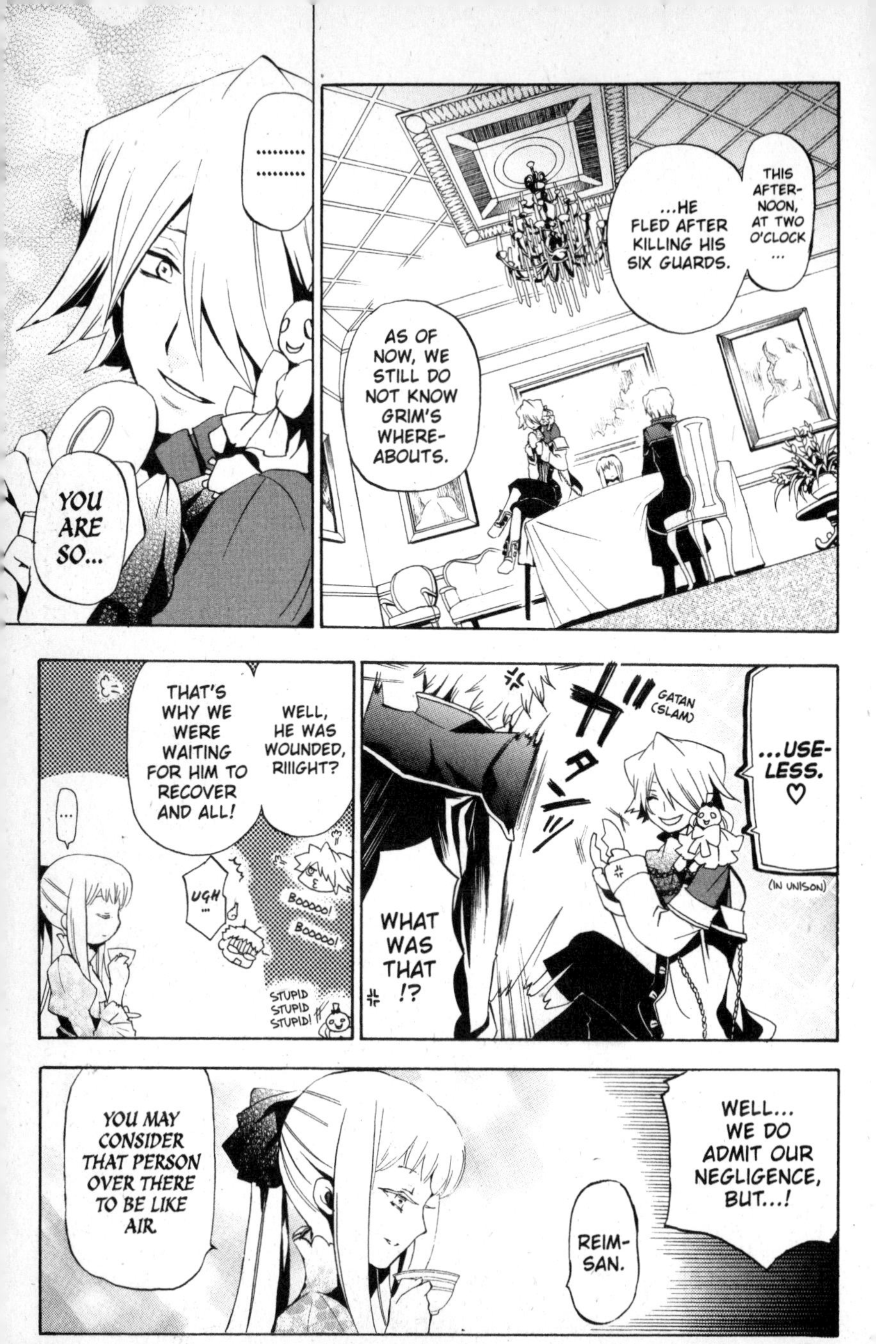
THIS AFTERNOON, AT TWO O'CLOCK...
...HE FLED AFTER KILLING HIS SIX GUARDS.
AS OF NOW, WE STILL DO NOT KNOW GRIM'S WHEREABOUTS.
....
....
YOU ARE SO...
GATAN (SLAM)
...USELESS. ♥
(IN UNISON)
WHAT WAS THAT!?
WELL, HE WAS WOUNDED, RIIIGHT?
THAT'S WHY WE WERE WAITING FOR HIM TO RECOVER AND ALL!
UGH...
Booooo!
Booooo!
...
STUPID STUPID STUPID!
WELL... WE DO ADMIT OUR NEGLIGENCE, BUT...!
REIM-SAN.
YOU MAY CONSIDER THAT PERSON OVER THERE TO BE LIKE AIR.

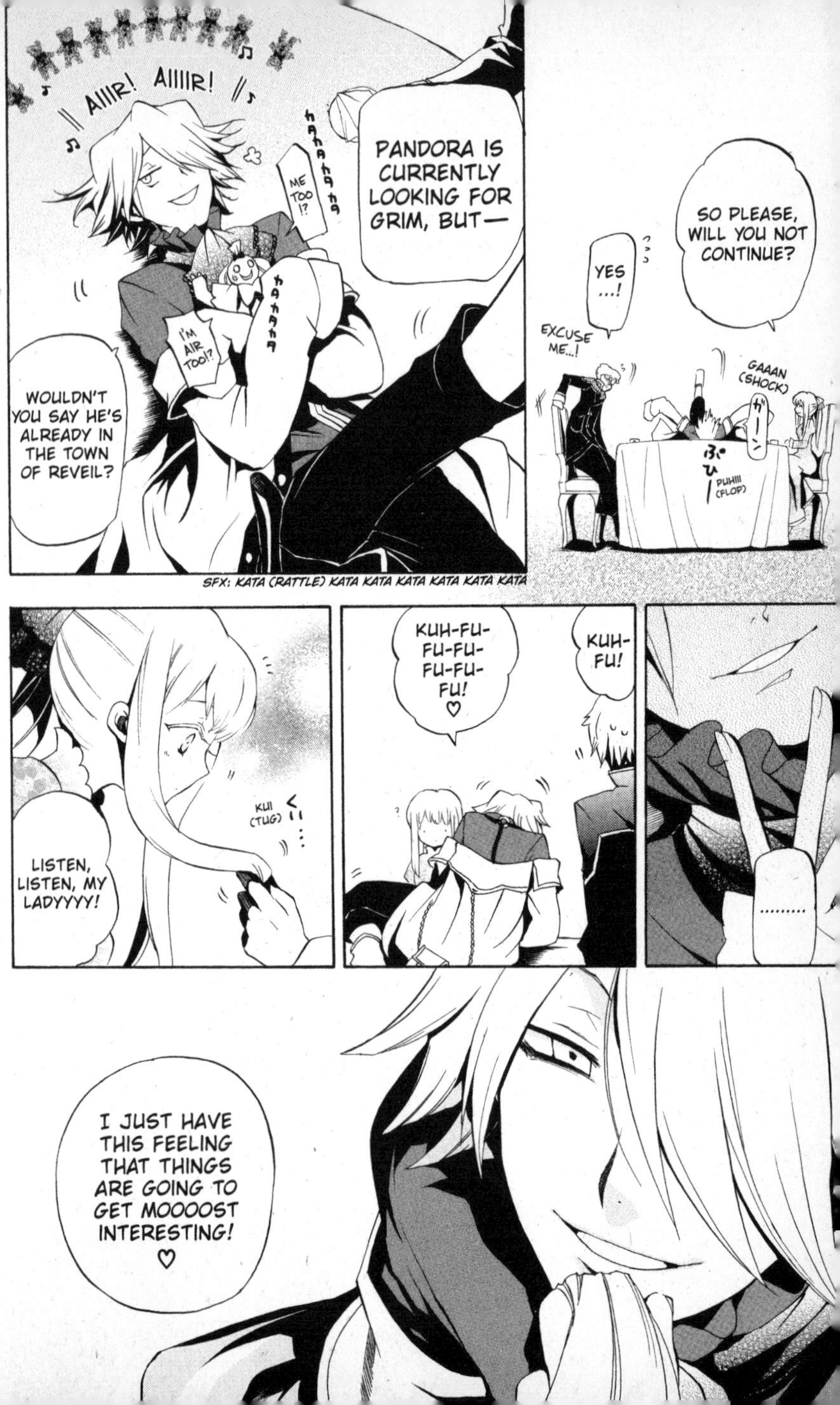
SO PLEASE, WILL YOU NOT CONTINUE?
YES ...!
EXCUSE ME...!
GAAAN (SHOCK)
PUHIII (FLOP)
PANDORA IS CURRENTLY LOOKING FOR GRIM, BUT—
AIIIR! AIIIR!
ME TOO!?
I'M AIR TOO!?
WOULDN'T YOU SAY HE'S ALREADY IN THE TOWN OF REVEIL?
SFX: KATA (RATTLE) KATA KATA KATA KATA KATA KATA
....
KUH-FU!
KUH-FU-FU-FU-FU-FU-FU! ♡
KUI (TUG)
LISTEN, LISTEN, MY LADYYYY!
I JUST HAVE THIS FEELING THAT THINGS ARE GOING TO GET MOOOOST INTERESTING! ♡

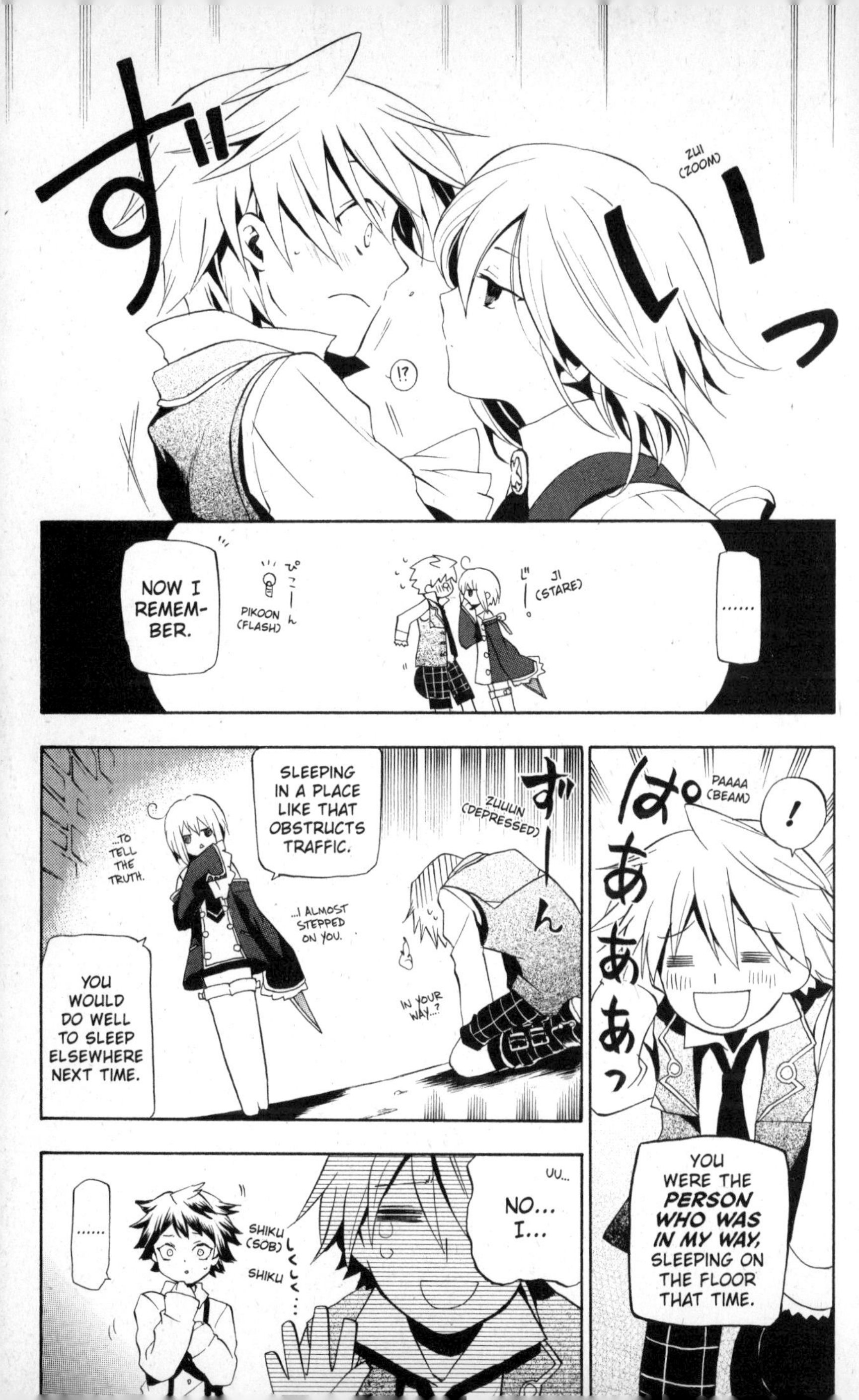

ずいっ
ZUI (ZOOM)
!?
......
じー
JI (STARE)
ぴこーん
PIKOON (FLASH)
NOW I REMEMBER.
ぱあああっ
PAAAA (BEAM)
!
YOU WERE THE PERSON WHO WAS IN MY WAY, SLEEPING ON THE FLOOR THAT TIME.
ずーん
ZUUUN (DEPRESSED)
SLEEPING IN A PLACE LIKE THAT OBSTRUCTS TRAFFIC.
...TO TELL THE TRUTH.
...I ALMOST STEPPED ON YOU.
IN YOUR WAY...?
YOU WOULD DO WELL TO SLEEP ELSEWHERE NEXT TIME.
UU...
NO... I...
しくしく...
SHIKU (SOB)
SHIKU
......

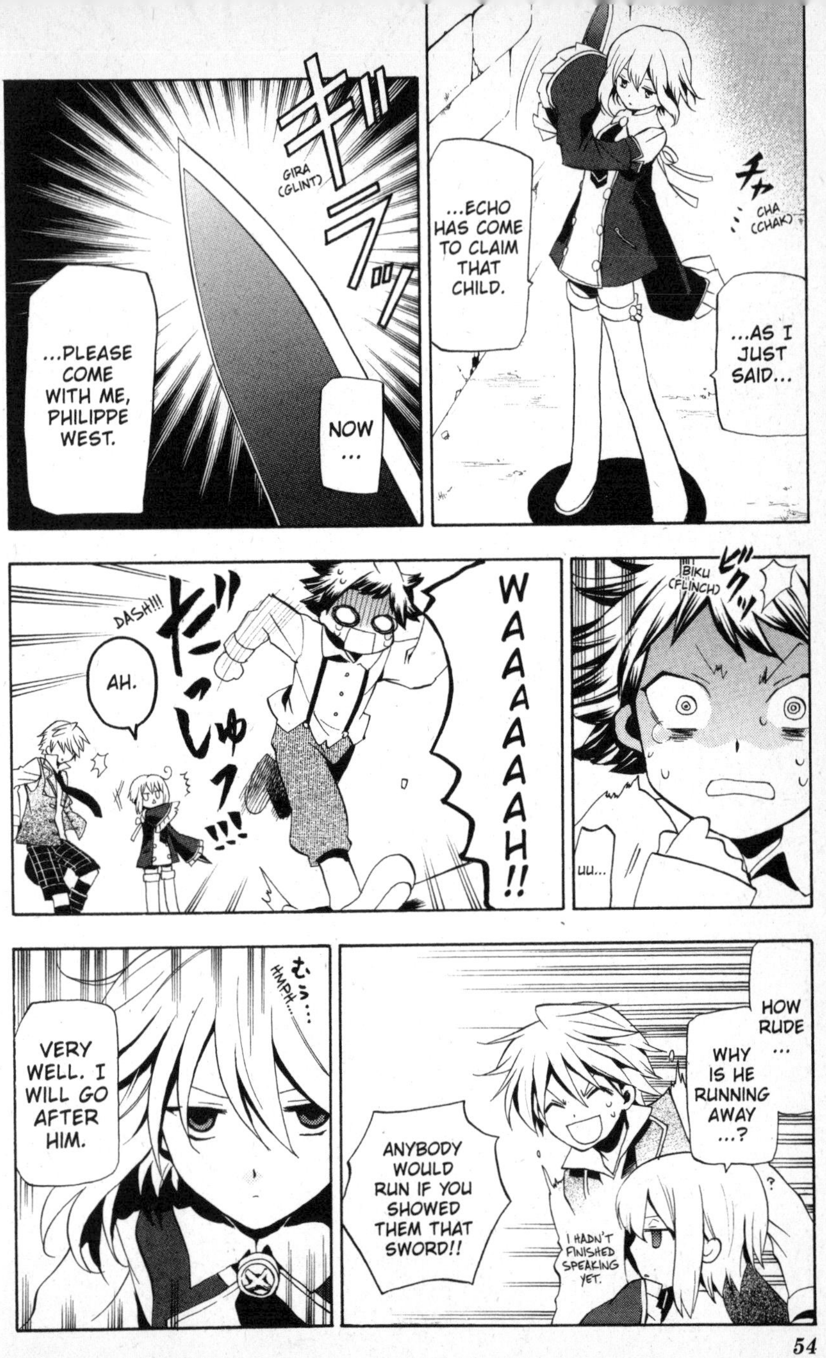
チャ
CHA (CHAK)
...AS I JUST SAID...
...ECHO HAS COME TO CLAIM THAT CHILD.
ギラッ
GIRA (GLINT)
NOW...
...PLEASE COME WITH ME, PHILIPPE WEST.
ビクッ
BIKU (FLINCH)
UU...
WAAAAAAAAH!!
だっしゅ!!!
DASH!!!
AH.
HOW RUDE...
WHY IS HE RUNNING AWAY...?
?
ANYBODY WOULD RUN IF YOU SHOWED THEM THAT SWORD!!
I HADN'T FINISHED SPEAKING YET.
むぅ...
HMPH...
VERY WELL. I WILL GO AFTER HIM.

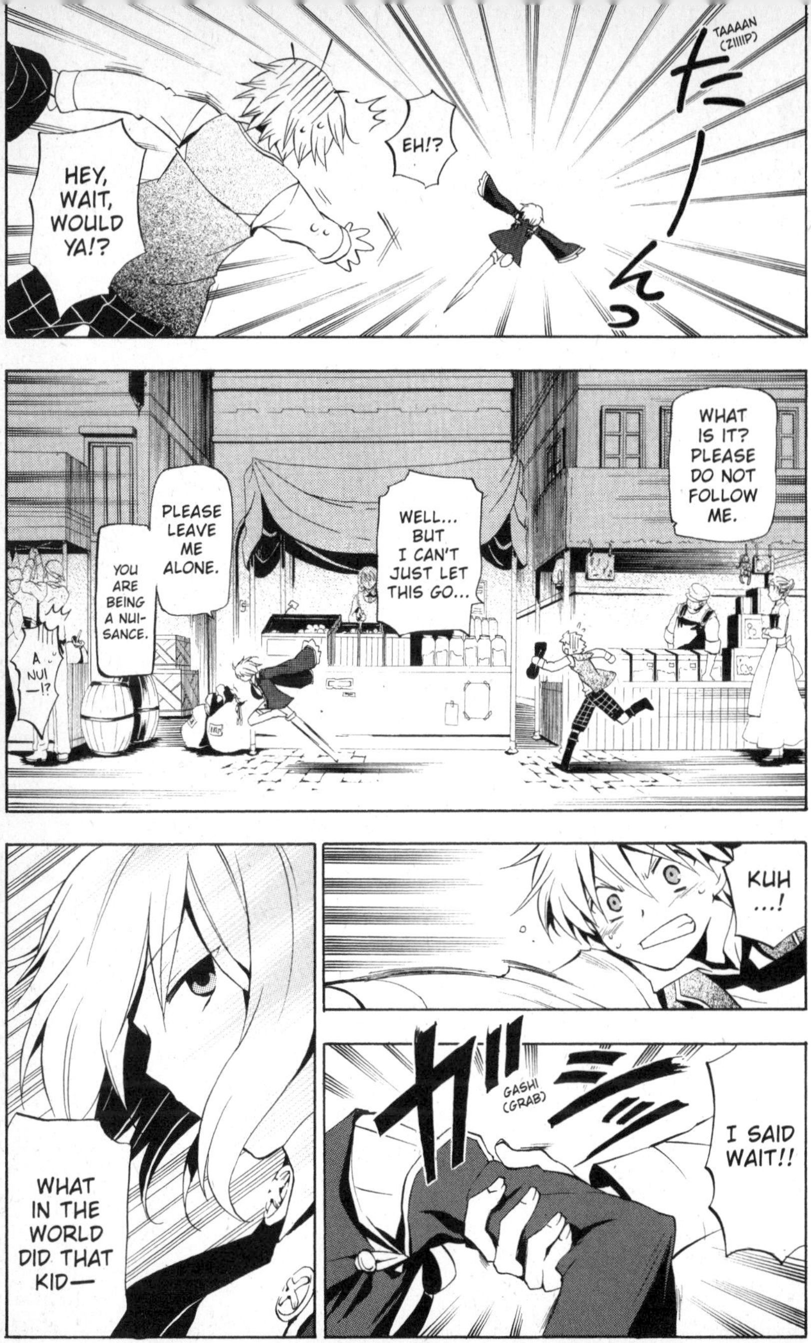

たーんっ
TAAAAN (ZIIIIP)
EH!?
HEY, WAIT, WOULD YA!?
WHAT IS IT? PLEASE DO NOT FOLLOW ME.
WELL... BUT I CAN'T JUST LET THIS GO...
PLEASE LEAVE ME ALONE.
YOU ARE BEING A NUI-SANCE.
A NUI—!?
KUH...!
GASHI (GRAB)
I SAID WAIT!!
WHAT IN THE WORLD DID THAT KID—

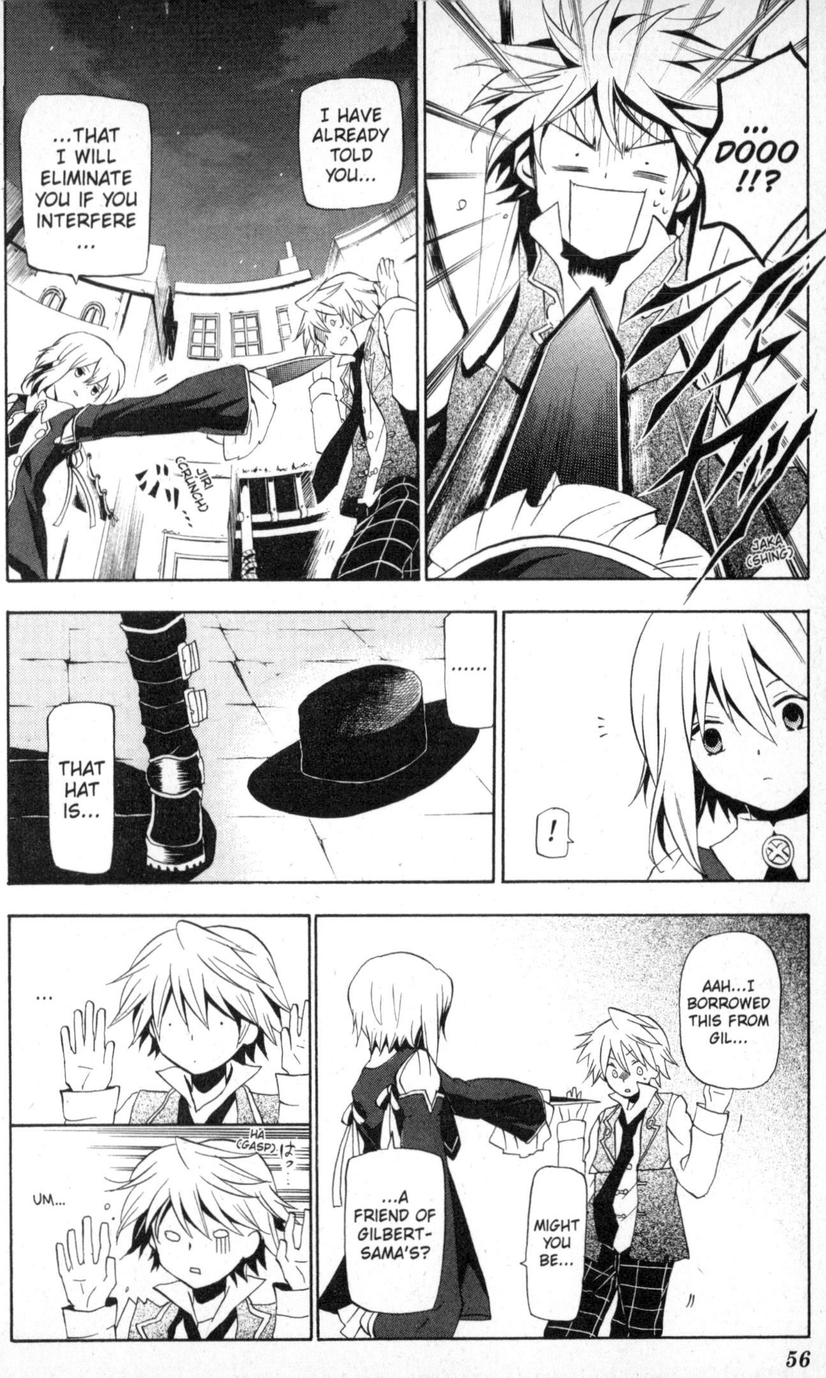
...DOOO!!?
JAKA (SHING)
I HAVE ALREADY TOLD YOU...
...THAT I WILL ELIMINATE YOU IF YOU INTERFERE...
JIRI (CRUNCH)
!
......
THAT HAT IS...
AAH...I BORROWED THIS FROM GIL...
MIGHT YOU BE...
...A FRIEND OF GILBERT-SAMA'S?
...
HA (GASP)
UM...

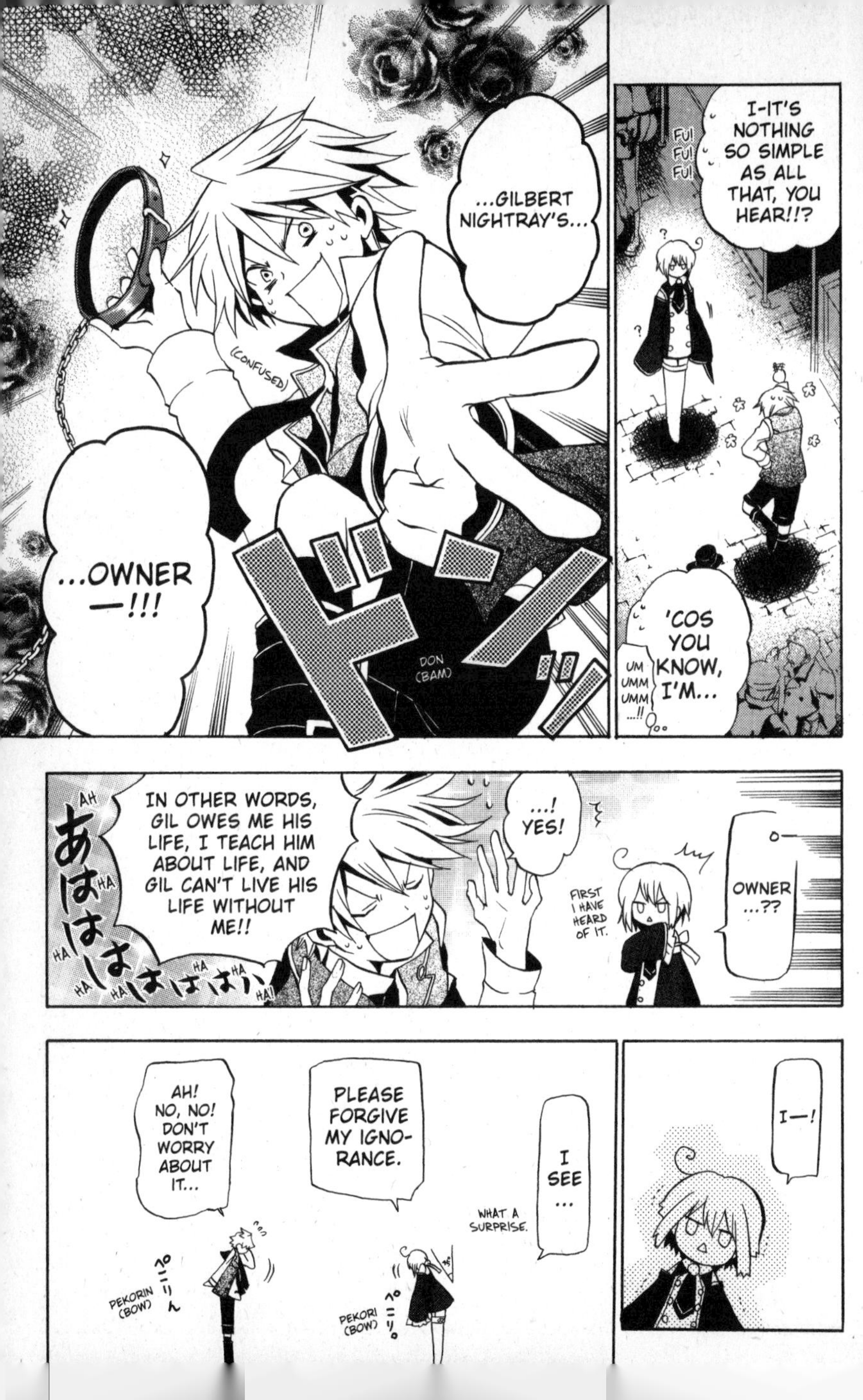
I-IT'S NOTHING SO SIMPLE AS ALL THAT, YOU HEAR!!?
FU! FU! FU!
'COS YOU KNOW, I'M...
UM UMM UMM ...!!
...GILBERT NIGHTRAY'S...
(CONFUSED)
...OWNER—!!!
DON (BAM)
O—OWNER ...??
FIRST I HAVE HEARD OF IT.
...! YES!
IN OTHER WORDS, GIL OWES ME HIS LIFE, I TEACH HIM ABOUT LIFE, AND GIL CAN'T LIVE HIS LIFE WITHOUT ME!!
あははははは
AH HA HA HA HA HA HA!
I—!
I SEE...
WHAT A SURPRISE.
PLEASE FORGIVE MY IGNO-RANCE.
PEKORI (BOW)
AH! NO, NO! DON'T WORRY ABOUT IT...
PEKORIN (BOW)

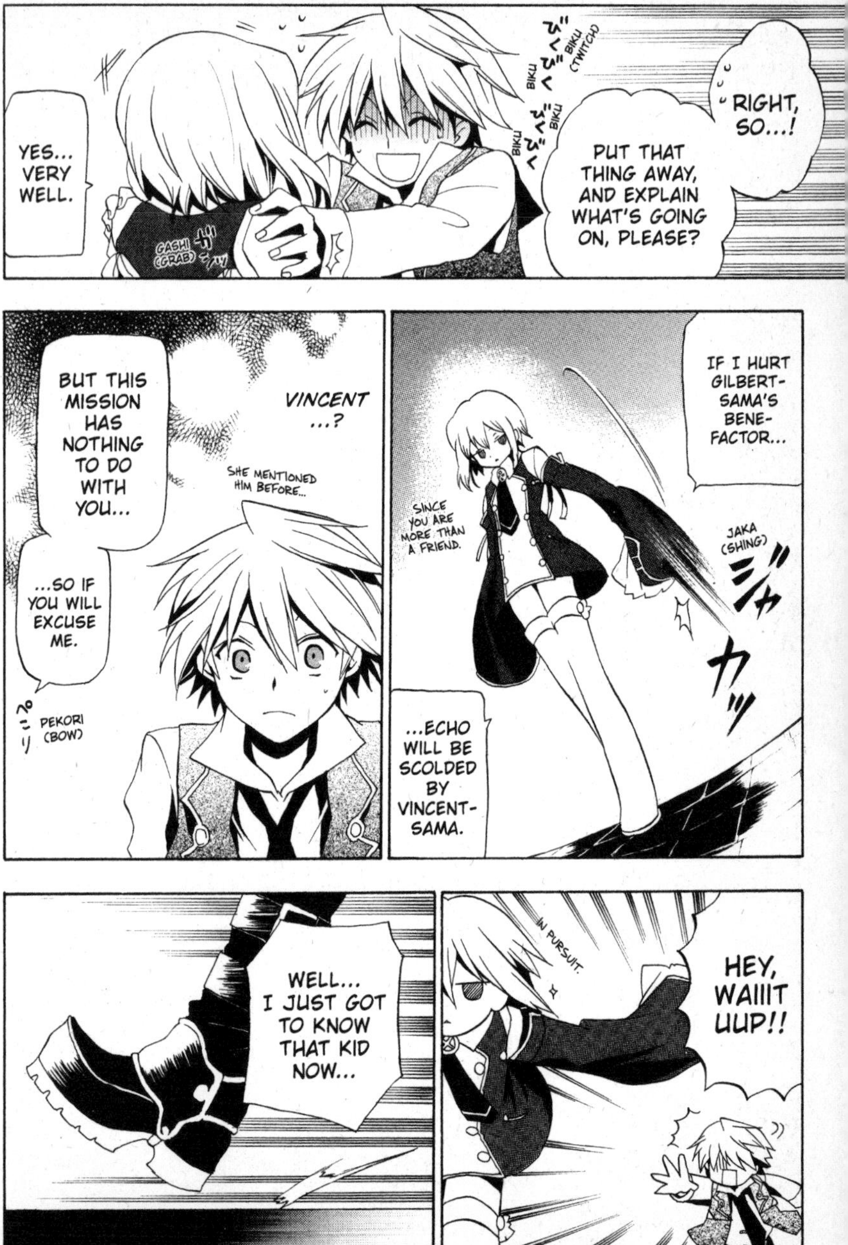
RIGHT, SO...!
PUT THAT THING AWAY, AND EXPLAIN WHAT'S GOING ON, PLEASE?
BIKU BIKU (TWITCH)
BIKU BIKU
YES... VERY WELL.
GASHI (GRAB)
IF I HURT GILBERT-SAMA'S BENE-FACTOR...
SINCE YOU ARE MORE THAN A FRIEND.
JAKA (SHING)
...ECHO WILL BE SCOLDED BY VINCENT-SAMA.
VINCENT...?
SHE MENTIONED HIM BEFORE...
BUT THIS MISSION HAS NOTHING TO DO WITH YOU...
...SO IF YOU WILL EXCUSE ME.
PEKORI (BOW)
HEY, WAIIIT UUP!!
IN PURSUIT.
WELL... I JUST GOT TO KNOW THAT KID NOW...

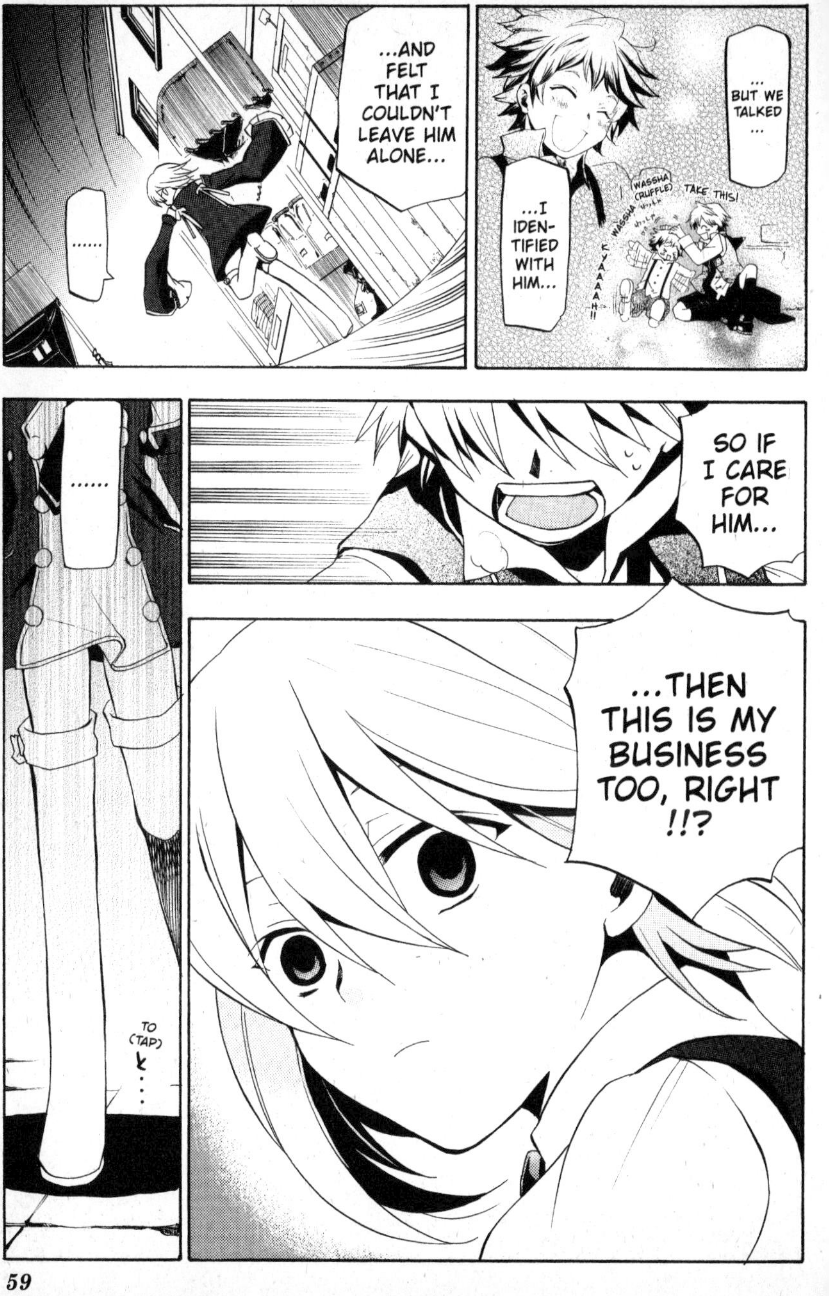
... BUT WE TALKED ...
...I IDENTIFIED WITH HIM...
WASSHA (RUFFLE)
TAKE THIS!
WASSHA
KYAAAAAH!!
...AND FELT THAT I COULDN'T LEAVE HIM ALONE...
......
SO IF I CARE FOR HIM...
...THEN THIS IS MY BUSINESS TOO, RIGHT !!?
......
TO (TAP)

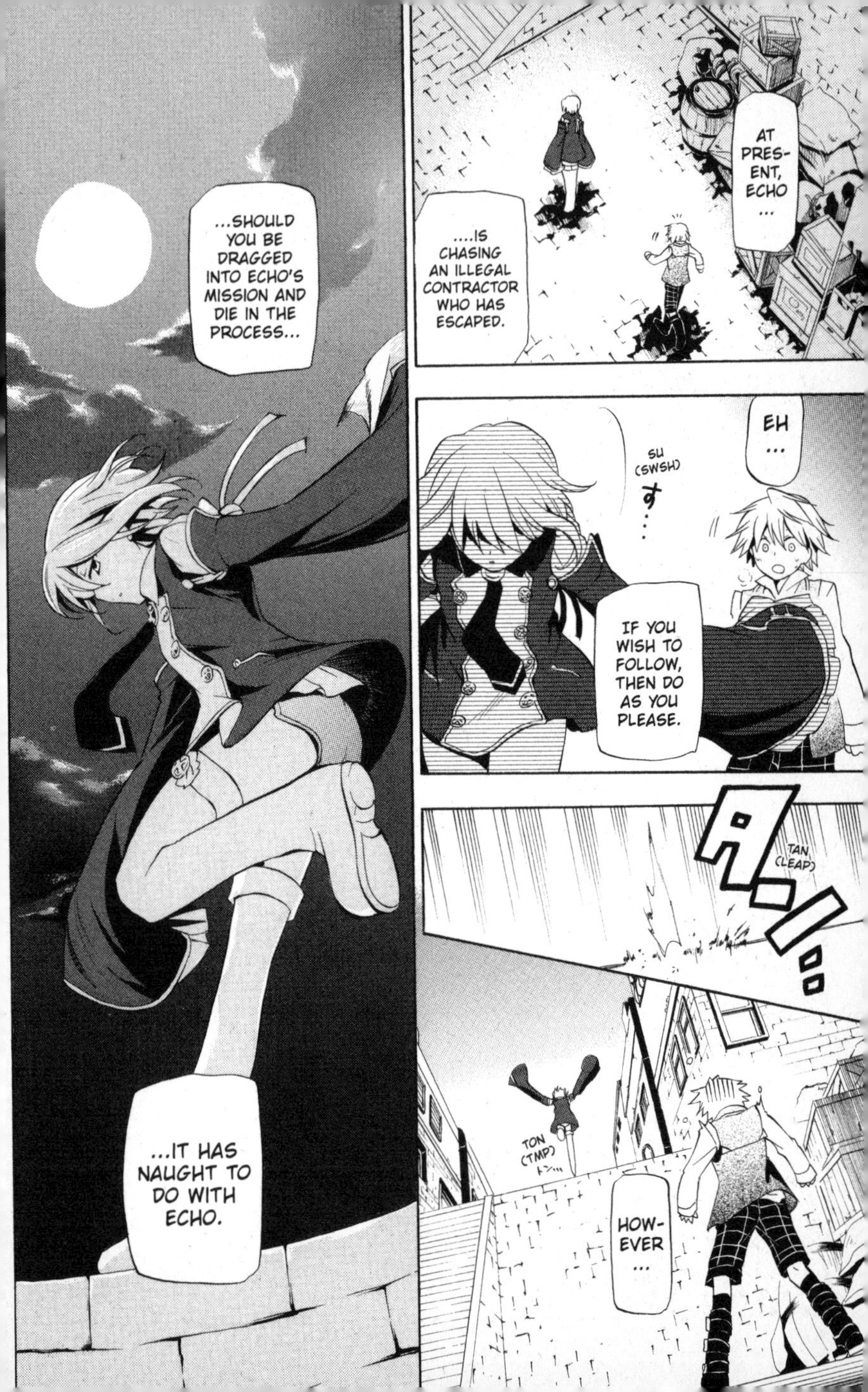
AT PRES-ENT, ECHO...
....IS CHASING AN ILLEGAL CONTRACTOR WHO HAS ESCAPED.
EH...
SU (SWSH)
す…
IF YOU WISH TO FOLLOW, THEN DO AS YOU PLEASE.
TAN (LEAP)
TON (TMP)
トン…
HOW-EVER...
...SHOULD YOU BE DRAGGED INTO ECHO'S MISSION AND DIE IN THE PROCESS...
...IT HAS NAUGHT TO DO WITH ECHO.

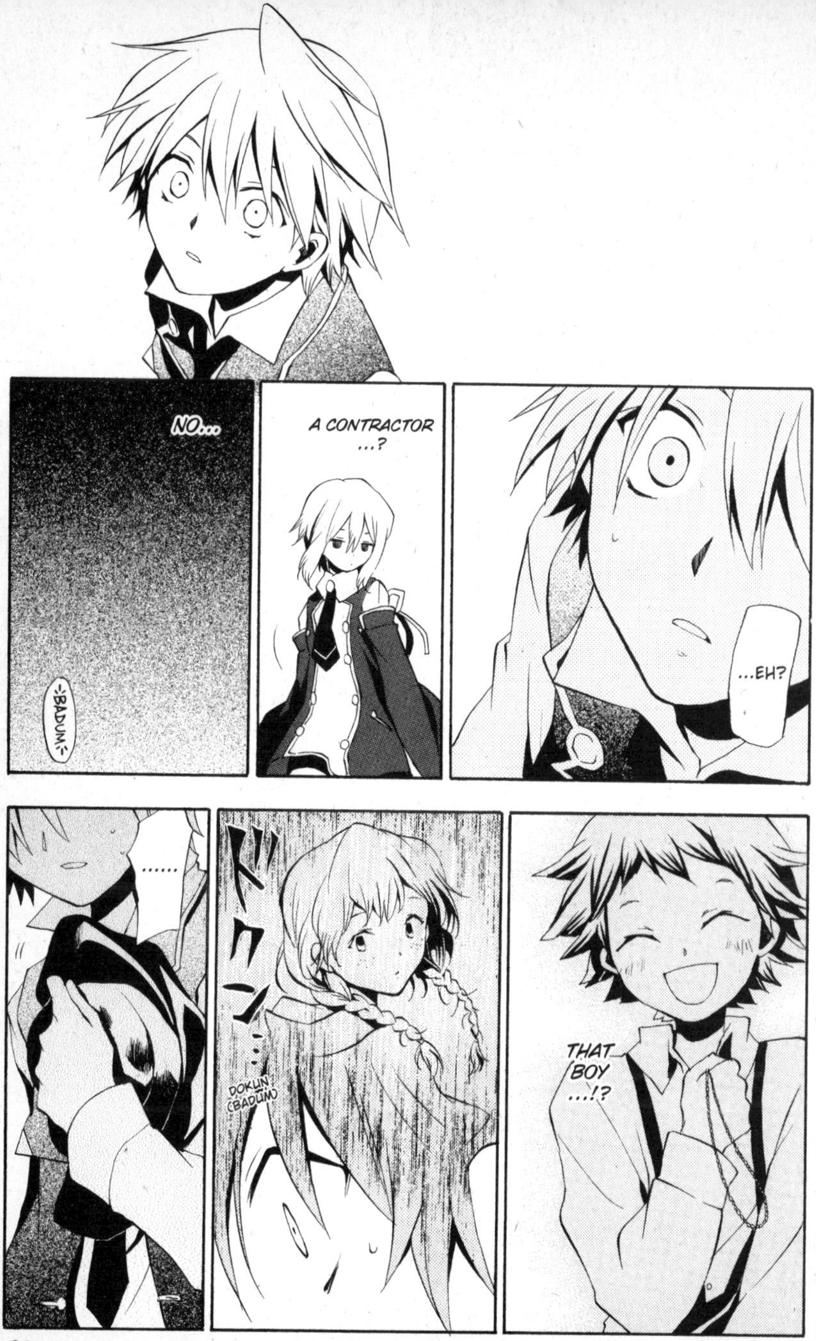

...EH?
A CONTRACTOR ...?
NO...
BADUM
THAT BOY ...!?
ドクン
DOKUN (BADUM)
......

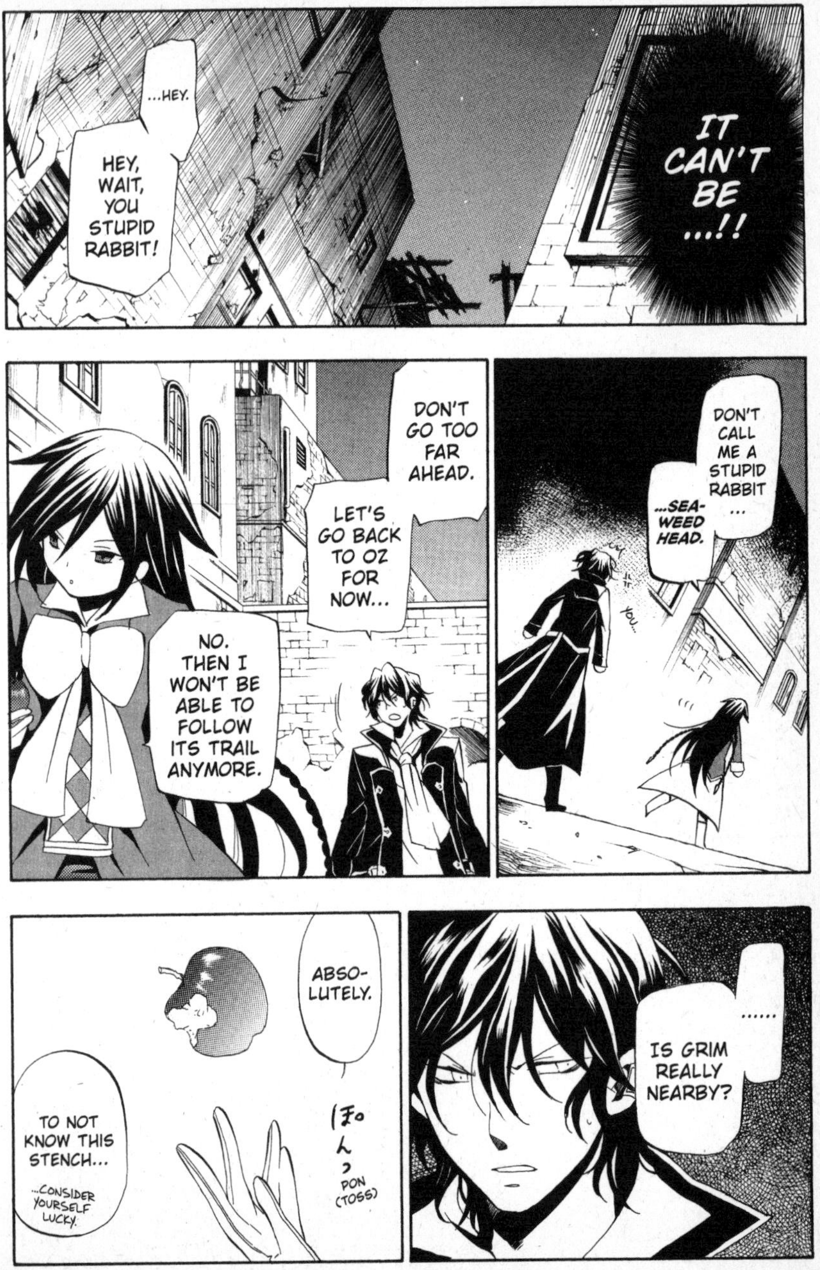
IT CAN'T BE ...!!
...HEY.
HEY, WAIT, YOU STUPID RABBIT!
DON'T CALL ME A STUPID RABBIT ...
...SEA-WEED HEAD.
YOU...
DON'T GO TOO FAR AHEAD.
LET'S GO BACK TO OZ FOR NOW...
NO. THEN I WON'T BE ABLE TO FOLLOW ITS TRAIL ANYMORE.
......
IS GRIM REALLY NEARBY?
ABSO-LUTELY.
ほんっ
PON (TOSS)
TO NOT KNOW THIS STENCH...
...CONSIDER YOURSELF LUCKY.

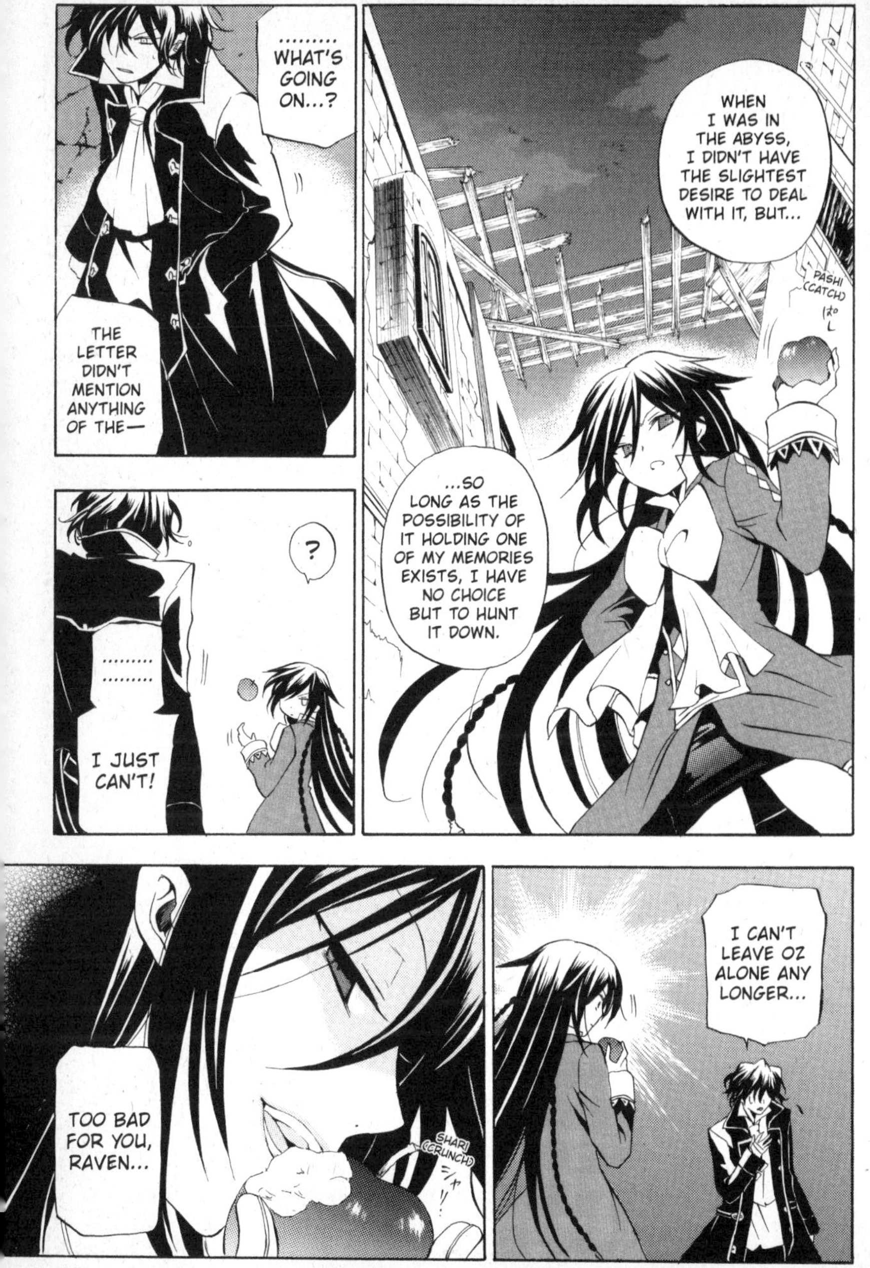
WHEN I WAS IN THE ABYSS, I DIDN'T HAVE THE SLIGHTEST DESIRE TO DEAL WITH IT, BUT...
PASHI (CATCH)
ぱし
...SO LONG AS THE POSSIBILITY OF IT HOLDING ONE OF MY MEMORIES EXISTS, I HAVE NO CHOICE BUT TO HUNT IT DOWN.
.... WHAT'S GOING ON...?
THE LETTER DIDN'T MENTION ANYTHING OF THE—
?
....
I JUST CAN'T!
I CAN'T LEAVE OZ ALONE ANY LONGER...
TOO BAD FOR YOU, RAVEN...
SHARI (CRUNCH)
シャ!!

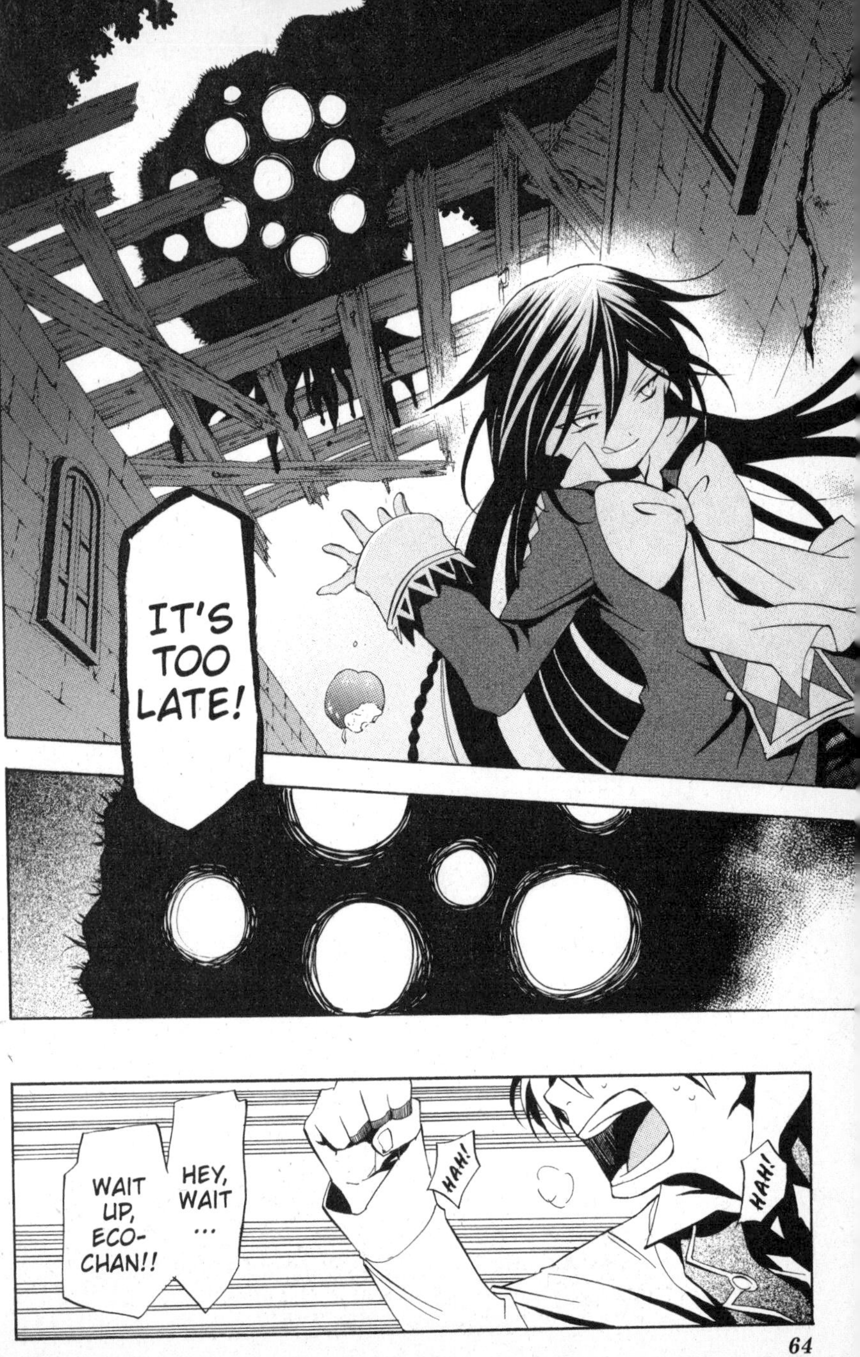
IT'S TOO LATE!
HAH!
HAH!
HEY, WAIT ...
WAIT UP, ECO-CHAN!!

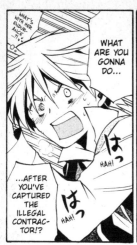

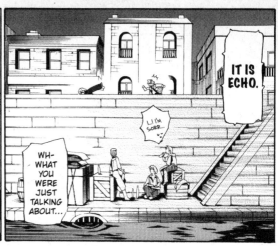

IT IS ECHO.
I...! I'M SORR...
WH-WHAT YOU WERE JUST TALKING ABOUT...
WHAT'S WITH HER ENDURANCE...?!
WHAT ARE YOU GONNA DO...
はっ
HAH!
はっ
HAH!
...AFTER YOU'VE CAPTURED THE ILLEGAL CONTRACTOR!?
THERE'S NO WAY... YOU'D KILL HIM, RIGHT...?
NOT A LITTLE KID LIKE THAT—!
?
ばっ
BA (LEAP)
!?

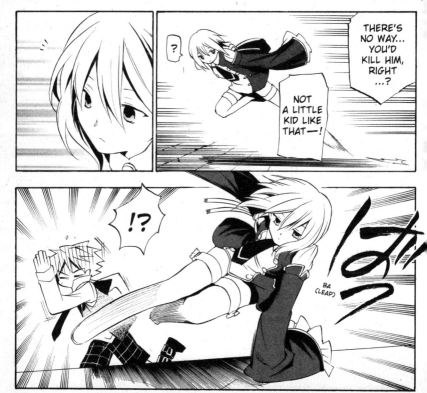

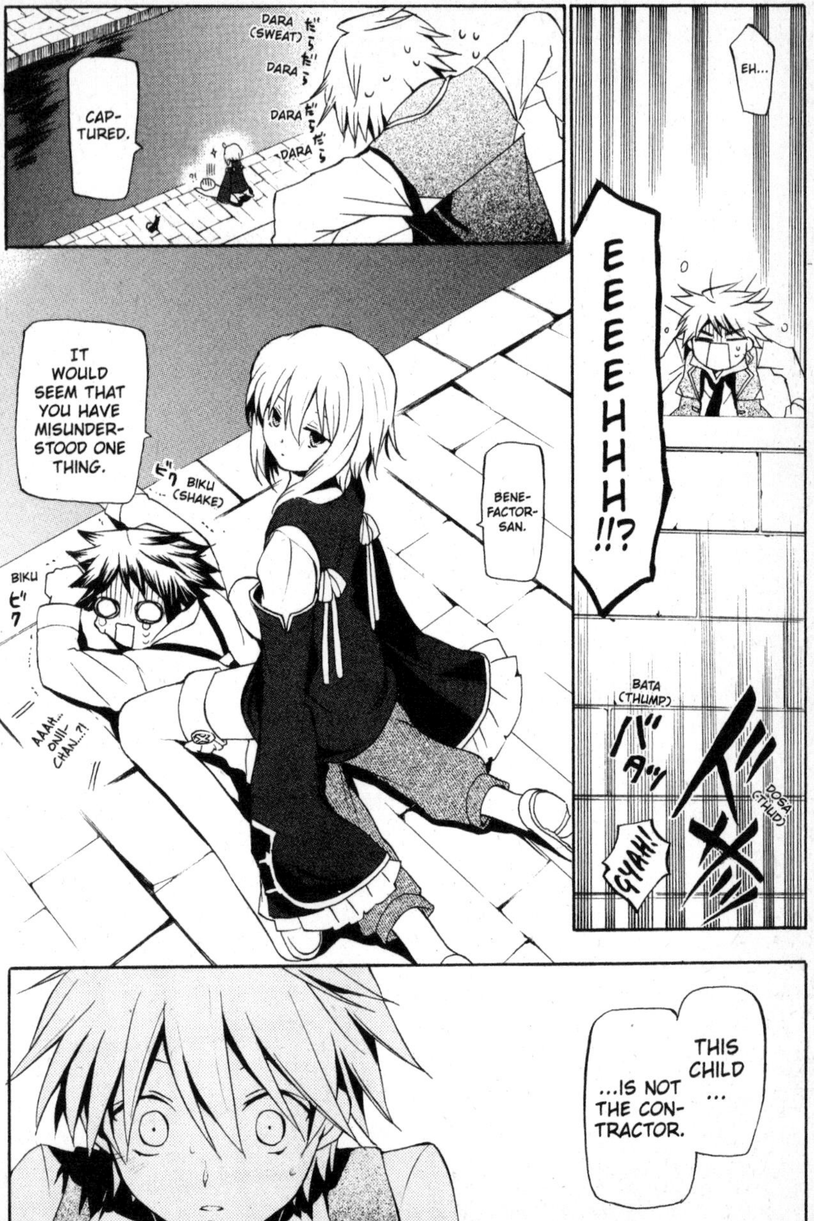

EH...
EEEEEHHHH!!?
BATA (THUMP)
GYAH!
DOSA (THUD)
DARA (SWEAT) DARA DARA DARA
CAP-TURED.
IT WOULD SEEM THAT YOU HAVE MISUNDER-STOOD ONE THING.
BENE-FACTOR-SAN.
BIKU (SHAKE)
BIKU
AAAH... ONII-CHAN...?!
THIS CHILD ...
...IS NOT THE CON-TRACTOR.

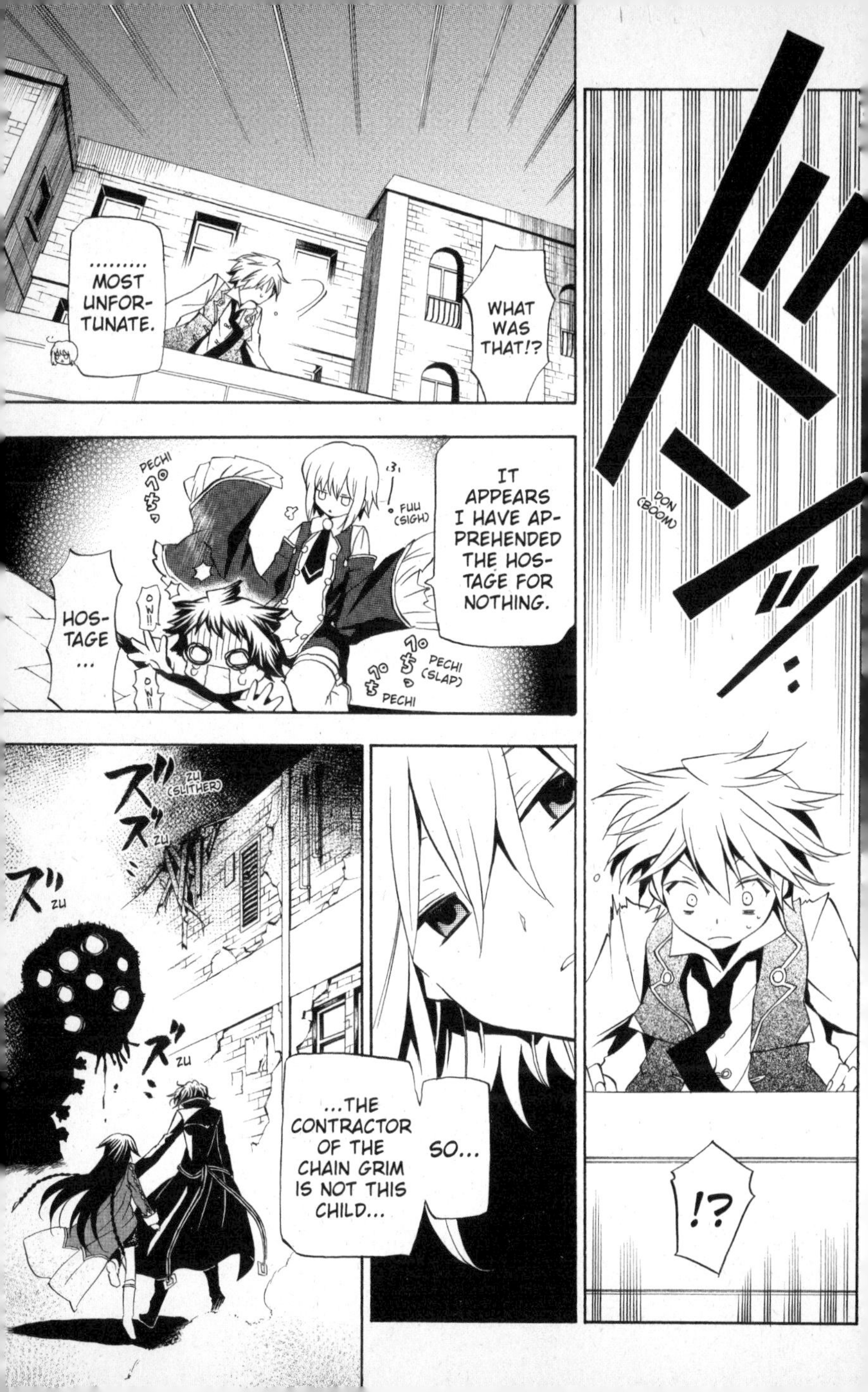
DON (BOOM)
WHAT WAS THAT!?
....
MOST UNFOR-TUNATE.
IT APPEARS I HAVE AP-PREHENDED THE HOS-TAGE FOR NOTHING.
FUU (SIGH)
PECHI (SLAP)
PECHI
PECHI
OW!!
OW!!
HOS-TAGE...
!?
SO...
...THE CONTRACTOR OF THE CHAIN GRIM IS NOT THIS CHILD...
ZU (SLITHER)
ZU
ZU
ZU

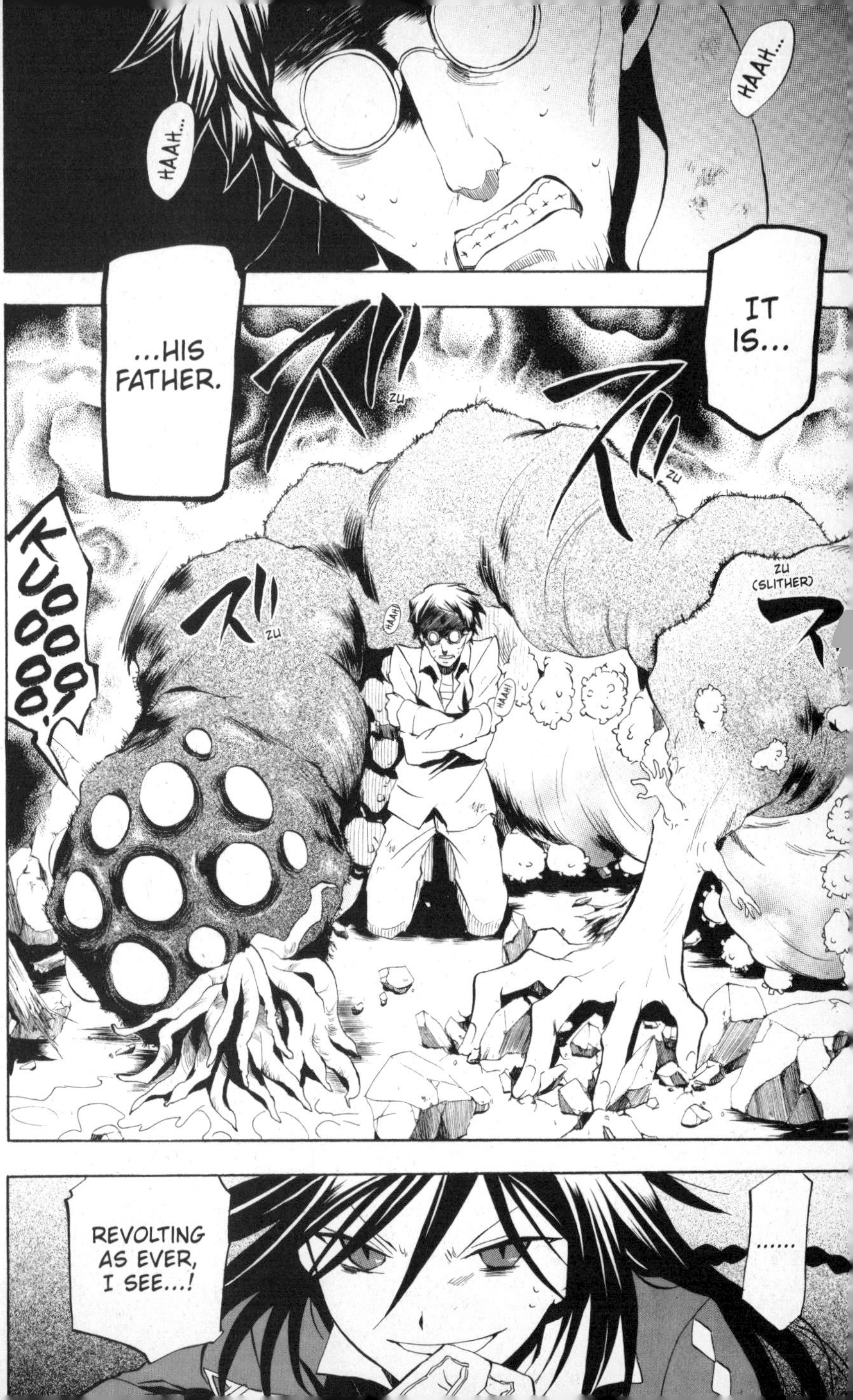
HAAH...
HAAH...
IT IS...
...HIS FATHER.
ZU
ZU
ZU (SLITHER)
HAAH
HAAH
ZU
KUOOOOOO!
......
REVOLTING AS EVER, I SEE...!

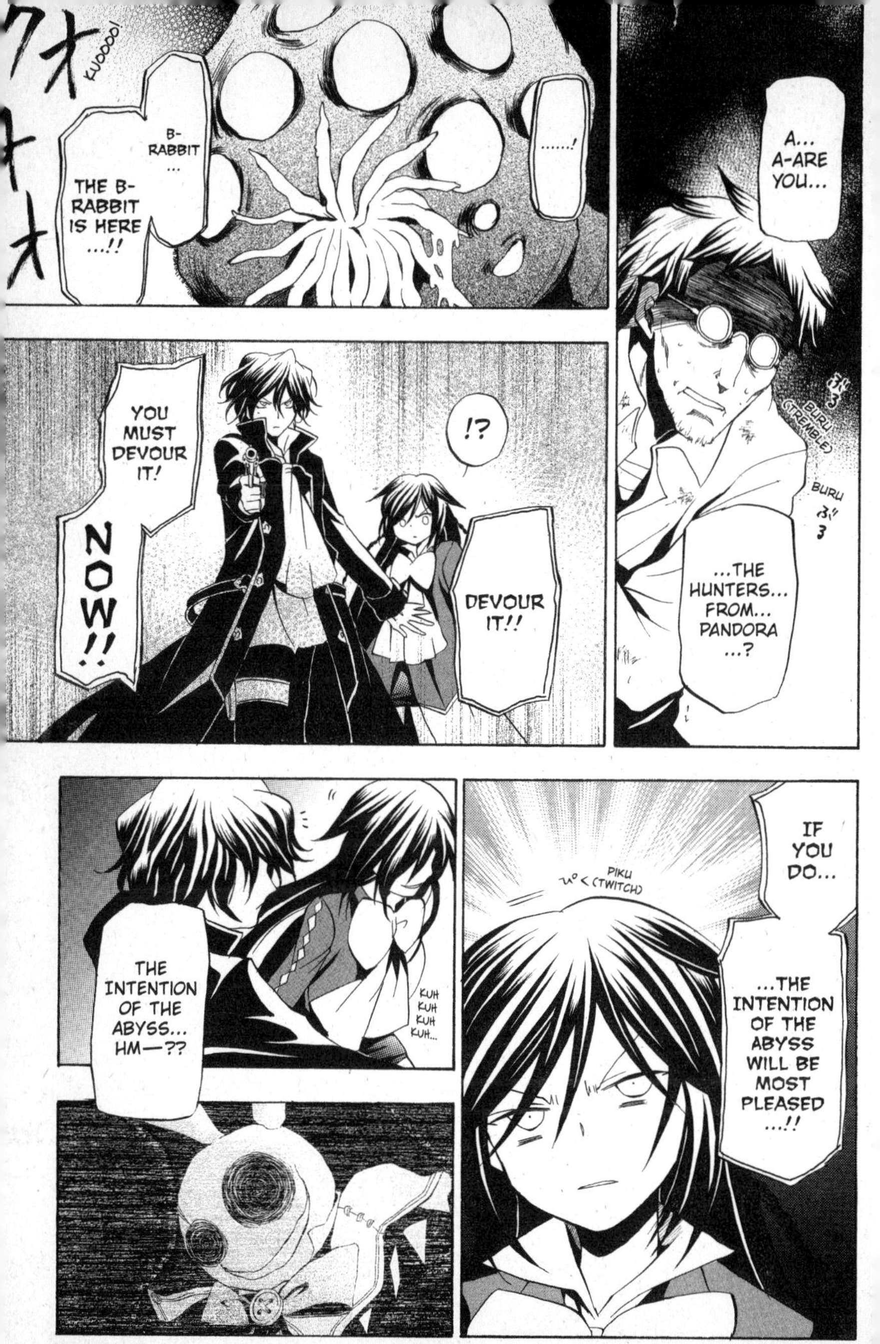

A... A-ARE YOU...
ぶる BURU (TREMBLE)
BURU ぶる
...THE HUNTERS... FROM... PANDORA ...?
......!
B-RABBIT ...
THE B-RABBIT IS HERE ...!!
KUOOOO!
!?
DEVOUR IT!!
YOU MUST DEVOUR IT!
NOW!!
IF YOU DO...
PIKU ぴく (TWITCH)
...THE INTENTION OF THE ABYSS WILL BE MOST PLEASED ...!!
THE INTENTION OF THE ABYSS... HM—??
KUH KUH KUH KUH...

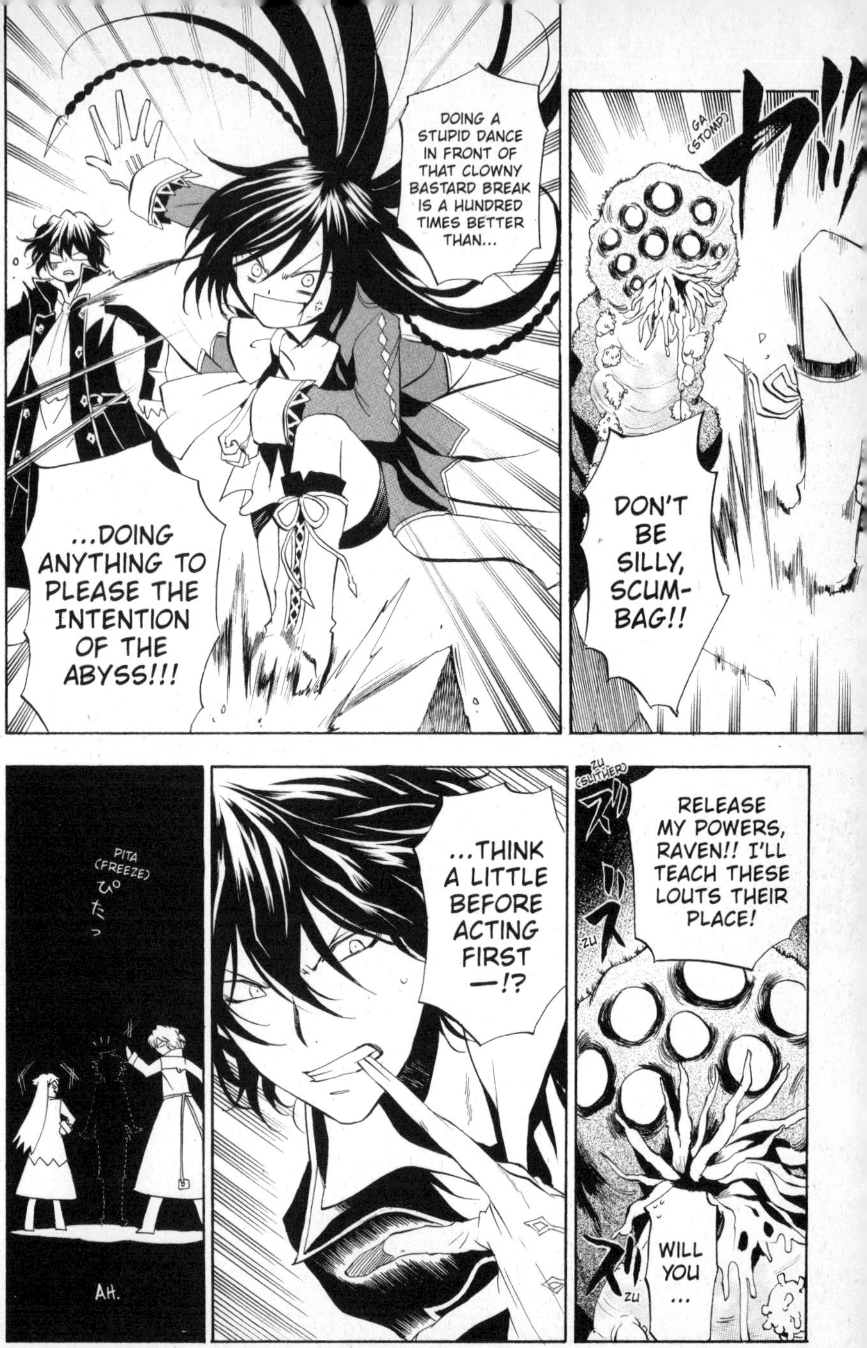
GA (STOMP)
DON'T BE SILLY, SCUM-BAG!!
DOING A STUPID DANCE IN FRONT OF THAT CLOWNY BASTARD BREAK IS A HUNDRED TIMES BETTER THAN...
...DOING ANYTHING TO PLEASE THE INTENTION OF THE ABYSS!!!
ZU (SLITHER)
RELEASE MY POWERS, RAVEN!! I'LL TEACH THESE LOUTS THEIR PLACE!
ZU
ZU
WILL YOU ...
...THINK A LITTLE BEFORE ACTING FIRST—!?
PITA (FREEZE)
ぴたっ
AH.

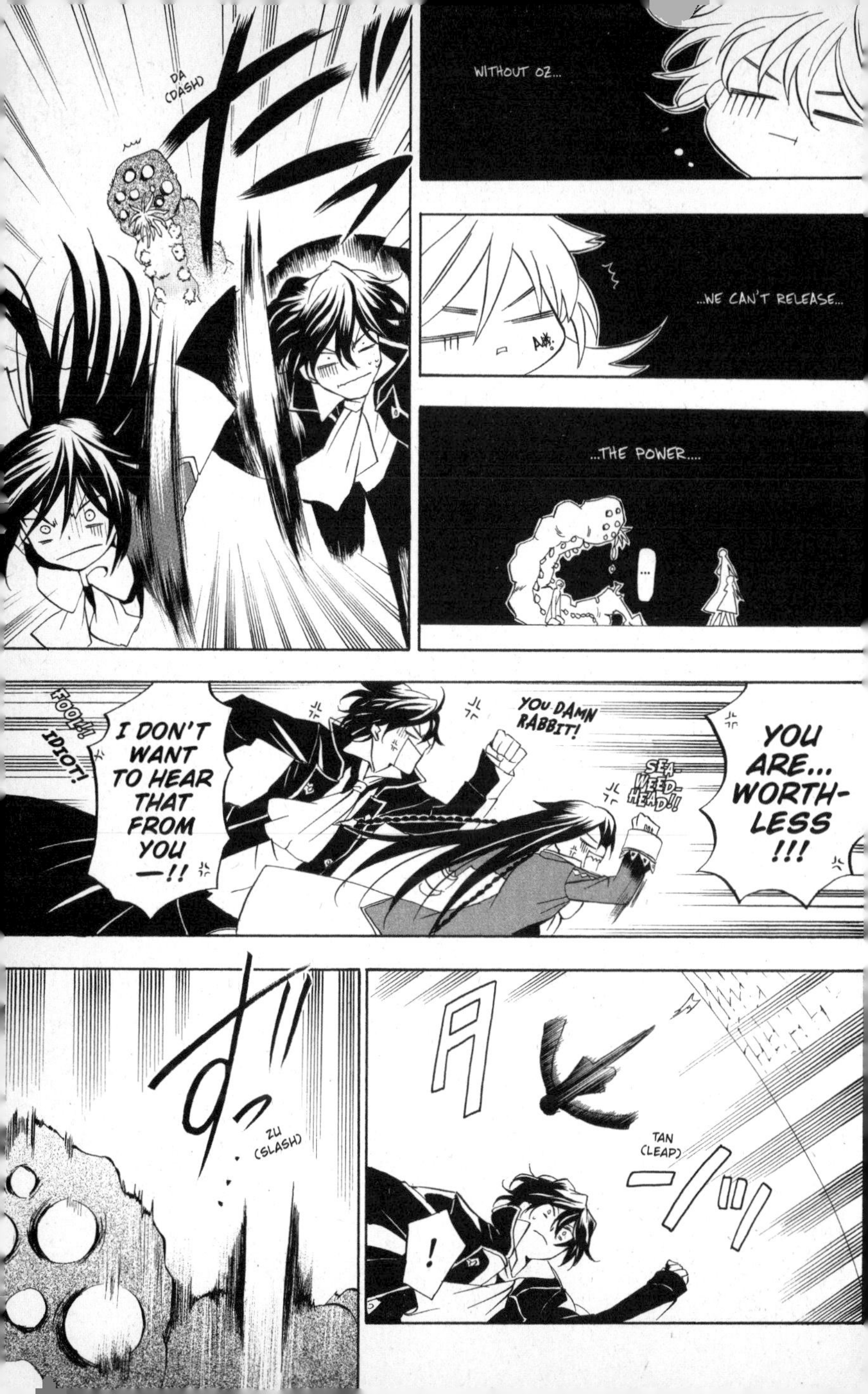
WITHOUT OZ...
...WE CAN'T RELEASE...
...THE POWER....
...
DA (DASH)
YOU ARE... WORTHLESS!!!
SEAWEED-HEAD!!
YOU DAMN RABBIT!
I DON'T WANT TO HEAR THAT FROM YOU—!!
FOOL!! IDIOT!
TAN (LEAP)
!
ZU (SLASH)

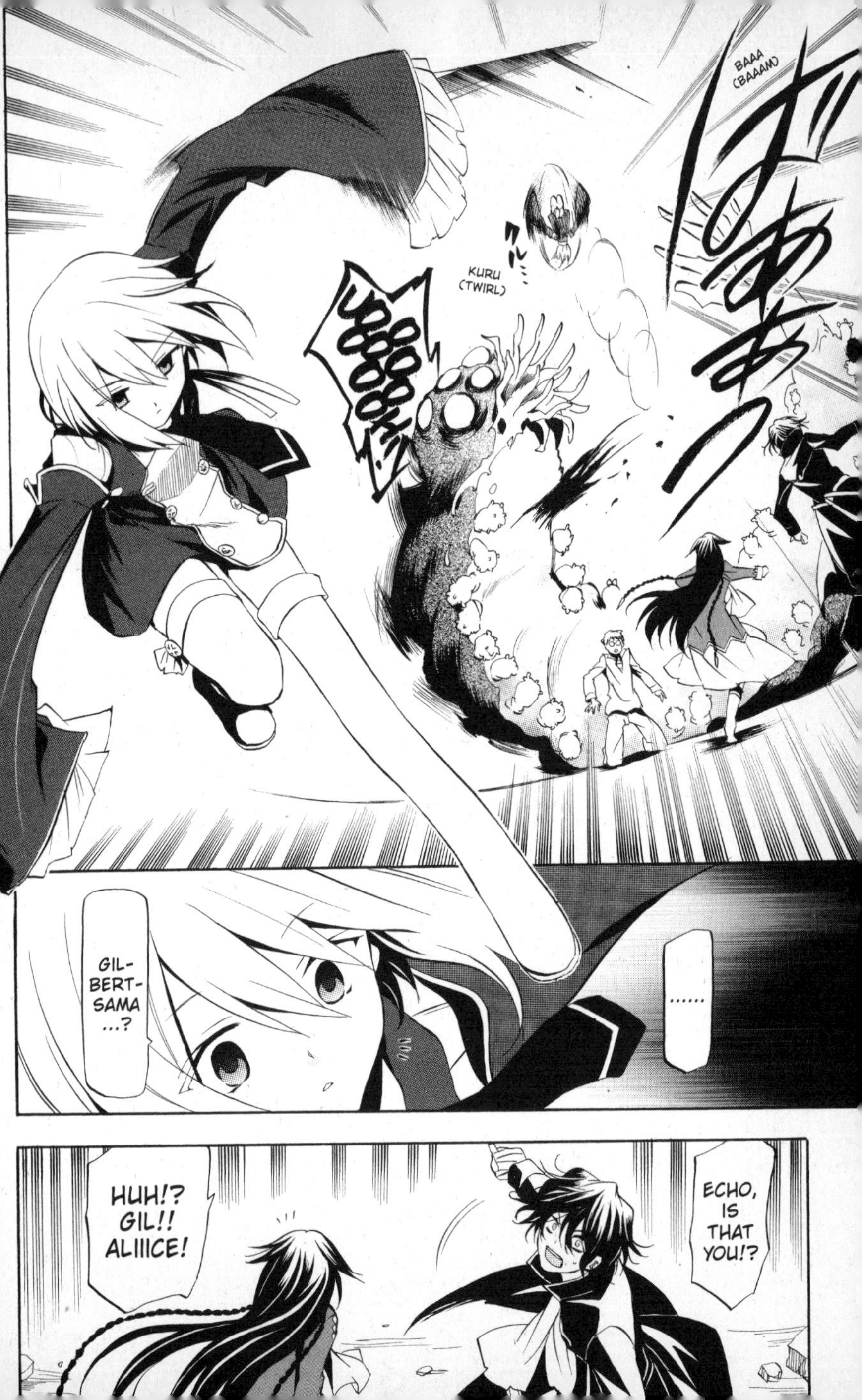
BAAA (BAAAM)
ばあっ
KURU (TWIRL)
くるっ
UOOOOOOOOH!?
......
GIL-BERT-SAMA ...?
ECHO, IS THAT YOU!?
HUH!? GIL!! ALIIICE!

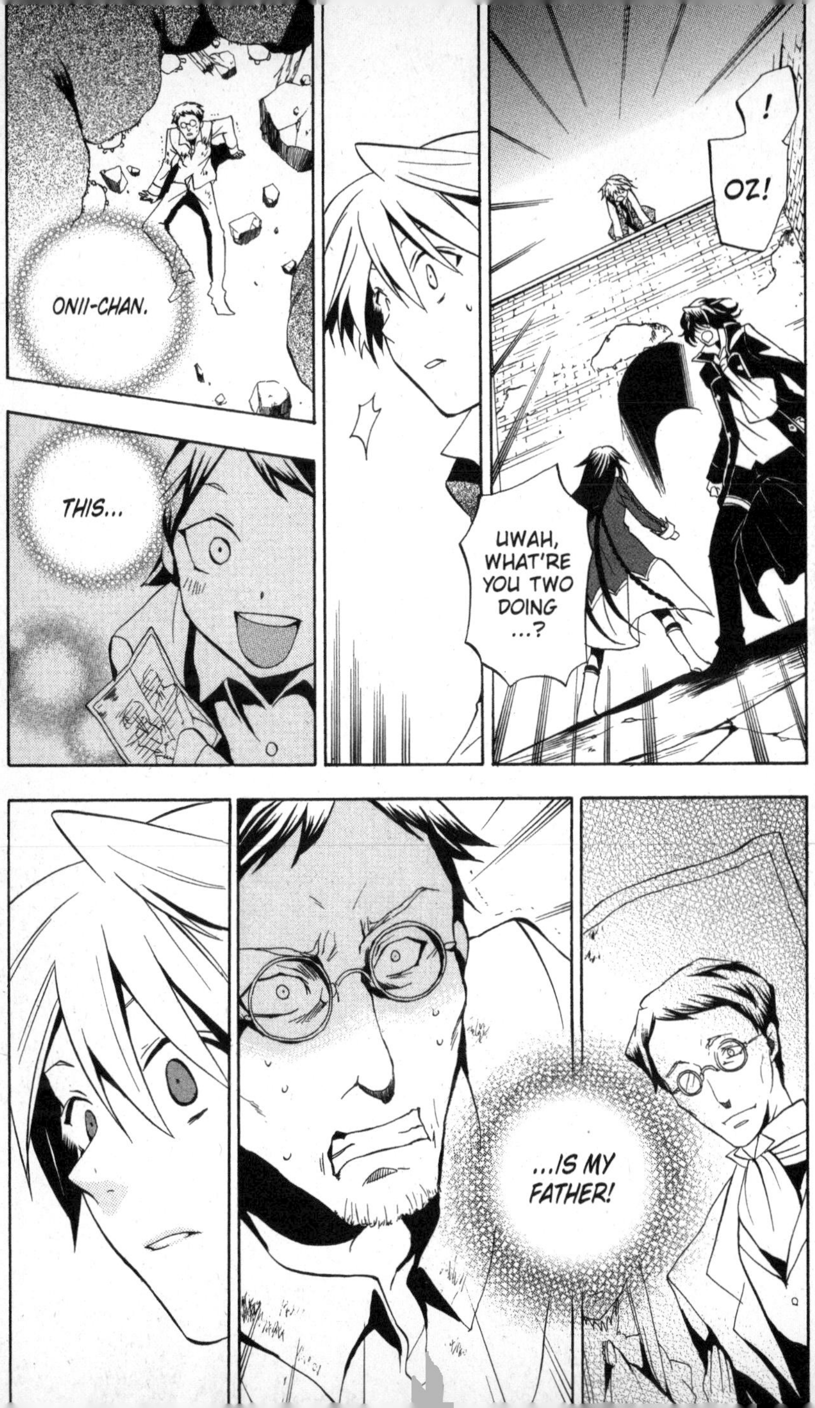
!
OZ!
UWAH, WHAT'RE YOU TWO DOING ...?
ONII-CHAN.
THIS...
...IS MY FATHER!

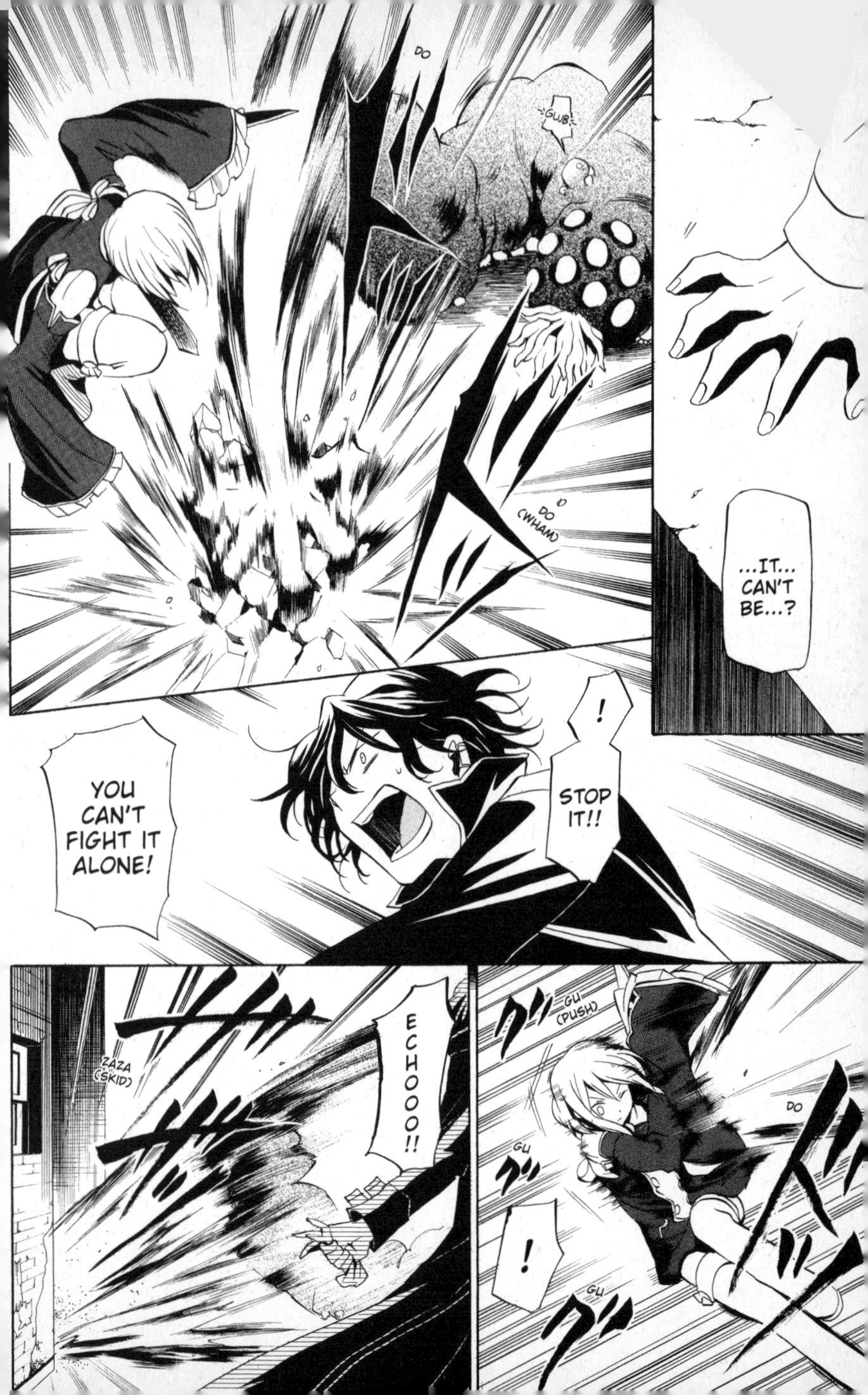
...IT... CAN'T BE...?
DO
GLUB
DO (WHAM)
!
STOP IT!!
YOU CAN'T FIGHT IT ALONE!
GU (PUSH)
DO
GU
!
GU
ECHOOOO!!
ZAZA (SKID)

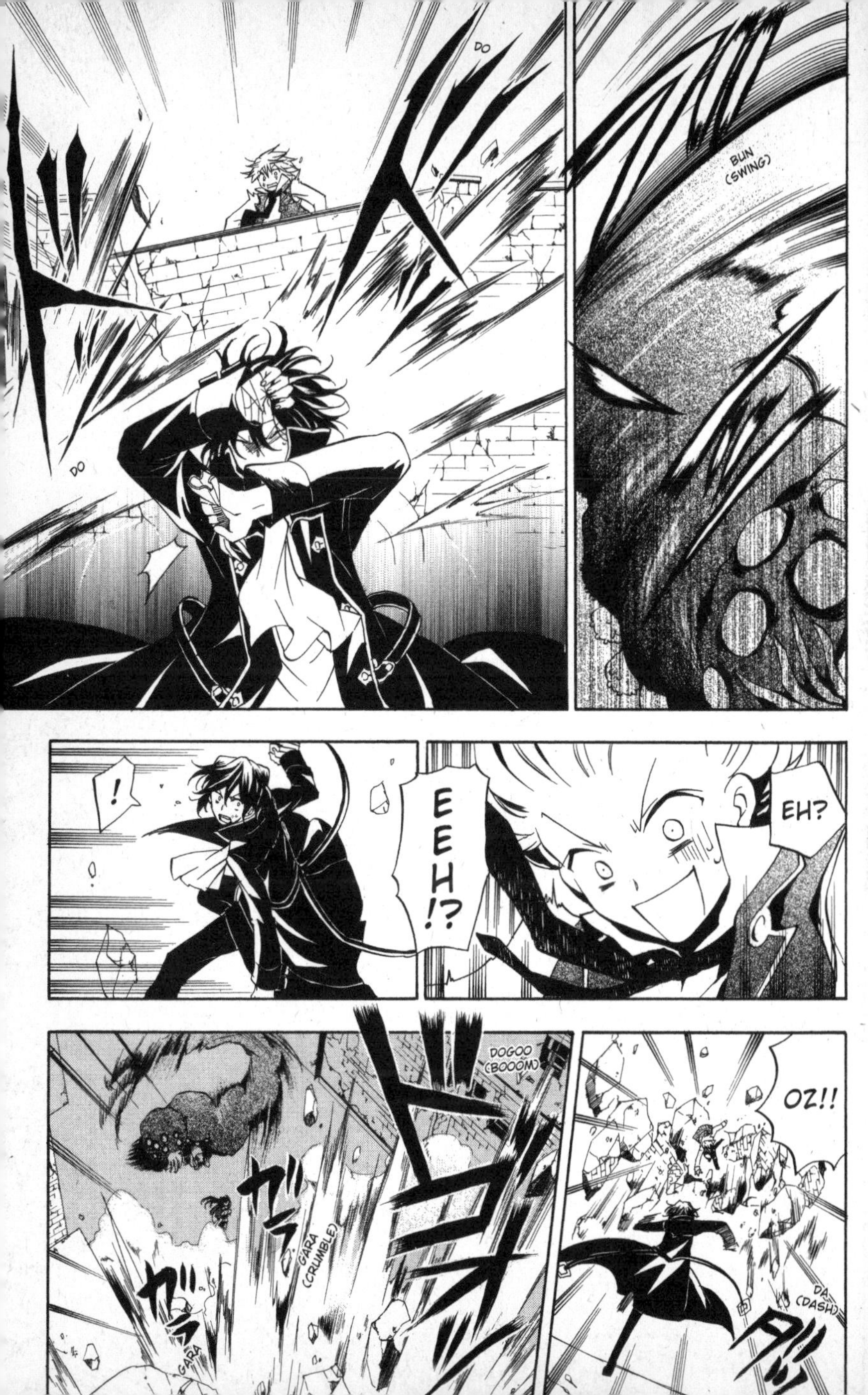
BUN (SWING)
DO
DO
EH?
EEH!?
!
OZ!!
DA (DASH)
DOGOO (BOOOM)
GARA (CRUMBLE)
GARA

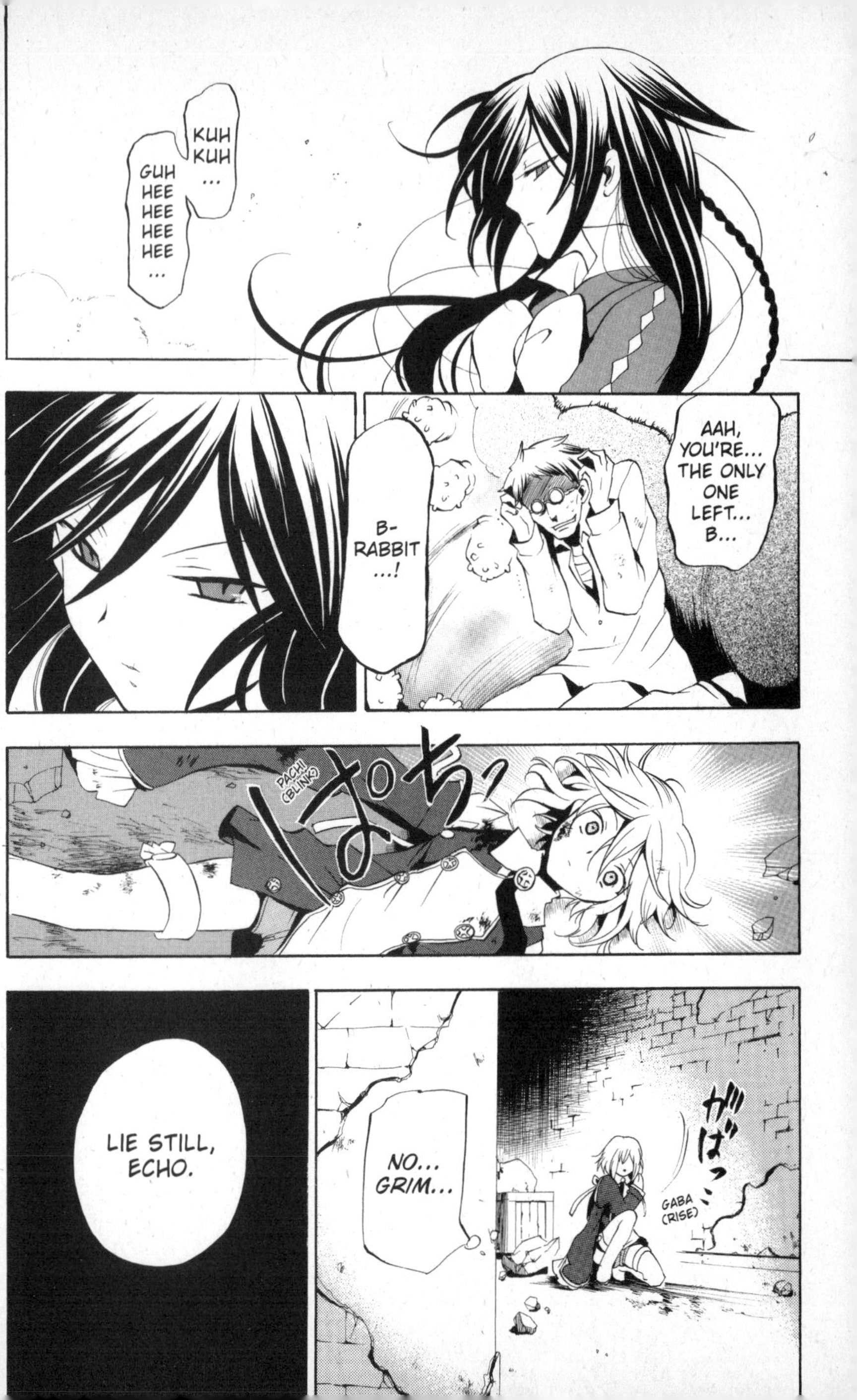
KUH KUH ...
GUH HEE HEE HEE HEE ...
AAH, YOU'RE... THE ONLY ONE LEFT... B...
B-RABBIT ...!
ぱちっ
PACHI (BLINK)
がばっ
GABA (RISE)
NO... GRIM...
LIE STILL, ECHO.

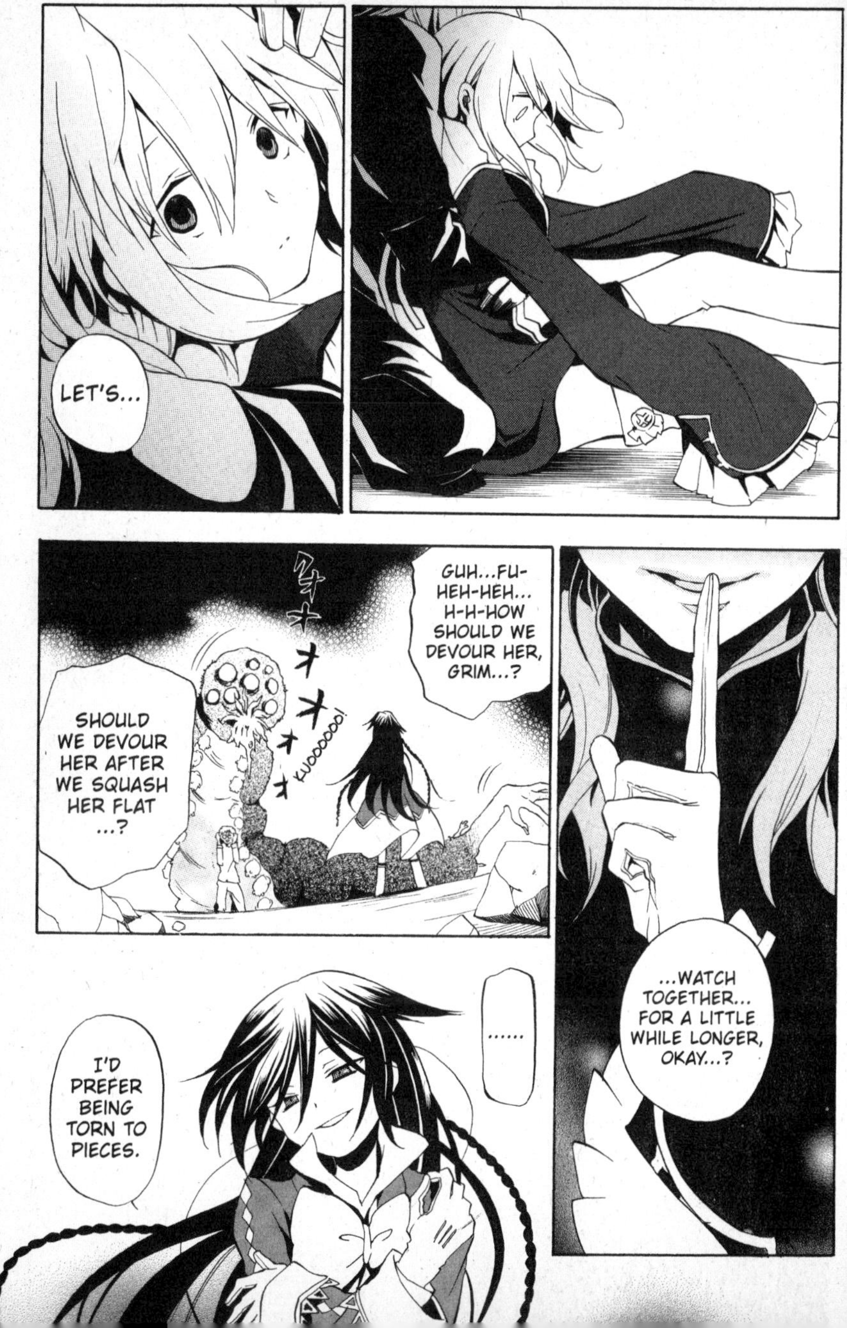
LET'S...
...WATCH TOGETHER... FOR A LITTLE WHILE LONGER, OKAY...?
GUH...FU-HEH-HEH... H-H-HOW SHOULD WE DEVOUR HER, GRIM...?
KUOOOOOO!
SHOULD WE DEVOUR HER AFTER WE SQUASH HER FLAT ...?
......
I'D PREFER BEING TORN TO PIECES.

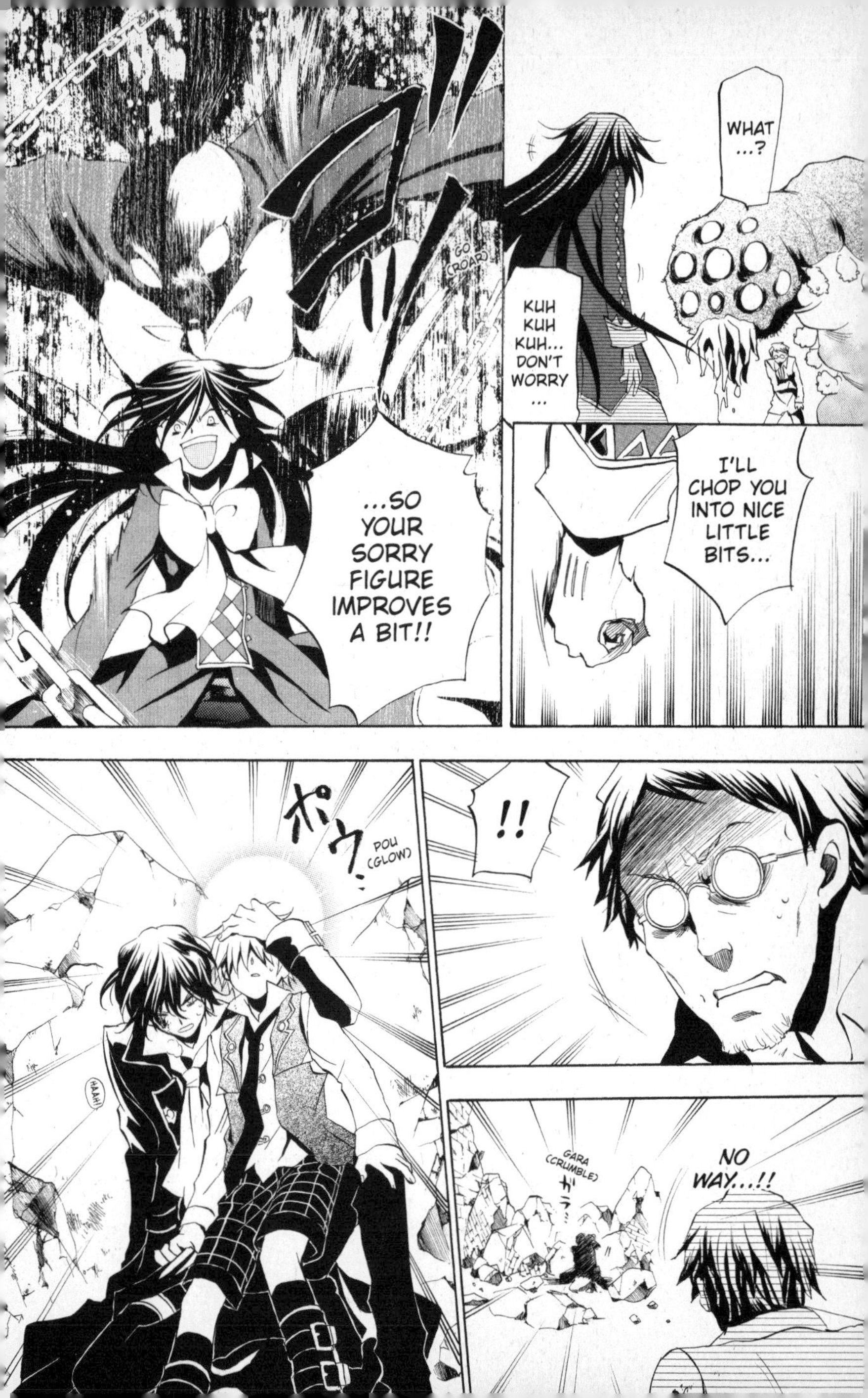
WHAT ...?
KUH KUH KUH... DON'T WORRY ...
I'LL CHOP YOU INTO NICE LITTLE BITS...
GO (ROAR)
...SO YOUR SORRY FIGURE IMPROVES A BIT!!
!!
POU (GLOW)
HAAH!
NO WAY...!!
GARA (CRUMBLE)

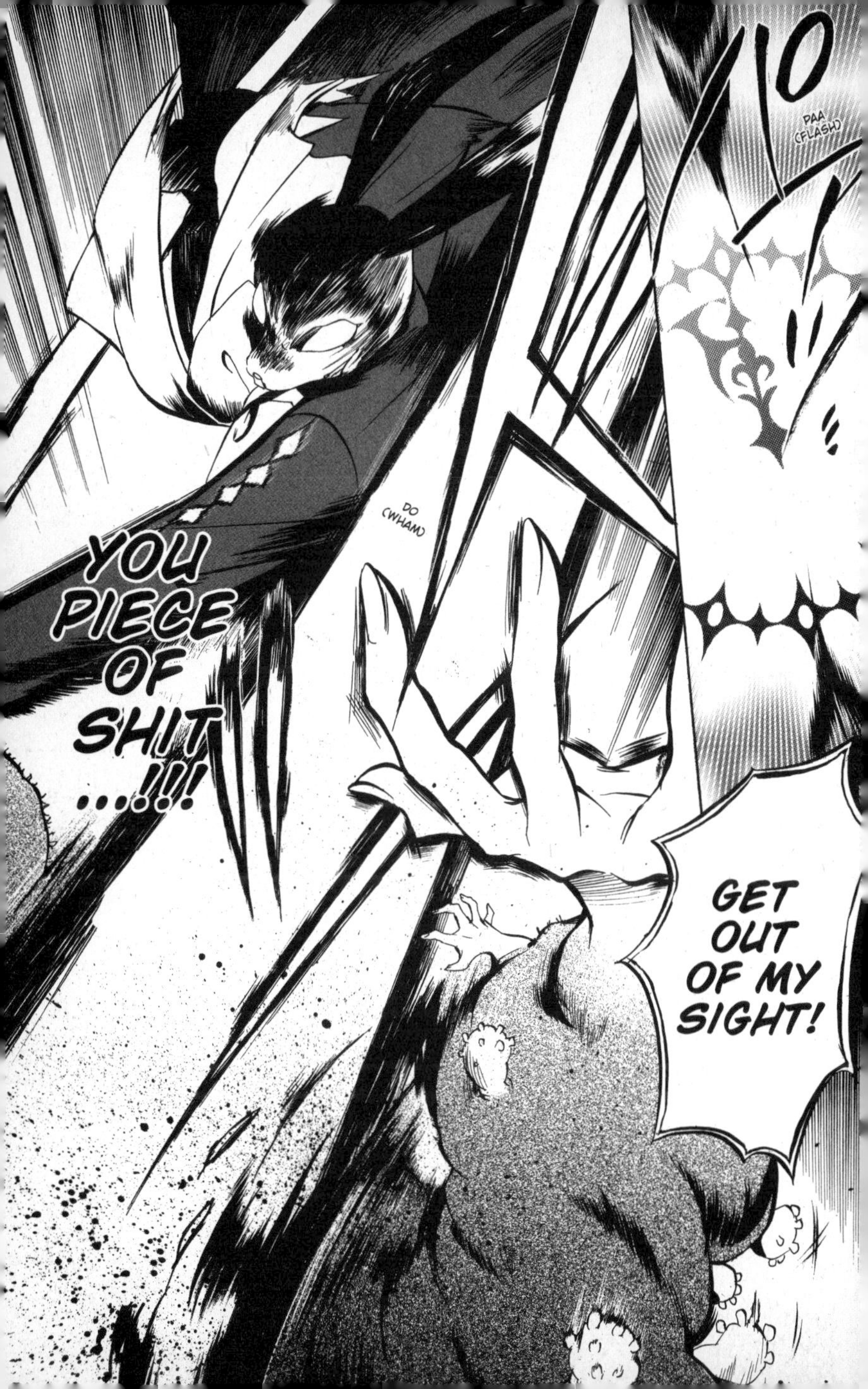
PAA
(FLASH)
GET OUT OF MY SIGHT!
DO
(WHAM)
YOU PIECE OF SHIT...!!!

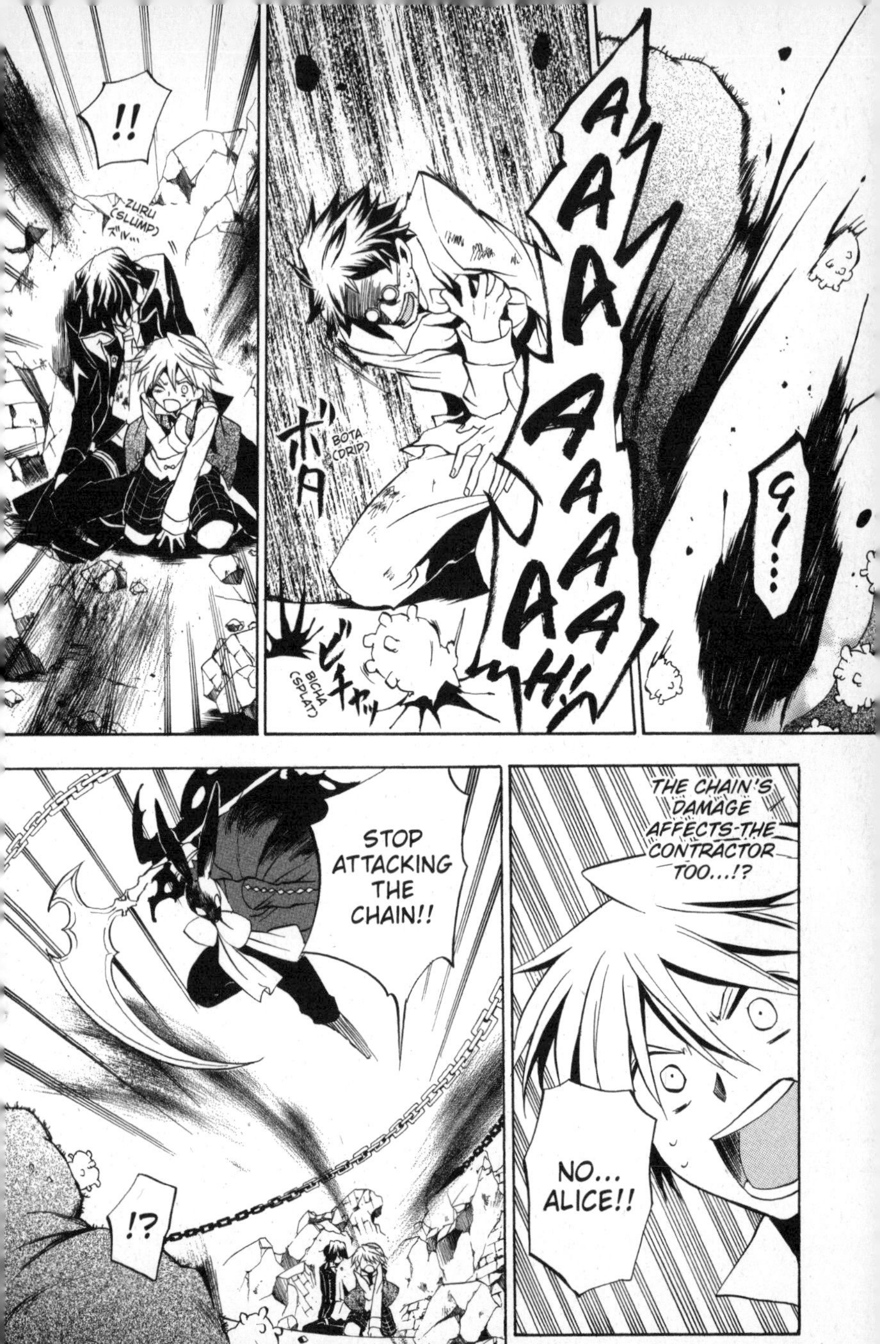
G...
AAAAAAAAAH!!
ボタ
BOTA (DRIP)
ビチャッ
BICHA (SPLAT)
!!
ZURU (SLUMP)
ズル…
THE CHAIN'S DAMAGE AFFECTS THE CONTRACTOR TOO...!?
NO... ALICE!!
STOP ATTACKING THE CHAIN!!
!?

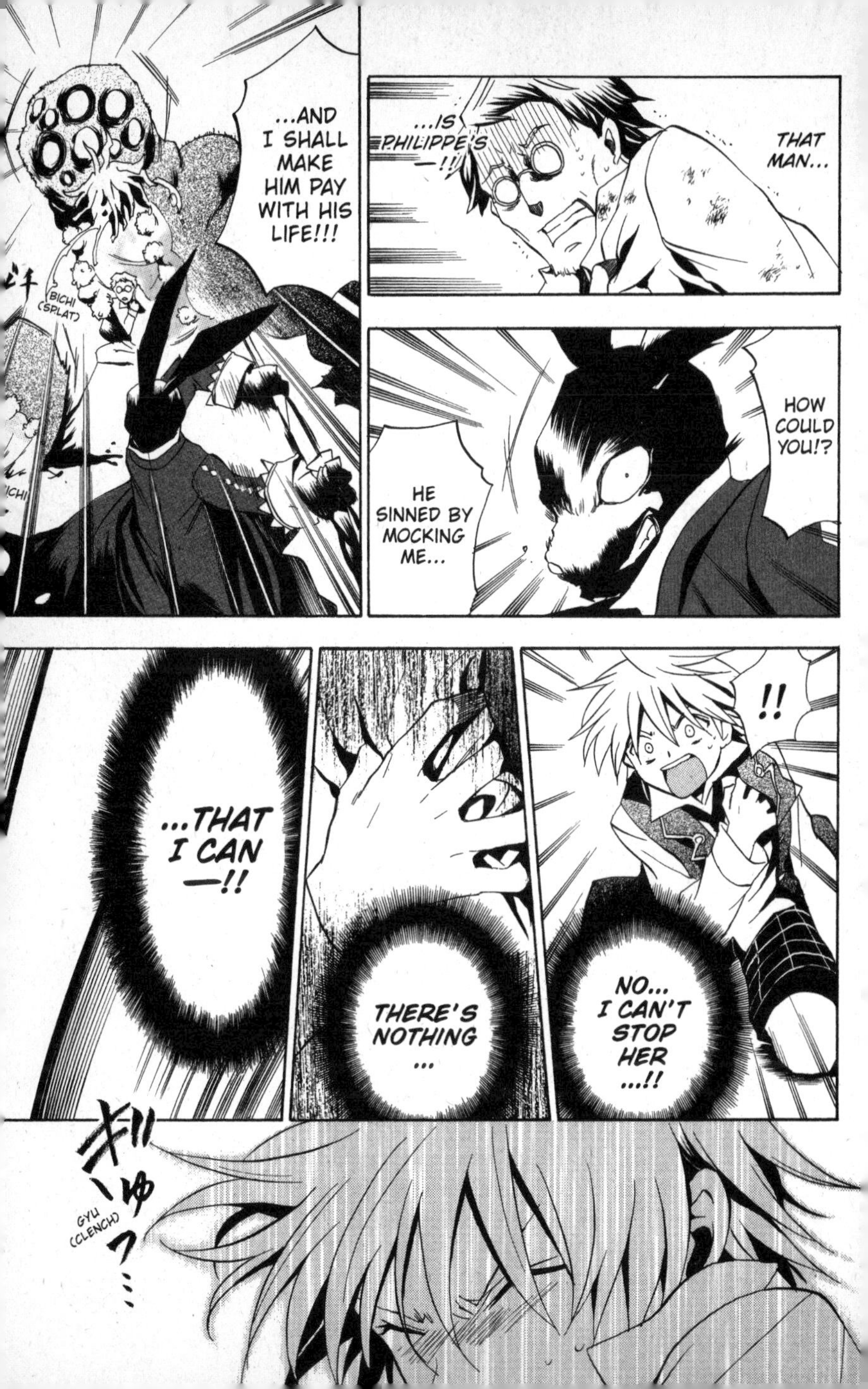
THAT MAN...
...IS PHILIPPE'S—!!
HOW COULD YOU!?
HE SINNED BY MOCKING ME...
...AND I SHALL MAKE HIM PAY WITH HIS LIFE!!!
BICHI (SPLAT)
!!
NO... I CAN'T STOP HER...!!
THERE'S NOTHING...
...THAT I CAN—!!
GYU (CLENCH)

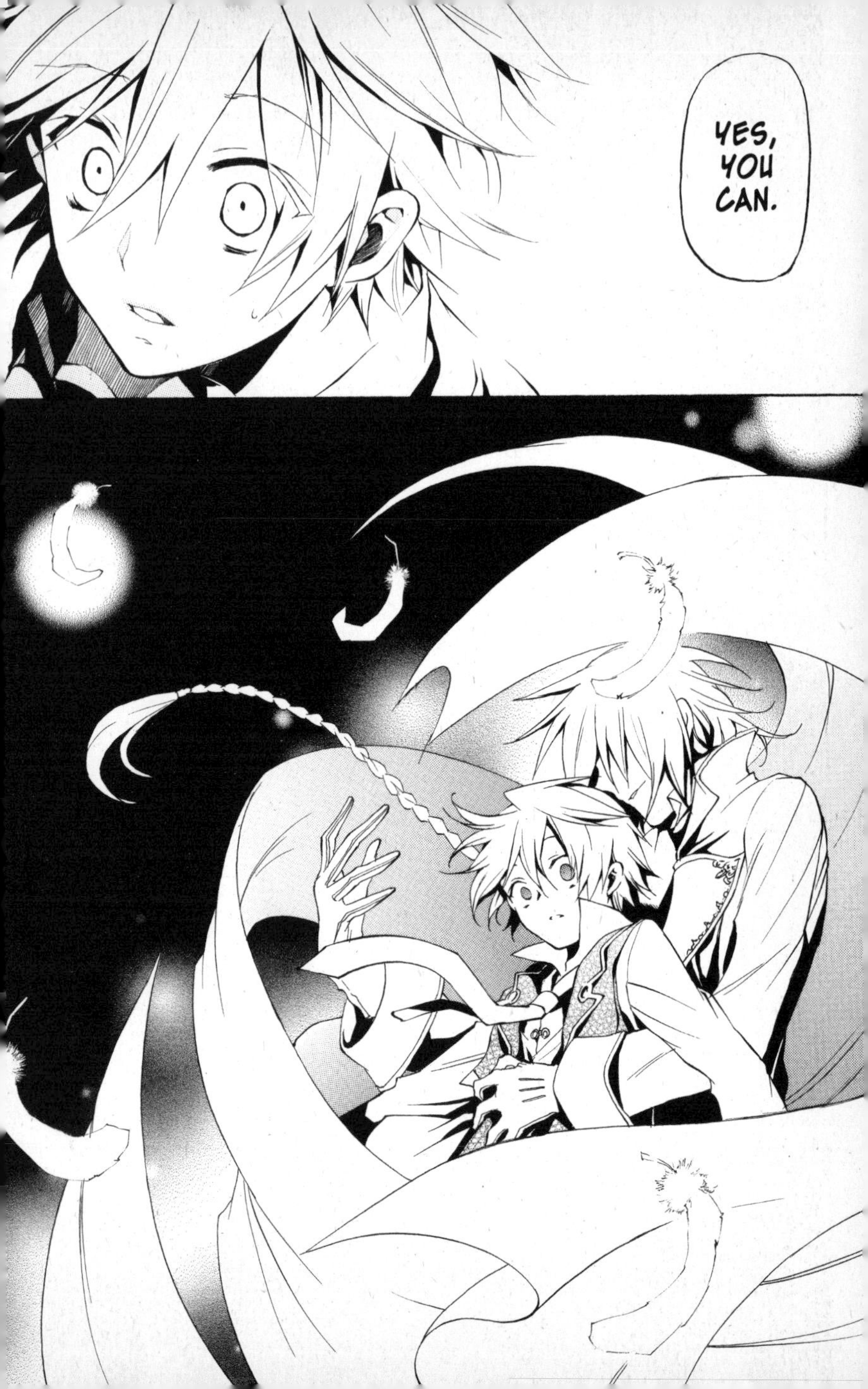
YES, YOU CAN.

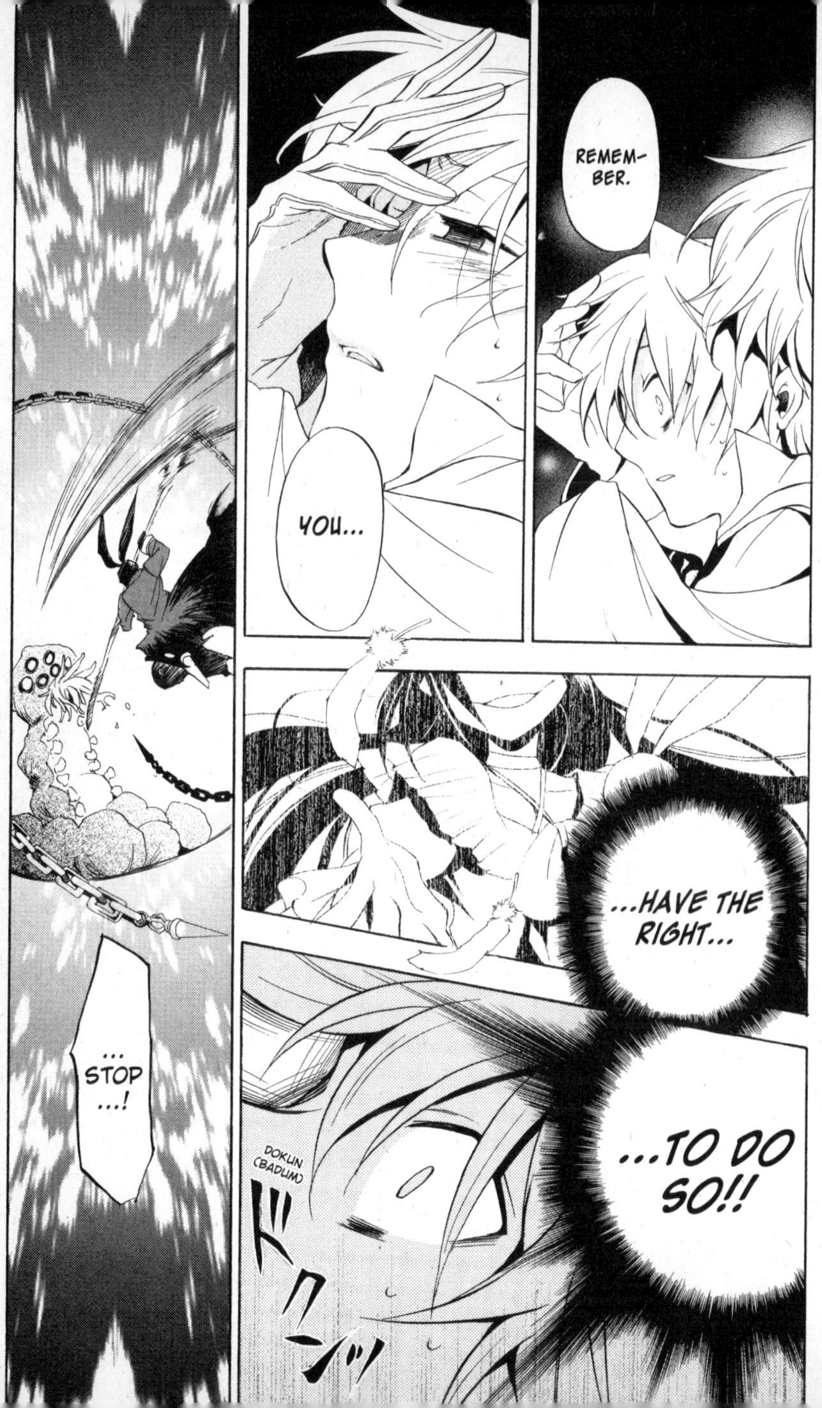
REMEMBER.
YOU...
...HAVE THE RIGHT...
...TO DO SO!!
DOKUN (BADUM)
...STOP...!

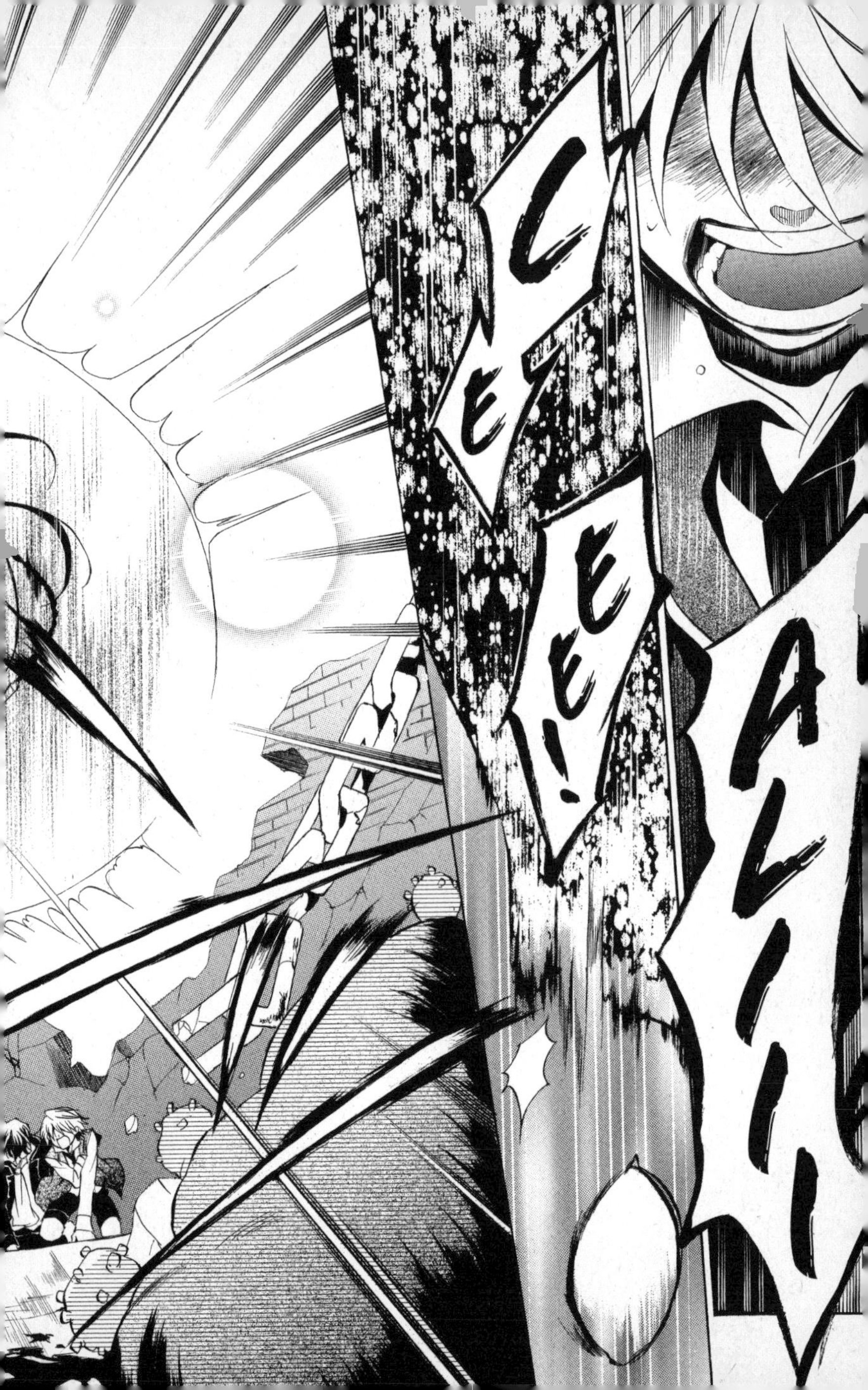
CEEEE!
AH!!

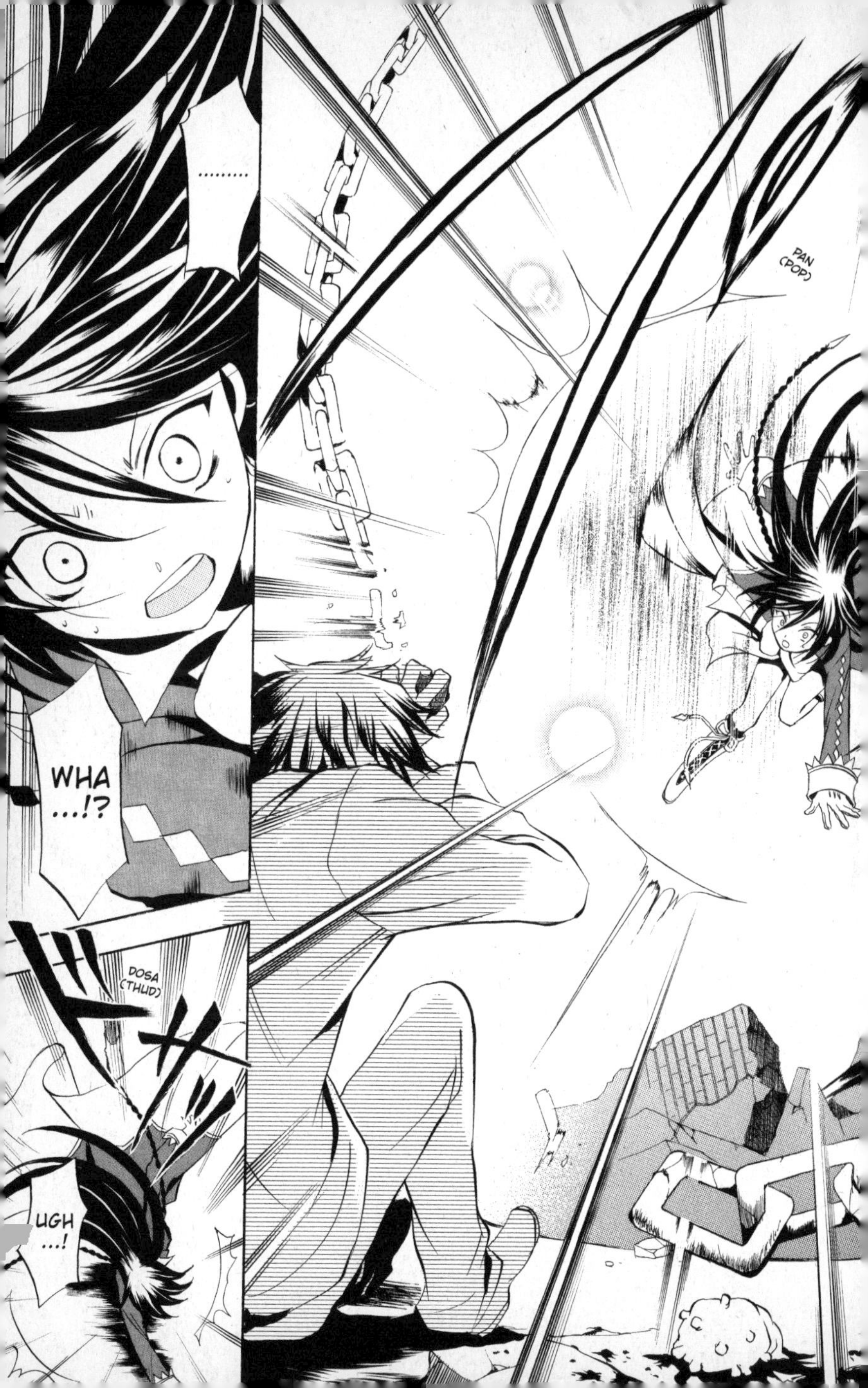
PAN (POP)
....
WHA ...!?
DOSA (THUD)
UGH ...!

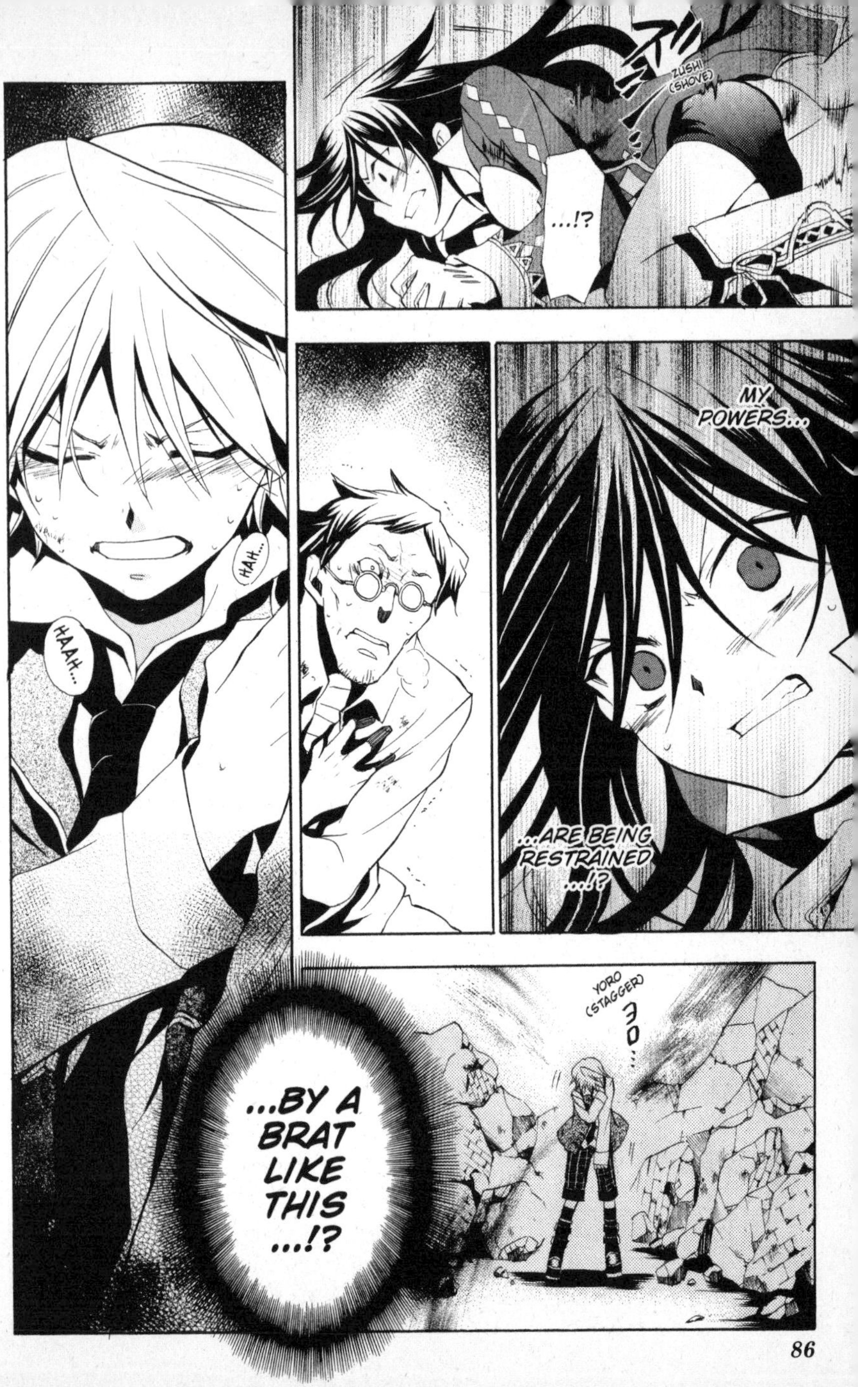
ZUSHI (SHOVE)
...!?
MY POWERS...
...ARE BEING RESTRAINED ...!?
YORO (STAGGER)
ヨロ...
...BY A BRAT LIKE THIS ...!?
HAH...
HAAH...

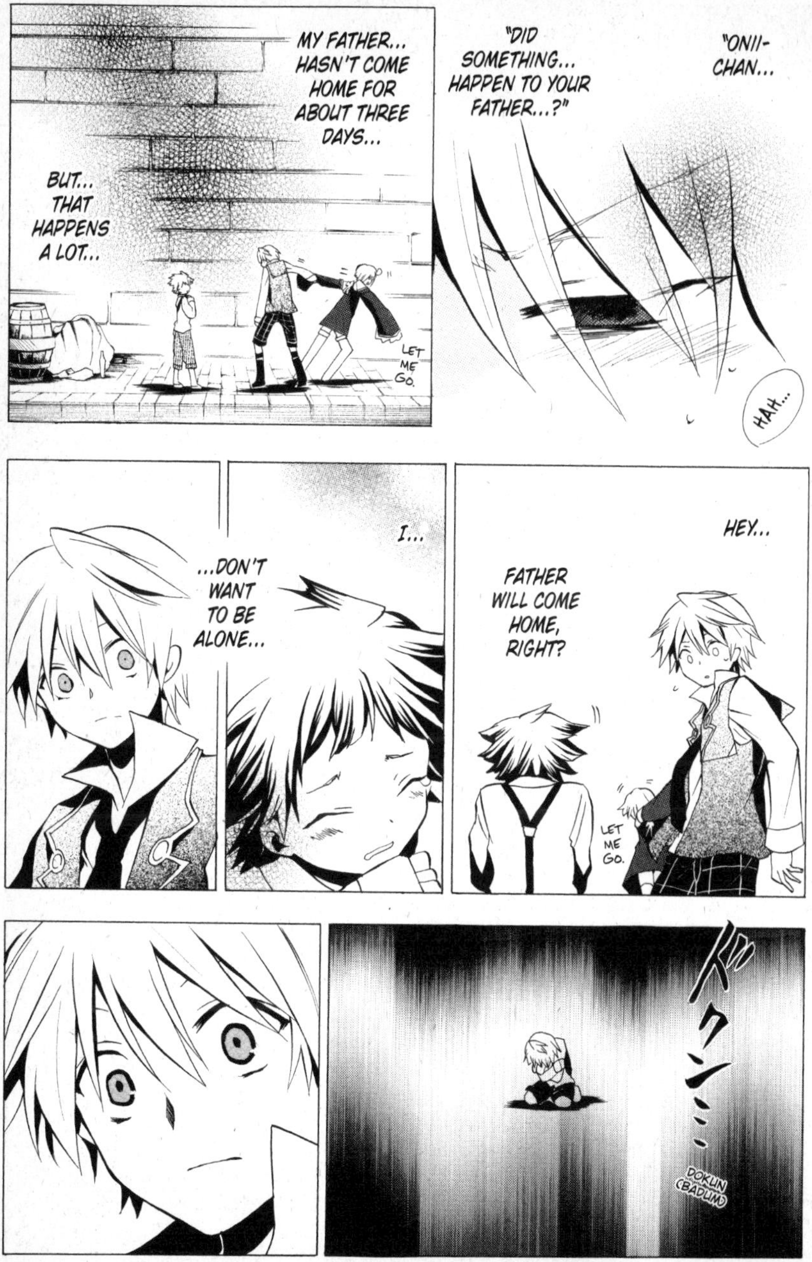
"ONII-CHAN...
"DID SOMETHING... HAPPEN TO YOUR FATHER...?"
HAH...
MY FATHER... HASN'T COME HOME FOR ABOUT THREE DAYS...
BUT... THAT HAPPENS A LOT...
LET ME GO.
HEY...
FATHER WILL COME HOME, RIGHT?
LET ME GO.
I...
...DON'T WANT TO BE ALONE...
ドクン…
DOKUN (BADUM)

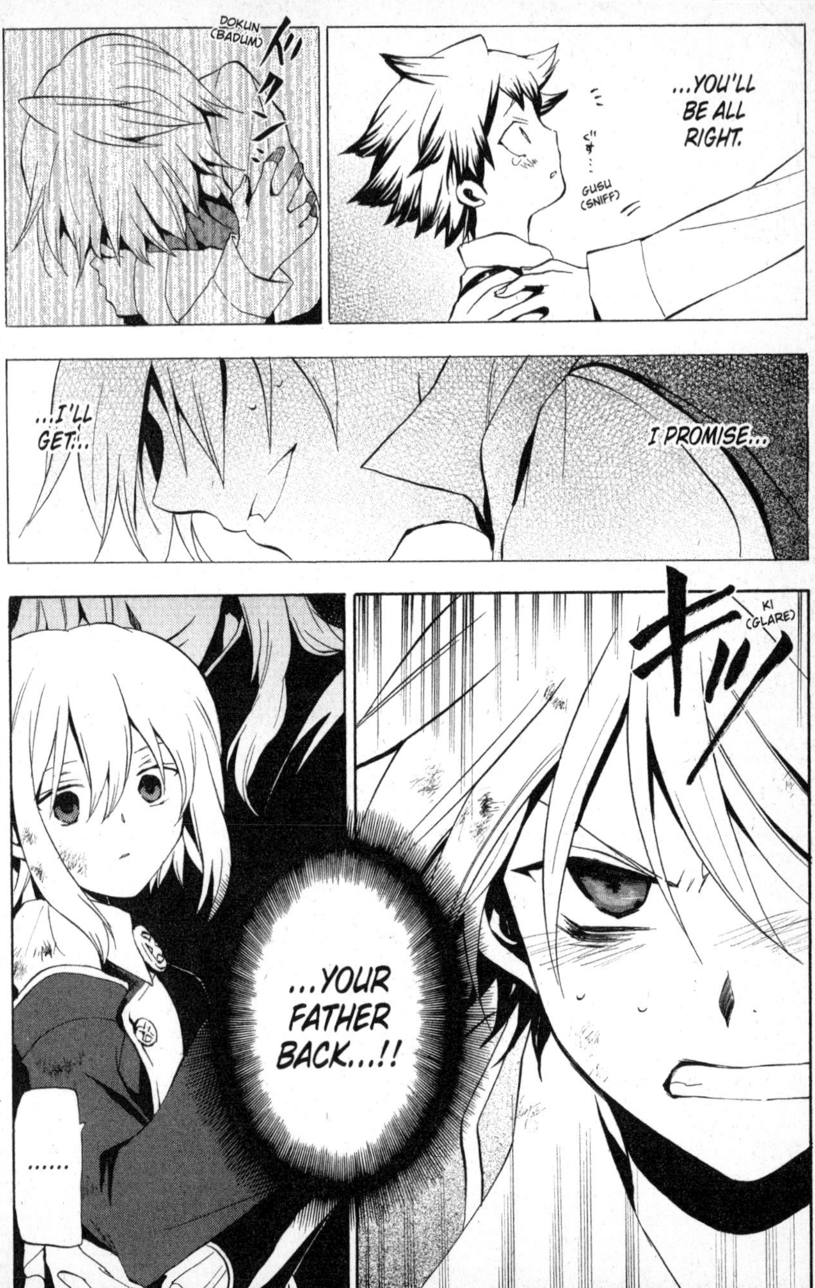
...YOU'LL BE ALL RIGHT.
GUSU (SNIFF)
DOKUN (BADUM)
I PROMISE...
...I'LL GET...
KI (GLARE)
キッ
...YOUR FATHER BACK...!!
......

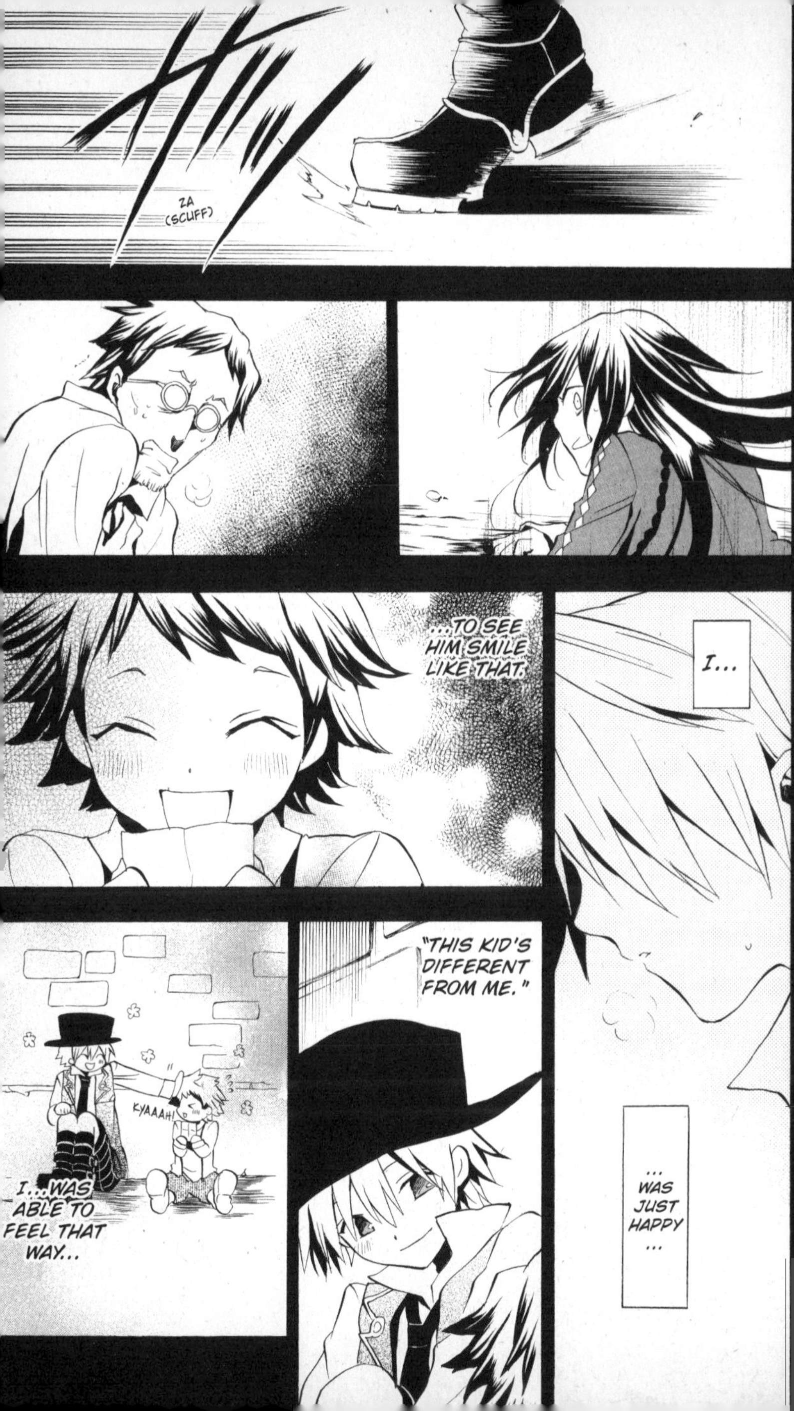
ZA (SCUFF)
I...
...WAS JUST HAPPY...
...TO SEE HIM SMILE LIKE THAT.
"THIS KID'S DIFFERENT FROM ME."
KYAAAH!
I...WAS ABLE TO FEEL THAT WAY...

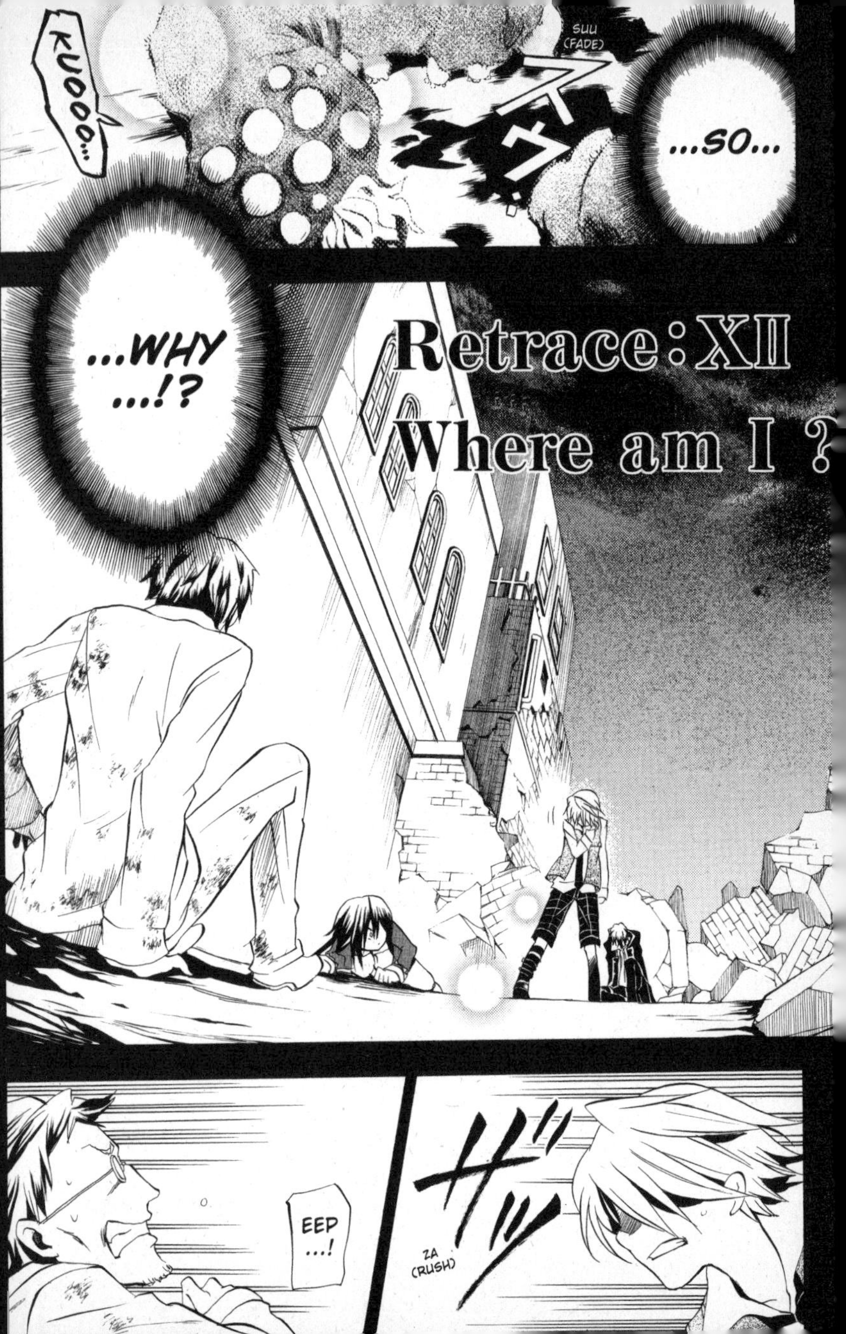
SUU (FADE)
...SO...
KUOOO...
Retrace: XII
Where am I ?
...WHY ...!?
ZA (RUSH)
EEP ...!

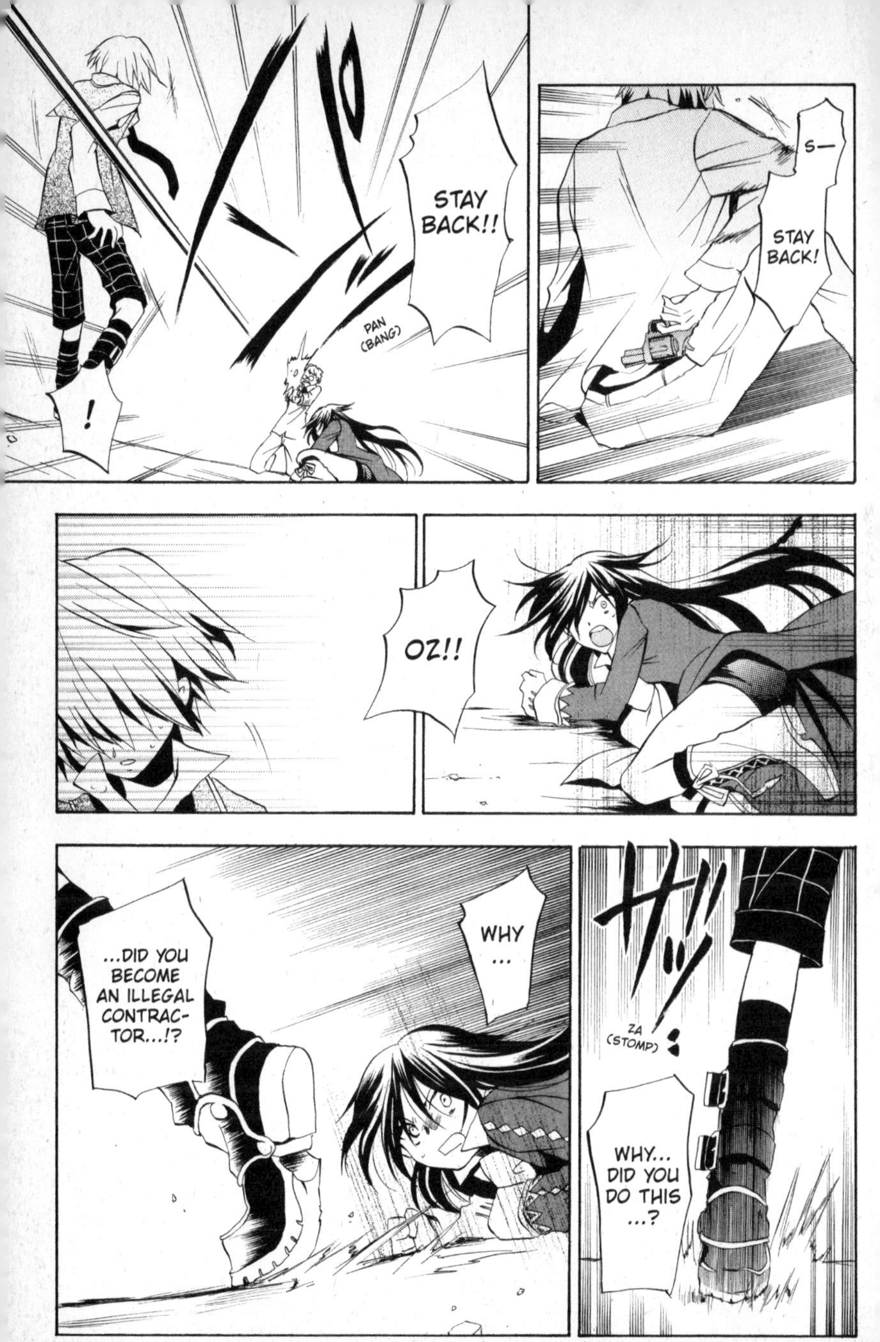
S—
STAY BACK!
STAY BACK!!
PAN (BANG)
!
OZ!!
ZA (STOMP)
WHY... DID YOU DO THIS ...?
WHY ...
...DID YOU BECOME AN ILLEGAL CONTRAC-TOR...!?

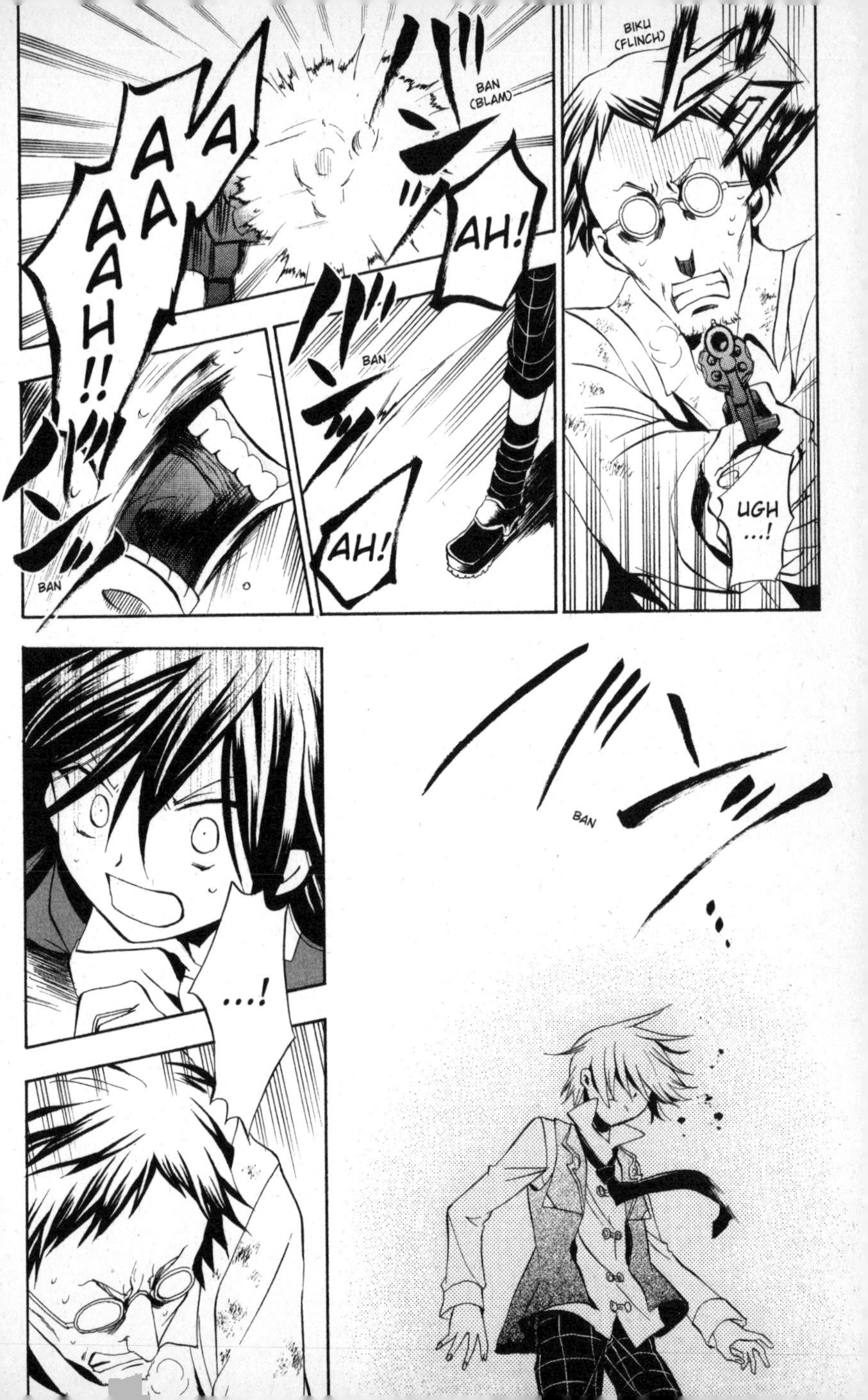
BIKU (FLINCH)
UGH ...!
BAN (BLAM)
AH!
BAN
AH!
AAAAAH!!
BAN
BAN
...!

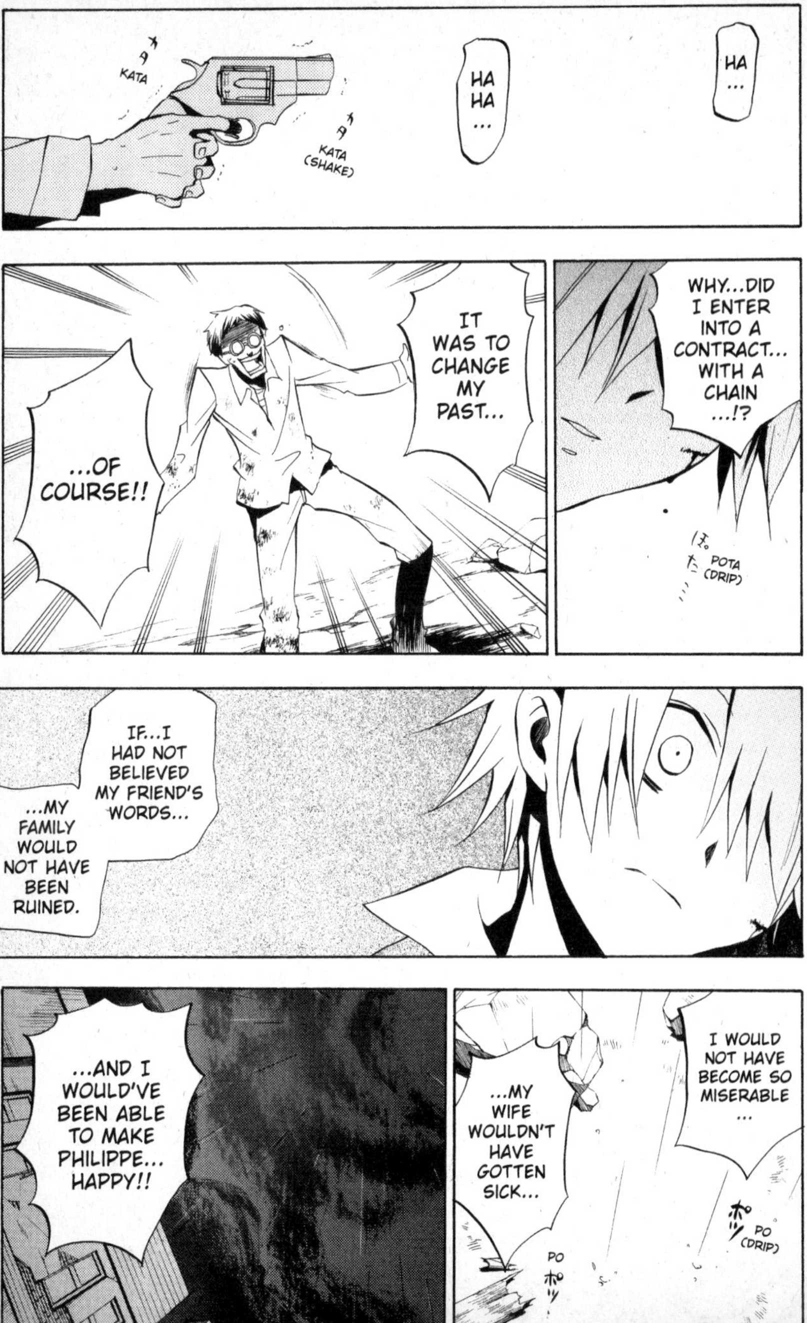
HA ...
HA HA ...
KATA (SHAKE)
KATA
WHY...DID I ENTER INTO A CONTRACT... WITH A CHAIN ...!?
POTA (DRIP)
IT WAS TO CHANGE MY PAST...
...OF COURSE!!
IF...I HAD NOT BELIEVED MY FRIEND'S WORDS...
...MY FAMILY WOULD NOT HAVE BEEN RUINED.
I WOULD NOT HAVE BECOME SO MISERABLE ...
...MY WIFE WOULDN'T HAVE GOTTEN SICK...
PO (DRIP)
PO
...AND I WOULD'VE BEEN ABLE TO MAKE PHILIPPE... HAPPY!!

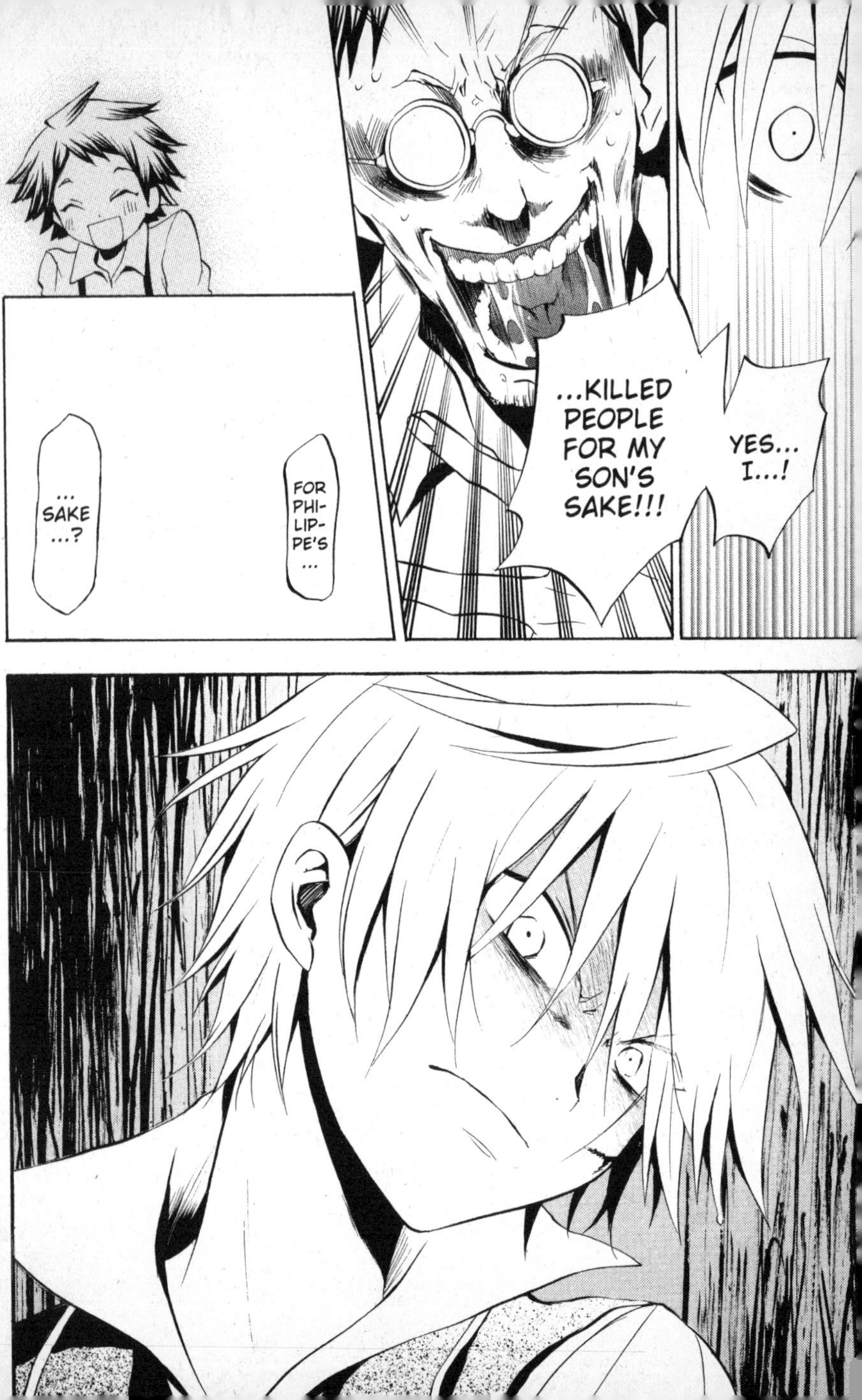
YES... I...!
...KILLED PEOPLE FOR MY SON'S SAKE!!!
FOR PHI-LIP-PE'S ...
... SAKE ...?

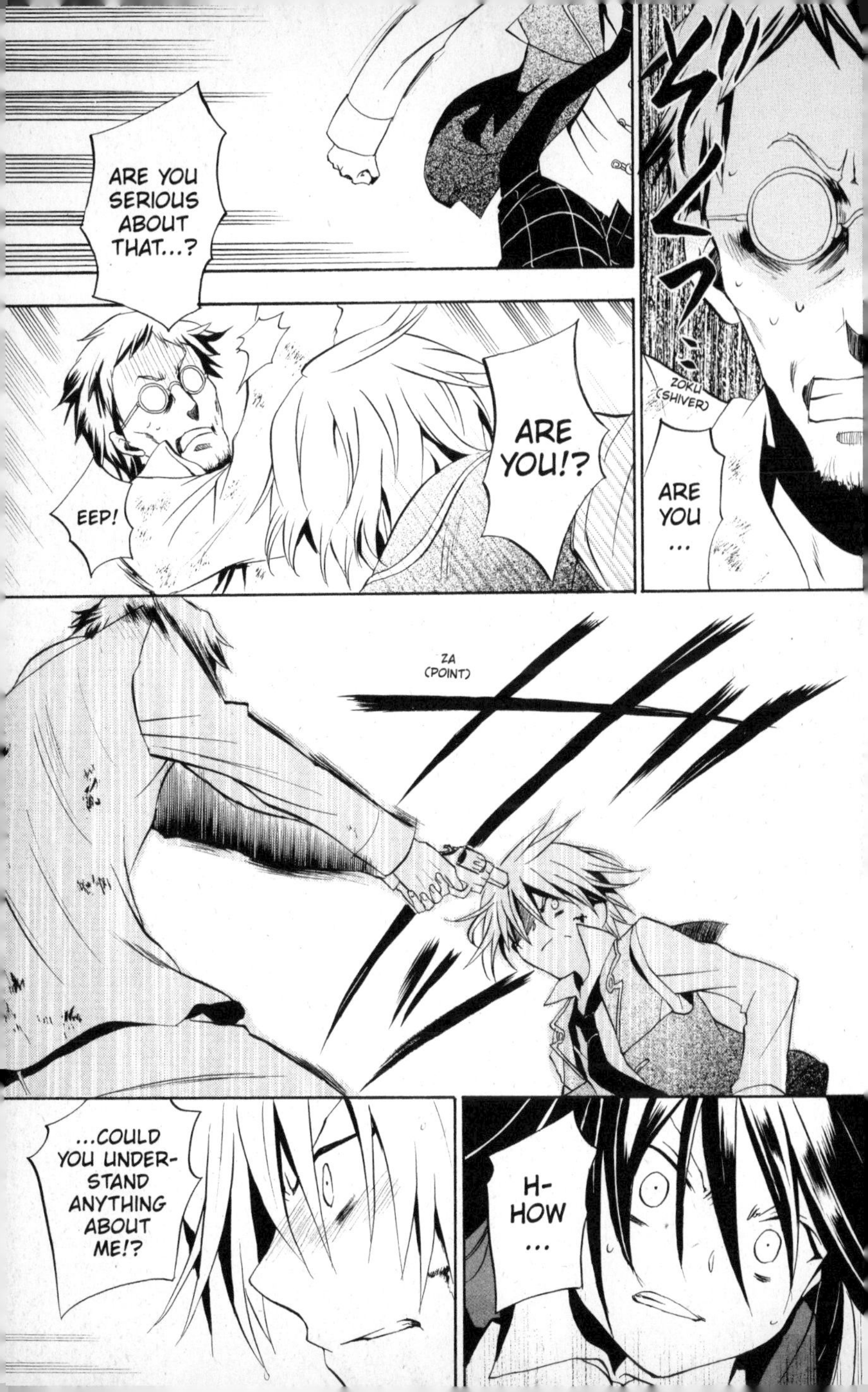
ZOKU (SHIVER)
ARE YOU ...
ARE YOU SERIOUS ABOUT THAT...?
ARE YOU!?
EEP!
ZA (POINT)
H-HOW ...
...COULD YOU UNDER-STAND ANYTHING ABOUT ME!?

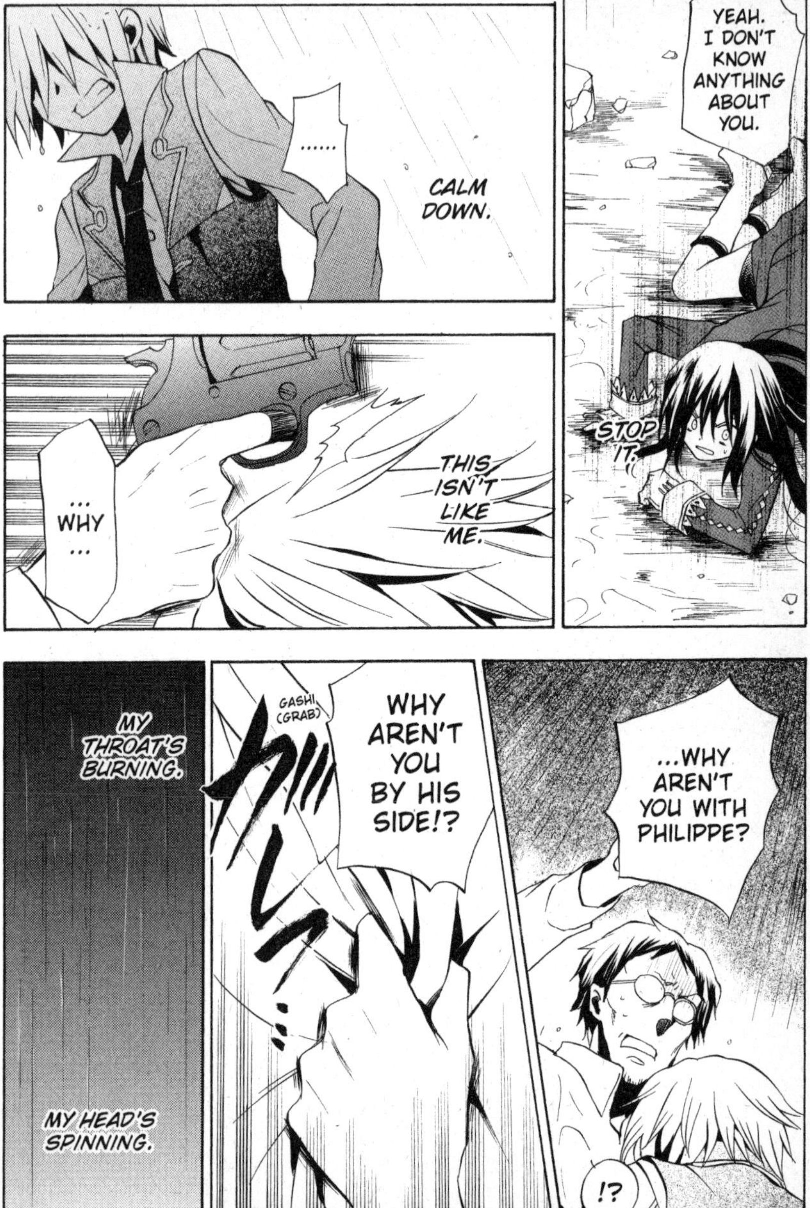
YEAH. I DON'T KNOW ANYTHING ABOUT YOU.
STOP IT.
......
CALM DOWN.
THIS ISN'T LIKE ME.
...WHY...
...WHY AREN'T YOU WITH PHILIPPE?
!?
GASHI (GRAB)
WHY AREN'T YOU BY HIS SIDE!?
MY THROAT'S BURNING.
MY HEAD'S SPINNING.

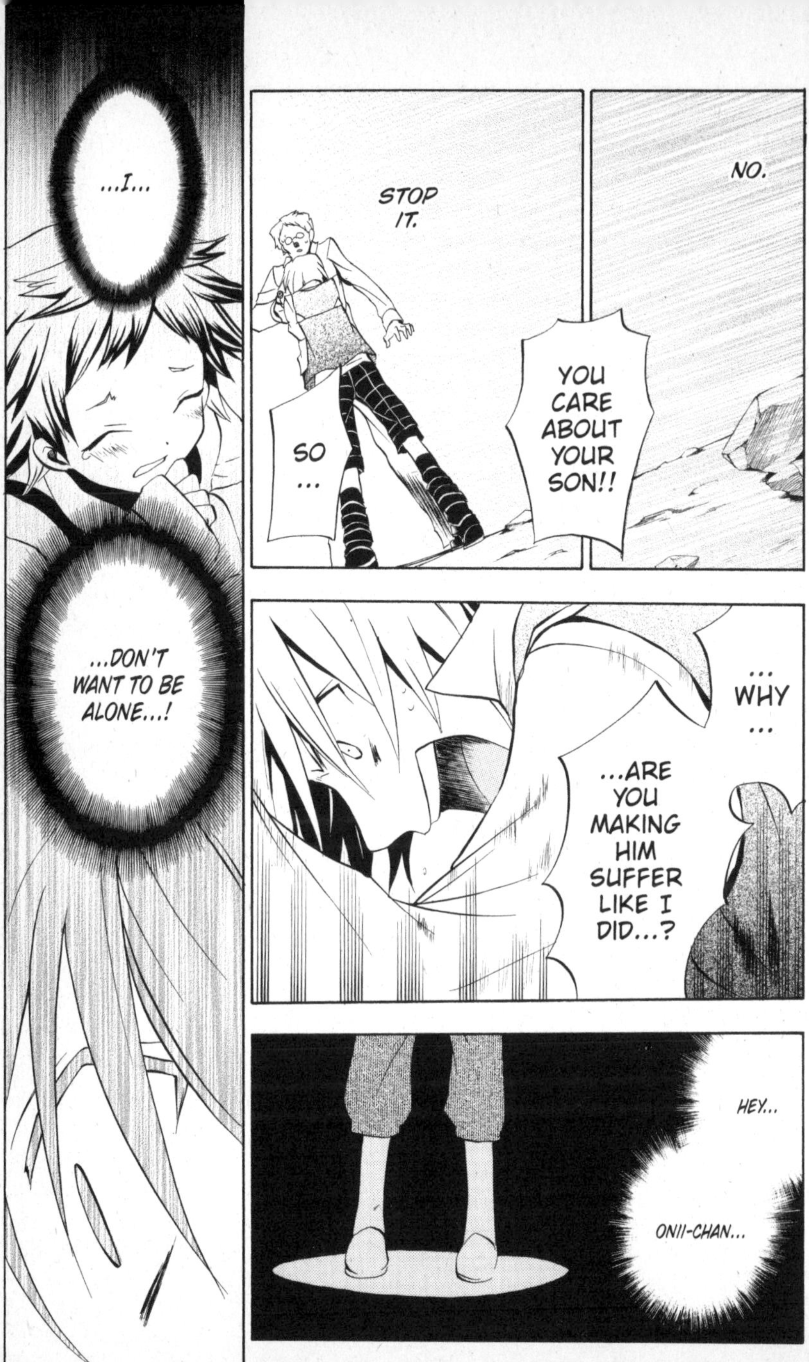
NO.
YOU CARE ABOUT YOUR SON!!
STOP IT.
SO ...
... WHY ...
...ARE YOU MAKING HIM SUFFER LIKE I DID...?
HEY...
ONII-CHAN...
...I...
...DON'T WANT TO BE ALONE...!

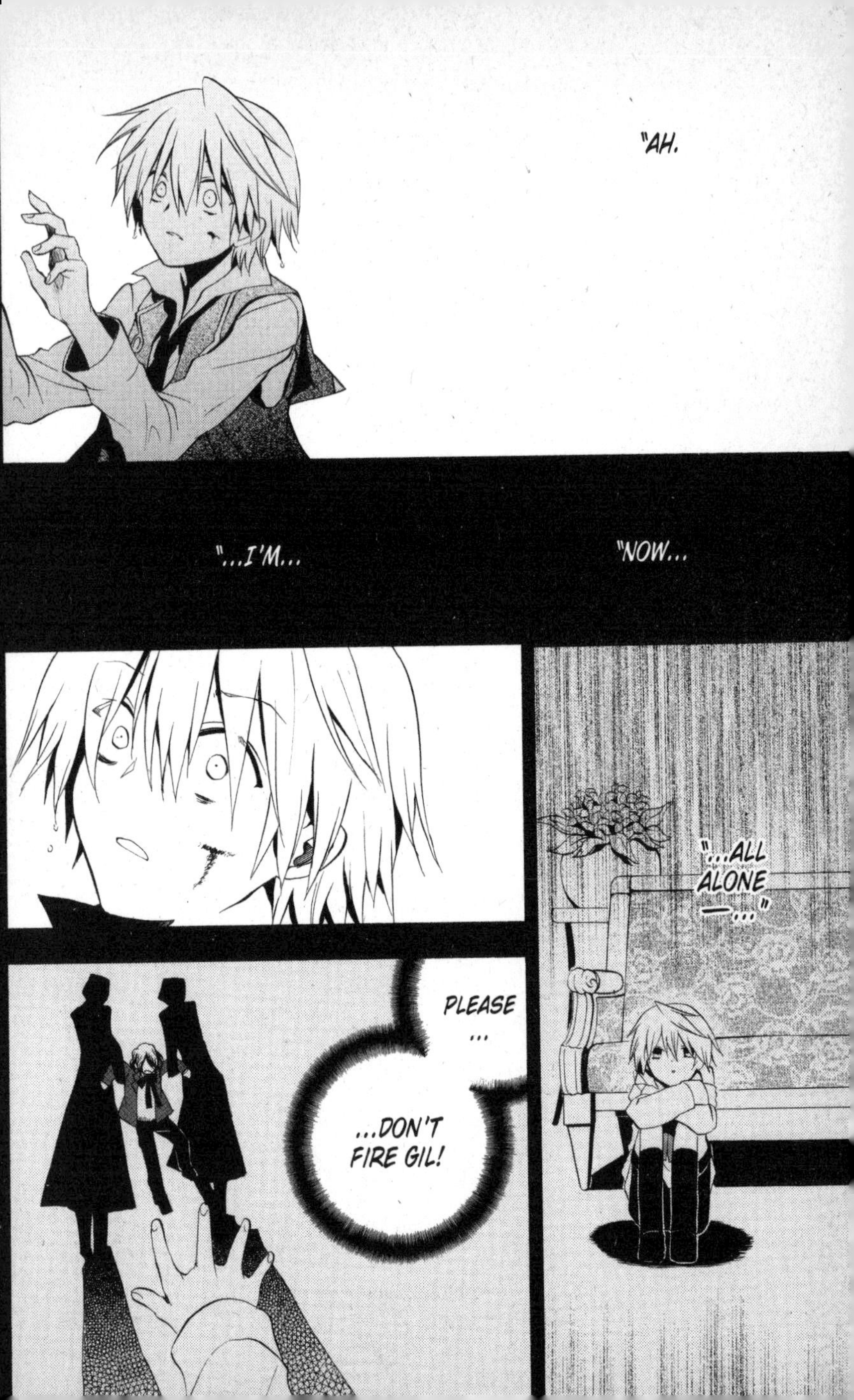
"AH.
"NOW...
"...I'M...
"...ALL ALONE —..."
PLEASE ...
...DON'T FIRE GIL!

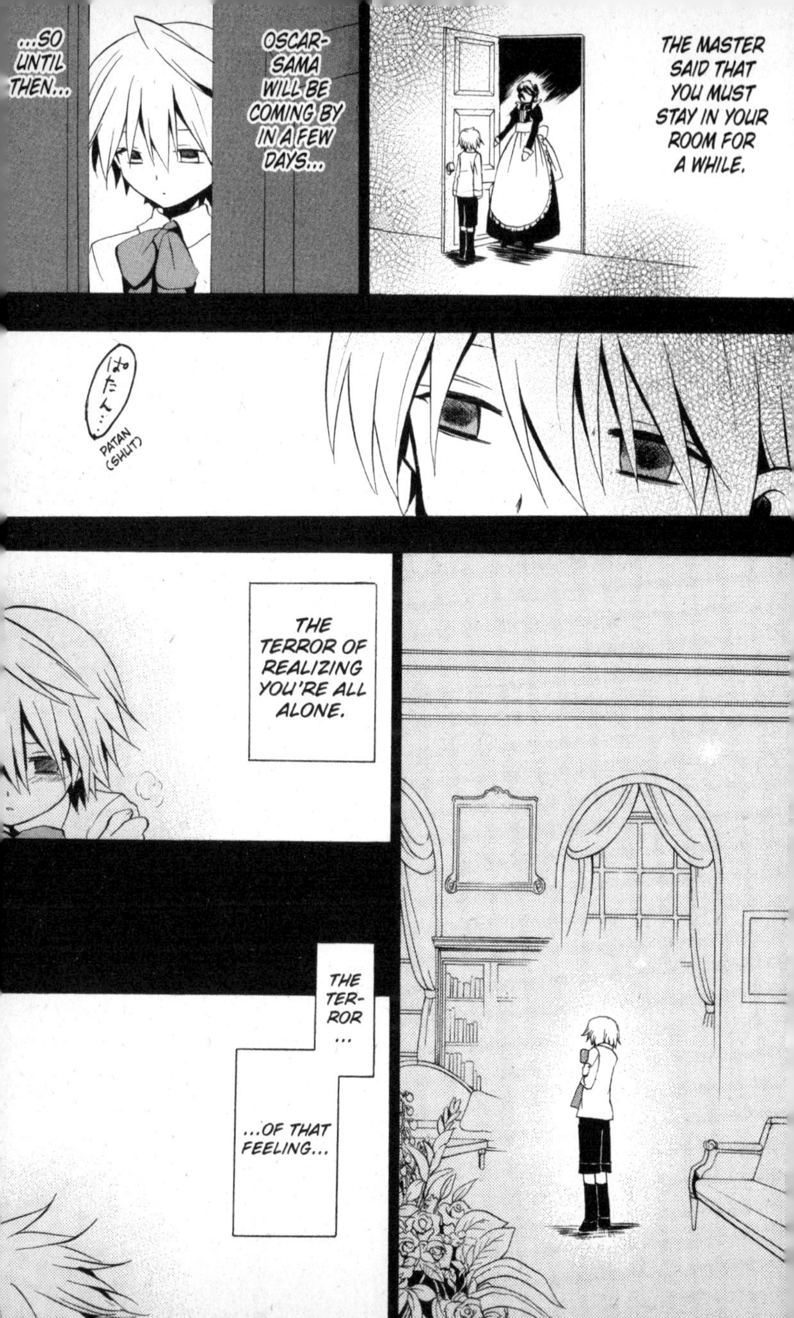
THE MASTER SAID THAT YOU MUST STAY IN YOUR ROOM FOR A WHILE.
OSCAR-SAMA WILL BE COMING BY IN A FEW DAYS...
...SO UNTIL THEN...
ぱたん…
PATAN (SHUT)
THE TERROR OF REALIZING YOU'RE ALL ALONE.
THE TER-ROR...
...OF THAT FEELING...

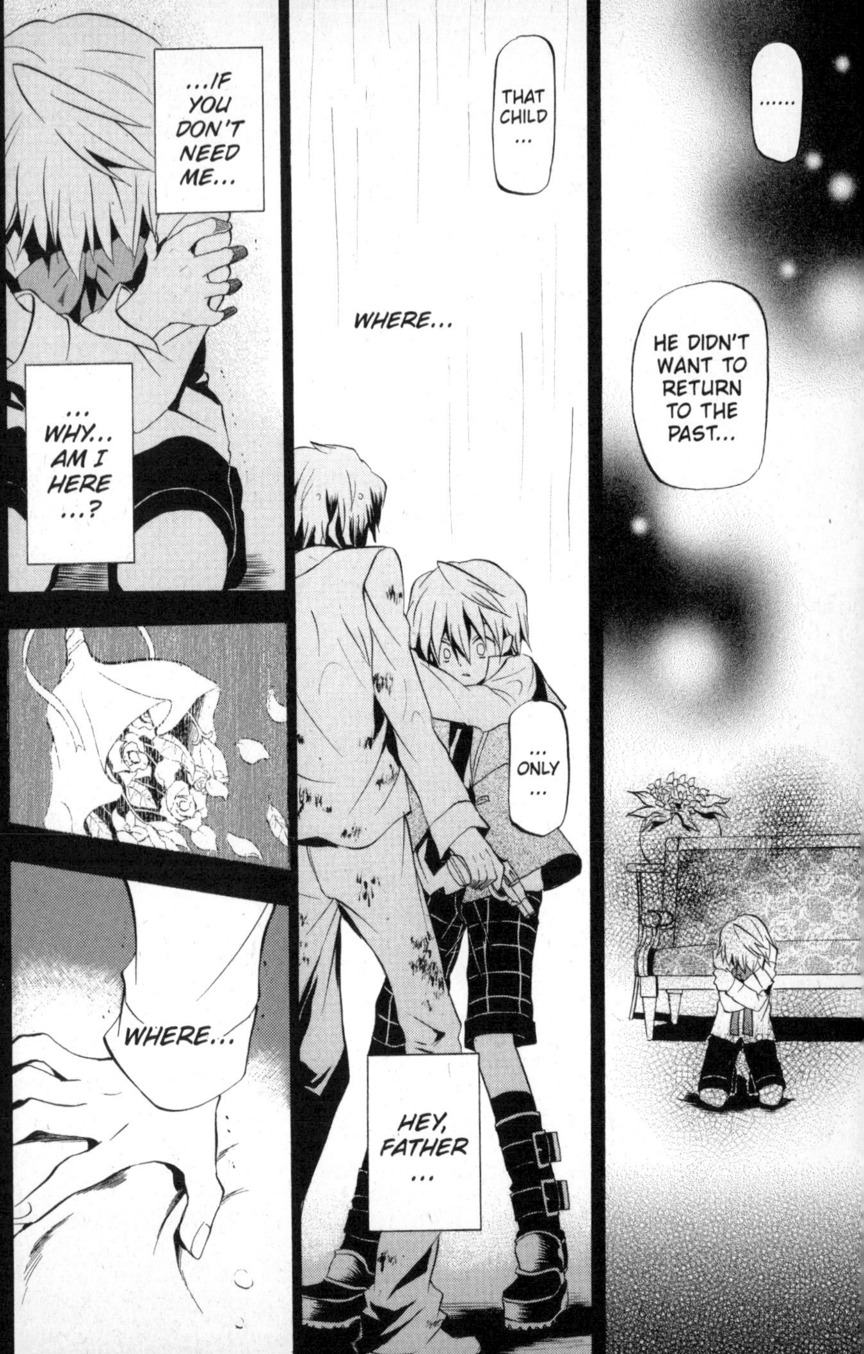
......
HE DIDN'T WANT TO RETURN TO THE PAST...
THAT CHILD...
WHERE...
...ONLY...
HEY, FATHER...
...IF YOU DON'T NEED ME...
...WHY... AM I HERE...?
WHERE...

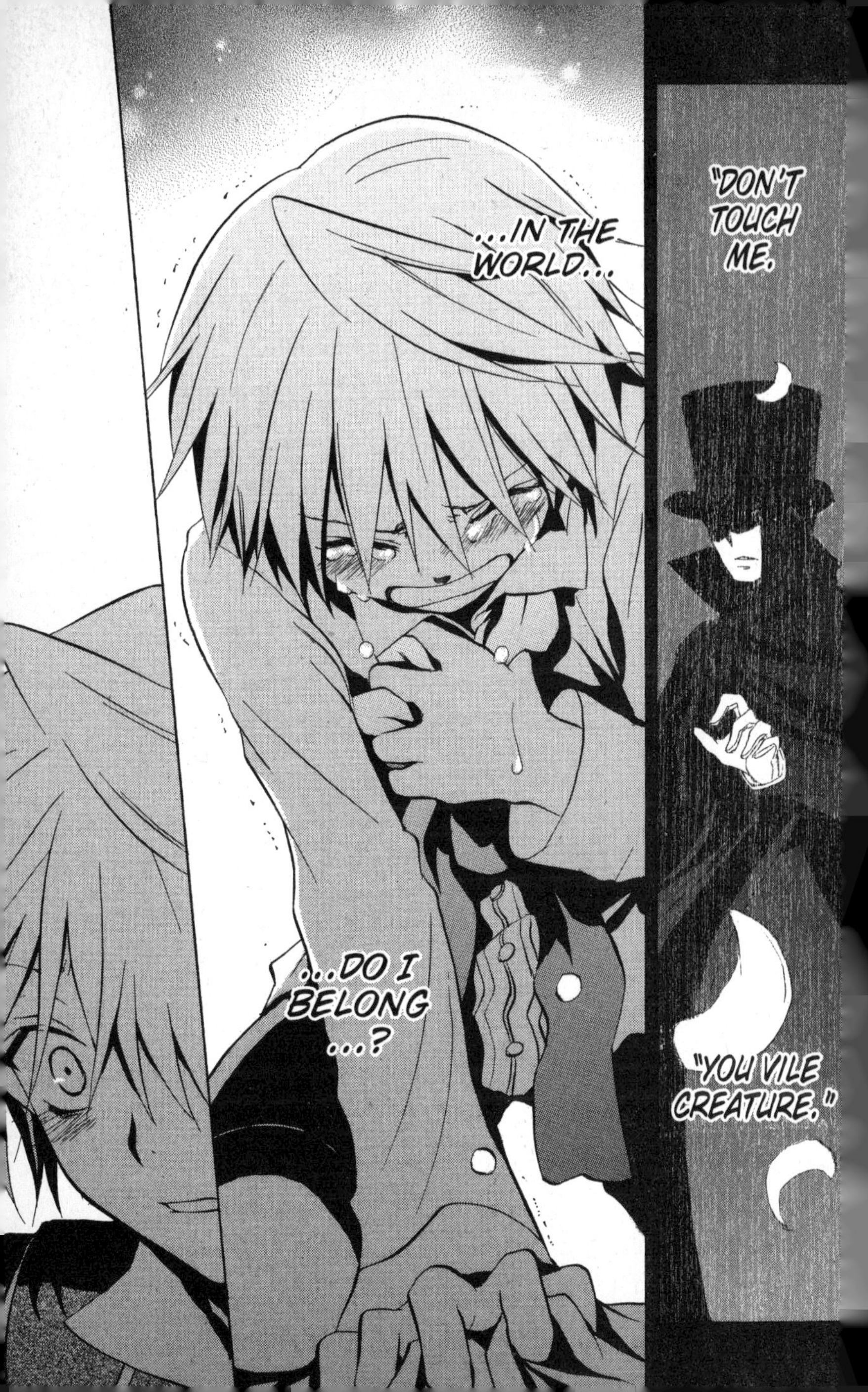
"DON'T TOUCH ME.
"YOU VILE CREATURE."
...IN THE WORLD...
...DO I BELONG ...?

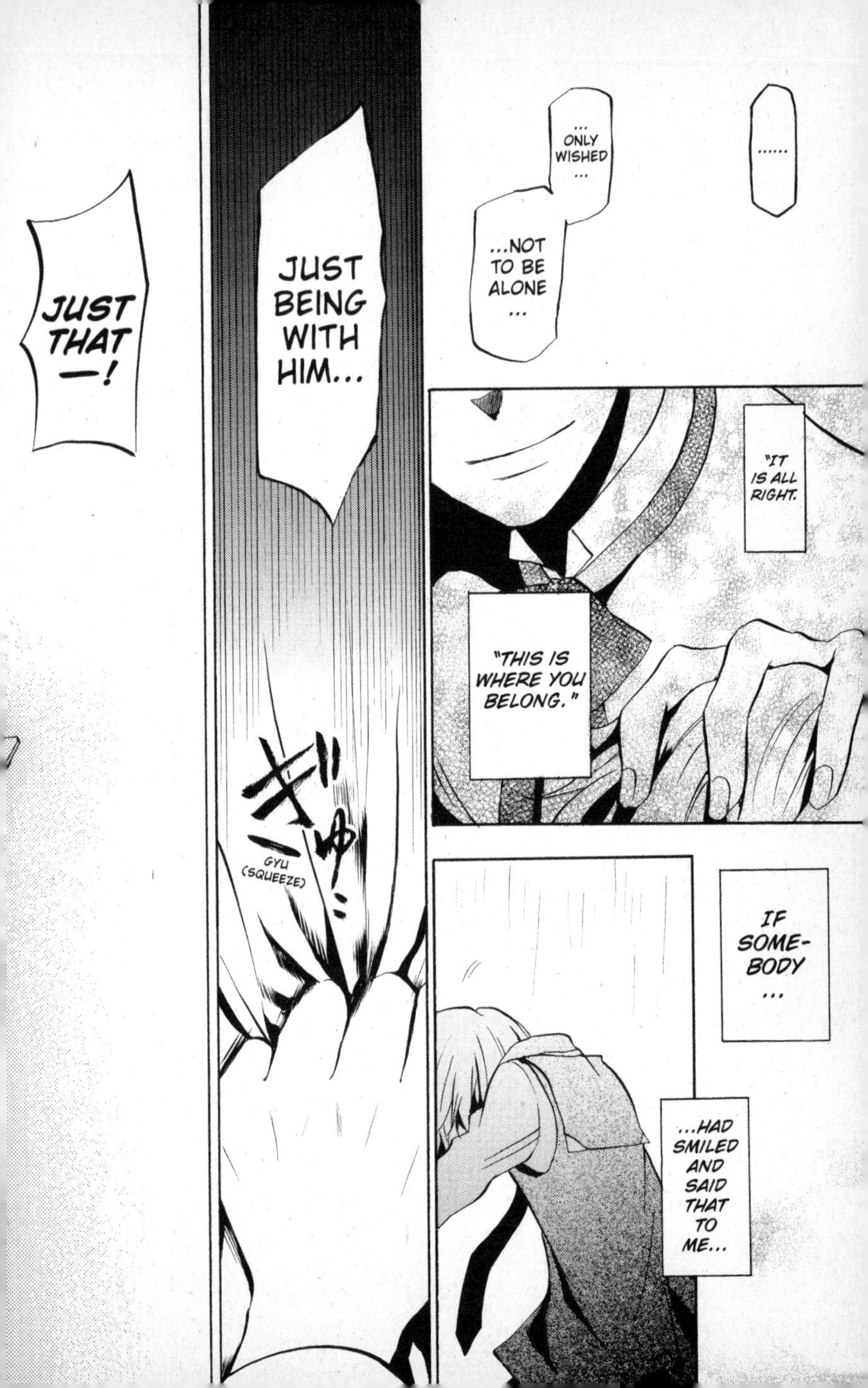
......
...ONLY WISHED...
...NOT TO BE ALONE...
"IT IS ALL RIGHT.
"THIS IS WHERE YOU BELONG."
IF SOMEBODY...
...HAD SMILED AND SAID THAT TO ME...
JUST BEING WITH HIM...
GYU (SQUEEZE)
JUST THAT—!

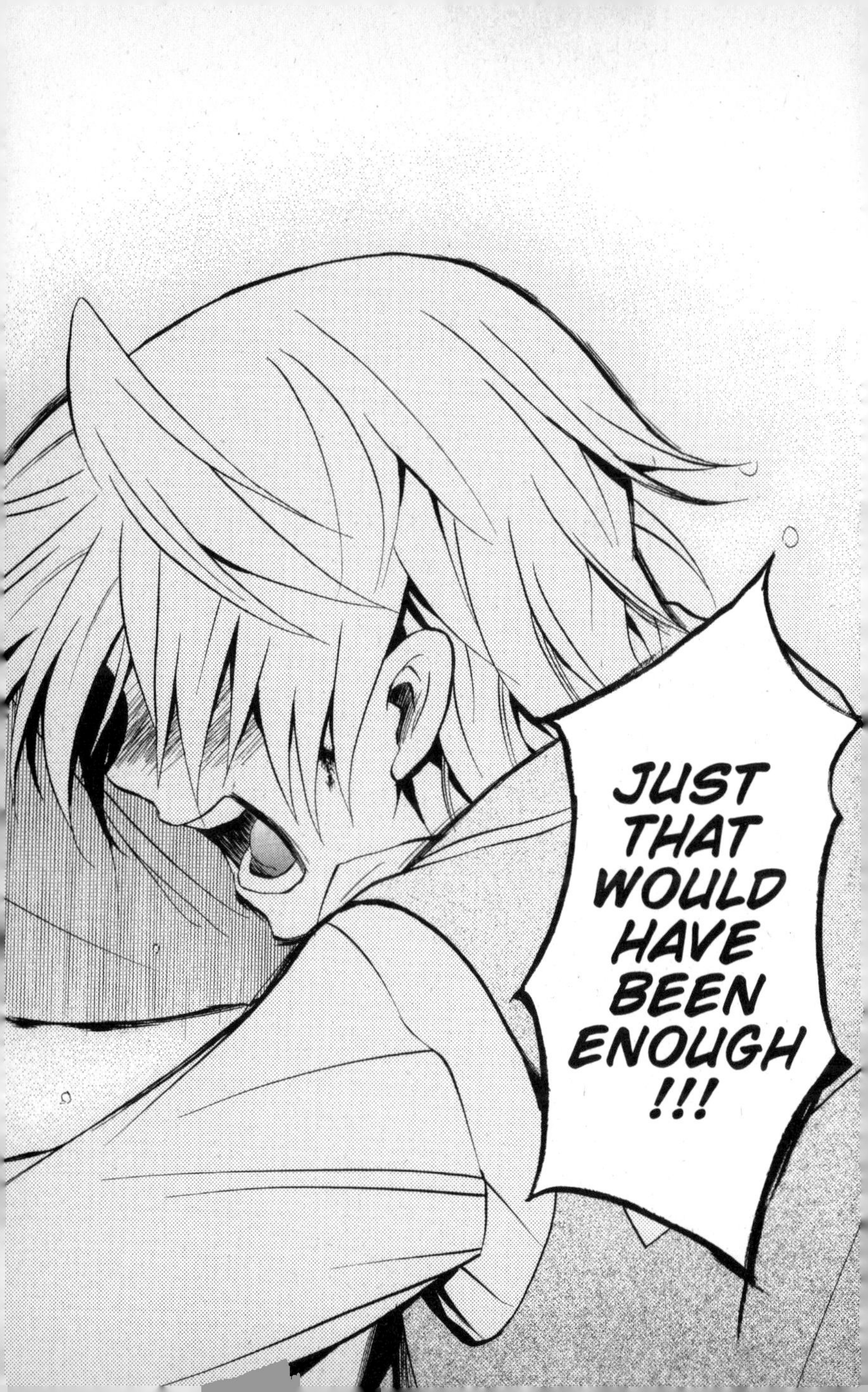
JUST THAT WOULD HAVE BEEN ENOUGH !!!

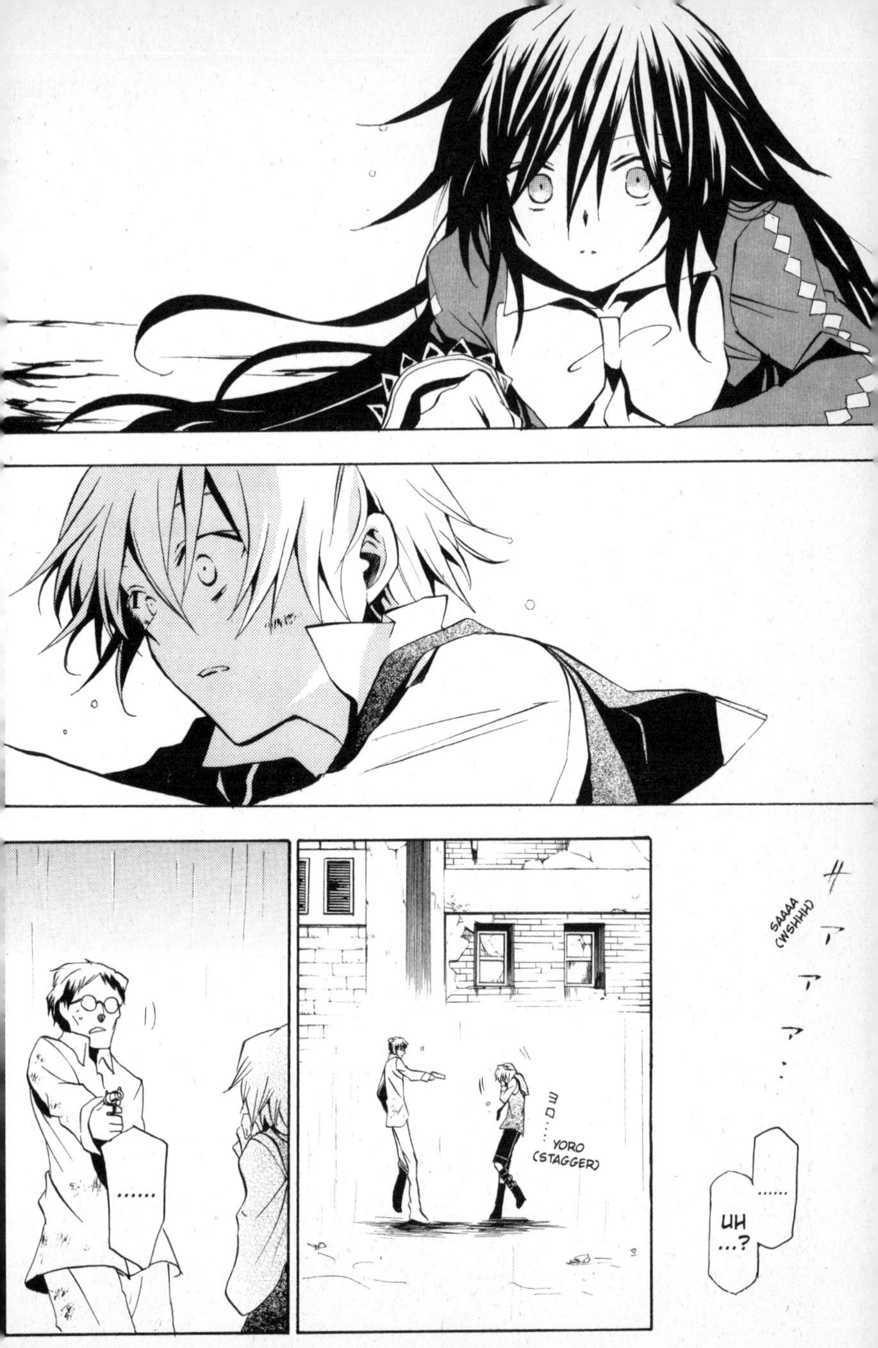
SAAAA (WSHHH)
...... UH ...?
YORO (STAGGER)
......

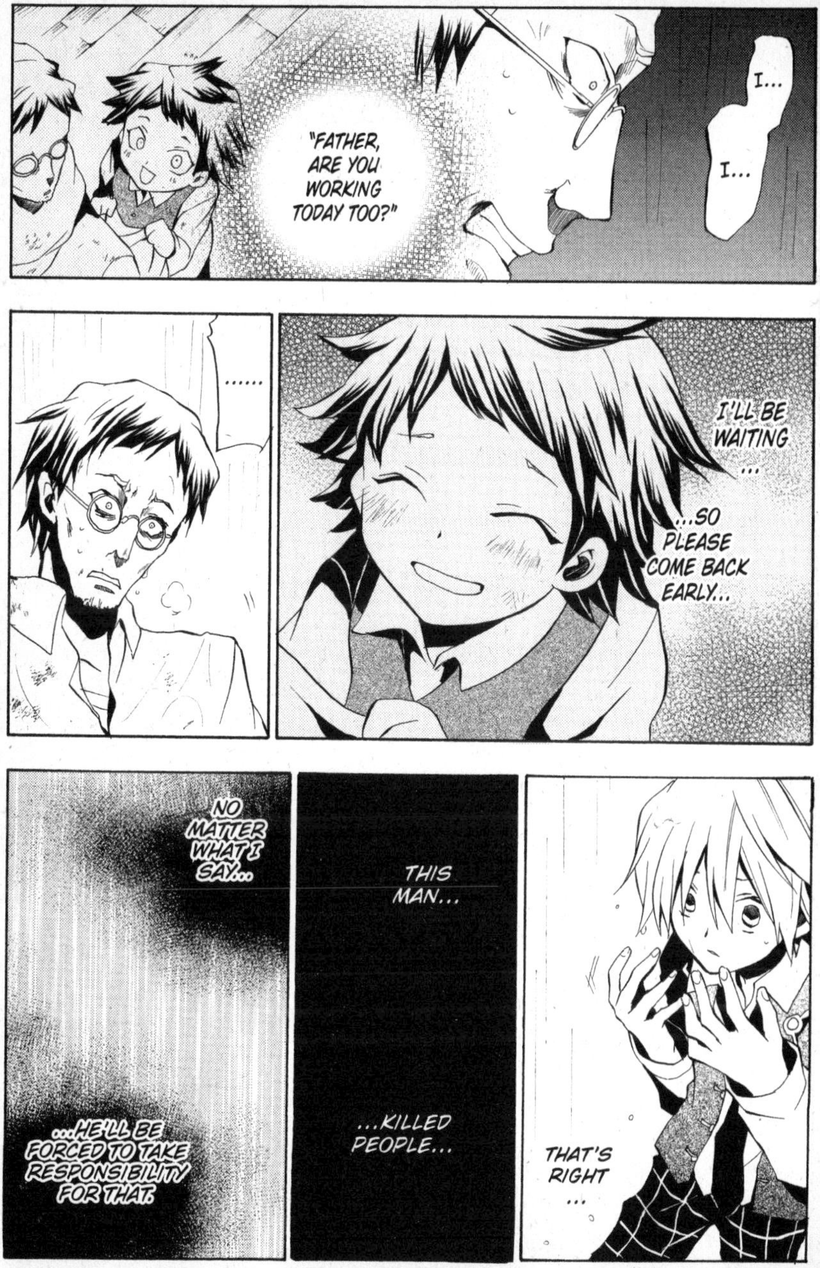
I...
I...
"FATHER, ARE YOU WORKING TODAY TOO?"
I'LL BE WAITING ...
...SO PLEASE COME BACK EARLY...
......
THAT'S RIGHT ...
THIS MAN...
...KILLED PEOPLE...
NO MATTER WHAT I SAY...
...HE'LL BE FORCED TO TAKE RESPONSIBILITY FOR THAT.

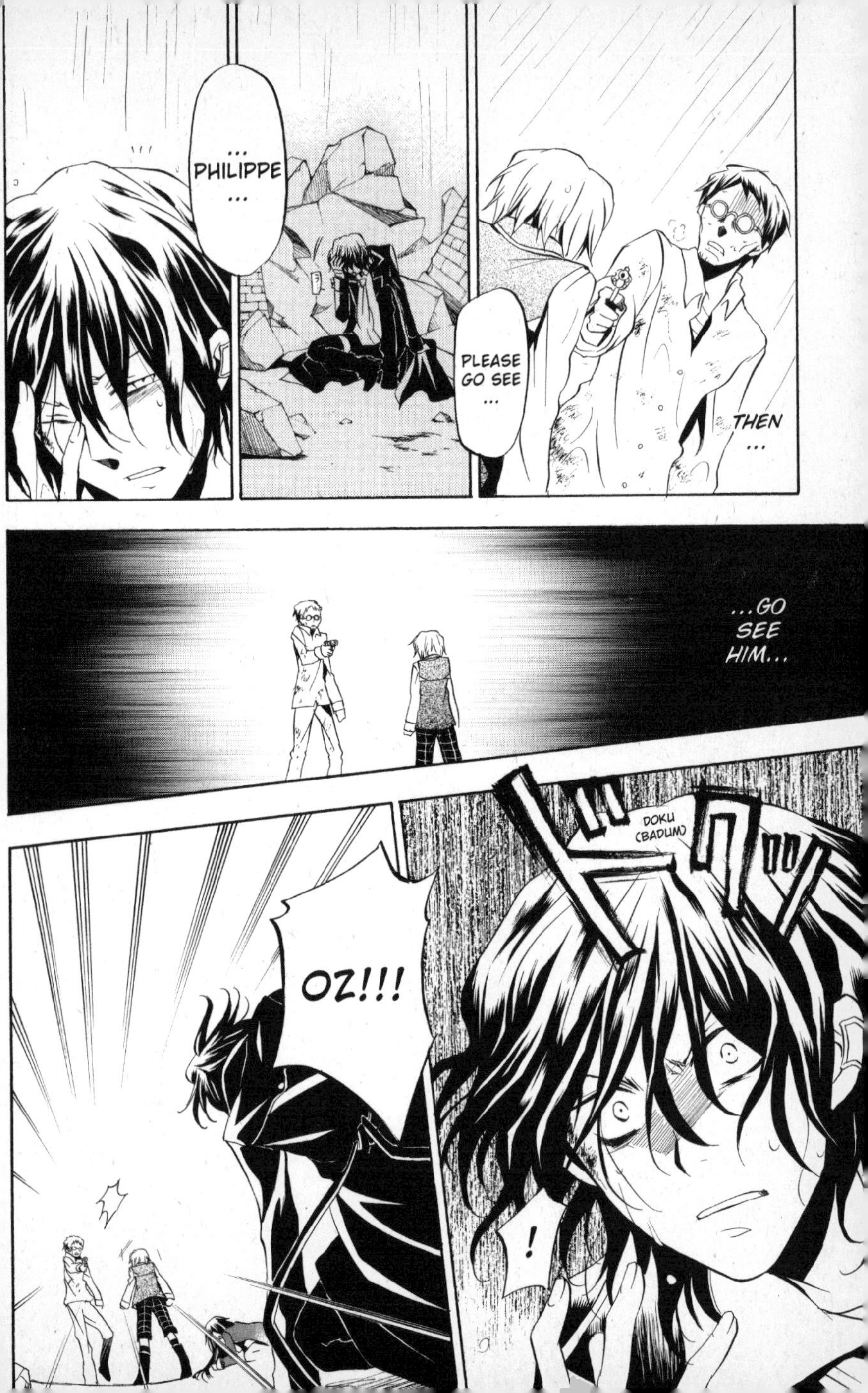
THEN ...
PLEASE GO SEE ...
... PHILIPPE ...
...GO SEE HIM...
DOKU (BADUM)
OZ!!!
!

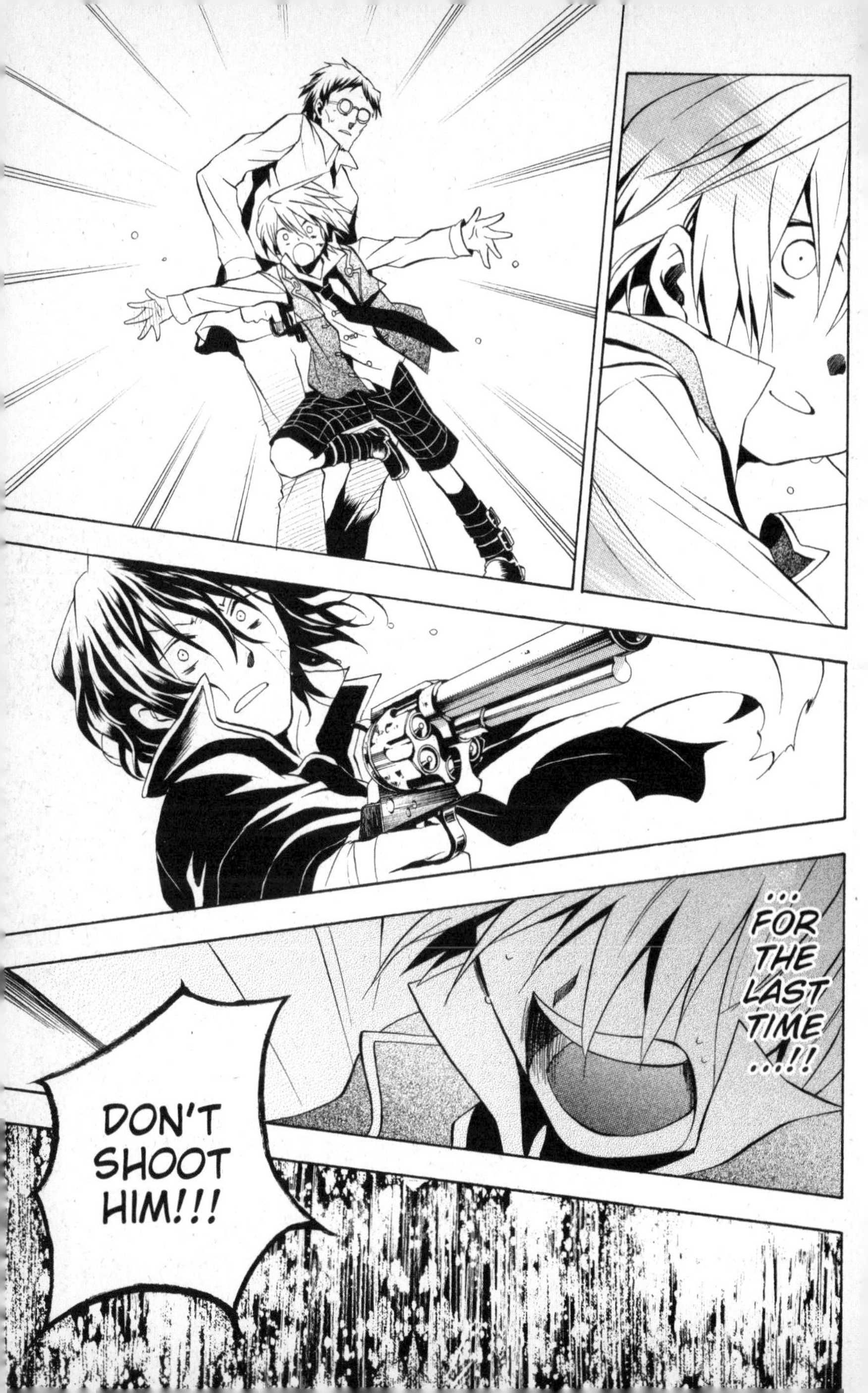
...FOR THE LAST TIME...!!
DON'T SHOOT HIM!!!

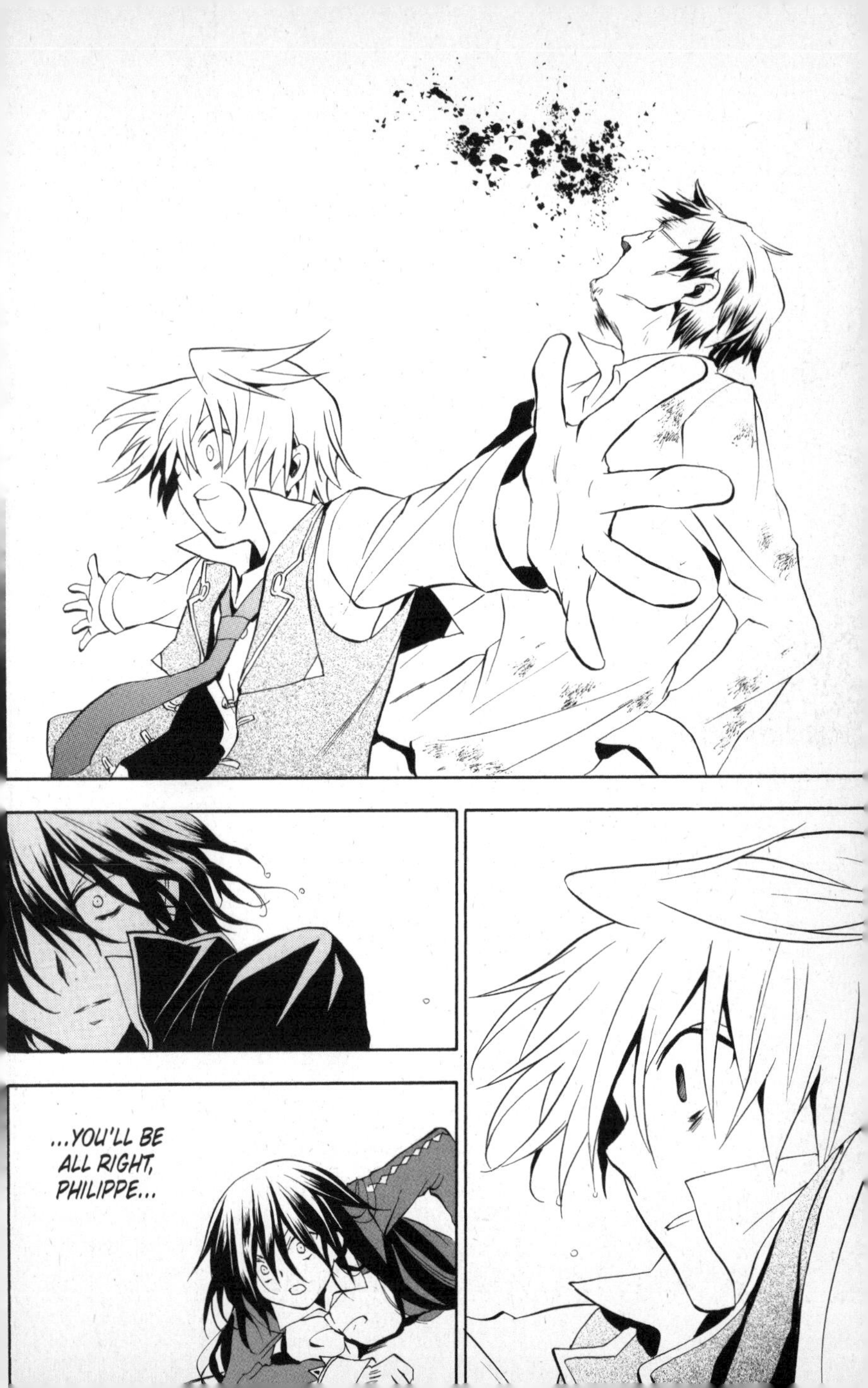
...YOU'LL BE ALL RIGHT, PHILIPPE...

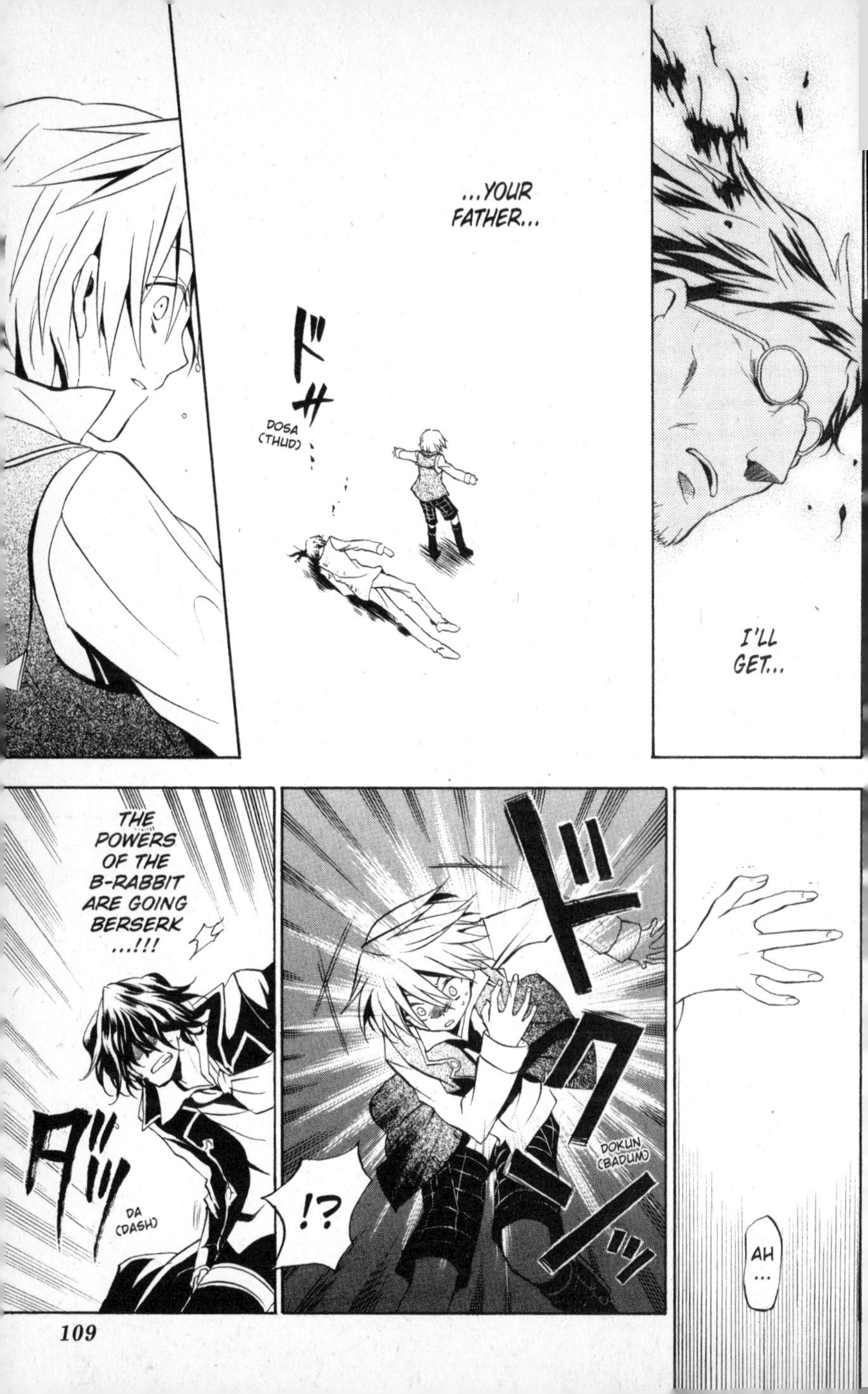
I'LL GET...
...YOUR FATHER...
ドサ
DOSA (THUD)
AH ...
ドクンッ
DOKUN (BADUM)
!?
THE POWERS OF THE B-RABBIT ARE GOING BERSERK ...!!!
ダッ
DA (DASH)

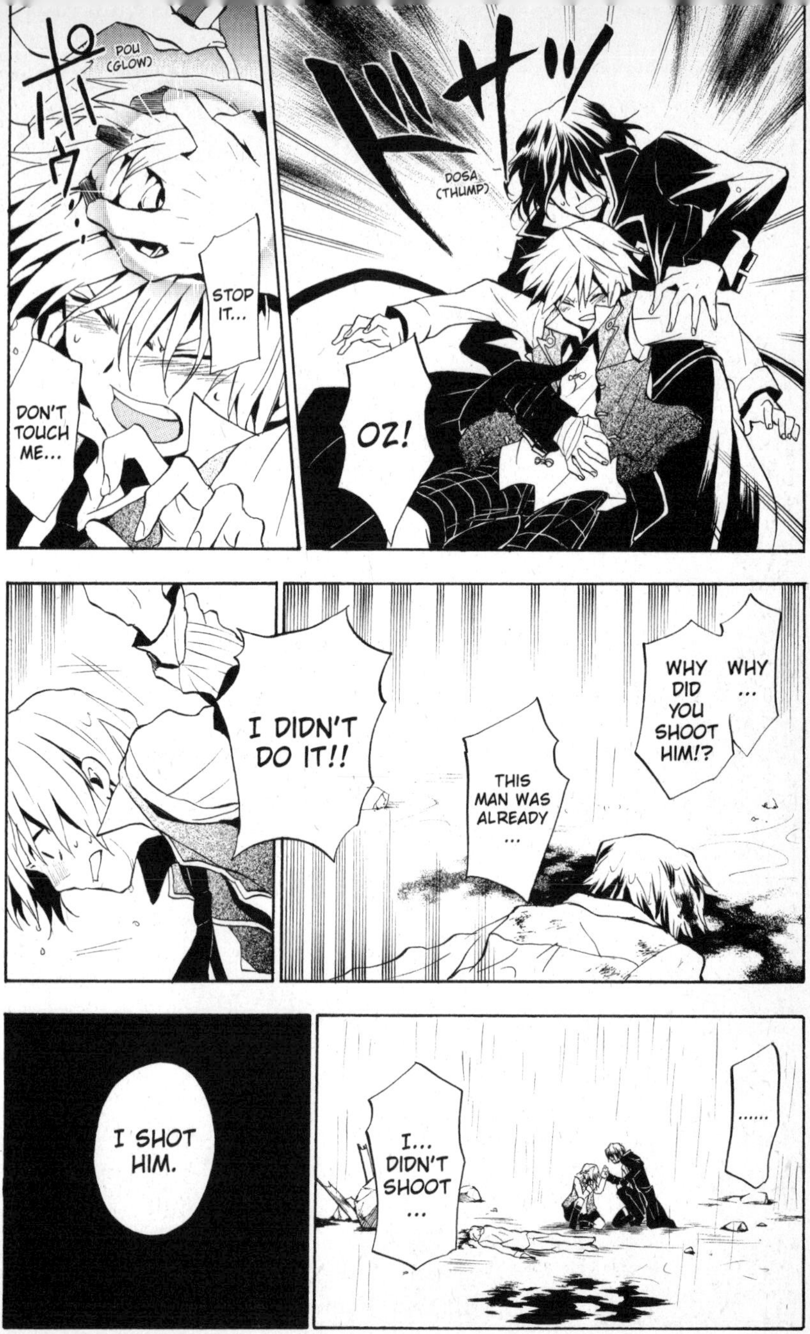
ドサッ
DOSA (THUMP)
OZ!
POU (GLOW)
STOP IT...
DON'T TOUCH ME...
WHY...
WHY DID YOU SHOOT HIM!?
THIS MAN WAS ALREADY...
I DIDN'T DO IT!!
......
I... DIDN'T SHOOT...
I SHOT HIM.

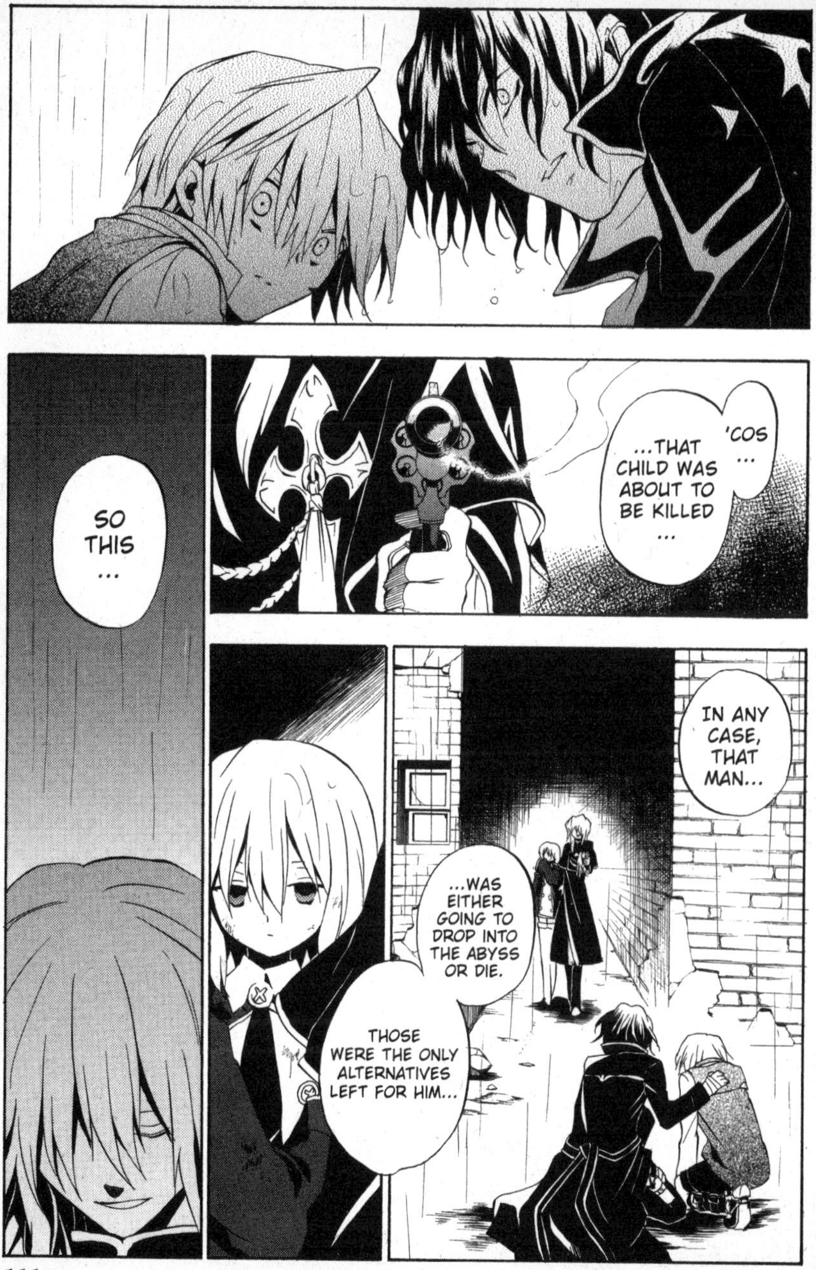
'COS...
...THAT CHILD WAS ABOUT TO BE KILLED...
IN ANY CASE, THAT MAN...
...WAS EITHER GOING TO DROP INTO THE ABYSS OR DIE.
THOSE WERE THE ONLY ALTERNATIVES LEFT FOR HIM...
SO THIS...

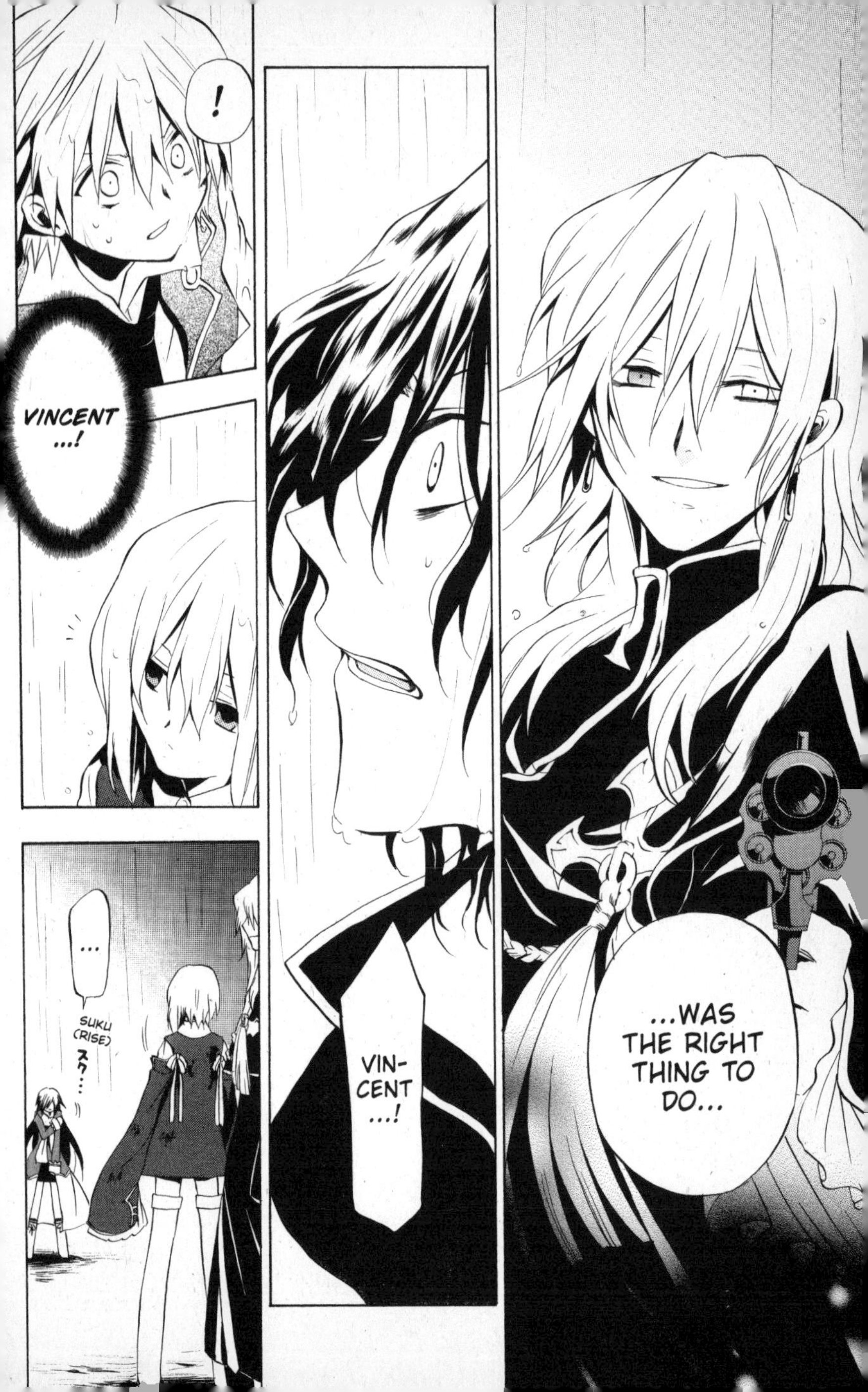
...WAS THE RIGHT THING TO DO...
VIN-CENT ...!
!
VINCENT ...!
...
SUKU (RISE)
スク…

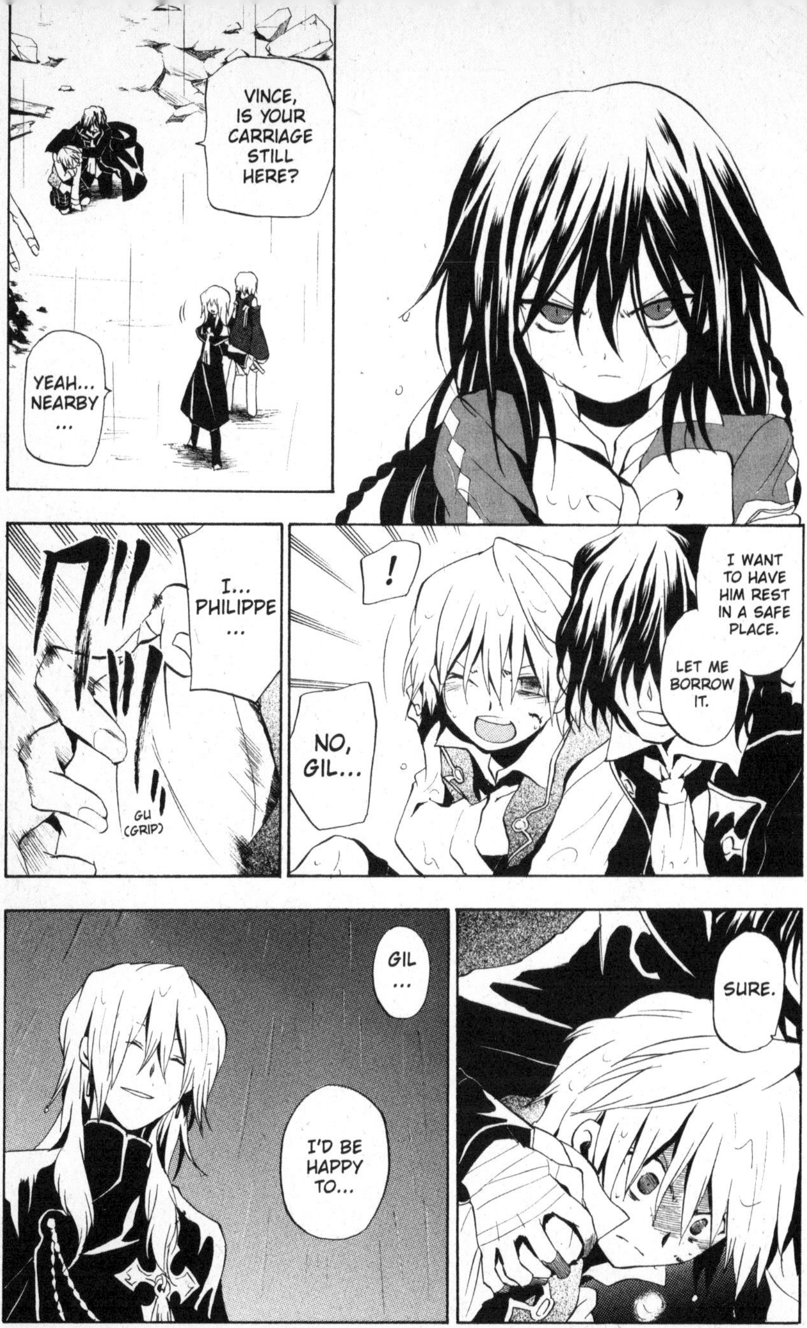
VINCE, IS YOUR CARRIAGE STILL HERE?
YEAH... NEARBY ...
!
I WANT TO HAVE HIM REST IN A SAFE PLACE.
LET ME BORROW IT.
NO, GIL...
I... PHILIPPE ...
GU (GRIP)
SURE.
GIL ...
I'D BE HAPPY TO...

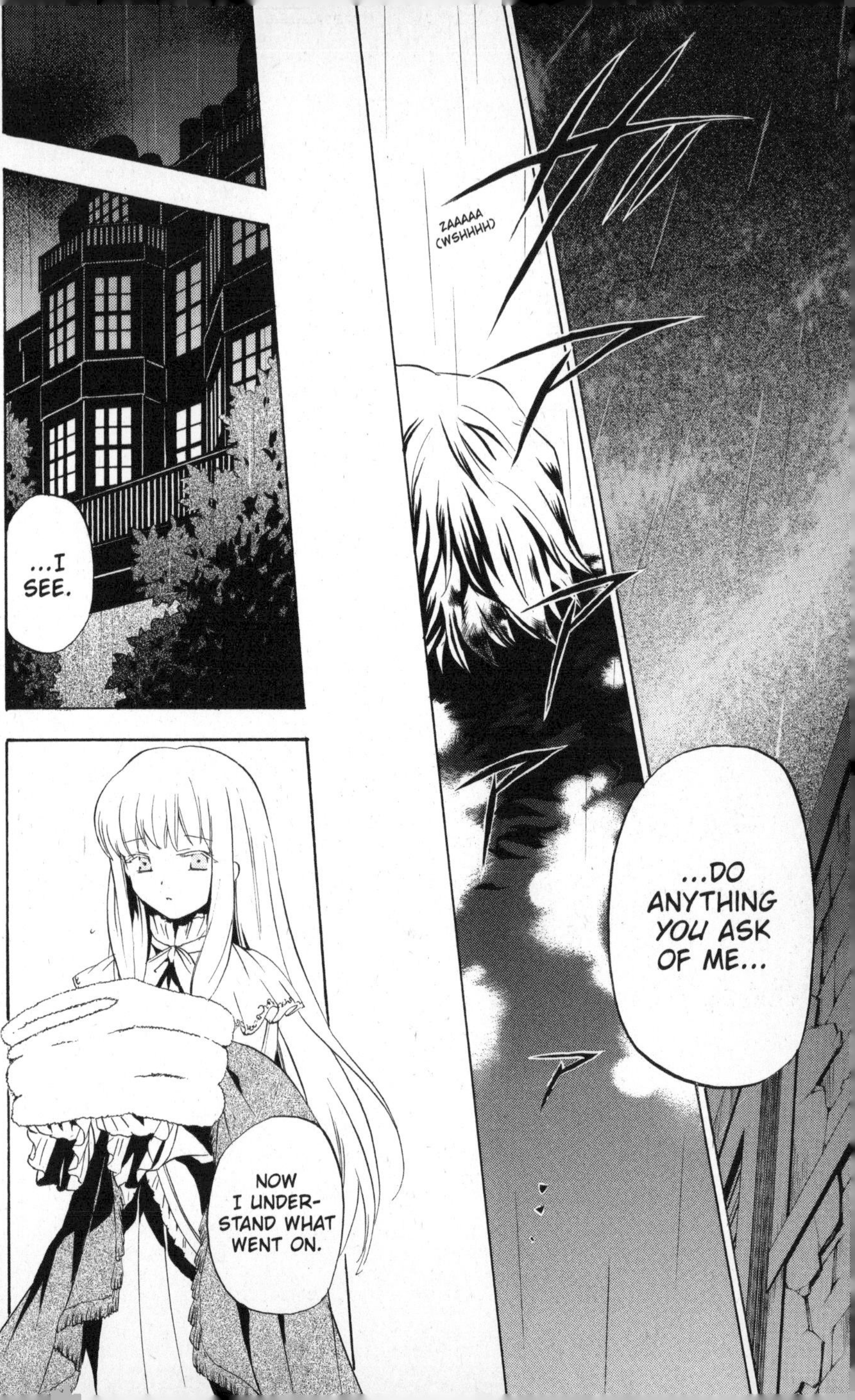
ZAAAAA (WSHHHH)
...DO ANYTHING YOU ASK OF ME...
...I SEE.
NOW I UNDER-STAND WHAT WENT ON.

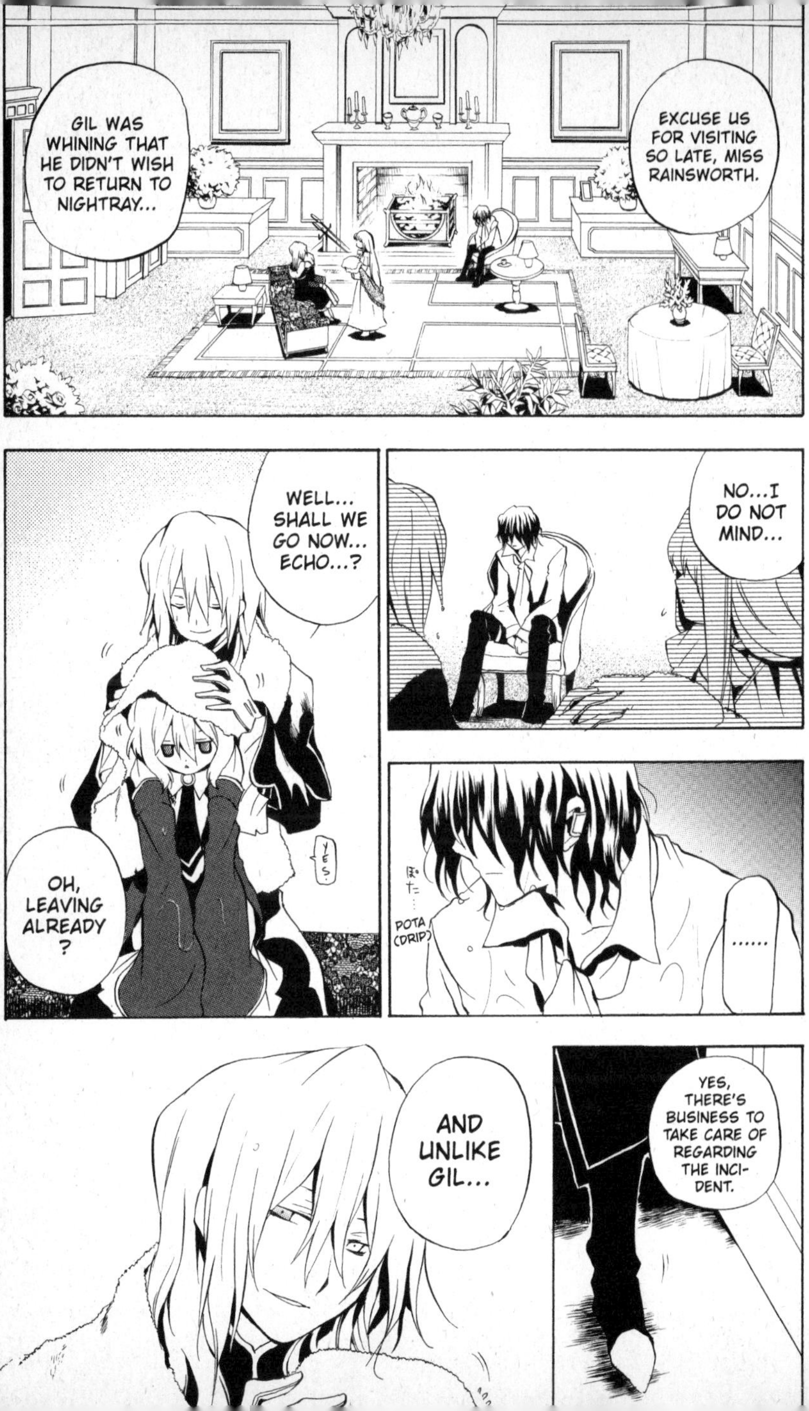
EXCUSE US FOR VISITING SO LATE, MISS RAINSWORTH.
GIL WAS WHINING THAT HE DIDN'T WISH TO RETURN TO NIGHTRAY...
NO...I DO NOT MIND...
ぽた...
POTA (DRIP)
......
WELL... SHALL WE GO NOW... ECHO...?
YES.
OH, LEAVING ALREADY?
YES, THERE'S BUSINESS TO TAKE CARE OF REGARDING THE INCI-DENT.
AND UNLIKE GIL...

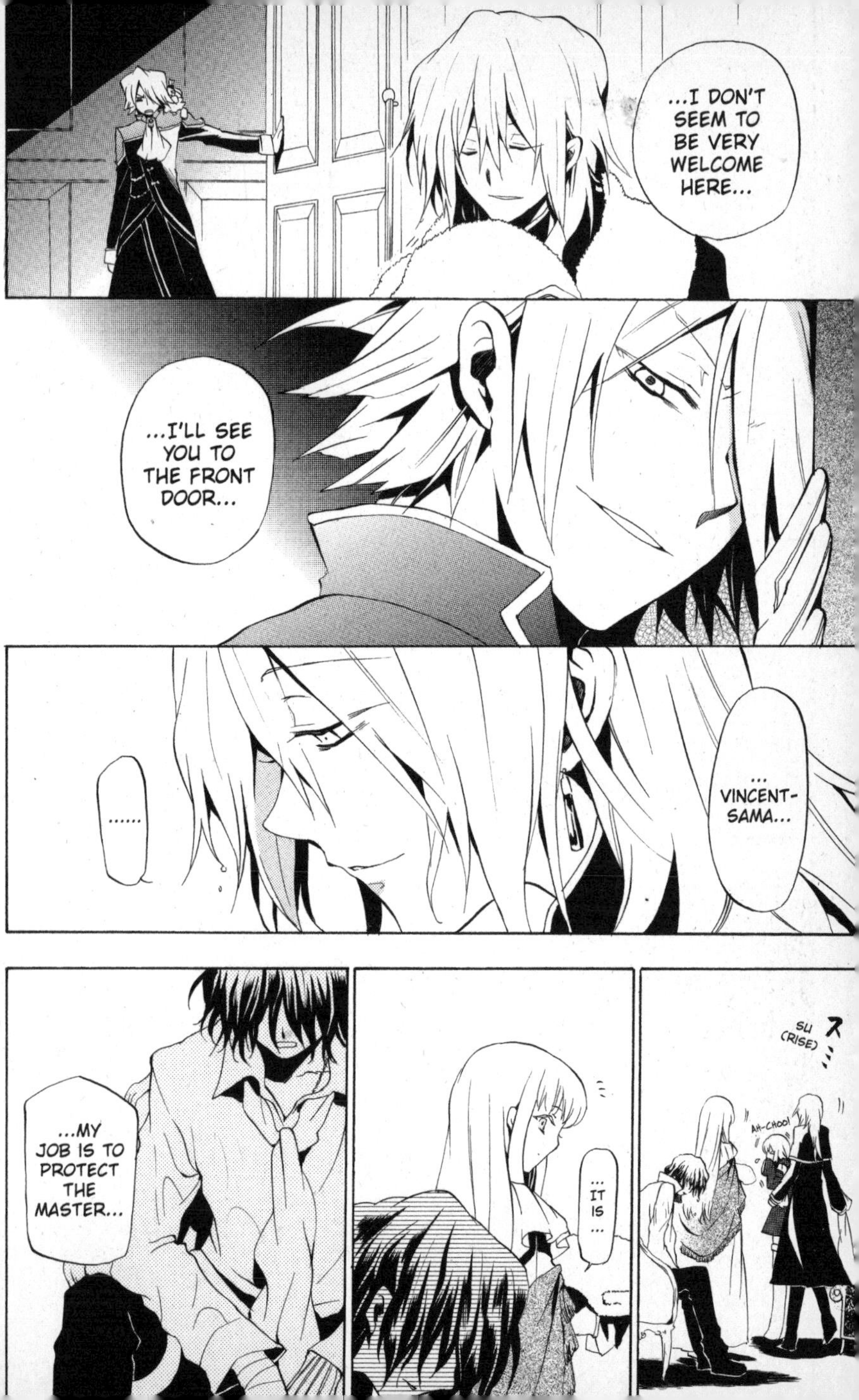
...I DON'T SEEM TO BE VERY WELCOME HERE...
...I'LL SEE YOU TO THE FRONT DOOR...
... VINCENT-SAMA...
......
SU (RISE)
AH-CHOO!
...IT IS...
...MY JOB IS TO PROTECT THE MASTER...

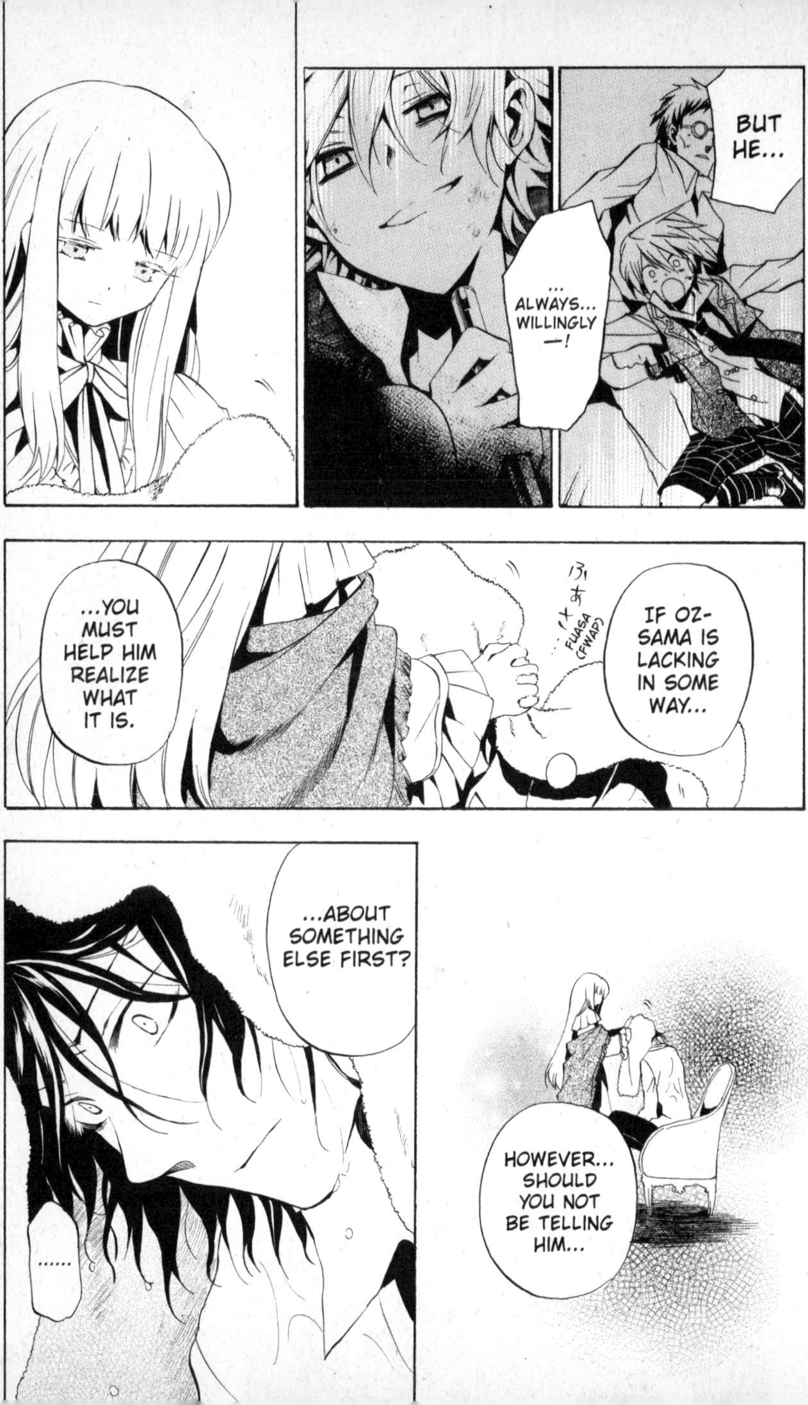
BUT HE...
...ALWAYS... WILLINGLY —!
IF OZ-SAMA IS LACKING IN SOME WAY...
ふぁさ
FUASA (FWAP)
...YOU MUST HELP HIM REALIZE WHAT IT IS.
HOWEVER... SHOULD YOU NOT BE TELLING HIM...
...ABOUT SOMETHING ELSE FIRST?
......

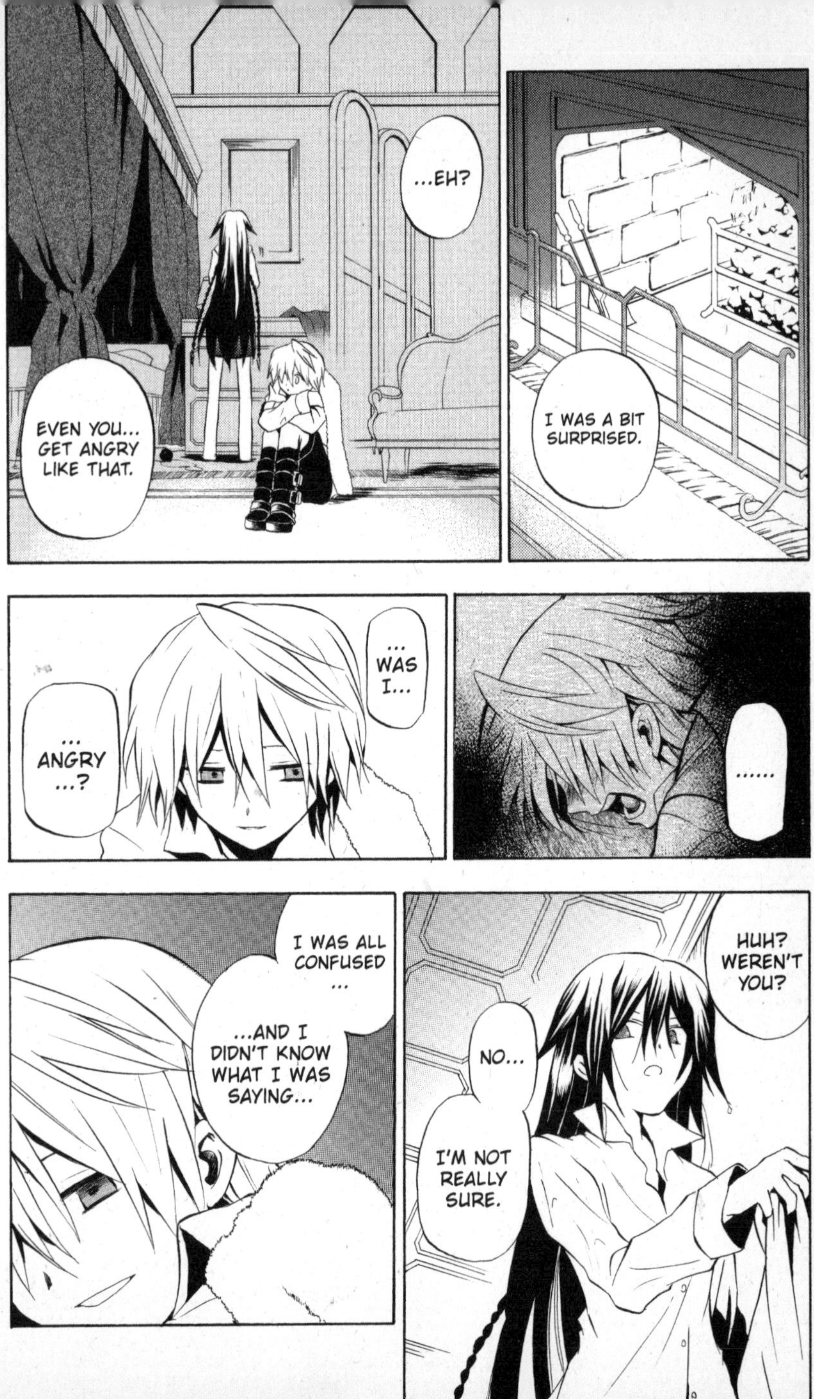
I WAS A BIT SURPRISED.
...EH?
EVEN YOU... GET ANGRY LIKE THAT.
......
...WAS I...
...ANGRY...?
HUH? WEREN'T YOU?
NO...
I'M NOT REALLY SURE.
I WAS ALL CONFUSED...
...AND I DIDN'T KNOW WHAT I WAS SAYING...

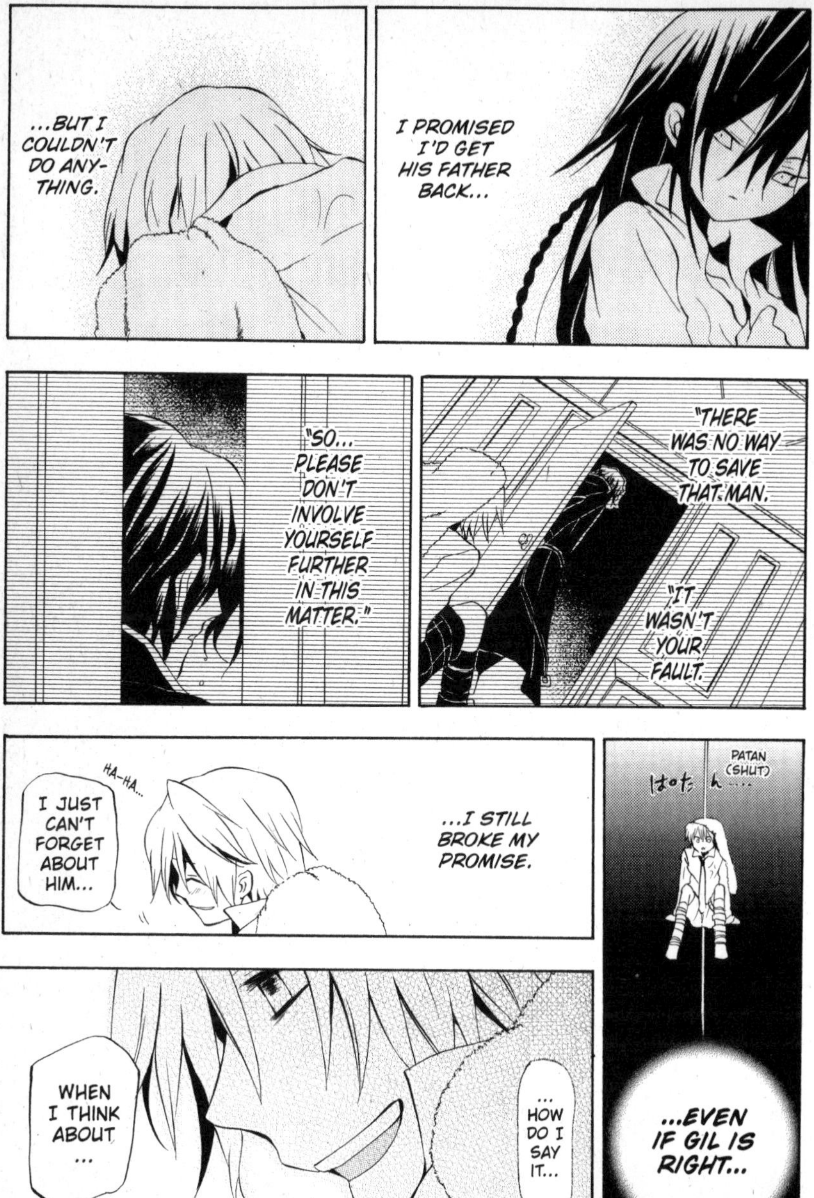
I PROMISED I'D GET HIS FATHER BACK...
...BUT I COULDN'T DO ANY-THING.
"THERE WAS NO WAY TO SAVE THAT MAN.
"IT WASN'T YOUR FAULT.
"SO... PLEASE DON'T INVOLVE YOURSELF FURTHER IN THIS MATTER."
ぱたん…
PATAN (SHUT)
...EVEN IF GIL IS RIGHT...
...I STILL BROKE MY PROMISE.
HA-HA...
I JUST CAN'T FORGET ABOUT HIM...
...HOW DO I SAY IT...
WHEN I THINK ABOUT ...

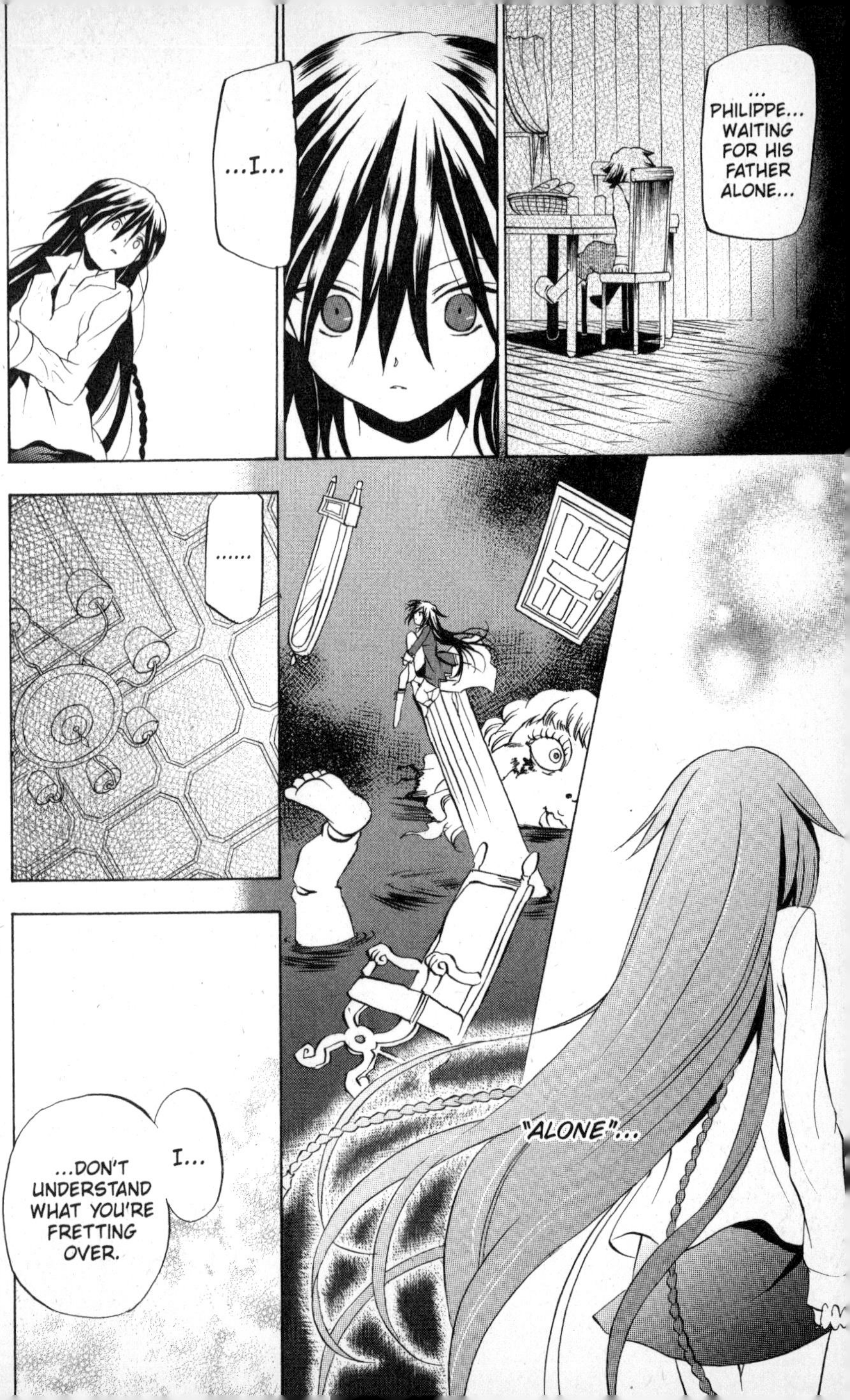

... PHILIPPE... WAITING FOR HIS FATHER ALONE...
...I...
"ALONE"...
......
I...
...DON'T UNDERSTAND WHAT YOU'RE FRETTING OVER.

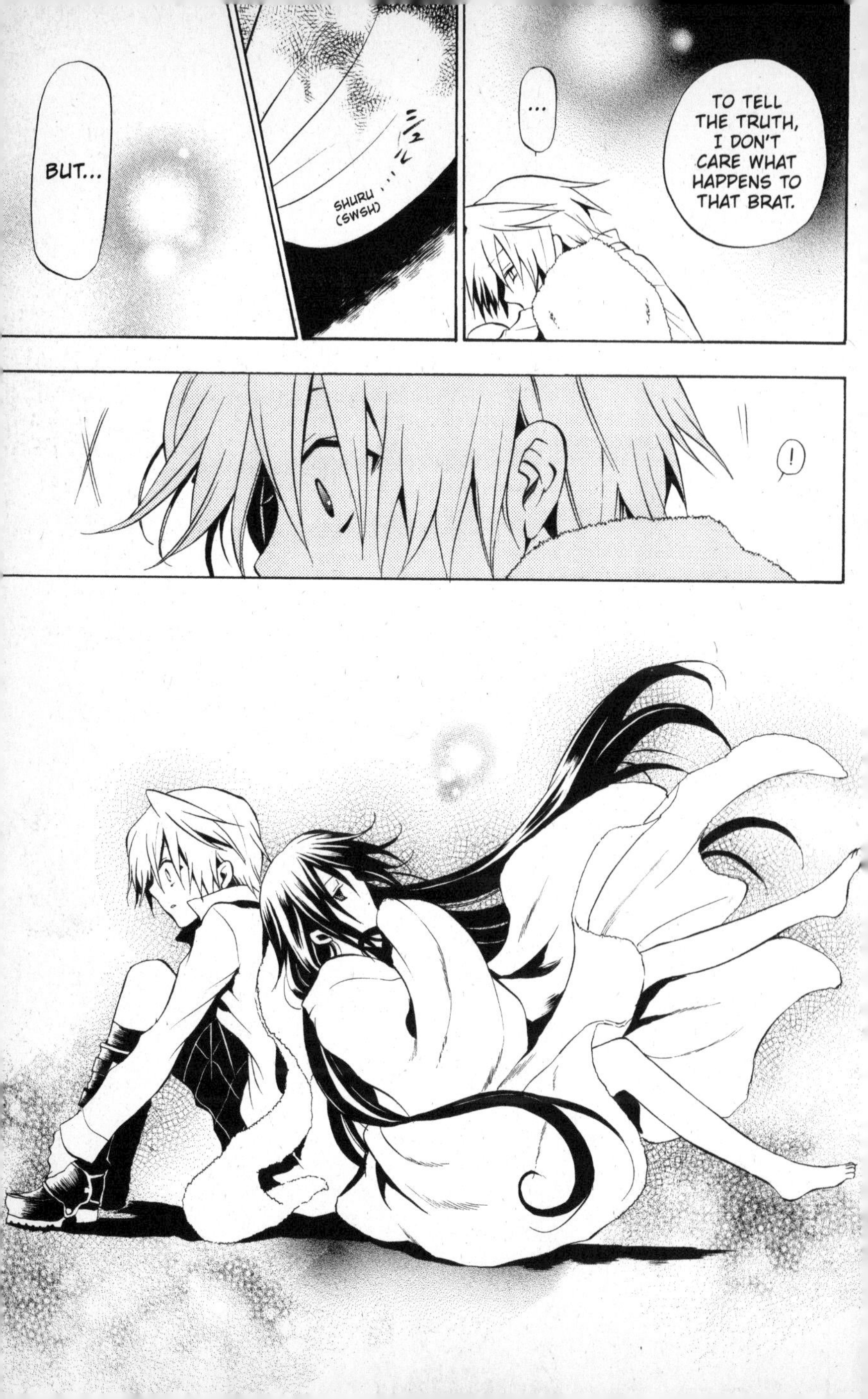
TO TELL THE TRUTH, I DON'T CARE WHAT HAPPENS TO THAT BRAT.
...
SHURU (SWSH)
BUT...
!

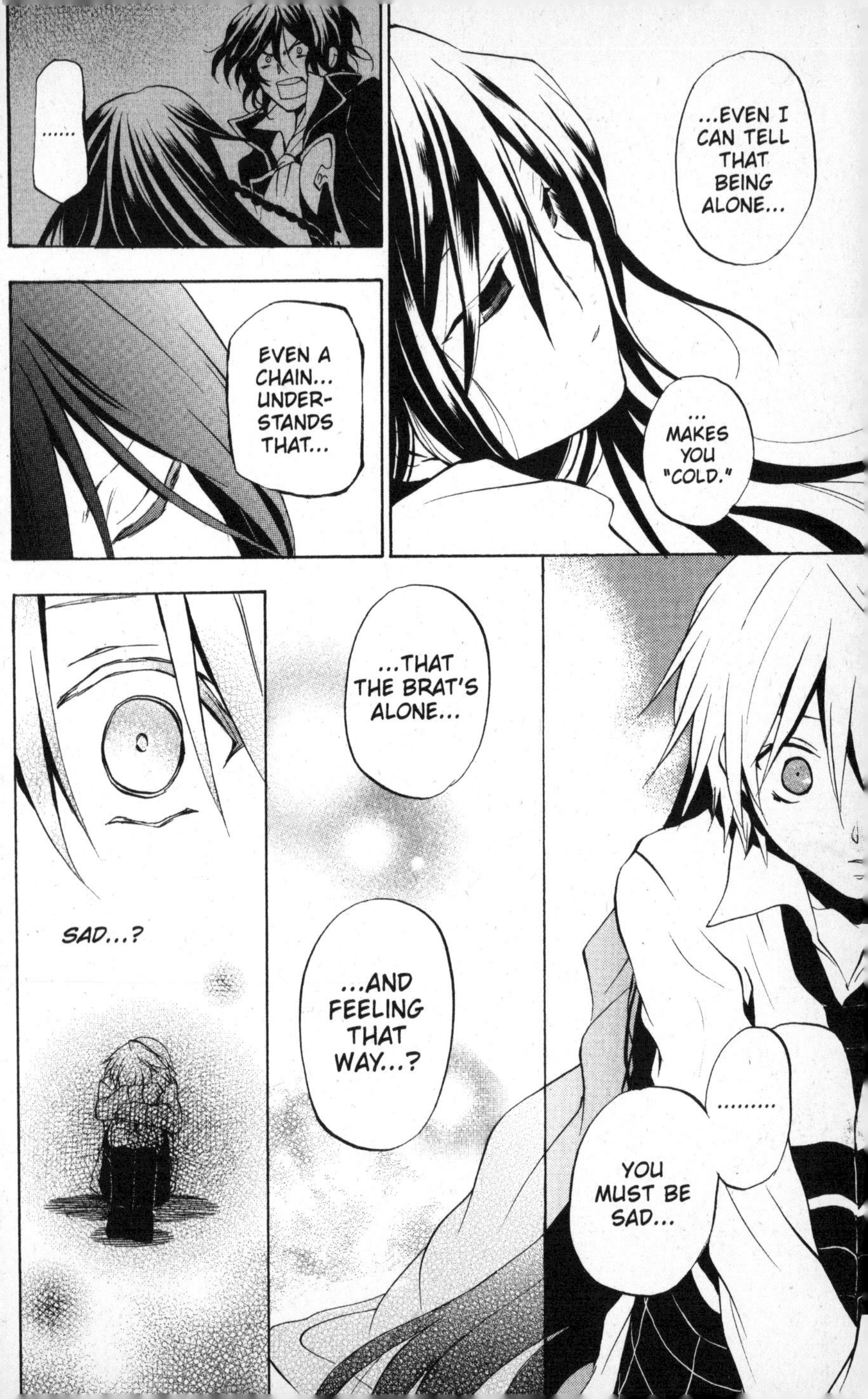
...EVEN I CAN TELL THAT BEING ALONE...
... MAKES YOU "COLD."
......
EVEN A CHAIN... UNDER-STANDS THAT...
....
YOU MUST BE SAD...
...THAT THE BRAT'S ALONE...
...AND FEELING THAT WAY...?
SAD...?

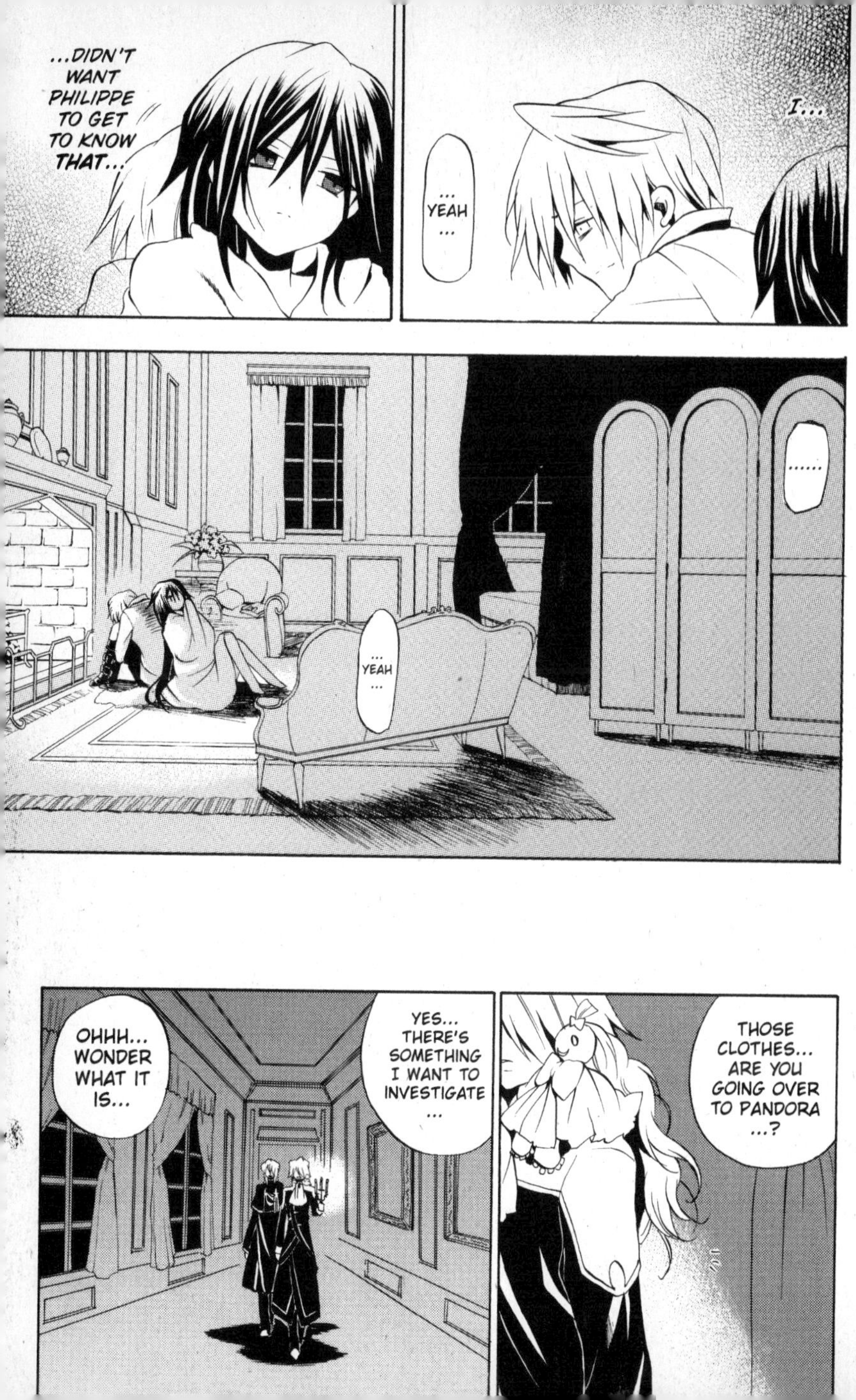
I...
...YEAH...
...DIDN'T WANT PHILIPPE TO GET TO KNOW THAT...
......
...YEAH...
THOSE CLOTHES... ARE YOU GOING OVER TO PANDORA...?
YES... THERE'S SOMETHING I WANT TO INVESTIGATE...
OHHH... WONDER WHAT IT IS...

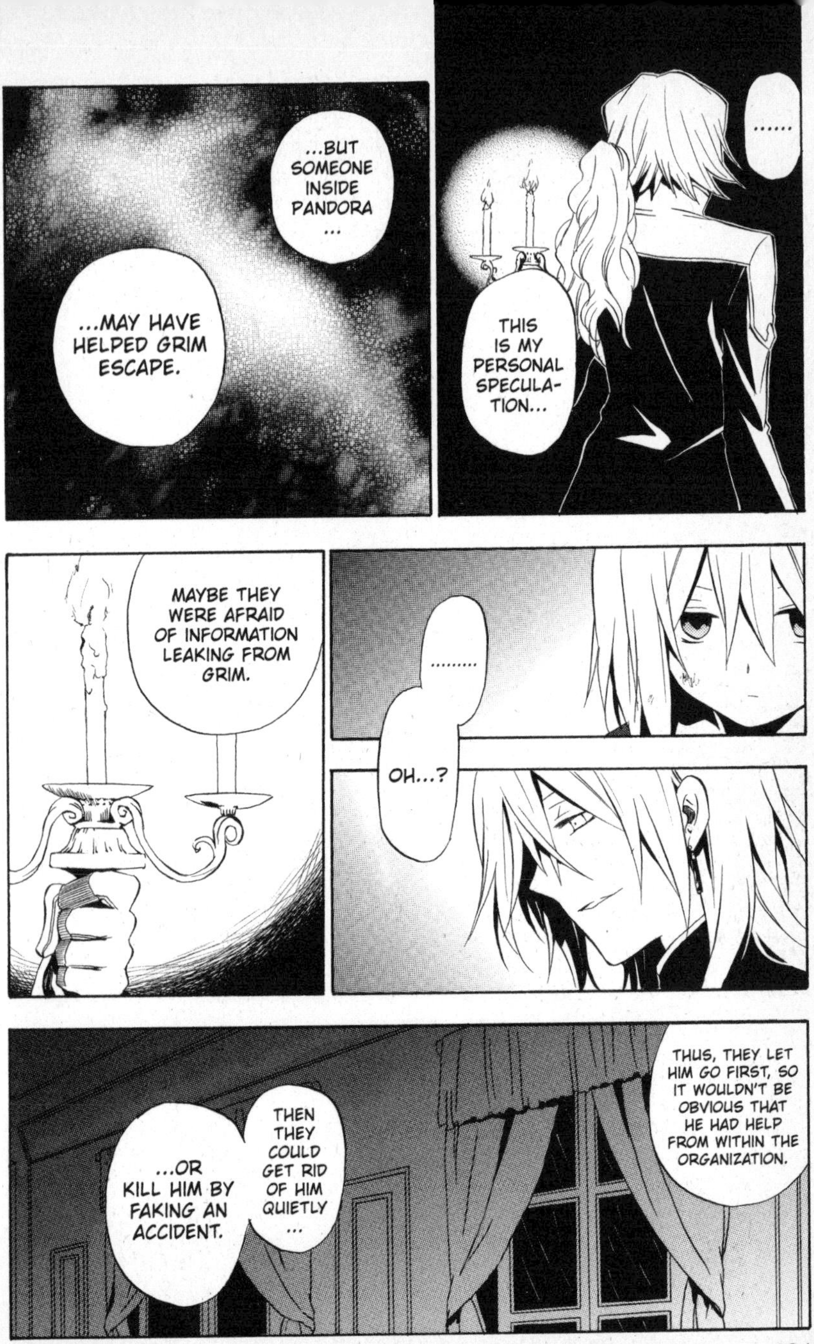
....
THIS IS MY PERSONAL SPECULATION...
...BUT SOMEONE INSIDE PANDORA...
...MAY HAVE HELPED GRIM ESCAPE.
....
OH...?
MAYBE THEY WERE AFRAID OF INFORMATION LEAKING FROM GRIM.
THUS, THEY LET HIM GO FIRST, SO IT WOULDN'T BE OBVIOUS THAT HE HAD HELP FROM WITHIN THE ORGANIZATION.
THEN THEY COULD GET RID OF HIM QUIETLY...
...OR KILL HIM BY FAKING AN ACCIDENT.

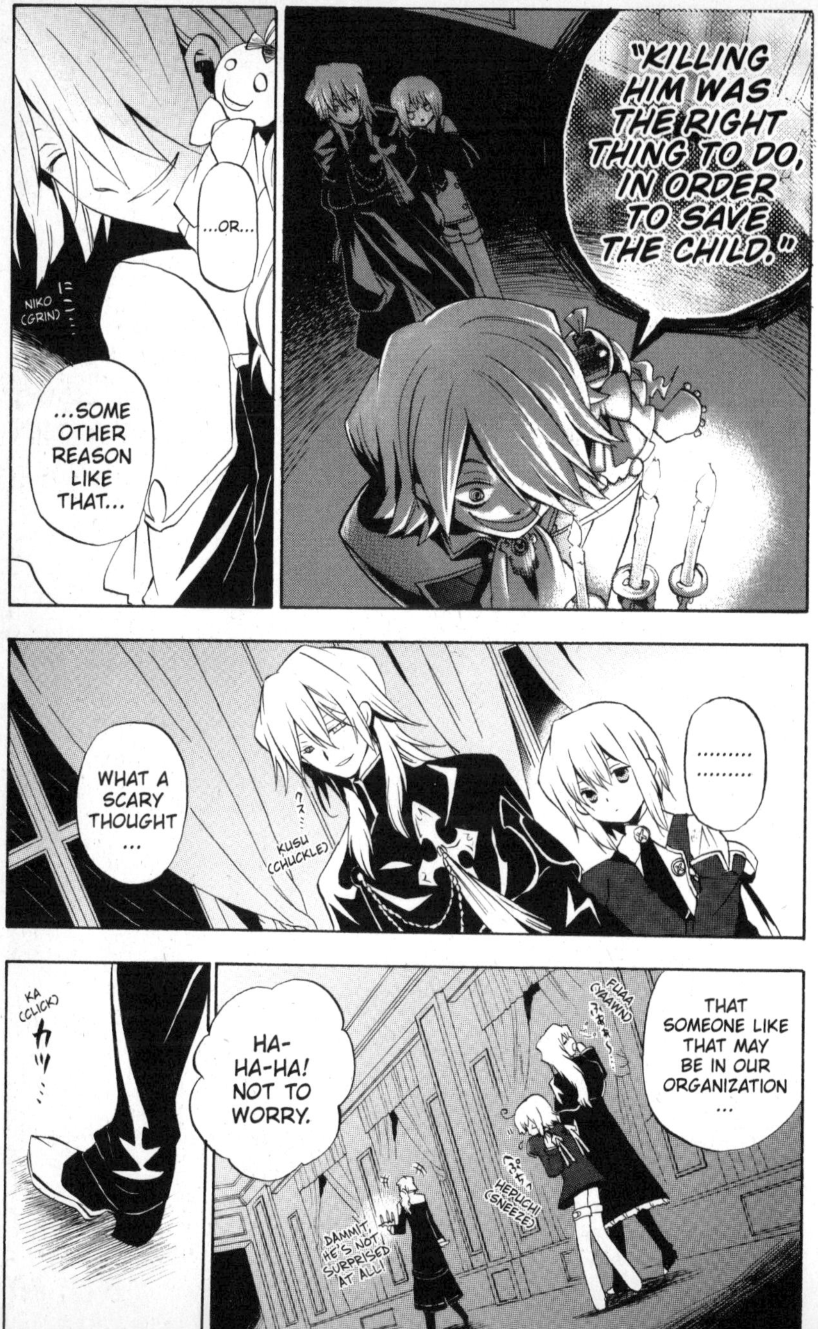
"KILLING HIM WAS THE RIGHT THING TO DO, IN ORDER TO SAVE THE CHILD."
...OR...
NIKO (GRIN)
...SOME OTHER REASON LIKE THAT...
....
....
KUSU (CHUCKLE)
WHAT A SCARY THOUGHT...
THAT SOMEONE LIKE THAT MAY BE IN OUR ORGANIZATION...
FUAA (YAAWN)
HA-HA-HA! NOT TO WORRY.
HEPUCHI (SNEEZE)
DAMMIT, HE'S NOT SURPRISED AT ALL!
KA (CLICK)

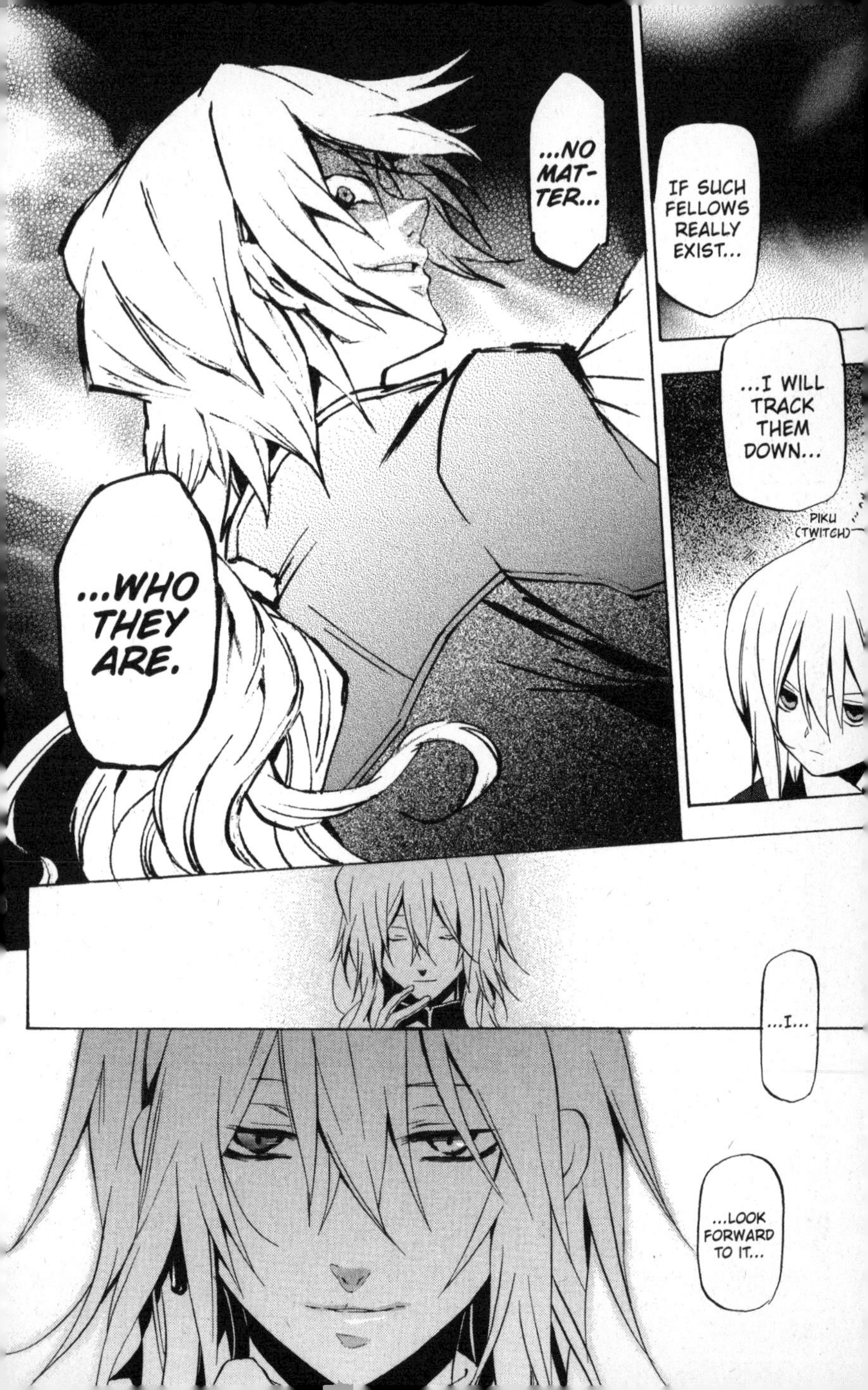
IF SUCH FELLOWS REALLY EXIST...
...NO MATTER...
...I WILL TRACK THEM DOWN...
PIKU (TWITCH)
...WHO THEY ARE.
...I...
...LOOK FORWARD TO IT...

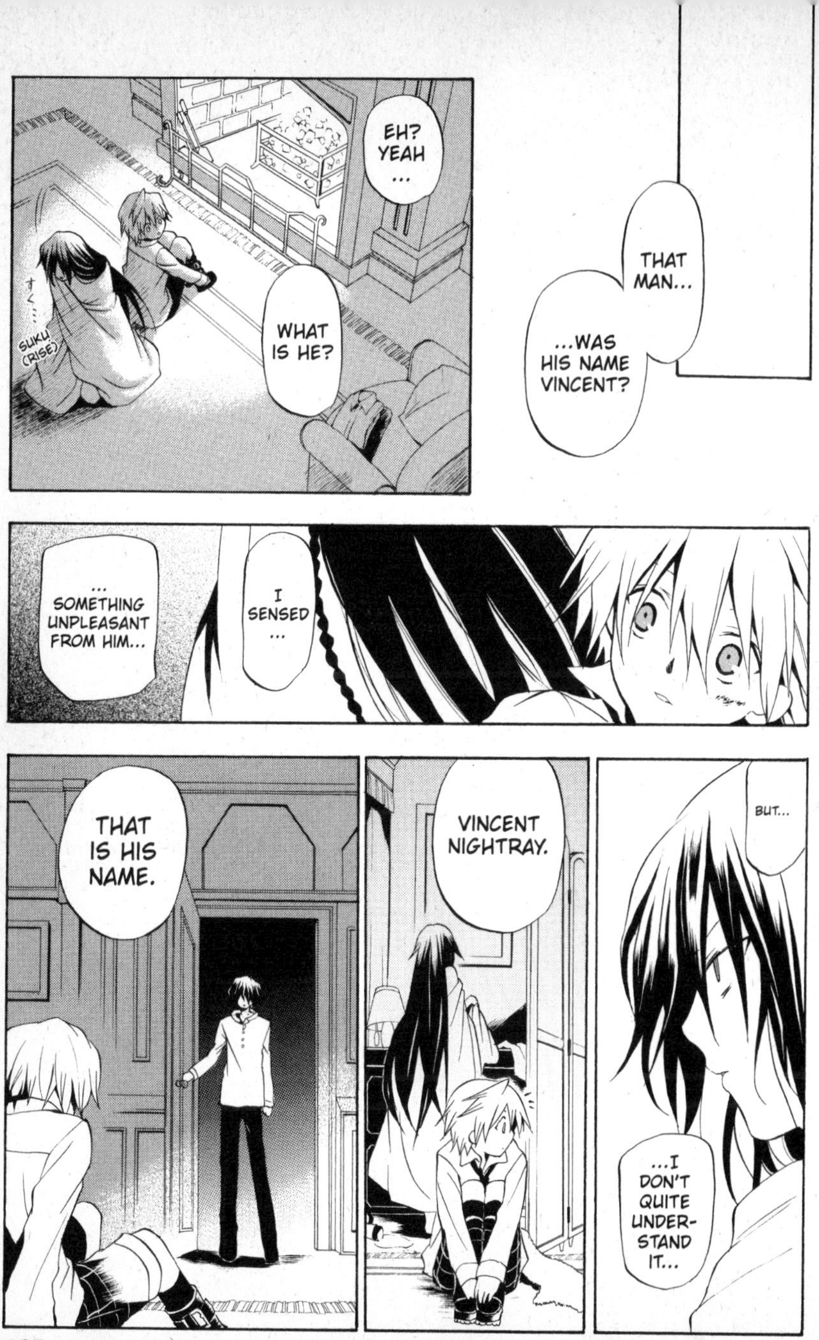
THAT MAN...
...WAS HIS NAME VINCENT?
EH? YEAH...
WHAT IS HE?
すく…
SUKU (RISE)
I SENSED...
...SOMETHING UNPLEASANT FROM HIM...
BUT...
...I DON'T QUITE UNDER-STAND IT...
VINCENT NIGHTRAY.
THAT IS HIS NAME.

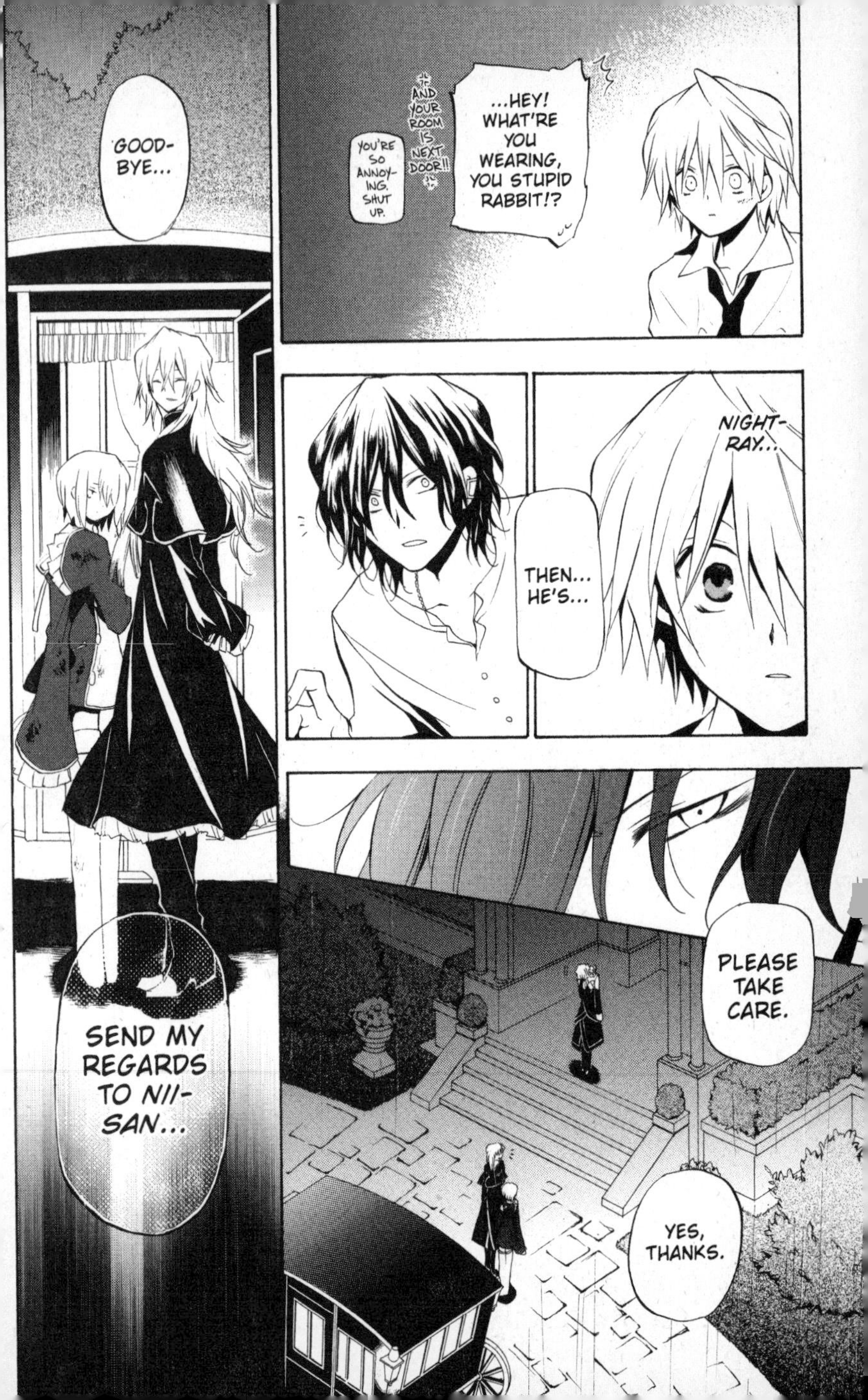
...HEY! WHAT'RE YOU WEARING, YOU STUPID RABBIT!?
AND YOUR ROOM IS NEXT DOOR!!
YOU'RE SO ANNOY-ING. SHUT UP.
NIGHT-RAY...
THEN... HE'S...
PLEASE TAKE CARE.
YES, THANKS.
GOOD-BYE...
SEND MY REGARDS TO NII-SAN...

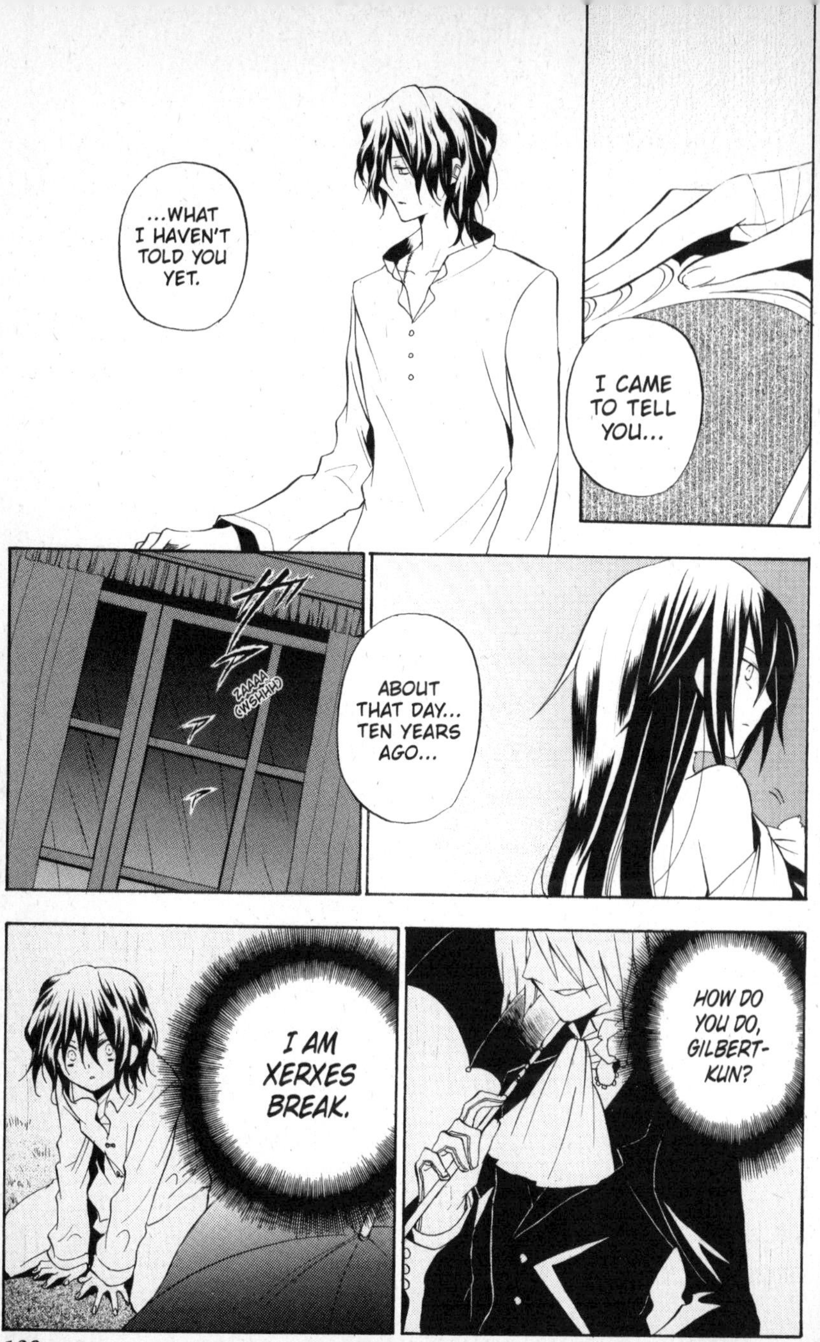
I CAME TO TELL YOU...
...WHAT I HAVEN'T TOLD YOU YET.
ABOUT THAT DAY... TEN YEARS AGO...
ZAAAA (WSHHH)
HOW DO YOU DO, GILBERT-KUN?
I AM XERXES BREAK.

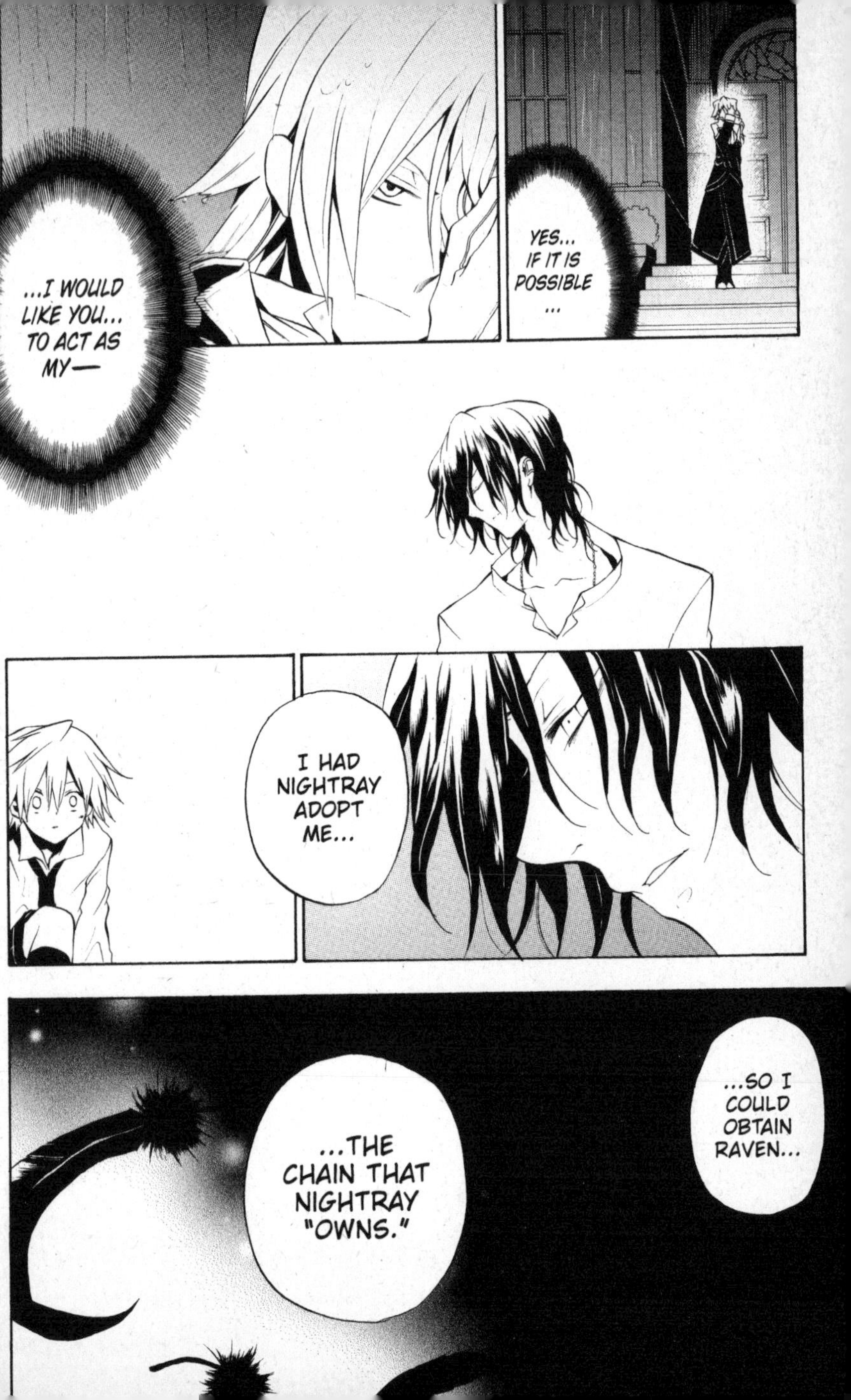
YES... IF IT IS POSSIBLE ...
...I WOULD LIKE YOU... TO ACT AS MY—
I HAD NIGHTRAY ADOPT ME...
...SO I COULD OBTAIN RAVEN...
...THE CHAIN THAT NIGHTRAY "OWNS."

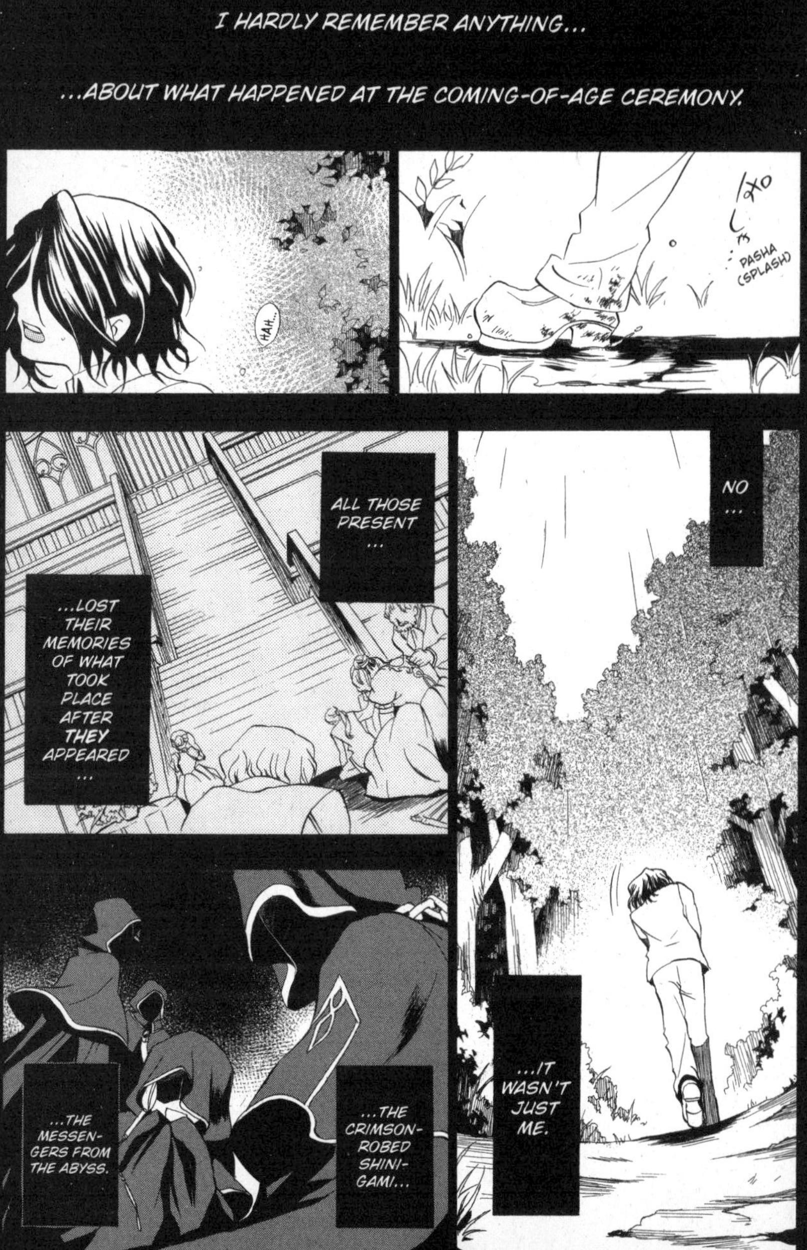
I HARDLY REMEMBER ANYTHING...
...ABOUT WHAT HAPPENED AT THE COMING-OF-AGE CEREMONY.
PASHA (SPLASH)
HAH...
NO...
...IT WASN'T JUST ME.
ALL THOSE PRESENT...
...LOST THEIR MEMORIES OF WHAT TOOK PLACE AFTER THEY APPEARED...
...THE CRIMSON-ROBED SHINIGAMI...
...THE MESSENGERS FROM THE ABYSS.

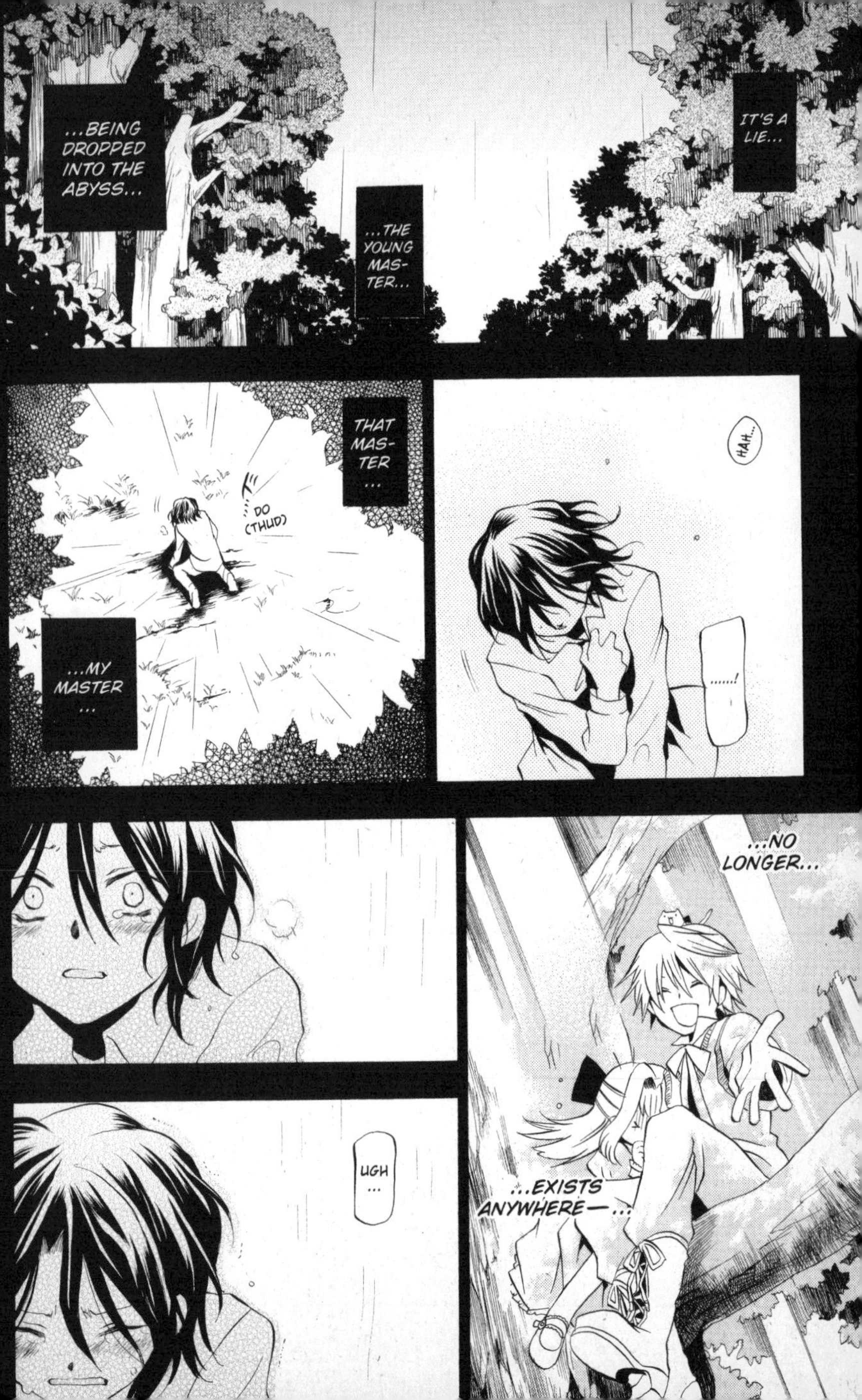
IT'S A LIE...
...THE YOUNG MAS-TER...
...BEING DROPPED INTO THE ABYSS...
HAH...
......!
THAT MAS-TER...
ド
DO (THUD)
...MY MASTER...
...NO LONGER...
...EXISTS ANYWHERE—...
UGH...

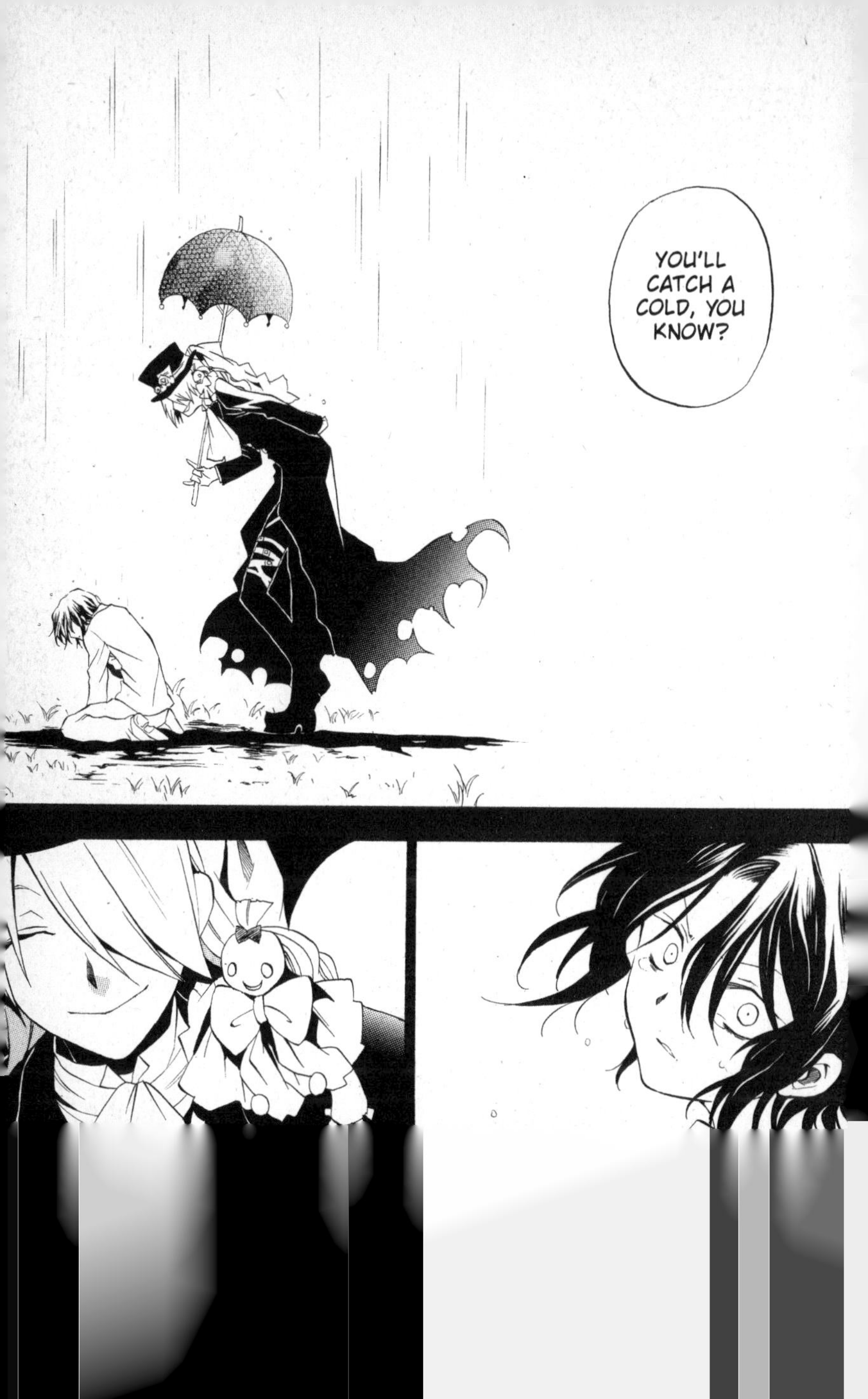
YOU'LL CATCH A COLD, YOU KNOW?

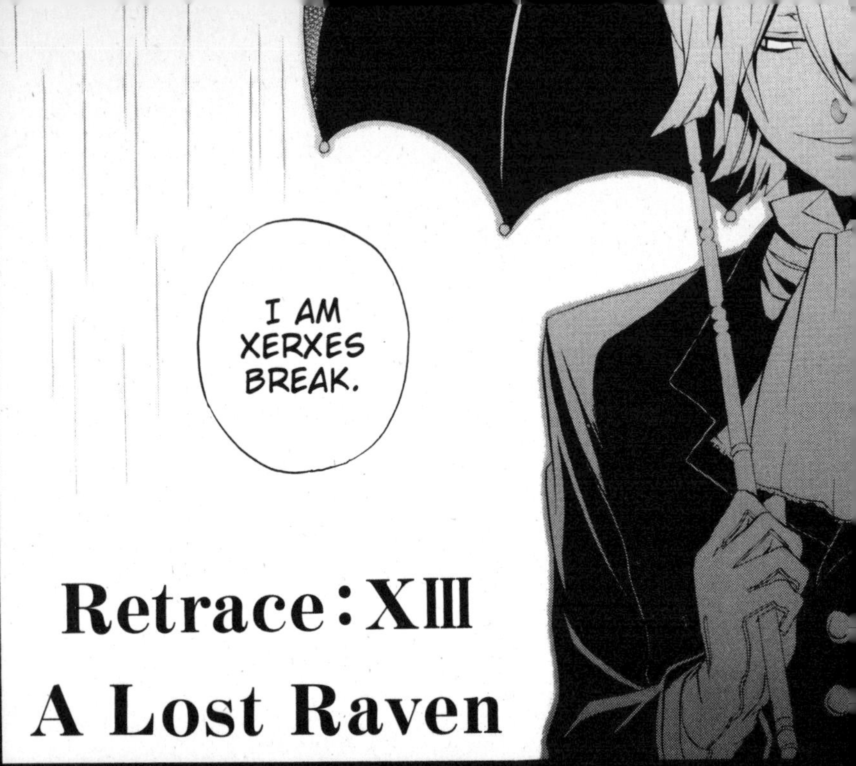
I AM XERXES BREAK.

Retrace: XIII
A Lost Raven

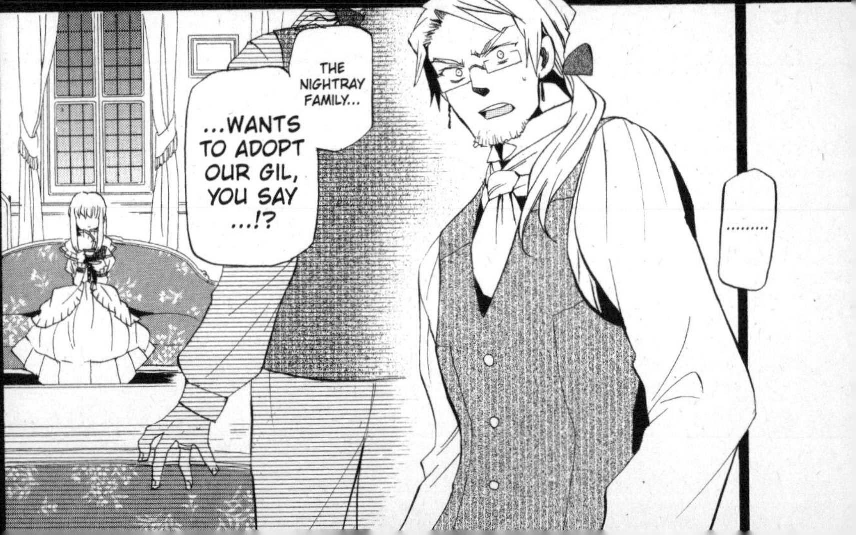
....
THE NIGHTRAY FAMILY...
...WANTS TO ADOPT OUR GIL, YOU SAY ...!?

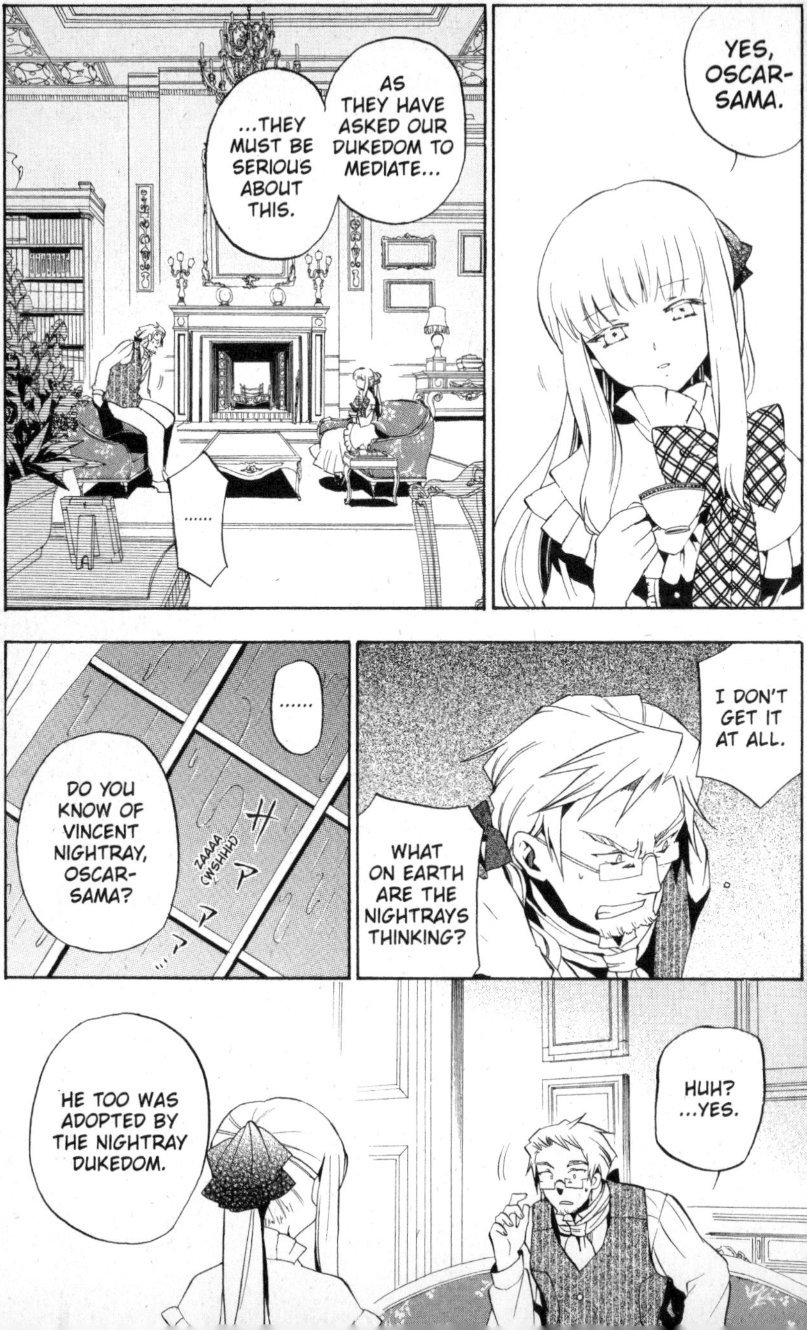
YES, OSCAR-SAMA.
AS THEY HAVE ASKED OUR DUKEDOM TO MEDIATE...
...THEY MUST BE SERIOUS ABOUT THIS.
......
I DON'T GET IT AT ALL.
WHAT ON EARTH ARE THE NIGHTRAYS THINKING?
......
DO YOU KNOW OF VINCENT NIGHTRAY, OSCAR-SAMA?
ZAAAA (WSHHH)
HUH? ...YES.
HE TOO WAS ADOPTED BY THE NIGHTRAY DUKEDOM.

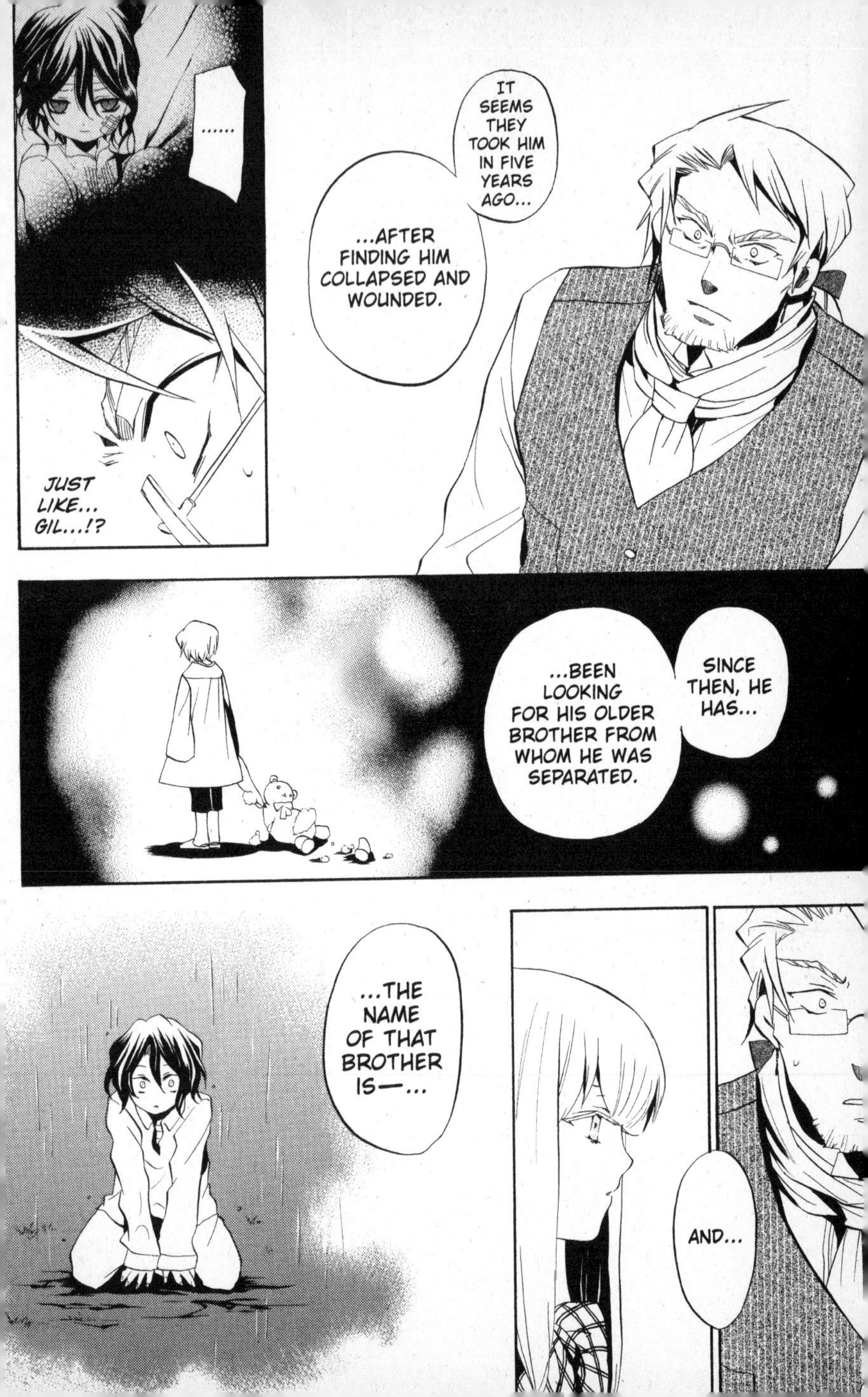
IT SEEMS THEY TOOK HIM IN FIVE YEARS AGO...
...AFTER FINDING HIM COLLAPSED AND WOUNDED.
......
JUST LIKE... GIL...!?
SINCE THEN, HE HAS...
...BEEN LOOKING FOR HIS OLDER BROTHER FROM WHOM HE WAS SEPARATED.
AND...
...THE NAME OF THAT BROTHER IS—...

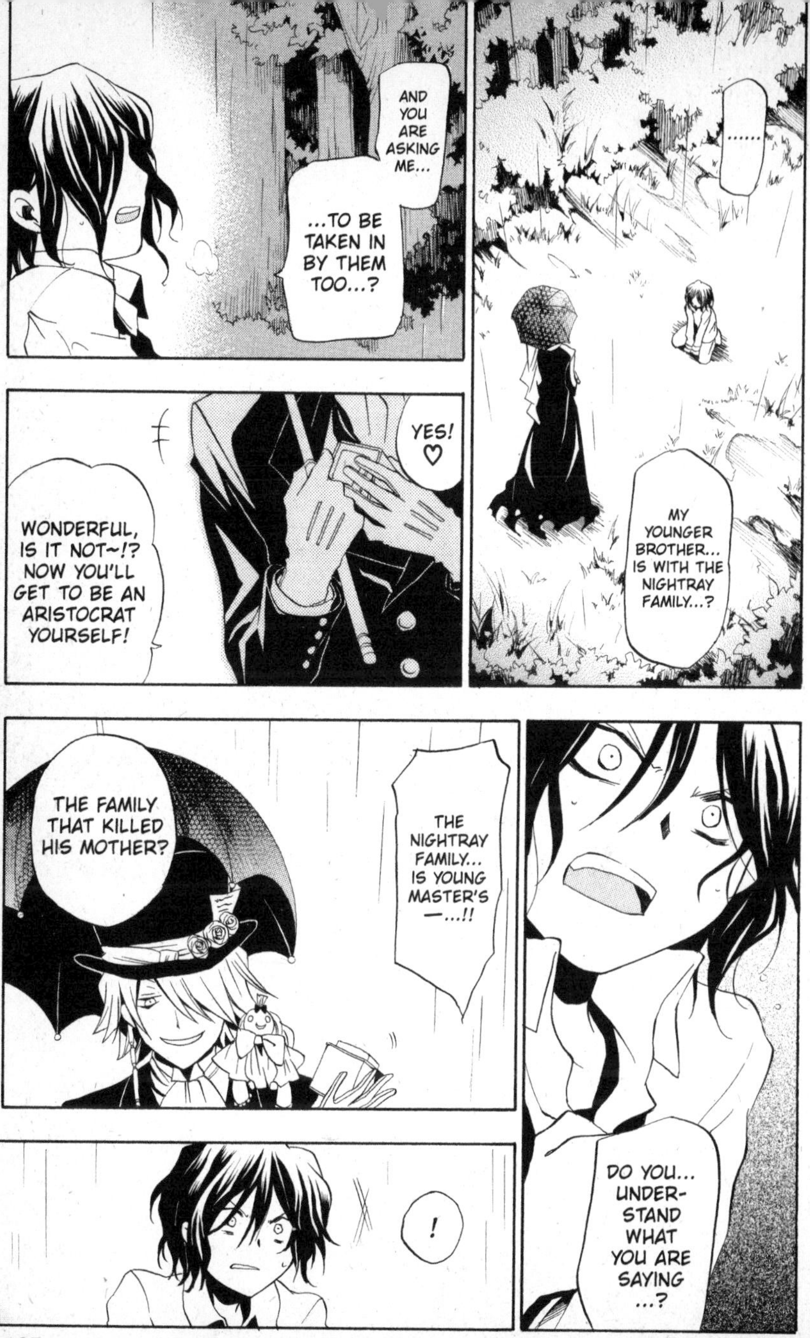
......
MY YOUNGER BROTHER... IS WITH THE NIGHTRAY FAMILY...?
AND YOU ARE ASKING ME...
...TO BE TAKEN IN BY THEM TOO...?
YES! ♡
WONDERFUL, IS IT NOT~!? NOW YOU'LL GET TO BE AN ARISTOCRAT YOURSELF!
DO YOU... UNDER-STAND WHAT YOU ARE SAYING ...?
THE NIGHTRAY FAMILY... IS YOUNG MASTER'S —...!!
THE FAMILY THAT KILLED HIS MOTHER?
!

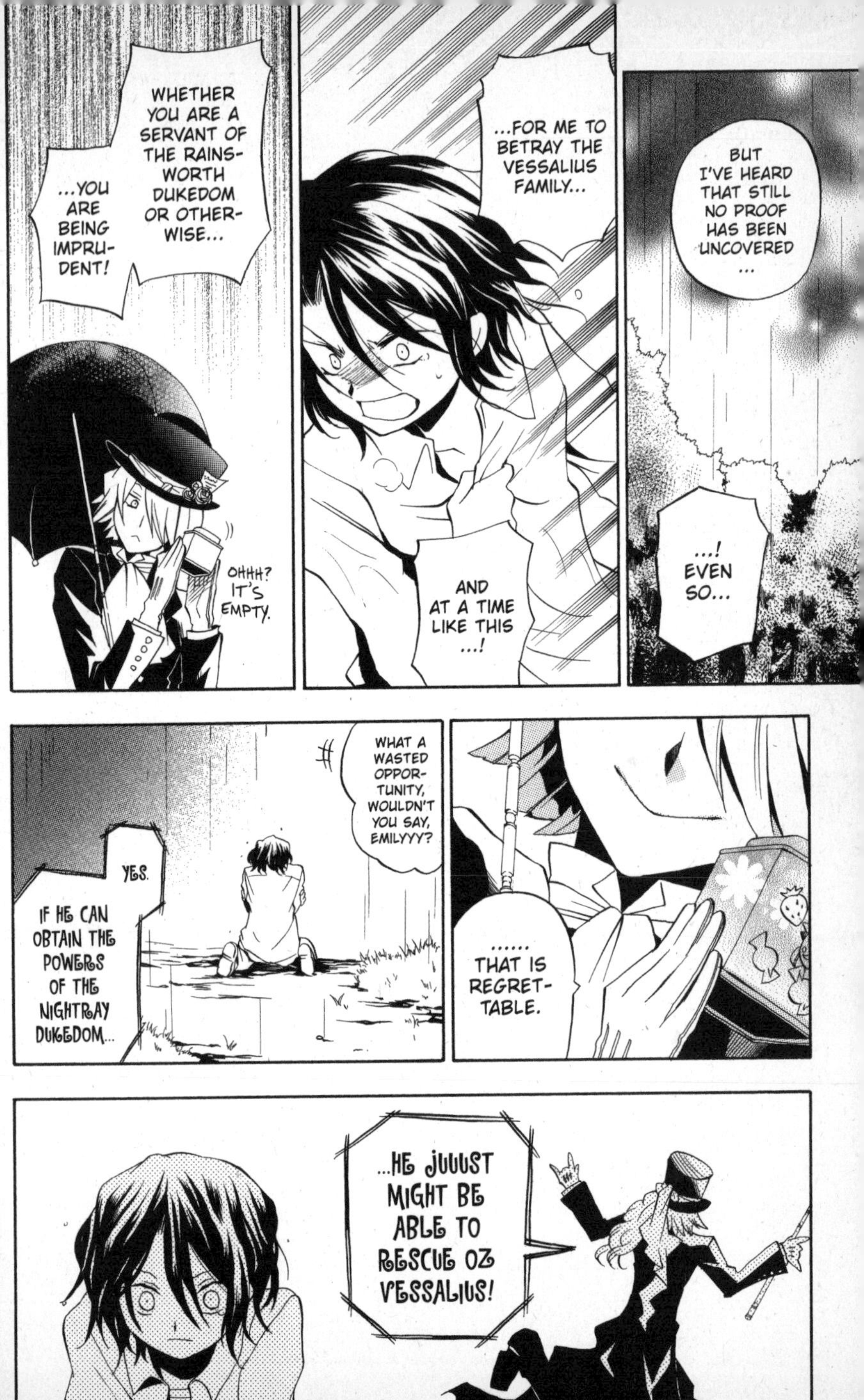
BUT I'VE HEARD THAT STILL NO PROOF HAS BEEN UNCOVERED ...
...! EVEN SO...
...FOR ME TO BETRAY THE VESSALIUS FAMILY...
AND AT A TIME LIKE THIS ...!
WHETHER YOU ARE A SERVANT OF THE RAINSWORTH DUKEDOM OR OTHERWISE...
...YOU ARE BEING IMPRUDENT!
OHHH? IT'S EMPTY.
...... THAT IS REGRETTABLE.
WHAT A WASTED OPPORTUNITY, WOULDN'T YOU SAY, EMILYYY?
YES.
IF HE CAN OBTAIN THE POWERS OF THE NIGHTRAY DUKEDOM...
...HE JUUUST MIGHT BE ABLE TO RESCUE OZ VESSALIUS!

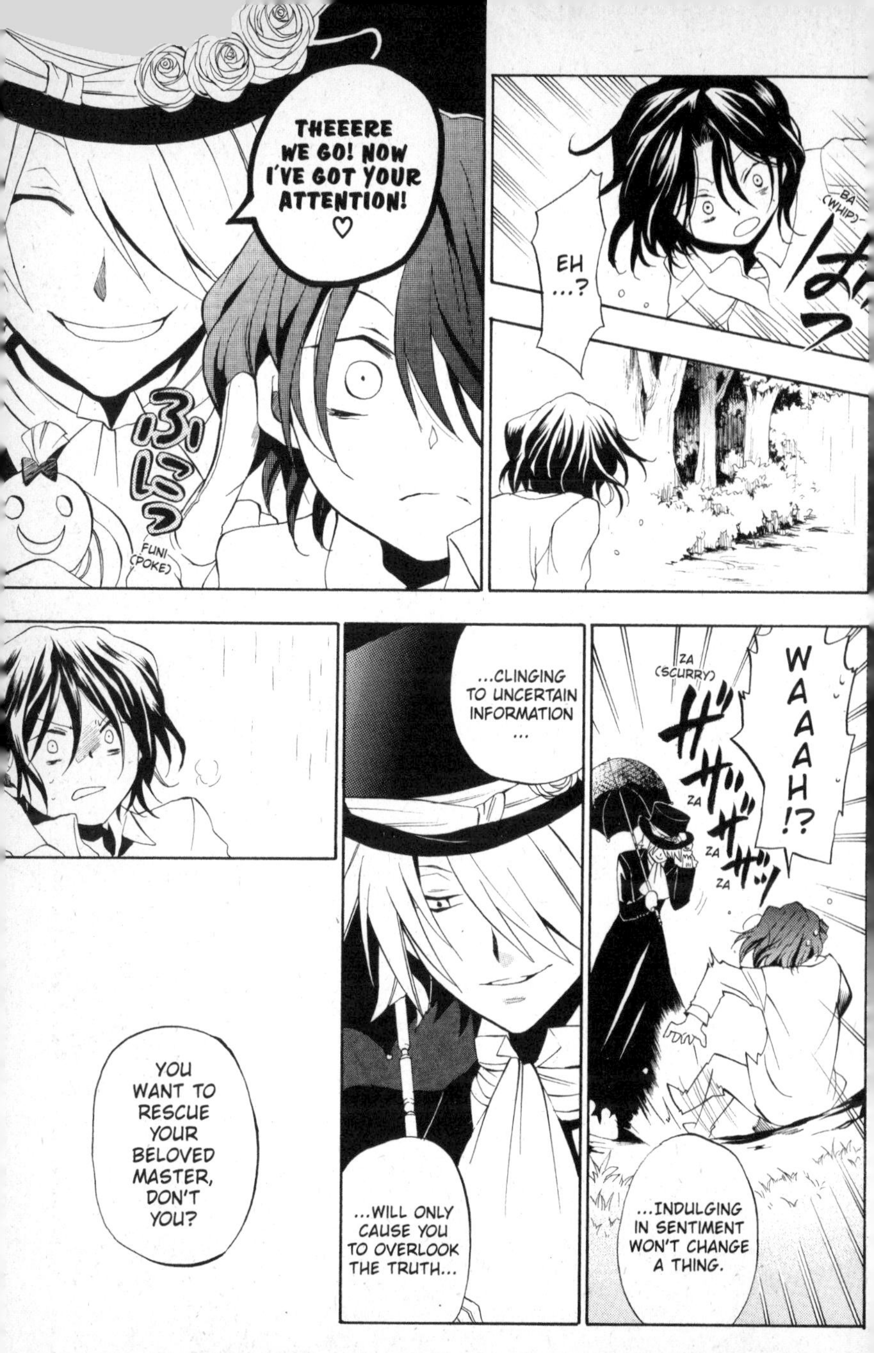
BA (WHIP)
EH …?
THEEERE WE GO! NOW I'VE GOT YOUR ATTENTION! ♡
FUNI (POKE)
WAAAAH!?
ZA (SCURRY)
ZA
ZA
ZA
…INDULGING IN SENTIMENT WON'T CHANGE A THING.
…CLINGING TO UNCERTAIN INFORMATION …
…WILL ONLY CAUSE YOU TO OVERLOOK THE TRUTH…
YOU WANT TO RESCUE YOUR BELOVED MASTER, DON'T YOU?

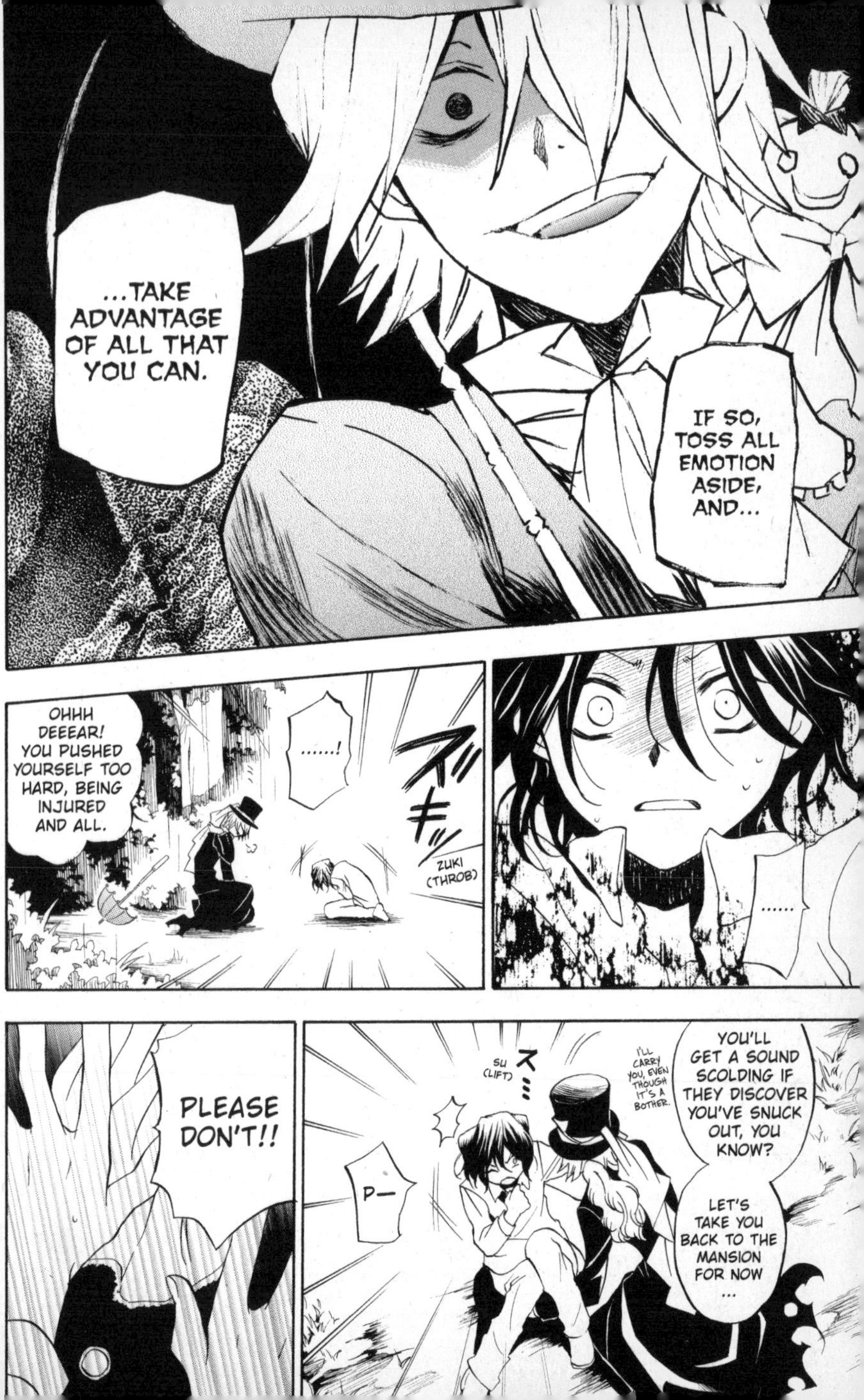
IF SO, TOSS ALL EMOTION ASIDE, AND...
...TAKE ADVANTAGE OF ALL THAT YOU CAN.
......
......!
ZUKI (THROB)
OHHH DEEEAR! YOU PUSHED YOURSELF TOO HARD, BEING INJURED AND ALL.
YOU'LL GET A SOUND SCOLDING IF THEY DISCOVER YOU'VE SNUCK OUT, YOU KNOW?
I'LL CARRY YOU, EVEN THOUGH IT'S A BOTHER.
SU (LIFT)
LET'S TAKE YOU BACK TO THE MANSION FOR NOW ...
P—
PLEASE DON'T!!

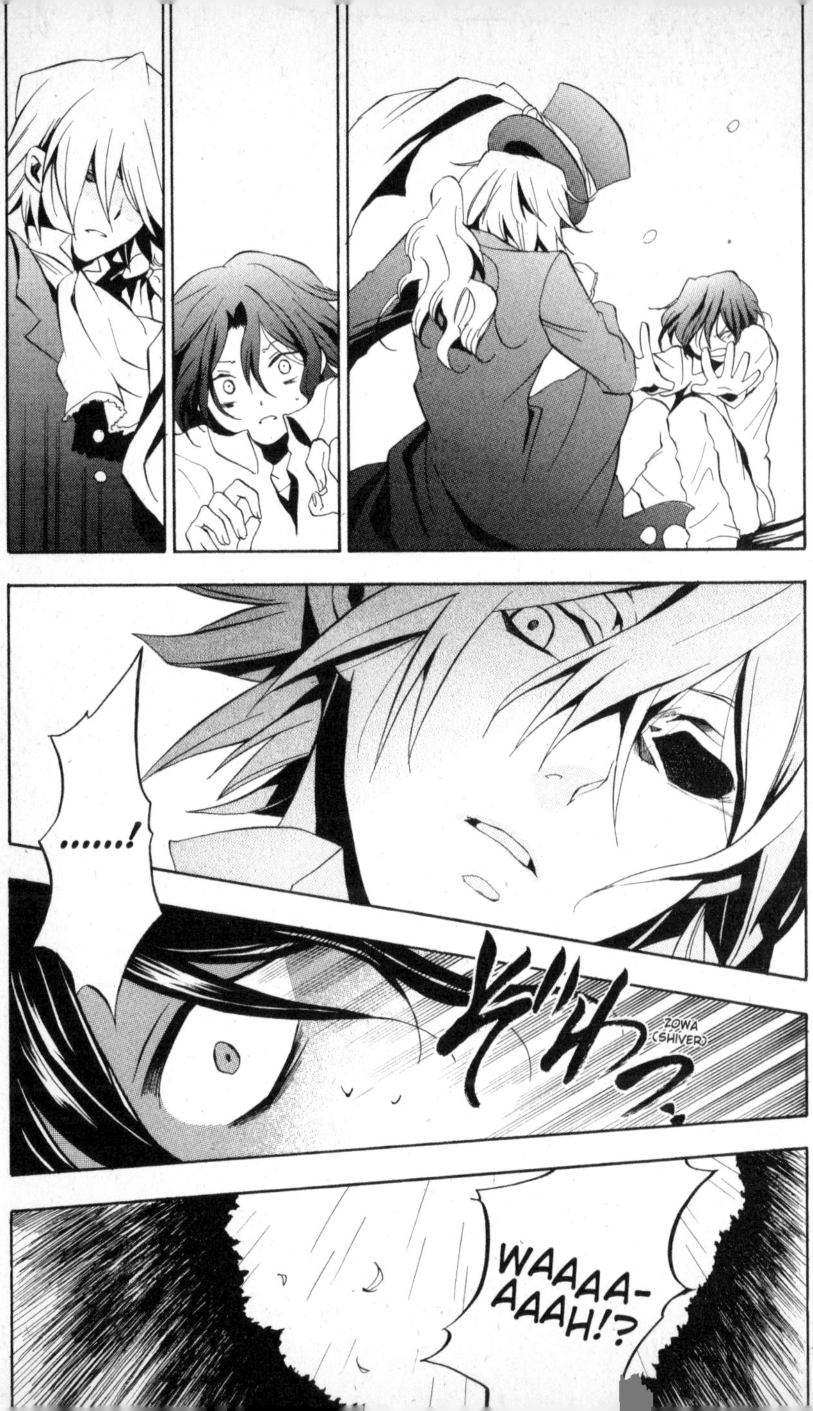
......!
ぞわっ
ZOWA (SHIVER)
WAAAA-AAAH!?

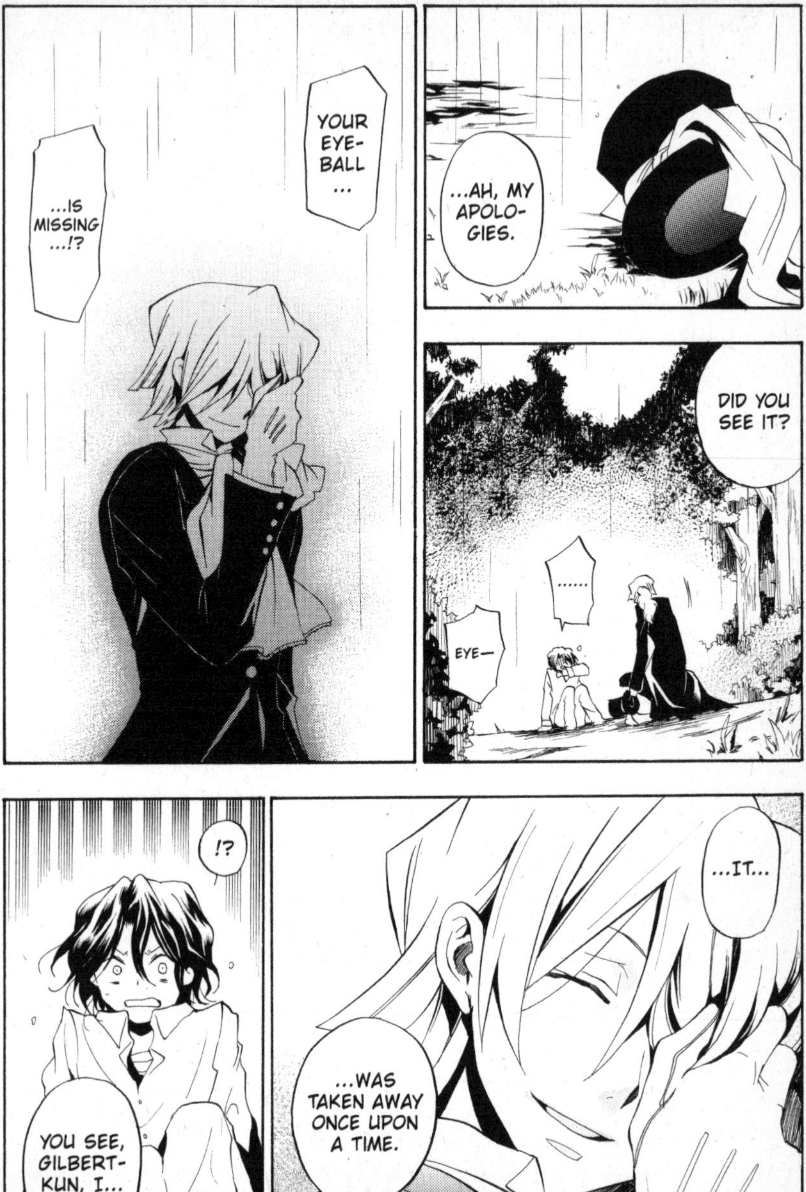
...AH, MY APOLOGIES.
DID YOU SEE IT?
......
EYE—
YOUR EYE-BALL ...
...IS MISSING ...!?
...IT...
...WAS TAKEN AWAY ONCE UPON A TIME.
!?
YOU SEE, GILBERT-KUN, I...

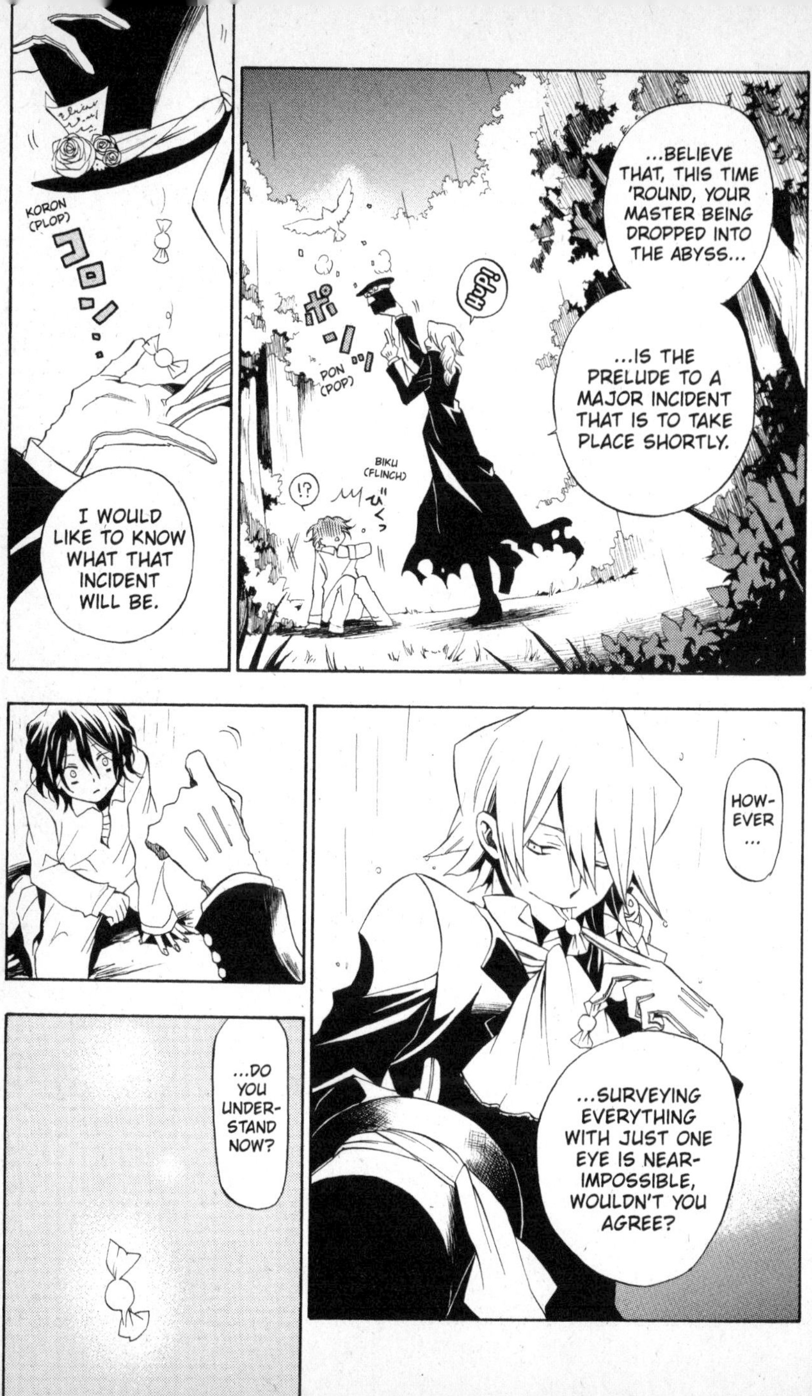
...BELIEVE THAT, THIS TIME 'ROUND, YOUR MASTER BEING DROPPED INTO THE ABYSS...
...IS THE PRELUDE TO A MAJOR INCIDENT THAT IS TO TAKE PLACE SHORTLY.
PON (POP)
BIKU (FLINCH)
!?
KORON (PLOP)
I WOULD LIKE TO KNOW WHAT THAT INCIDENT WILL BE.
HOW-EVER...
...SURVEYING EVERYTHING WITH JUST ONE EYE IS NEAR-IMPOSSIBLE, WOULDN'T YOU AGREE?
...DO YOU UNDER-STAND NOW?

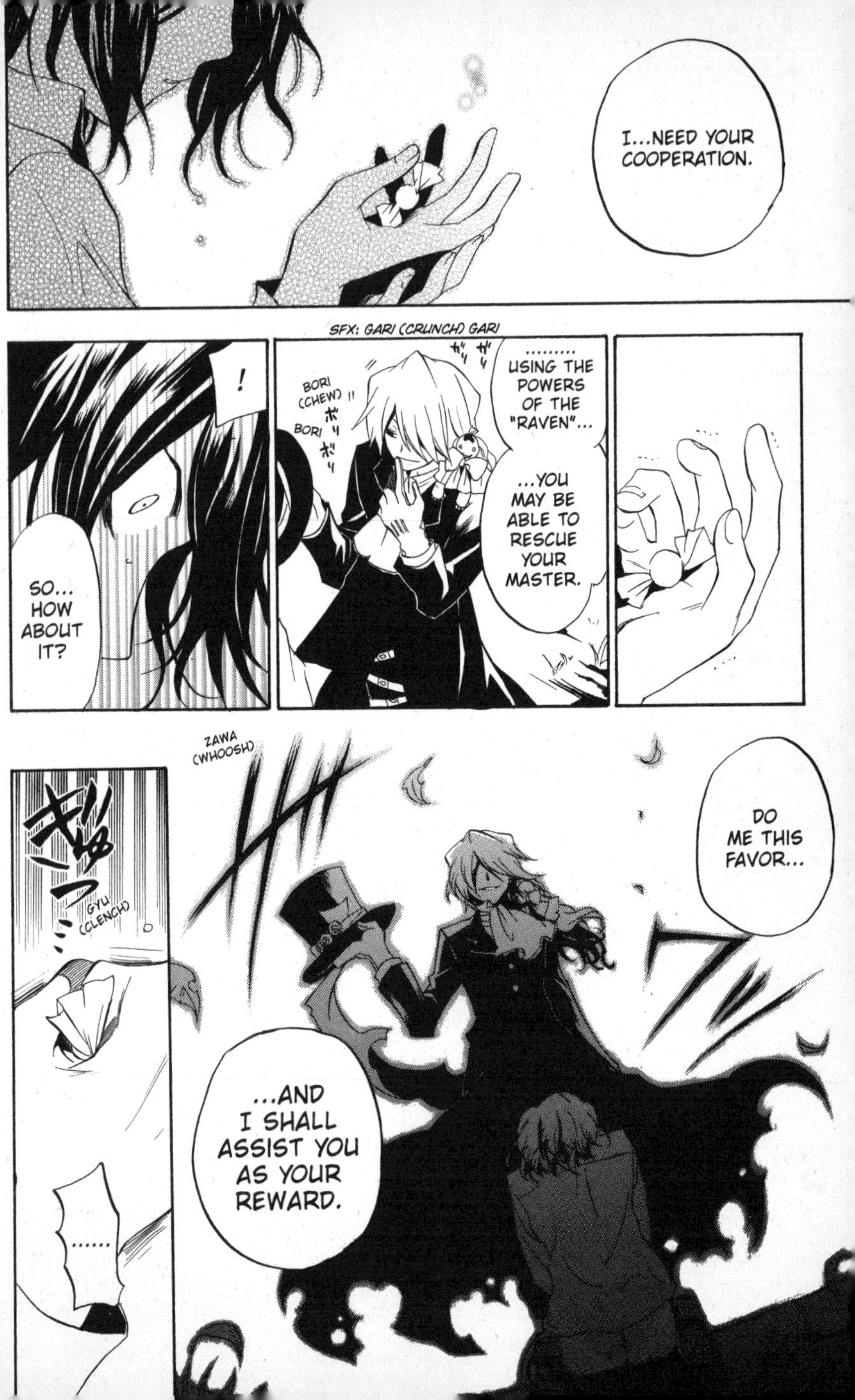
I...NEED YOUR COOPERATION.
SFX: GARI (CRUNCH) GARI
BORI (CHEW) BORI
.... USING THE POWERS OF THE "RAVEN"...
...YOU MAY BE ABLE TO RESCUE YOUR MASTER.
SO... HOW ABOUT IT?
ZAWA (WHOOSH)
DO ME THIS FAVOR...
...AND I SHALL ASSIST YOU AS YOUR REWARD.
GYU (CLENCH)
......

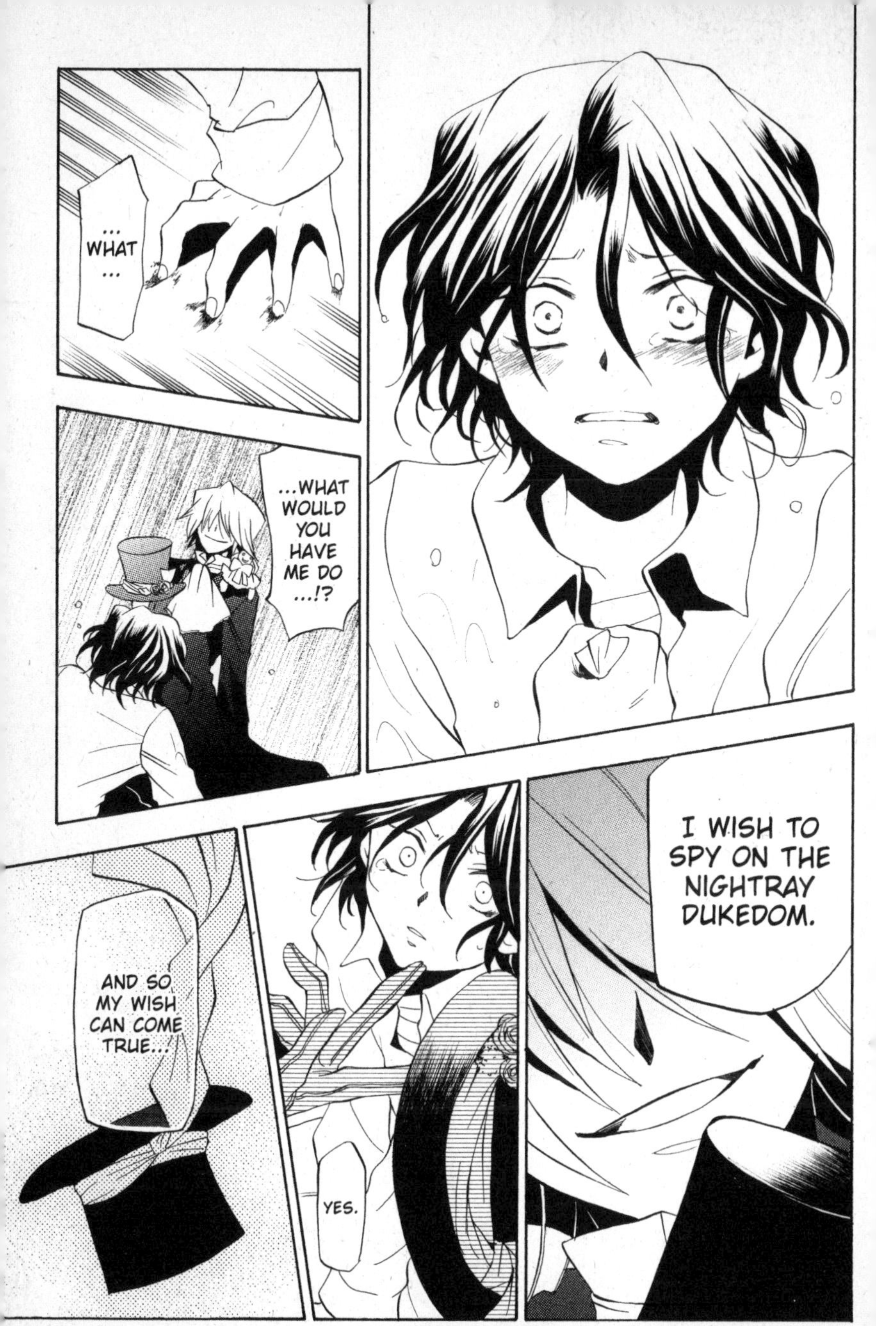
... WHAT ...
...WHAT WOULD YOU HAVE ME DO ...!?
I WISH TO SPY ON THE NIGHTRAY DUKEDOM.
YES.
AND SO MY WISH CAN COME TRUE...

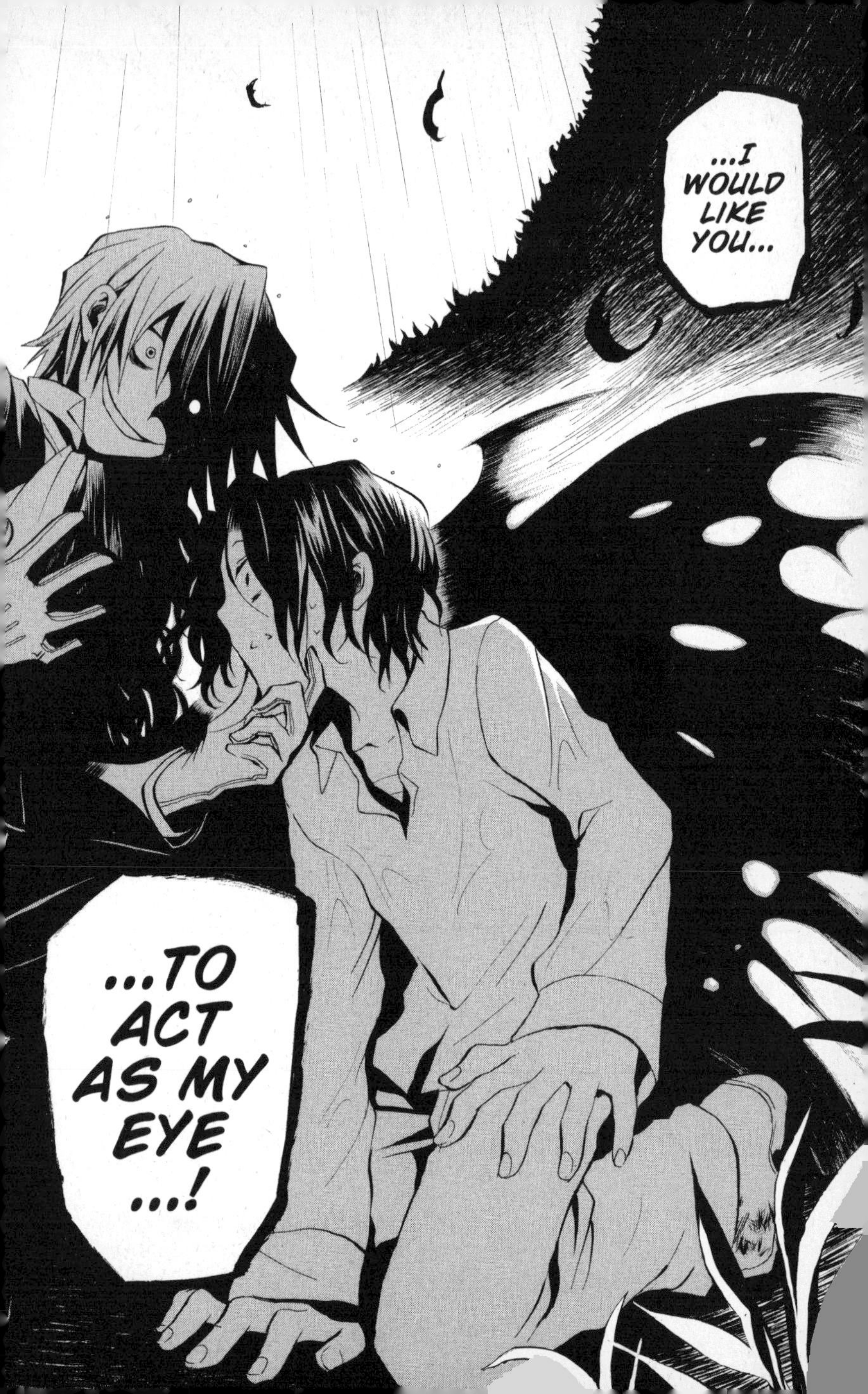
...I WOULD LIKE YOU...
...TO ACT AS MY EYE ...!

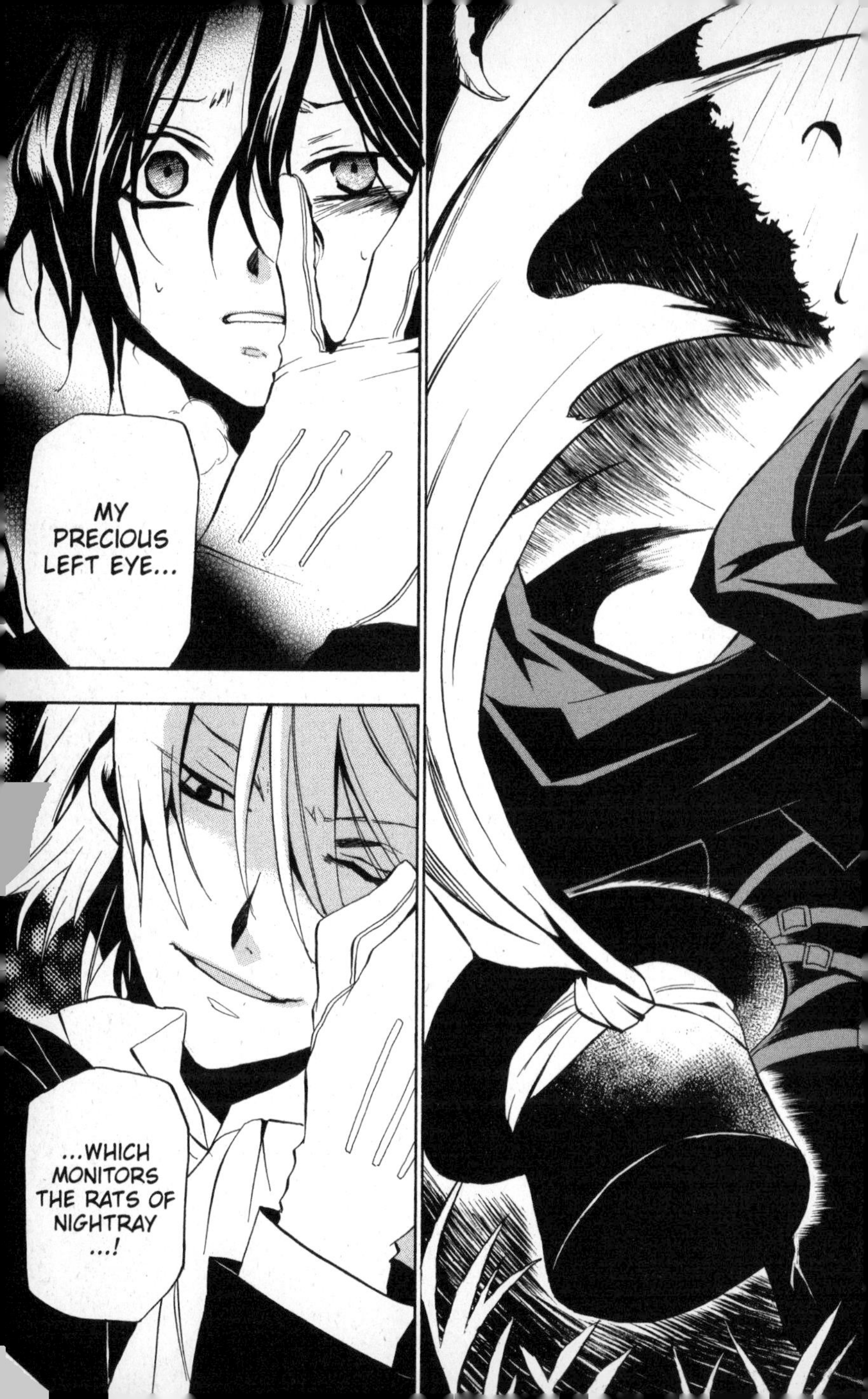
MY PRECIOUS LEFT EYE...
...WHICH MONITORS THE RATS OF NIGHTRAY ...!

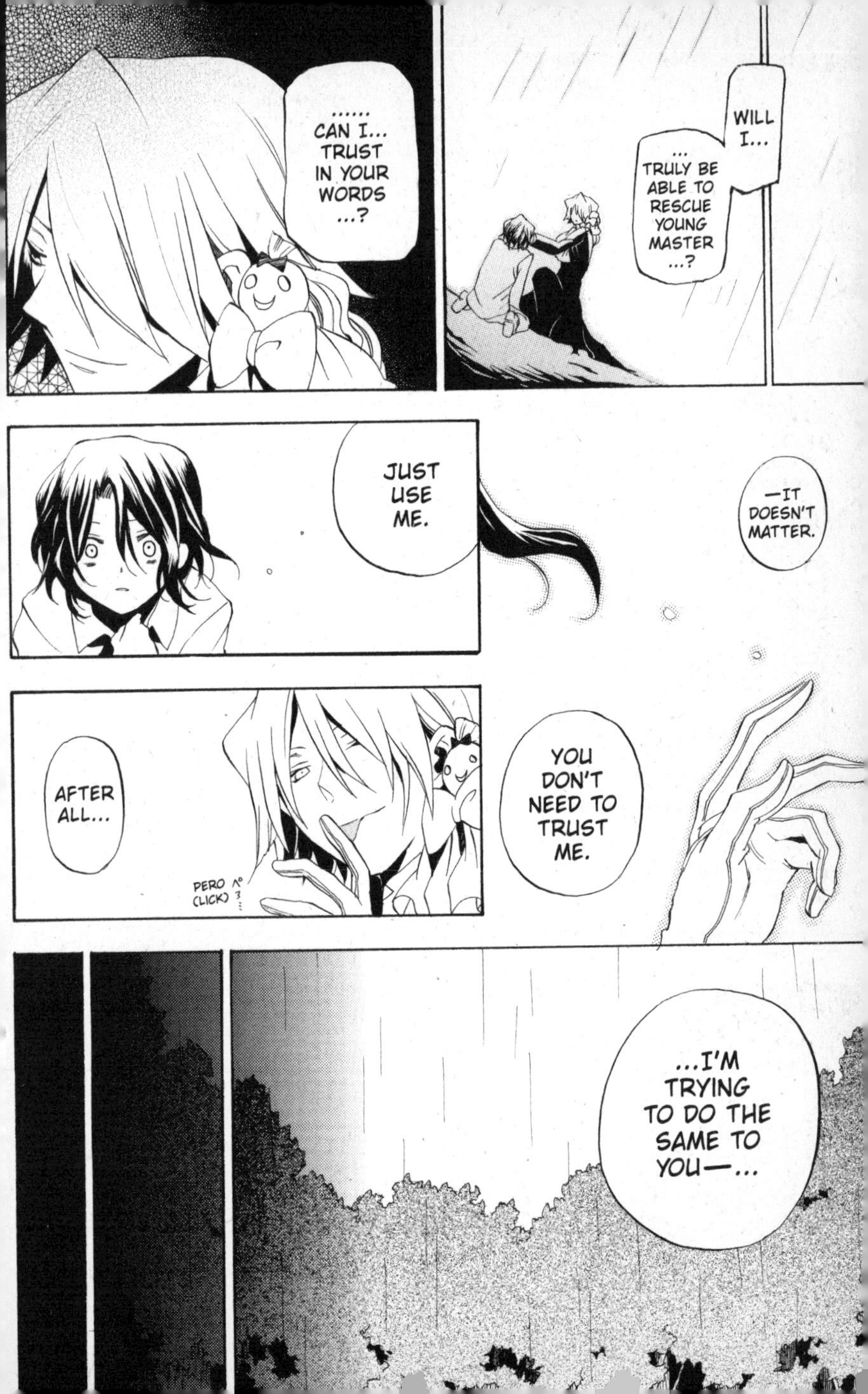
WILL I...
...TRULY BE ABLE TO RESCUE YOUNG MASTER...?
......CAN I... TRUST IN YOUR WORDS...?
—IT DOESN'T MATTER.
JUST USE ME.
YOU DON'T NEED TO TRUST ME.
AFTER ALL...
PERO (LICK)
...I'M TRYING TO DO THE SAME TO YOU—...

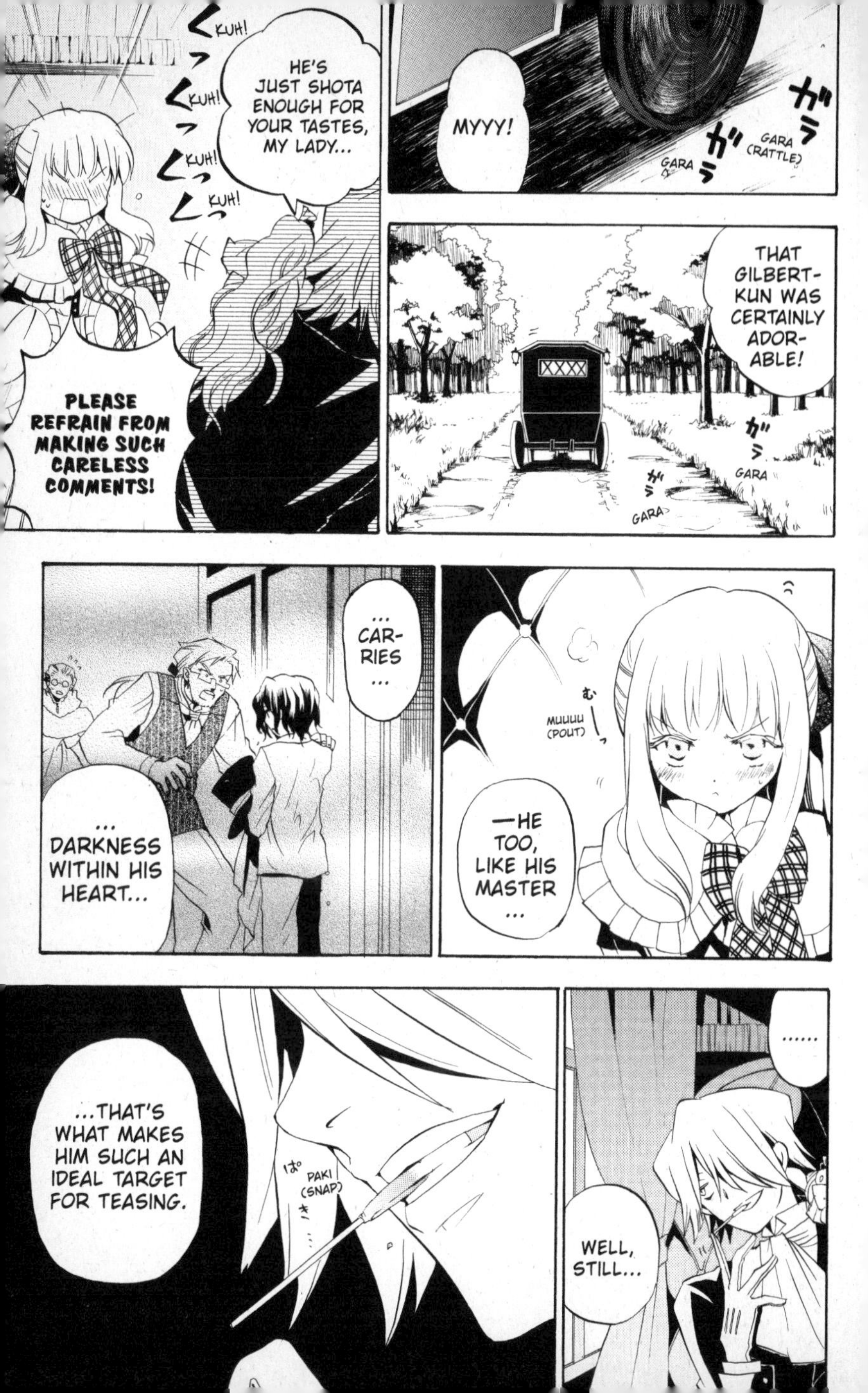
MYYY!
GARA (RATTLE)
GARA
THAT GILBERT-KUN WAS CERTAINLY ADORABLE!
GARA
GARA
HE'S JUST SHOTA ENOUGH FOR YOUR TASTES, MY LADY...
KUH!
KUH!
KUH!
KUH!
PLEASE REFRAIN FROM MAKING SUCH CARELESS COMMENTS!
MUUUU (POUT)
—HE TOO, LIKE HIS MASTER ...
... CARRIES ...
... DARKNESS WITHIN HIS HEART...
......
WELL, STILL...
PAKI (SNAP)
...THAT'S WHAT MAKES HIM SUCH AN IDEAL TARGET FOR TEASING.

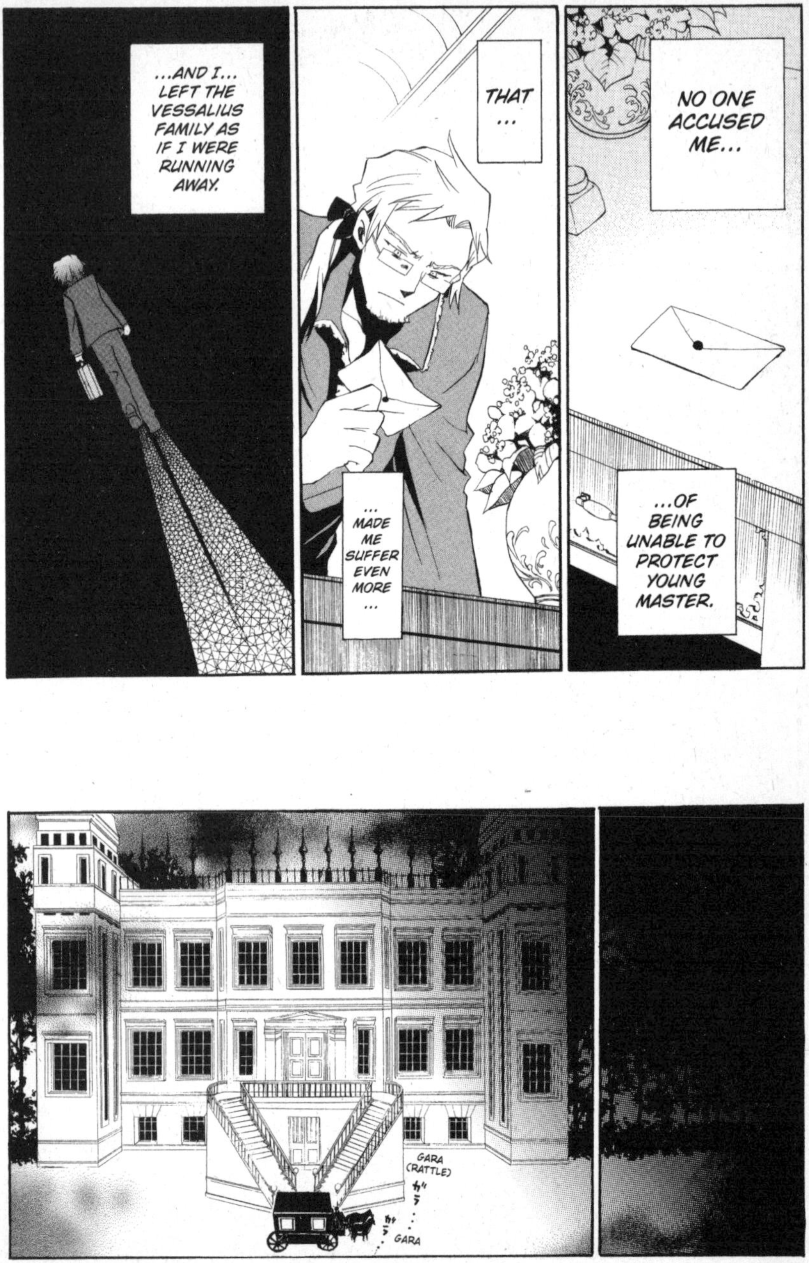
NO ONE ACCUSED ME...
...OF BEING UNABLE TO PROTECT YOUNG MASTER.
THAT...
...MADE ME SUFFER EVEN MORE...
...AND I... LEFT THE VESSALIUS FAMILY AS IF I WERE RUNNING AWAY.
GARA (RATTLE)
GARA

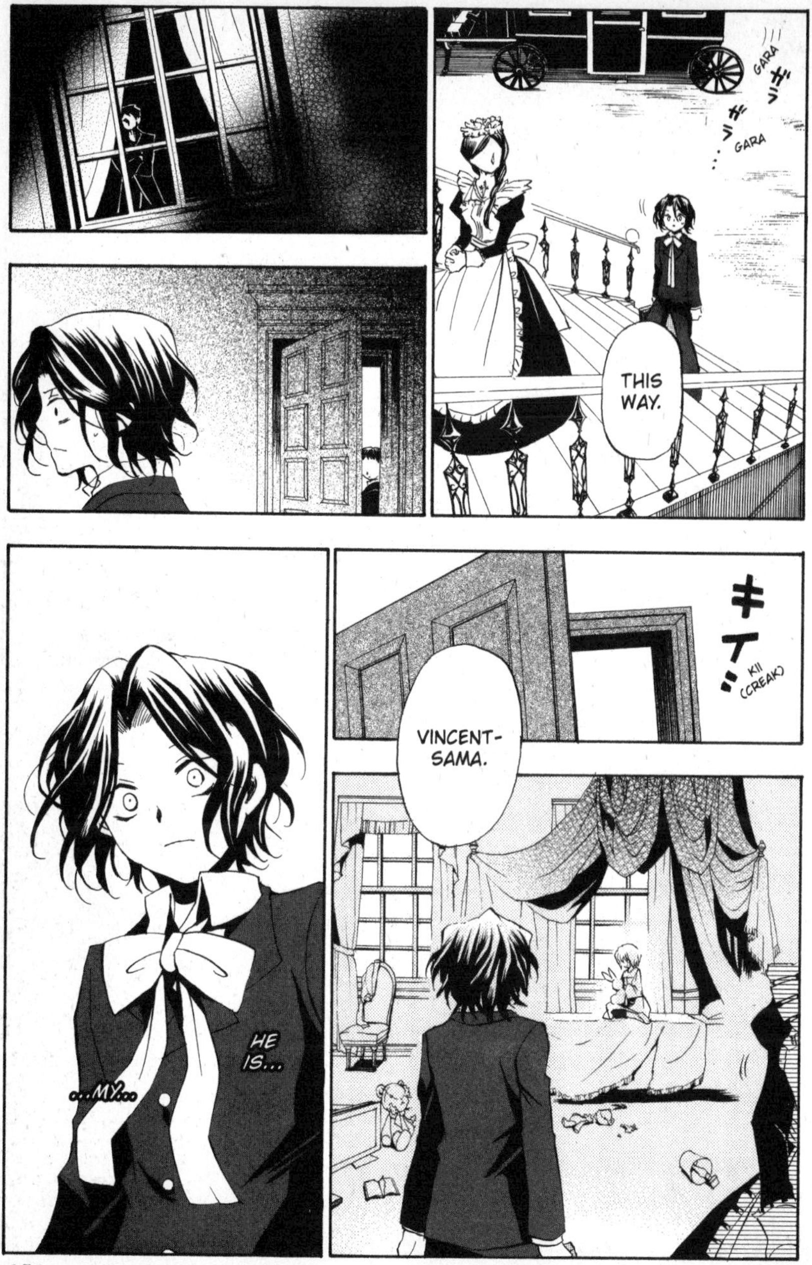
GARA
GARA
THIS WAY.
KII (CREAK)
VINCENT-SAMA.
HE IS...
...MY...

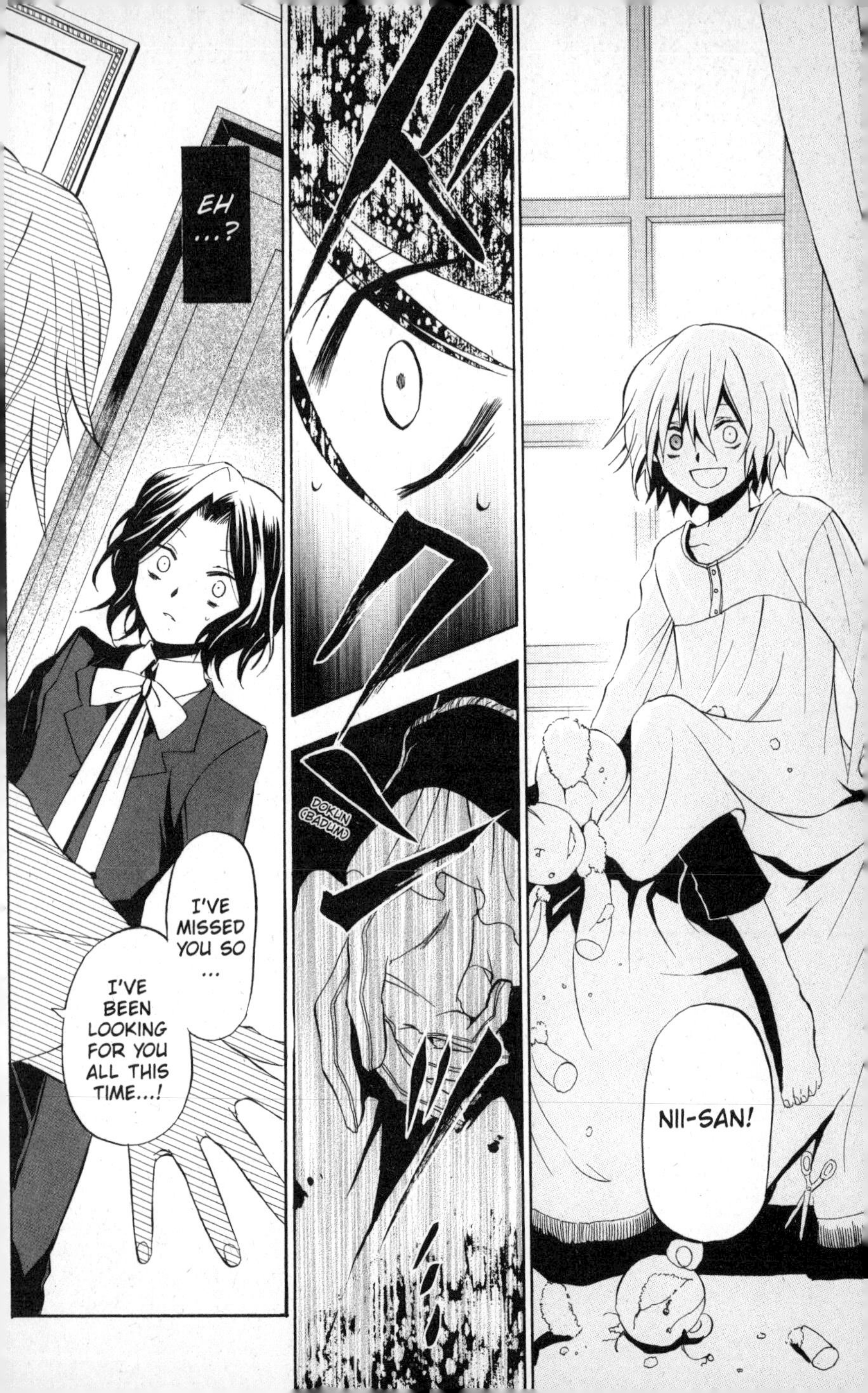
NII-SAN!
DOKUN (BADUMP)
EH ...?
I'VE MISSED YOU SO ...
I'VE BEEN LOOKING FOR YOU ALL THIS TIME...!

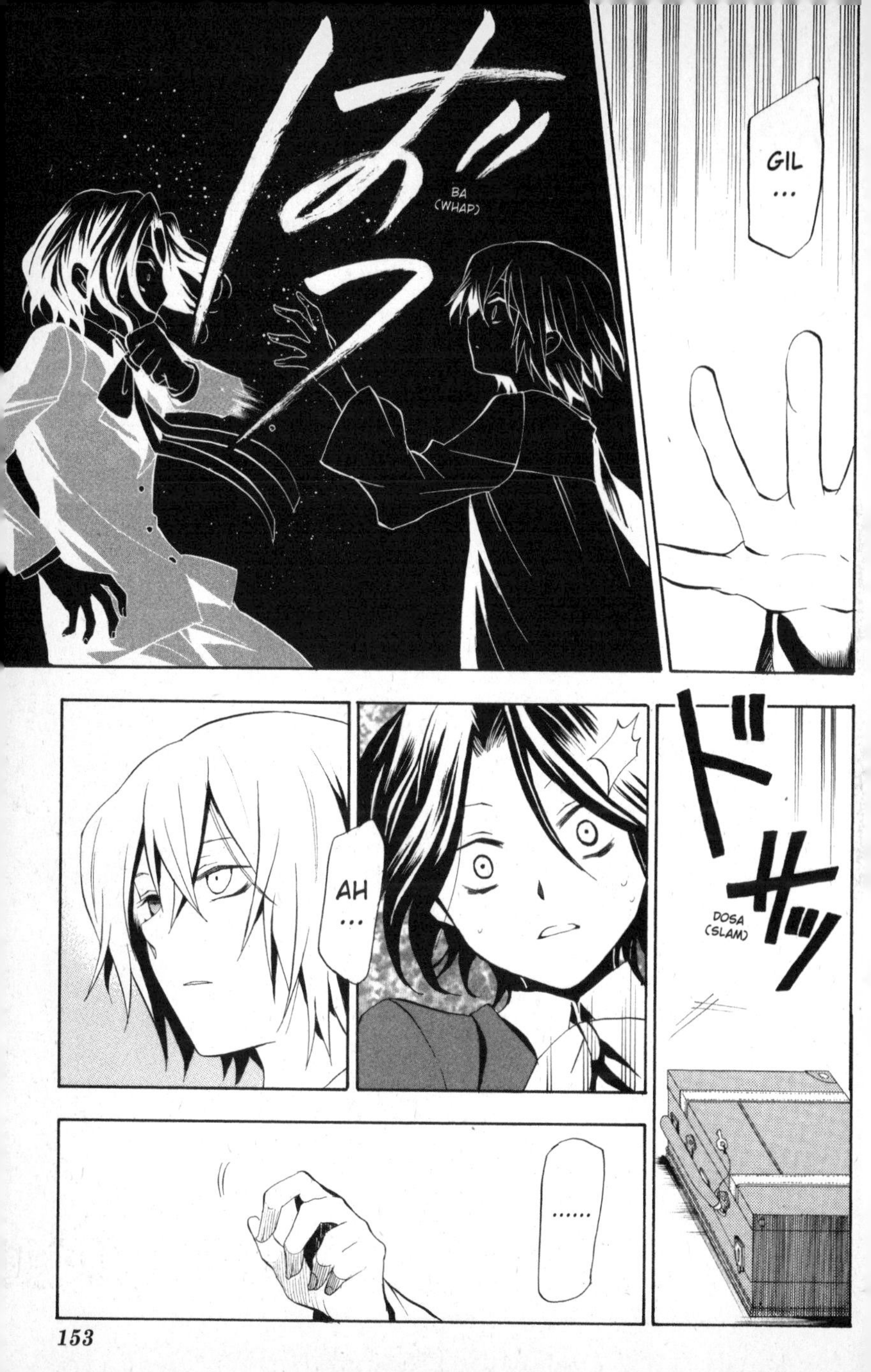
GIL ...
ばっ
BA (WHAP)
ドサッ
DOSA (SLAM)
AH ...
......

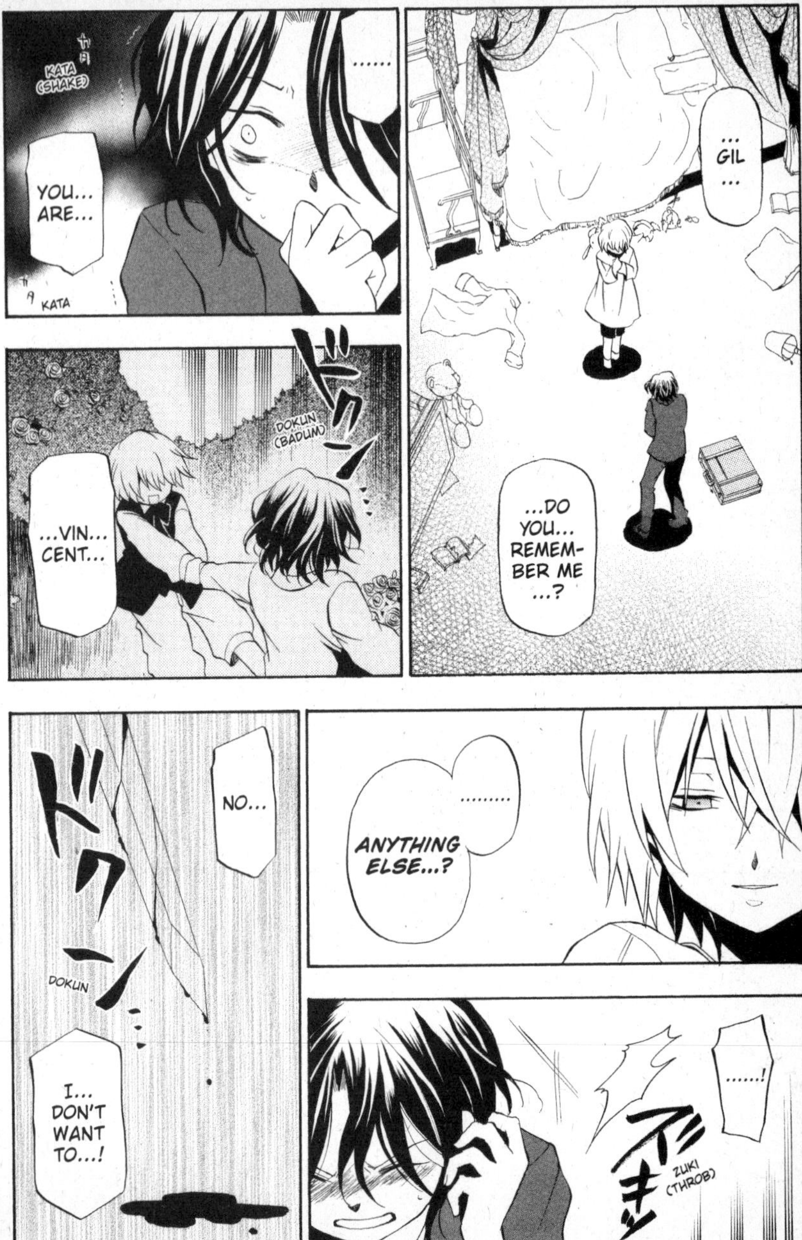
... GIL ...
...DO YOU... REMEMBER ME ...?
......
KATA (SHAKE)
YOU... ARE...
KATA
DOKUN (BADUM)
...VIN... CENT...
....
ANYTHING ELSE...?
......!
ZUKI (THROB)
NO...
DOKUN
I... DON'T WANT TO...!

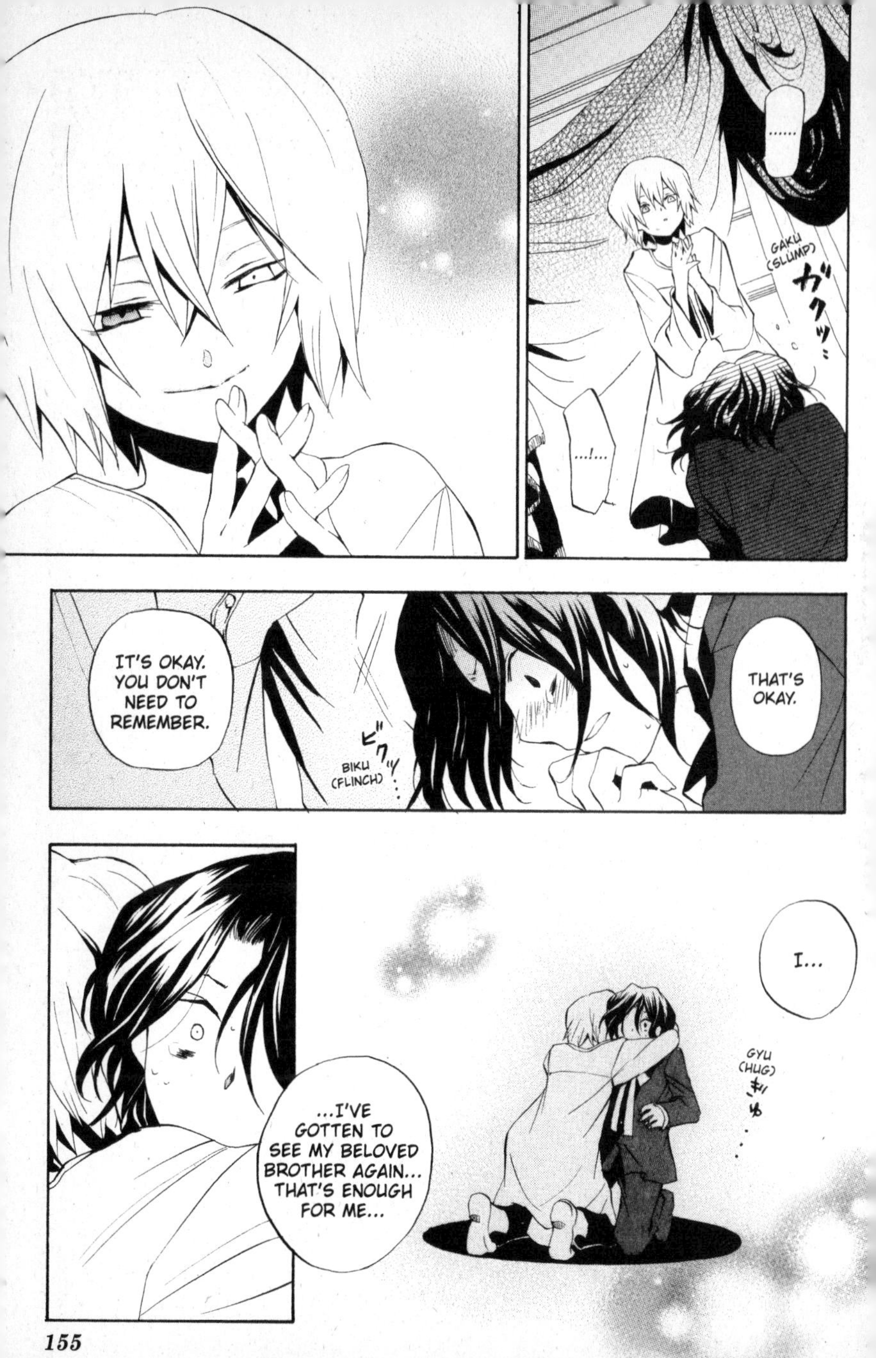
......
GAKU (SLUMP)
...!...
THAT'S OKAY.
BIKU (FLINCH)
IT'S OKAY. YOU DON'T NEED TO REMEMBER.
I...
GYU (HUG)
...I'VE GOTTEN TO SEE MY BELOVED BROTHER AGAIN... THAT'S ENOUGH FOR ME...

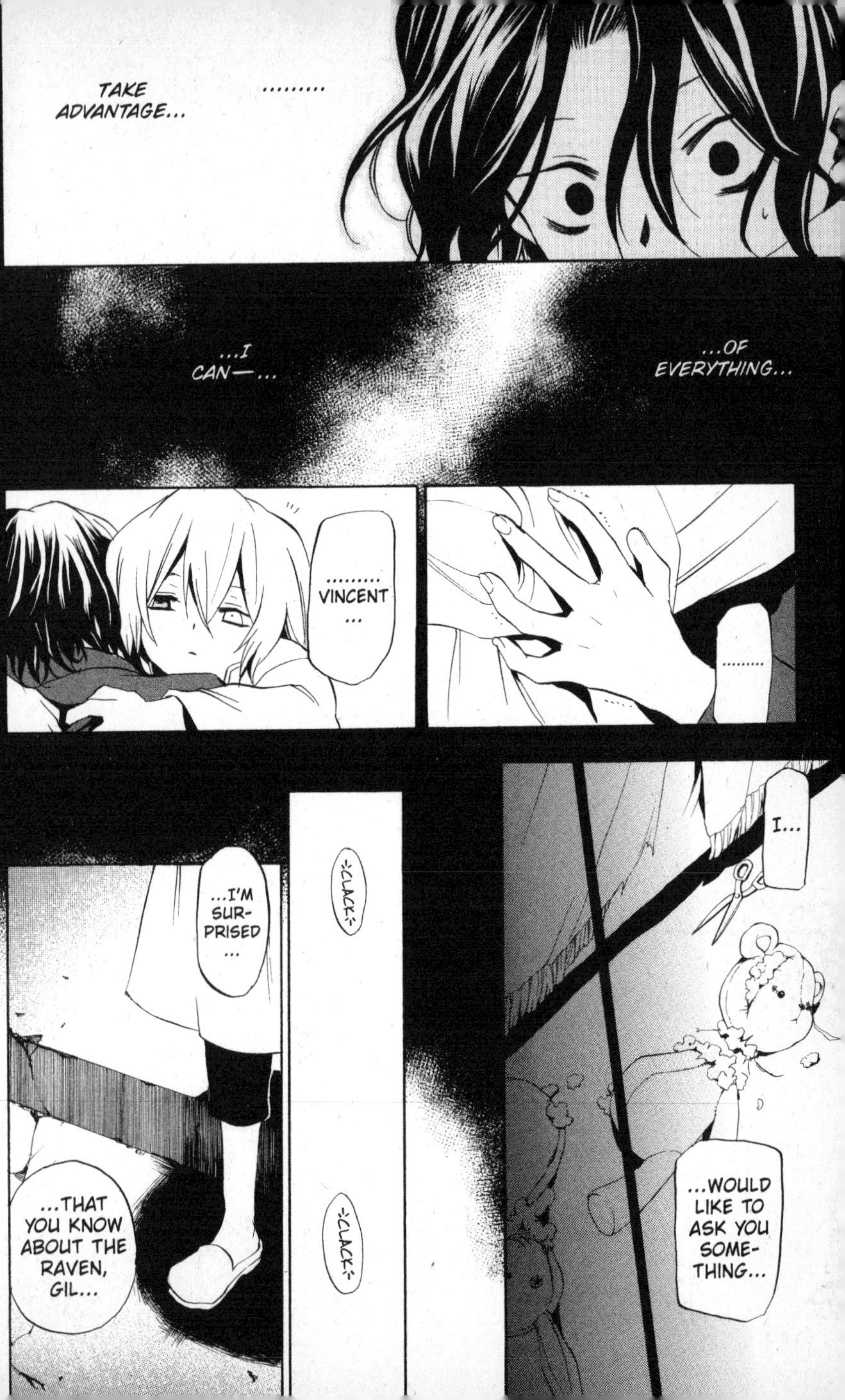
....
TAKE ADVANTAGE...
...OF EVERYTHING...
...I CAN—...
....
.... VINCENT ...
I...
...WOULD LIKE TO ASK YOU SOME-THING...
CLACK
CLACK
...I'M SUR-PRISED ...
...THAT YOU KNOW ABOUT THE RAVEN, GIL...

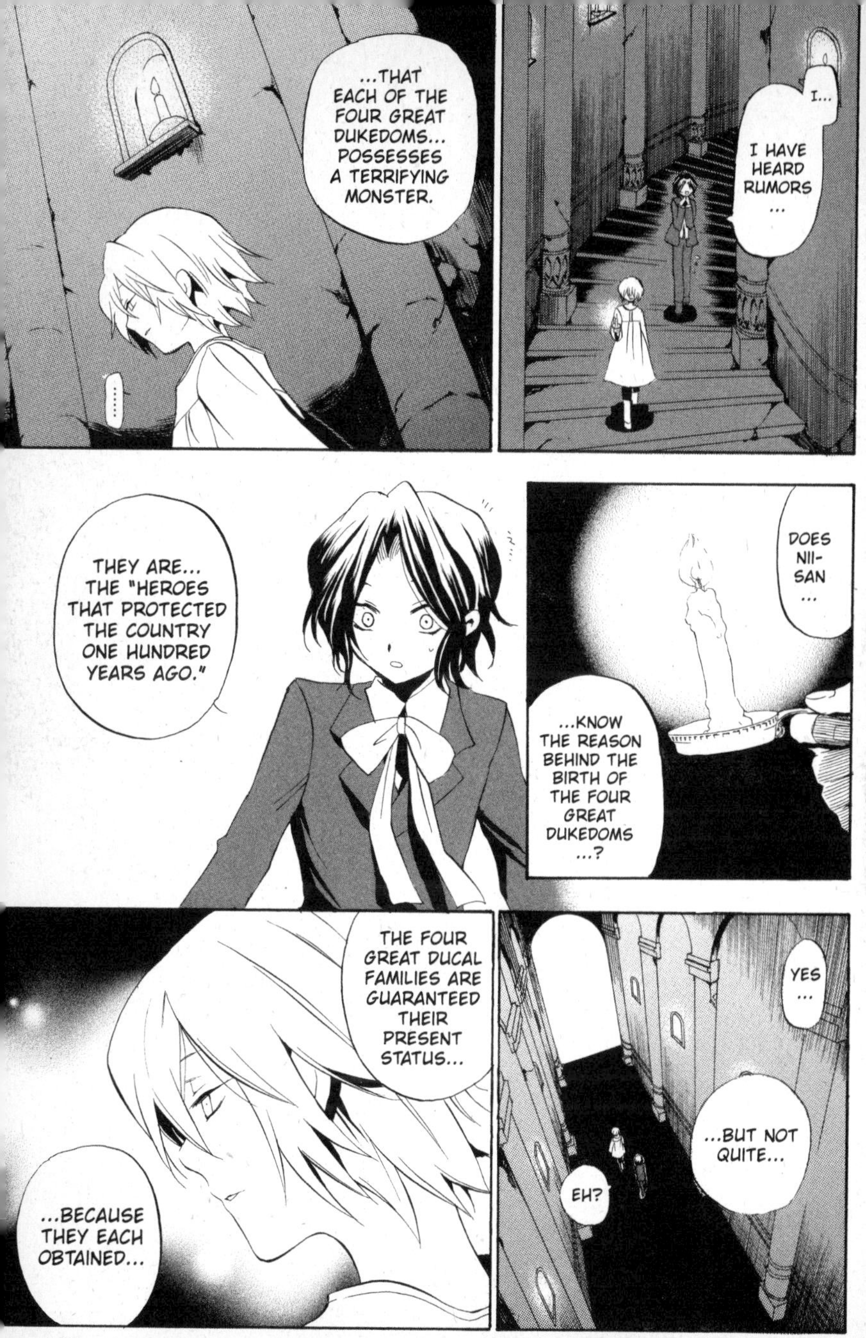
I...
I HAVE HEARD RUMORS...
...THAT EACH OF THE FOUR GREAT DUKEDOMS... POSSESSES A TERRIFYING MONSTER.
......
DOES NII-SAN...
...KNOW THE REASON BEHIND THE BIRTH OF THE FOUR GREAT DUKEDOMS...?
THEY ARE... THE "HEROES THAT PROTECTED THE COUNTRY ONE HUNDRED YEARS AGO."
YES...
...BUT NOT QUITE...
EH?
THE FOUR GREAT DUCAL FAMILIES ARE GUARANTEED THEIR PRESENT STATUS...
...BECAUSE THEY EACH OBTAINED...

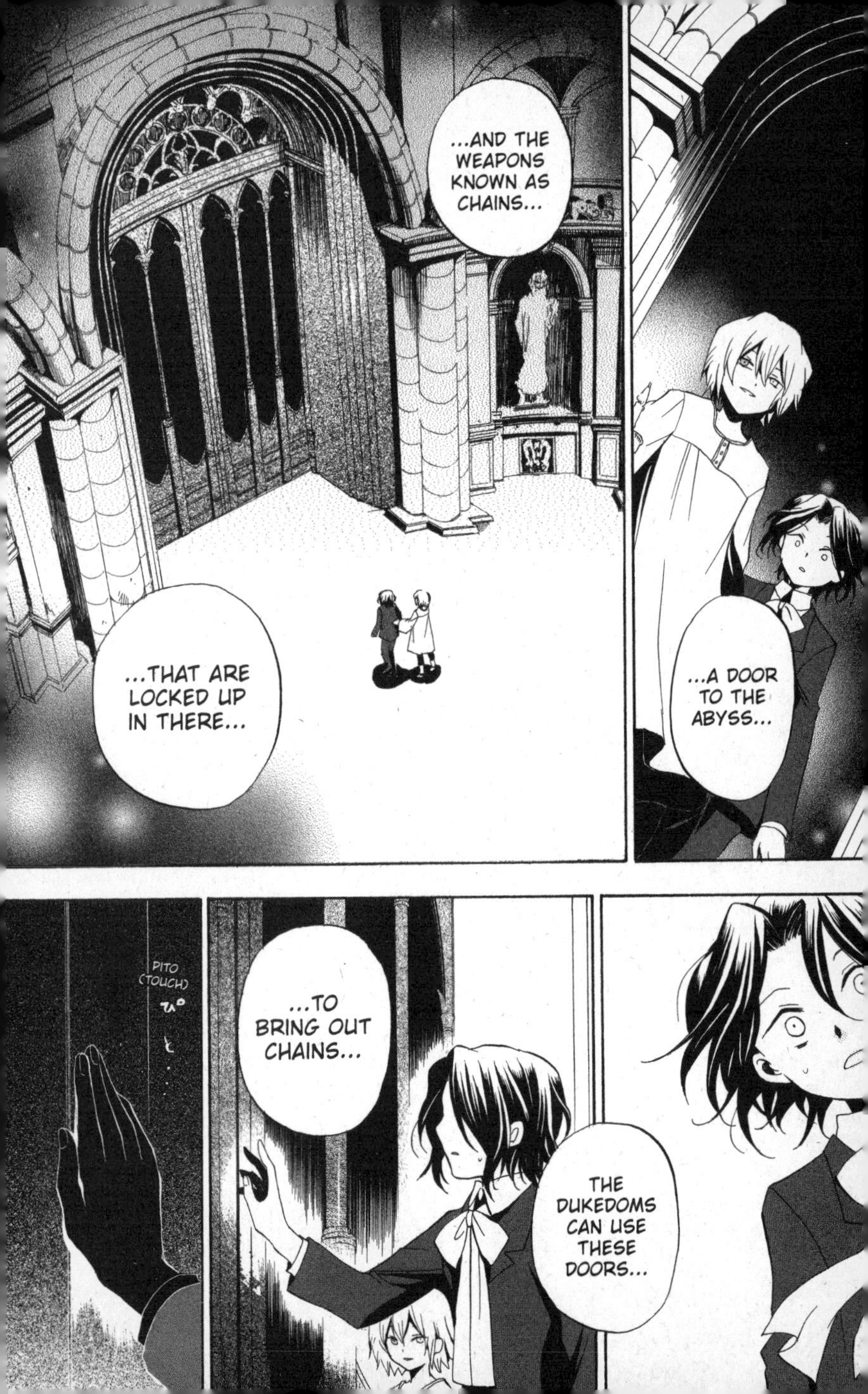
...A DOOR TO THE ABYSS...
...AND THE WEAPONS KNOWN AS CHAINS...
...THAT ARE LOCKED UP IN THERE...
THE DUKEDOMS CAN USE THESE DOORS...
...TO BRING OUT CHAINS...
PITO (TOUCH)

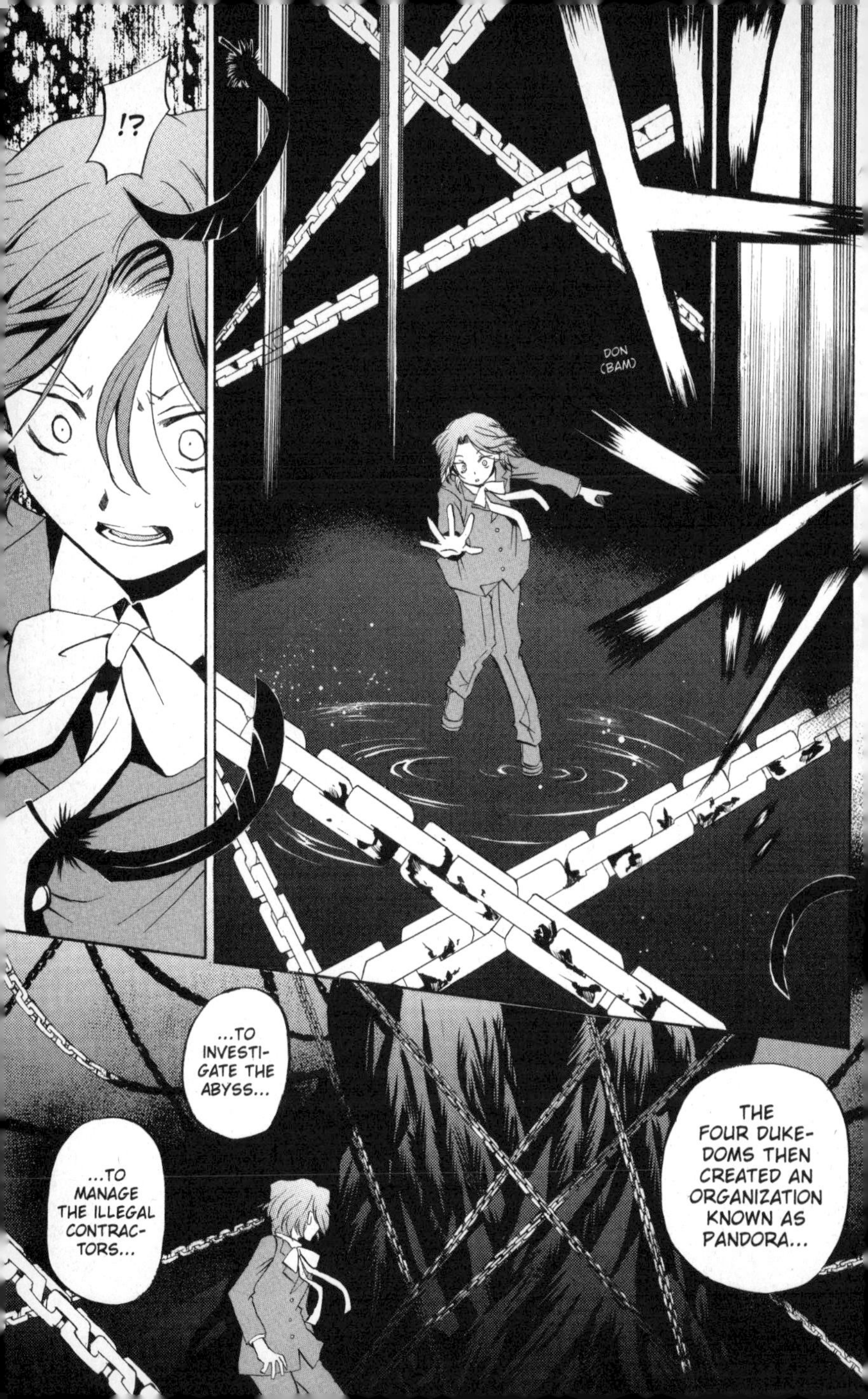
DON (BAM)
!?
THE FOUR DUKE-DOMS THEN CREATED AN ORGANIZATION KNOWN AS PANDORA...
...TO INVESTI-GATE THE ABYSS...
...TO MANAGE THE ILLEGAL CONTRAC-TORS...

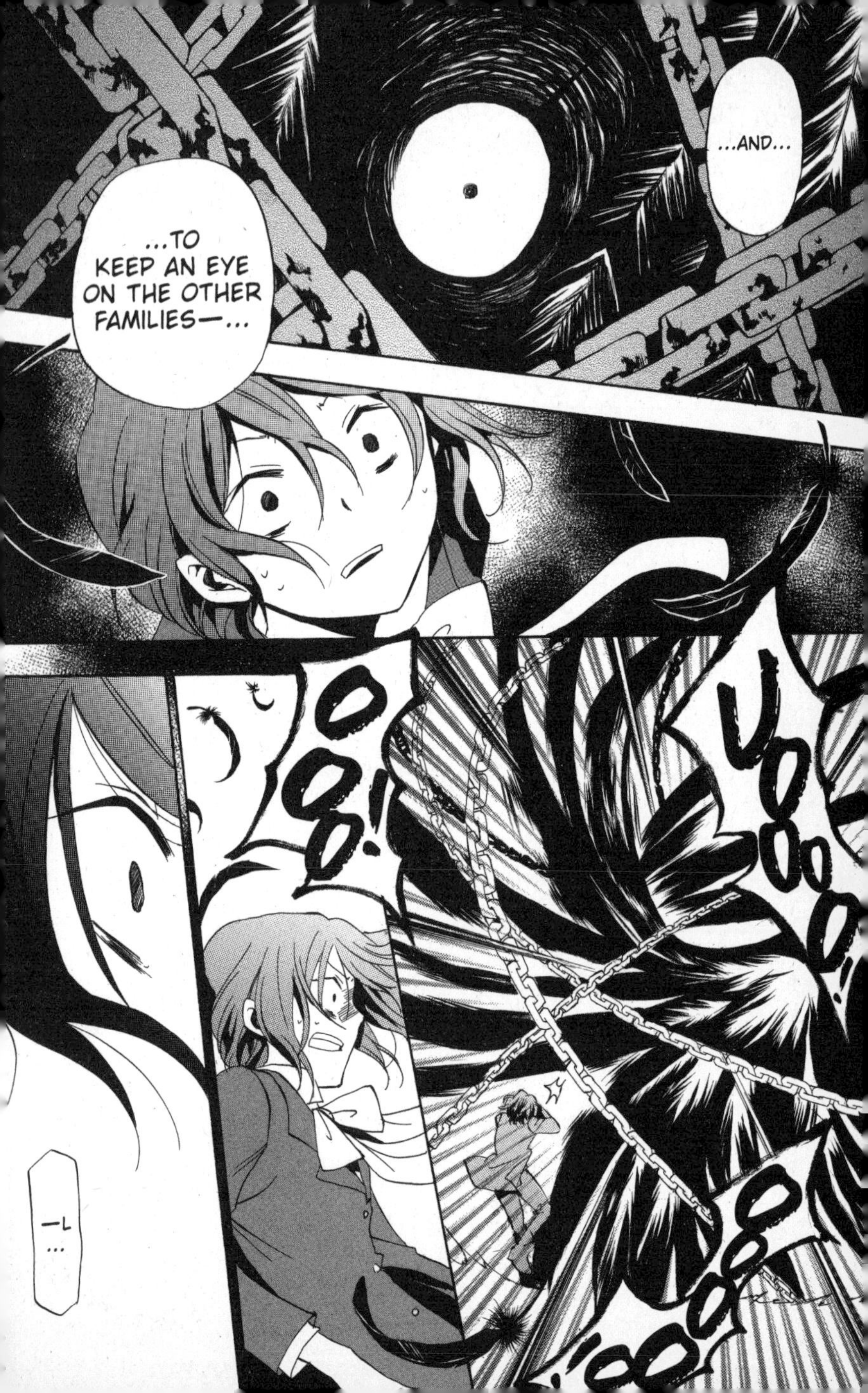
...AND...
...TO KEEP AN EYE ON THE OTHER FAMILIES—...
—L ...

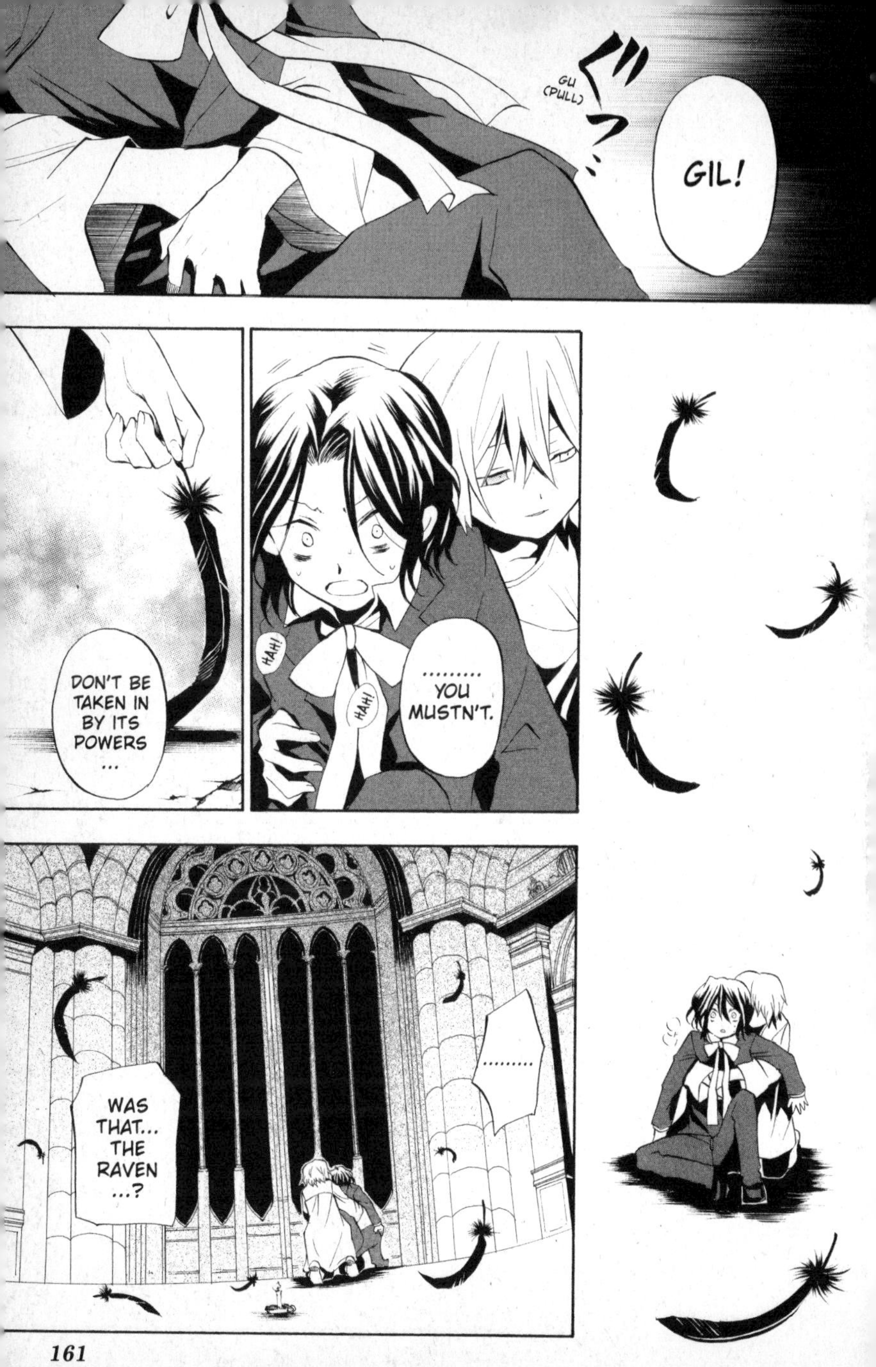
GIL!
GU (PULL)
HAH!
HAH!
.... YOU MUSTN'T.
DON'T BE TAKEN IN BY ITS POWERS ...
....
WAS THAT... THE RAVEN ...?

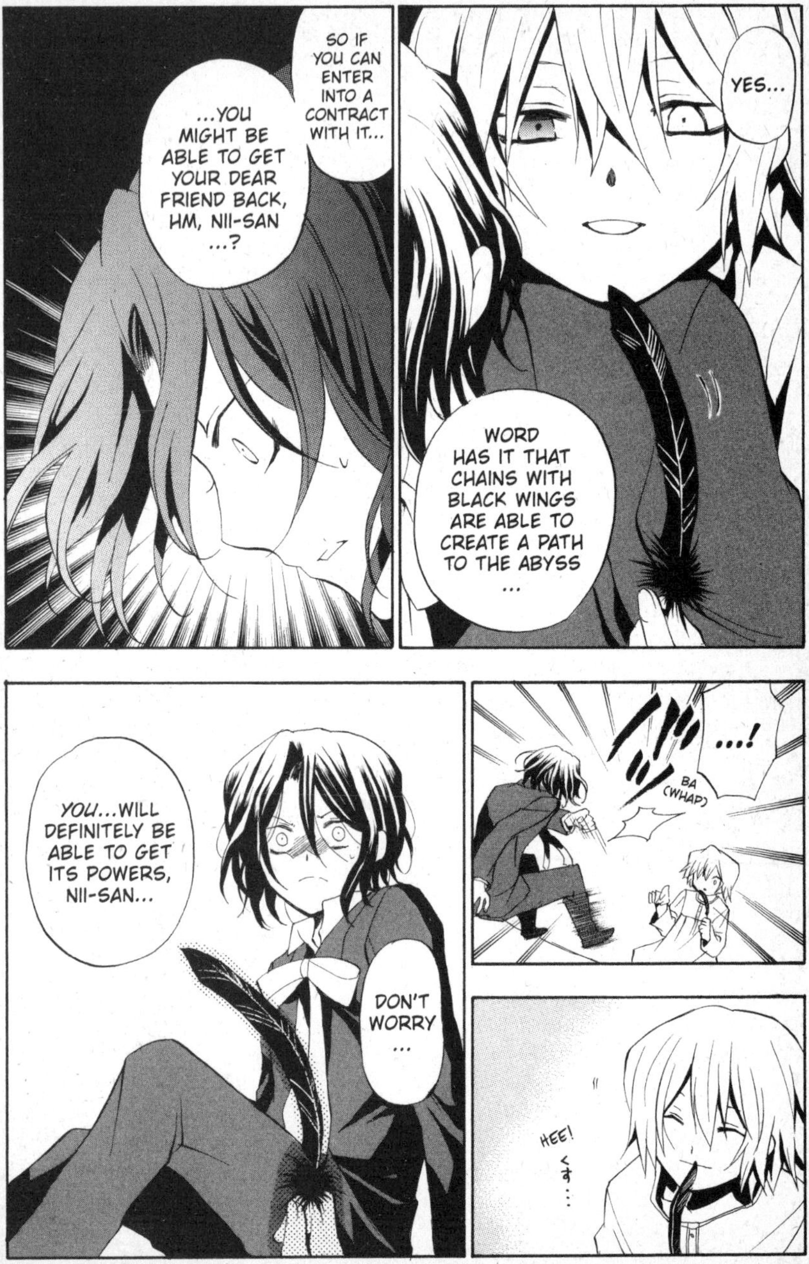
YES...
WORD HAS IT THAT CHAINS WITH BLACK WINGS ARE ABLE TO CREATE A PATH TO THE ABYSS ...
SO IF YOU CAN ENTER INTO A CONTRACT WITH IT...
...YOU MIGHT BE ABLE TO GET YOUR DEAR FRIEND BACK, HM, NII-SAN ...?
...!
BA (WHAP)
HEE!
くす...
DON'T WORRY ...
YOU...WILL DEFINITELY BE ABLE TO GET ITS POWERS, NII-SAN...

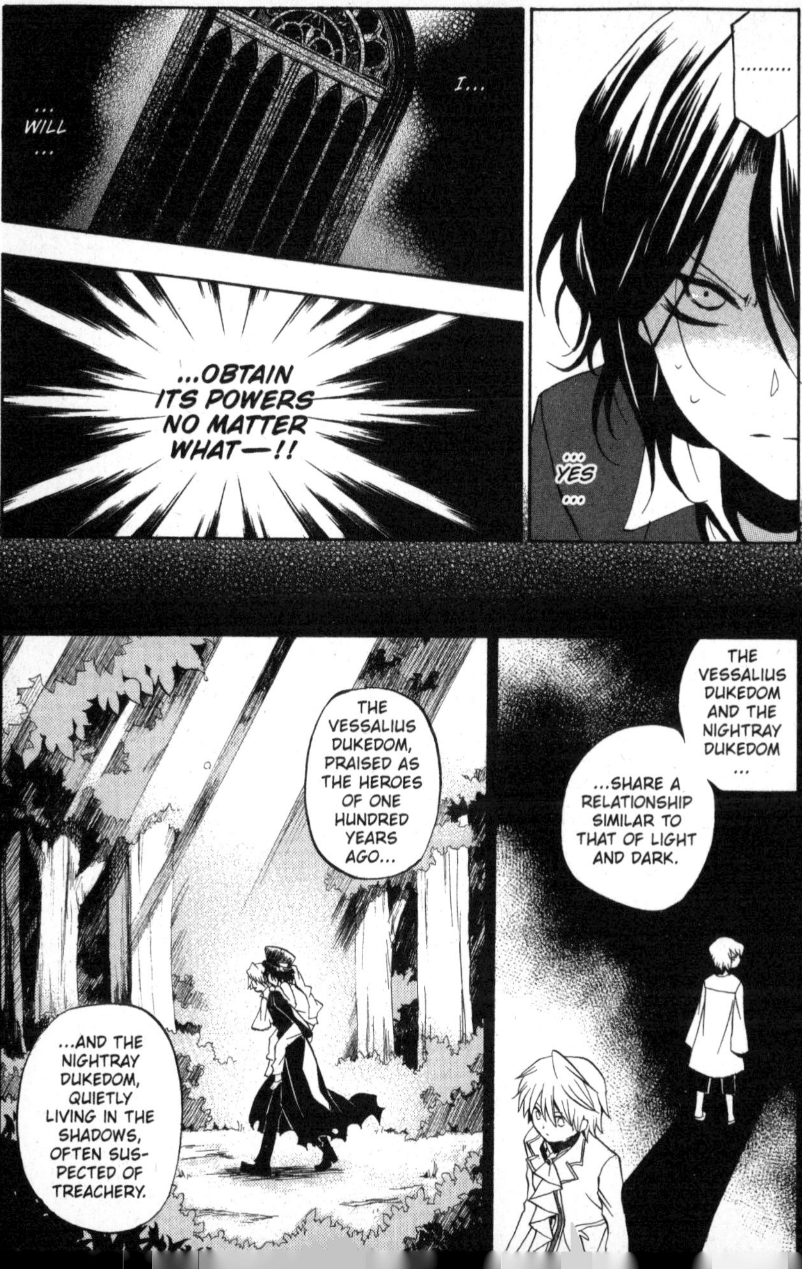
....
...YES...
I...
...WILL...
...OBTAIN ITS POWERS NO MATTER WHAT—!!
THE VESSALIUS DUKEDOM AND THE NIGHTRAY DUKEDOM...
...SHARE A RELATIONSHIP SIMILAR TO THAT OF LIGHT AND DARK.
THE VESSALIUS DUKEDOM, PRAISED AS THE HEROES OF ONE HUNDRED YEARS AGO...
...AND THE NIGHTRAY DUKEDOM, QUIETLY LIVING IN THE SHADOWS, OFTEN SUS-PECTED OF TREACHERY.

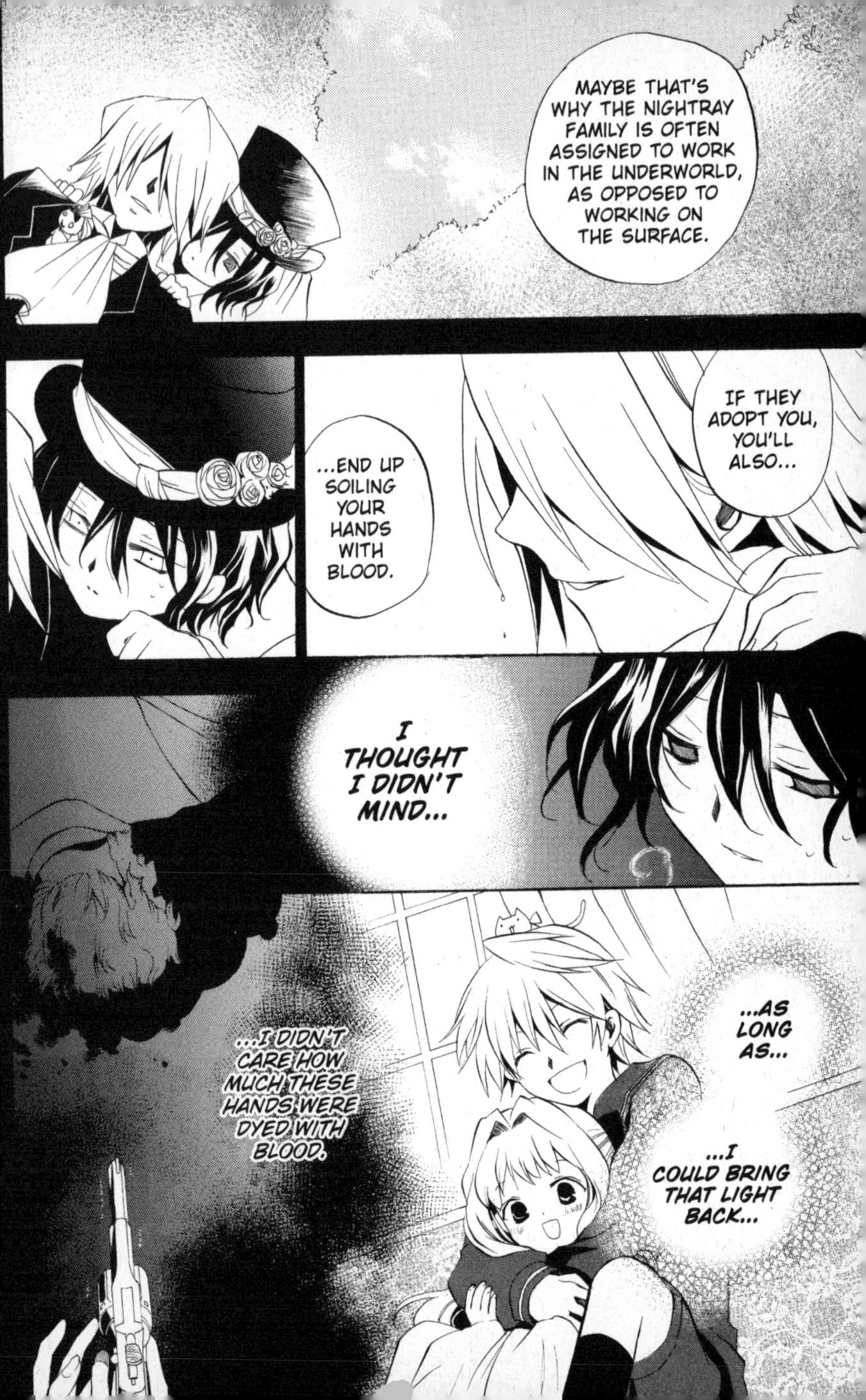
MAYBE THAT'S WHY THE NIGHTRAY FAMILY IS OFTEN ASSIGNED TO WORK IN THE UNDERWORLD, AS OPPOSED TO WORKING ON THE SURFACE.
IF THEY ADOPT YOU, YOU'LL ALSO...
...END UP SOILING YOUR HANDS WITH BLOOD.
I THOUGHT I DIDN'T MIND...
...AS LONG AS...
...I COULD BRING THAT LIGHT BACK...
...I DIDN'T CARE HOW MUCH THESE HANDS WERE DYED WITH BLOOD.

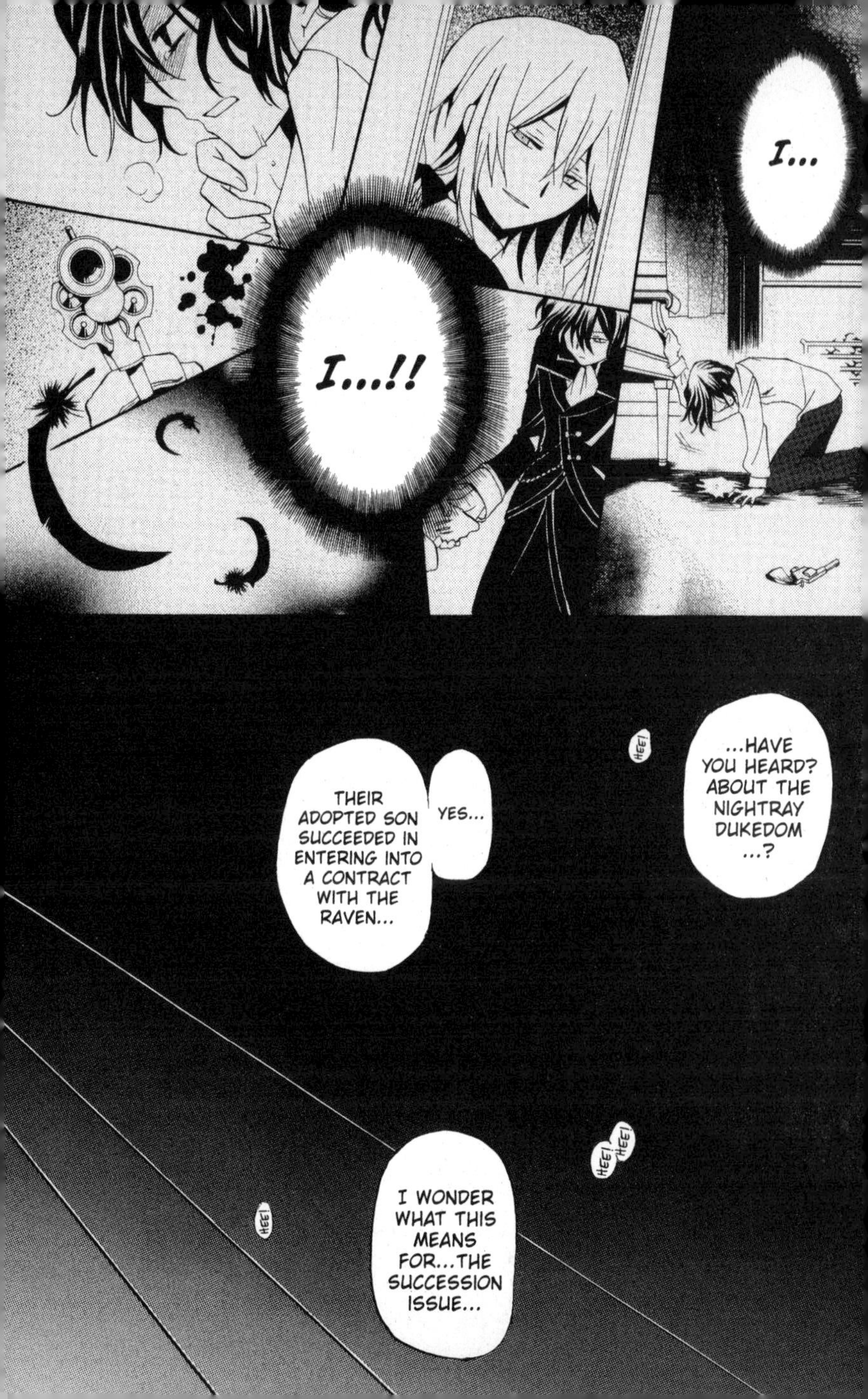
I...
I...!!
...HAVE YOU HEARD? ABOUT THE NIGHTRAY DUKEDOM ...?
HEE!
YES...
THEIR ADOPTED SON SUCCEEDED IN ENTERING INTO A CONTRACT WITH THE RAVEN...
HEE!
HEE!
I WONDER WHAT THIS MEANS FOR...THE SUCCESSION ISSUE...
HEE!

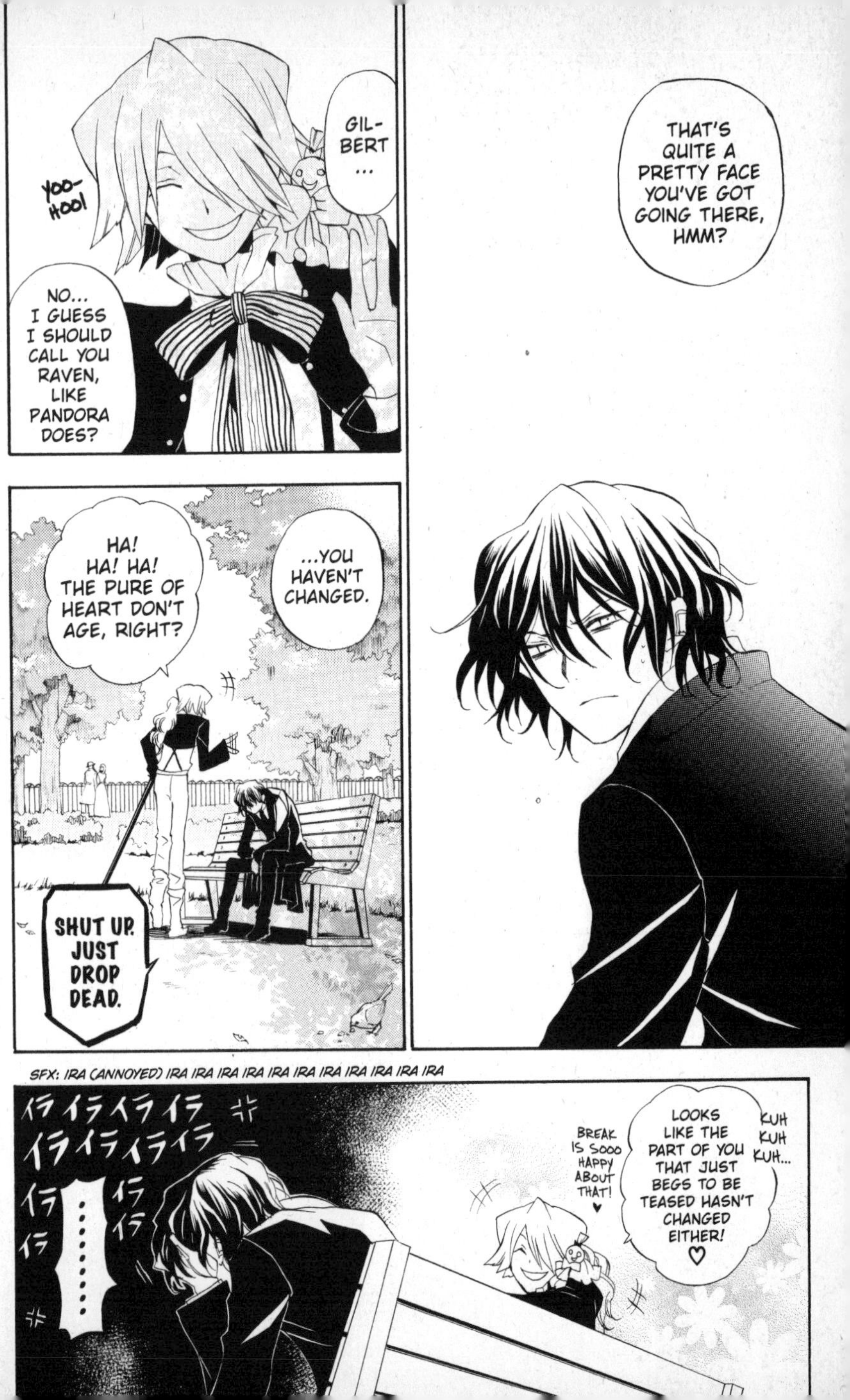
THAT'S QUITE A PRETTY FACE YOU'VE GOT GOING THERE, HMM?
GIL-BERT ...
YOO-HOO!
NO... I GUESS I SHOULD CALL YOU RAVEN, LIKE PANDORA DOES?
...YOU HAVEN'T CHANGED.
HA! HA! HA! THE PURE OF HEART DON'T AGE, RIGHT?
SHUT UP. JUST DROP DEAD.
SFX: IRA (ANNOYED) IRA IRA IRA IRA IRA IRA IRA IRA IRA IRA IRA
KUH KUH KUH...
LOOKS LIKE THE PART OF YOU THAT JUST BEGS TO BE TEASED HASN'T CHANGED EITHER! ♡
BREAK IS SOOO HAPPY ABOUT THAT! ♥
イライライライラ
イライライライラ
イラ イラ
イラ
....

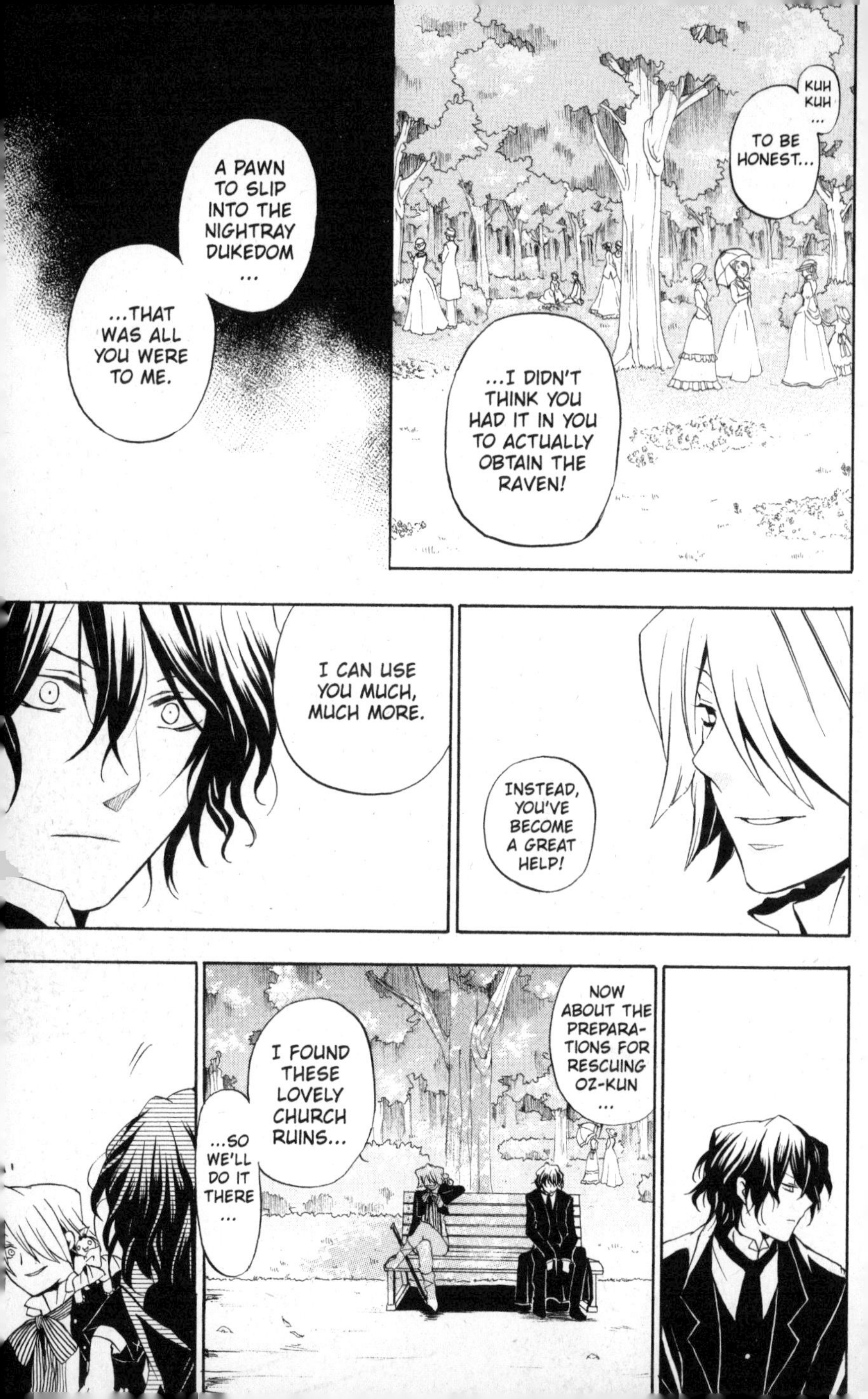
KUH KUH ...
TO BE HONEST...
...I DIDN'T THINK YOU HAD IT IN YOU TO ACTUALLY OBTAIN THE RAVEN!
A PAWN TO SLIP INTO THE NIGHTRAY DUKEDOM ...
...THAT WAS ALL YOU WERE TO ME.
INSTEAD, YOU'VE BECOME A GREAT HELP!
I CAN USE YOU MUCH, MUCH MORE.
NOW ABOUT THE PREPARATIONS FOR RESCUING OZ-KUN ...
I FOUND THESE LOVELY CHURCH RUINS...
...SO WE'LL DO IT THERE ...

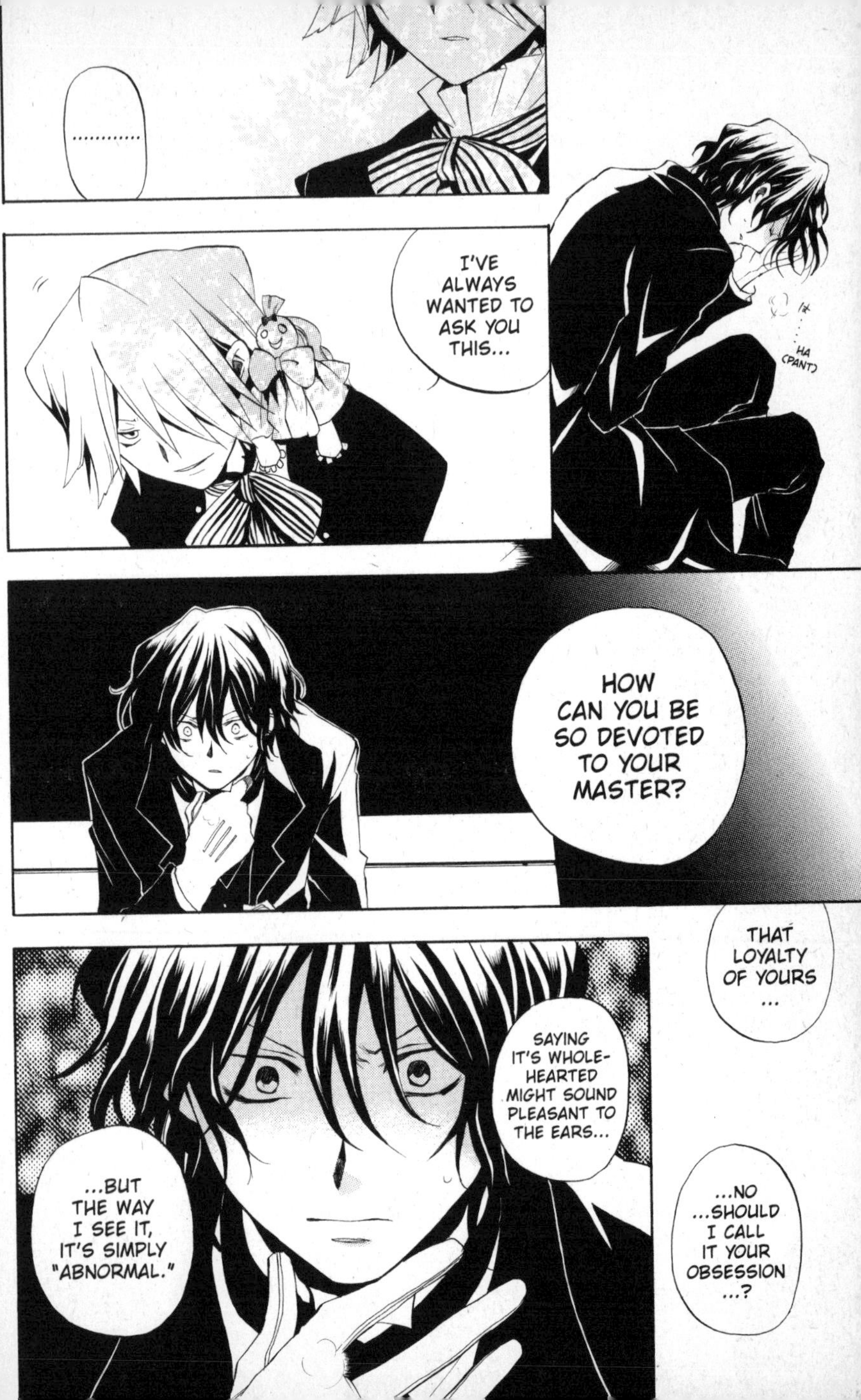
....
HA (PANT)
I'VE ALWAYS WANTED TO ASK YOU THIS...
HOW CAN YOU BE SO DEVOTED TO YOUR MASTER?
THAT LOYALTY OF YOURS ...
SAYING IT'S WHOLE-HEARTED MIGHT SOUND PLEASANT TO THE EARS...
...BUT THE WAY I SEE IT, IT'S SIMPLY "ABNORMAL."
...NO ...SHOULD I CALL IT YOUR OBSESSION ...?

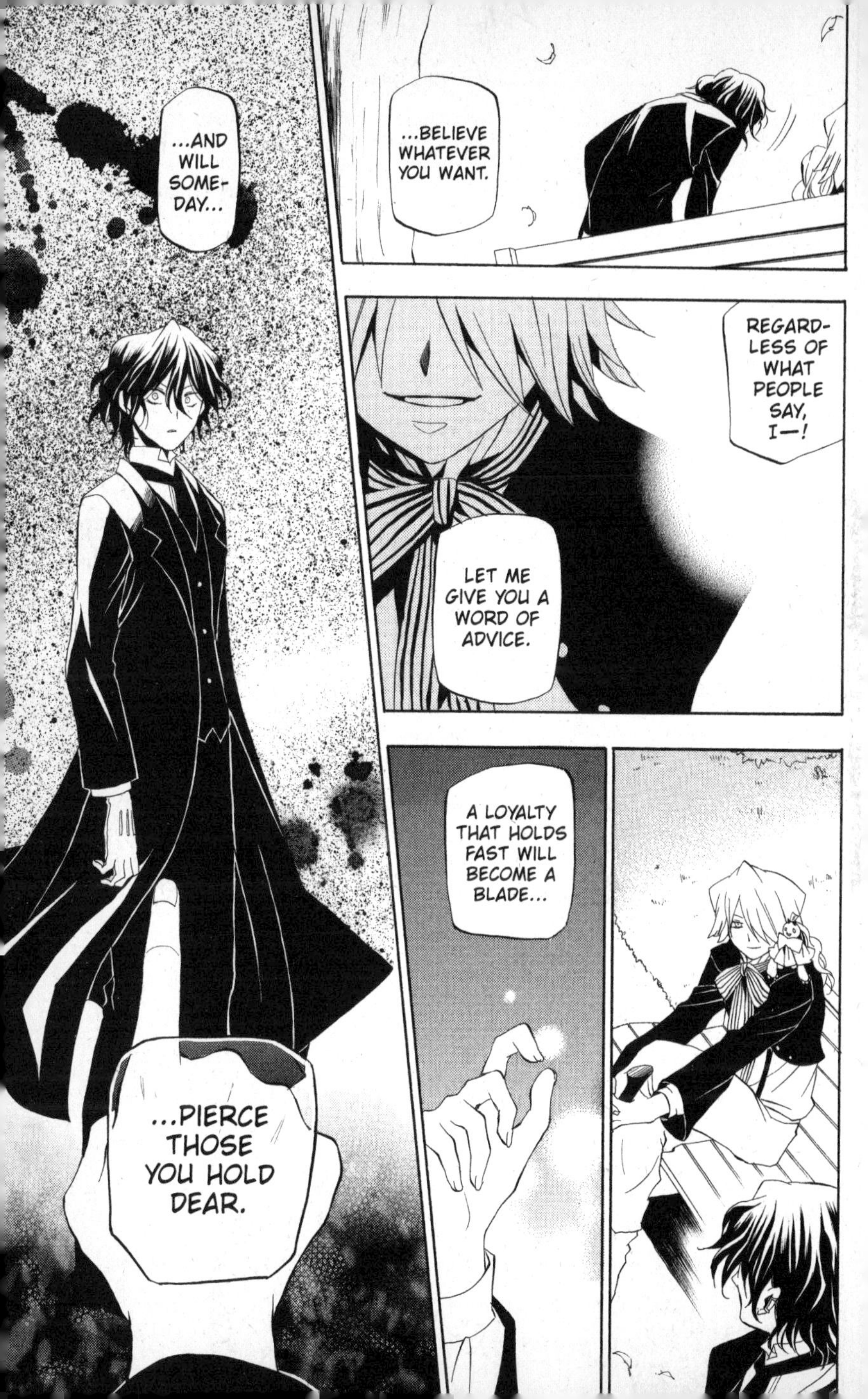
...BELIEVE WHATEVER YOU WANT.
REGARDLESS OF WHAT PEOPLE SAY, I—!
LET ME GIVE YOU A WORD OF ADVICE.
A LOYALTY THAT HOLDS FAST WILL BECOME A BLADE...
...AND WILL SOME-DAY...
...PIERCE THOSE YOU HOLD DEAR.

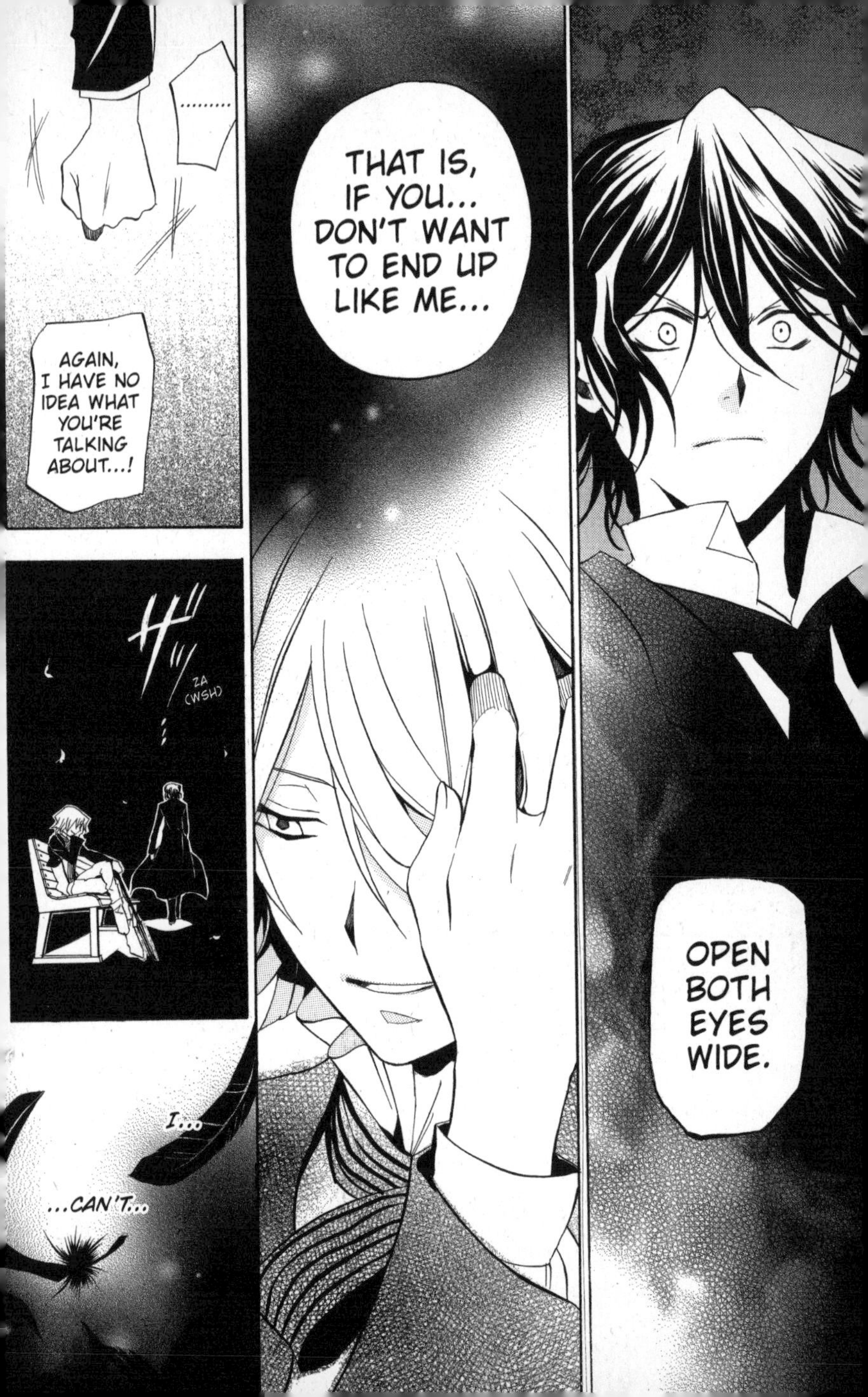
OPEN BOTH EYES WIDE.
THAT IS, IF YOU... DON'T WANT TO END UP LIKE ME...
....
AGAIN, I HAVE NO IDEA WHAT YOU'RE TALKING ABOUT...!
ZA (WSH)
I...
...CAN'T...

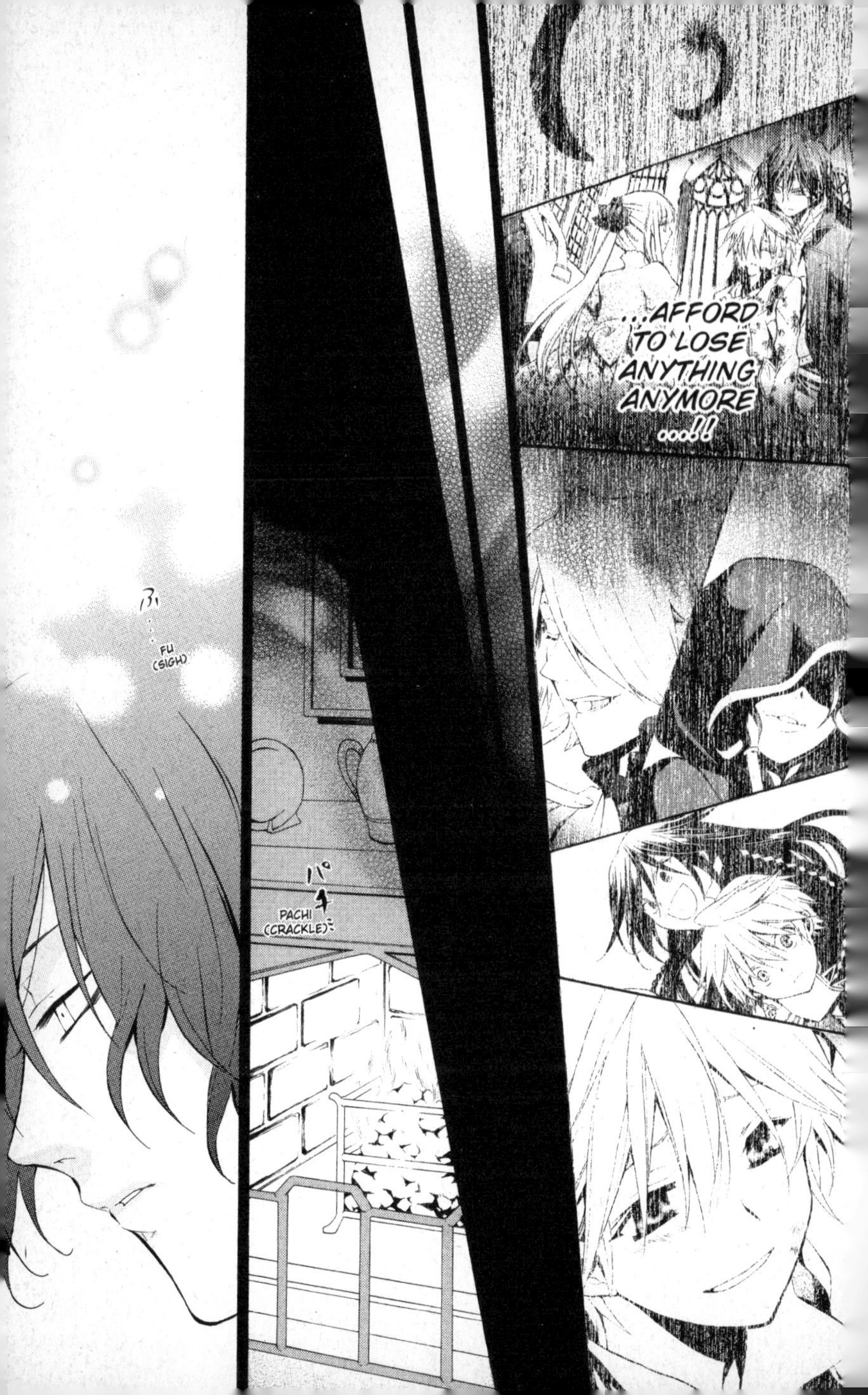
...AFFORD TO LOSE ANYTHING ANYMORE ...!!
パチ
PACHI (CRACKLE)
ふ...
FU (SIGH)

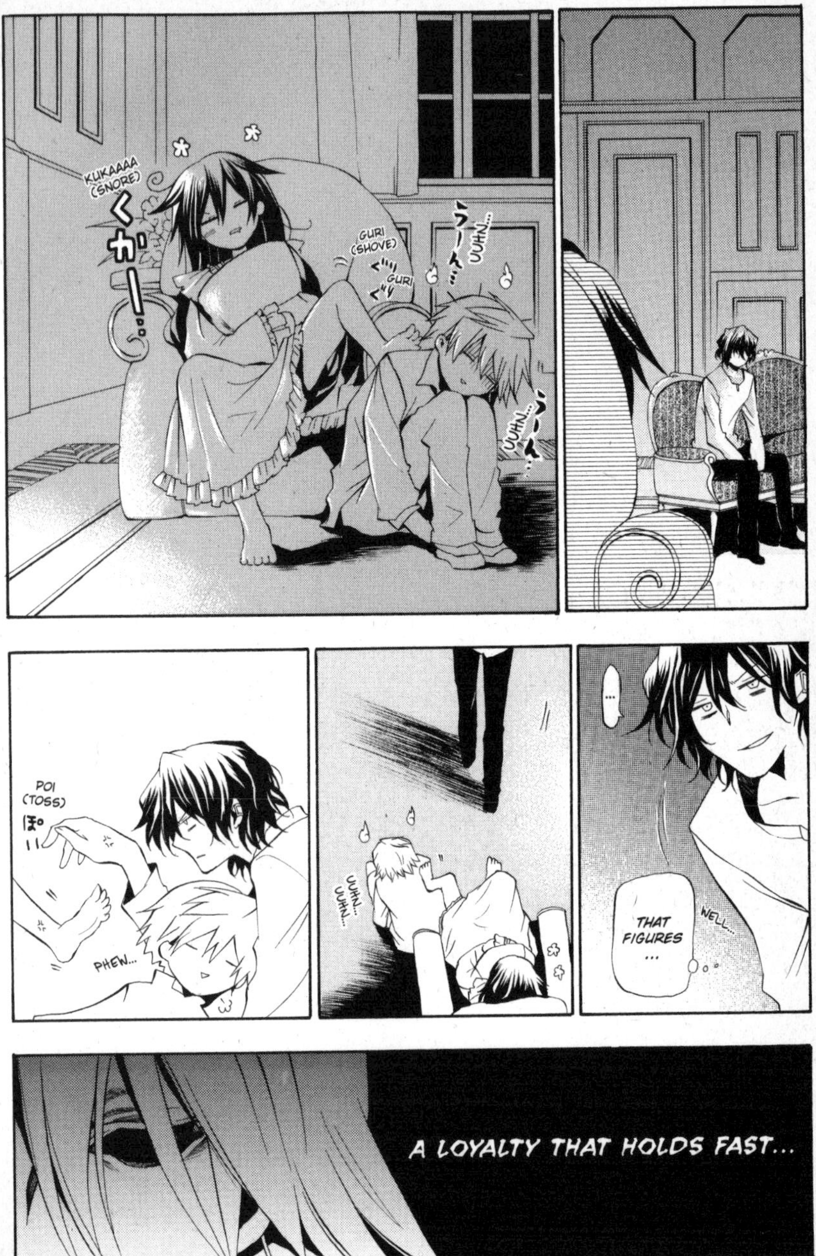
UUHN...
うーん…
GURI (SHOVE)
ぐり
GURI
ぐり
KUKAAAA (SNORE)
くかー!!
UUHN...
うーん…
...
WELL...
THAT FIGURES ...
UUHN... UUHN...
POI (TOSS)
ぽい
PHEW...
A LOYALTY THAT HOLDS FAST...

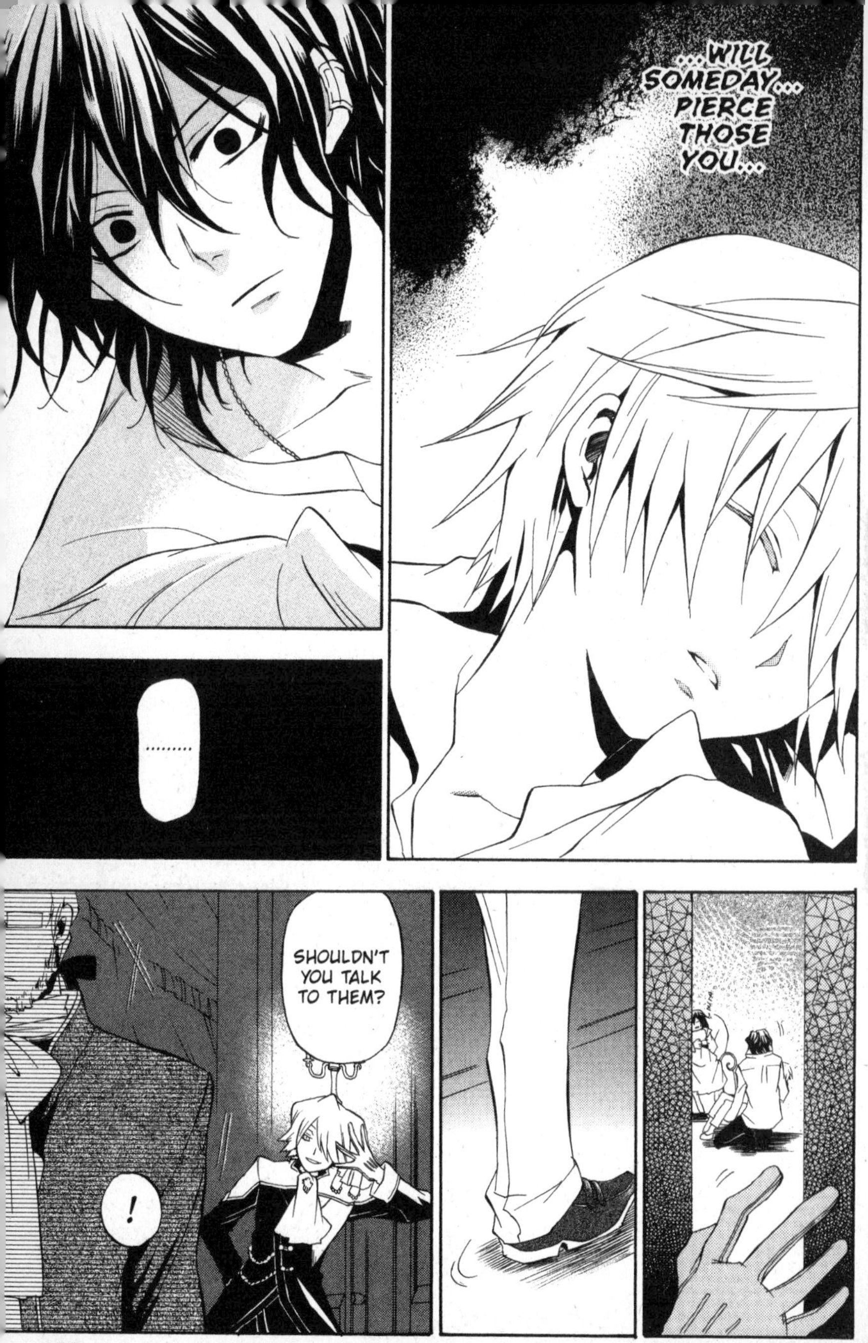

...WILL SOMEDAY... PIERCE THOSE YOU...
....
SHOULDN'T YOU TALK TO THEM?
!

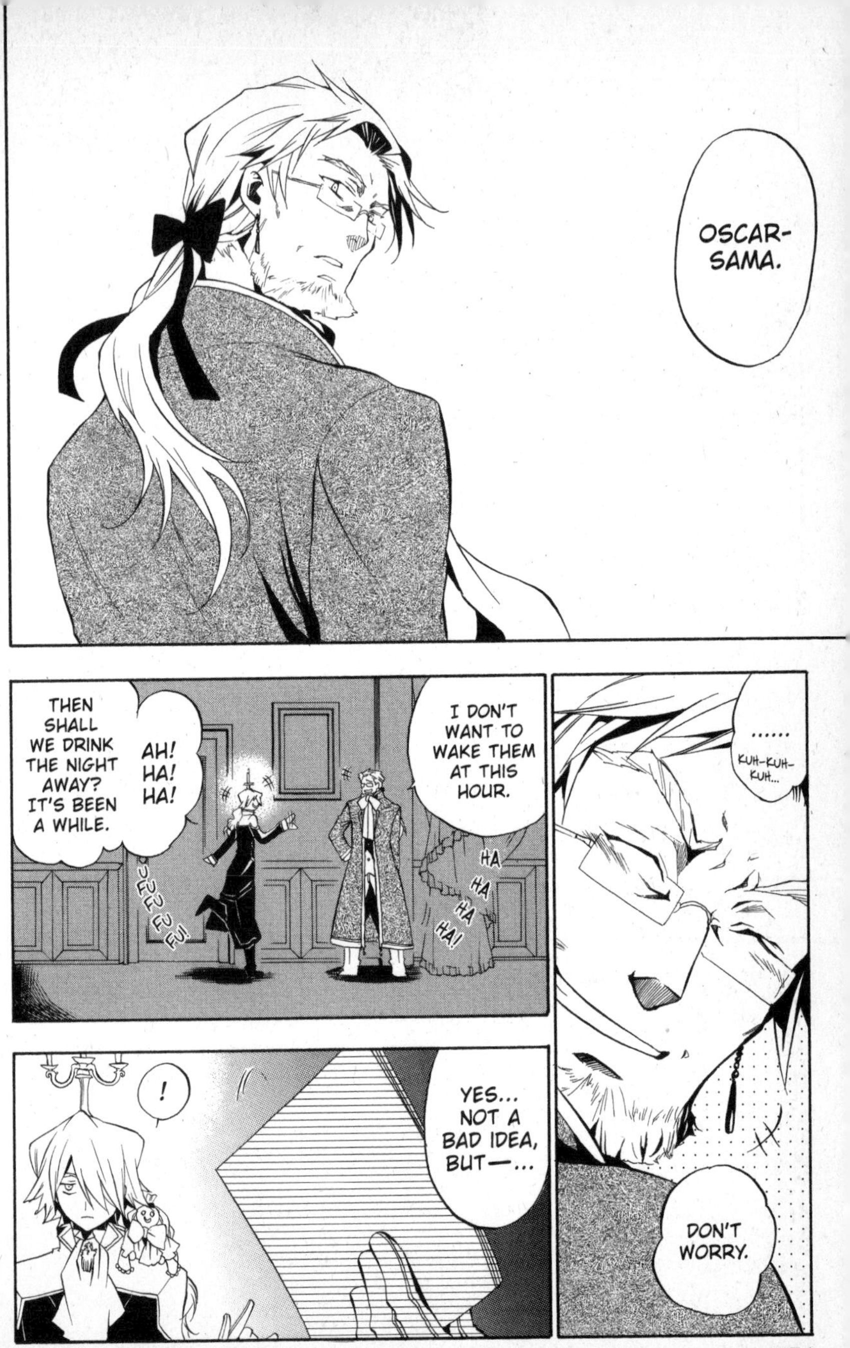
OSCAR-SAMA.
......
KUH-KUH-KUH...
DON'T WORRY.
I DON'T WANT TO WAKE THEM AT THIS HOUR.
HA HA HA HA!
AH! HA! HA!
THEN SHALL WE DRINK THE NIGHT AWAY? IT'S BEEN A WHILE.
UFUFUFUFU!
YES... NOT A BAD IDEA, BUT—...
!

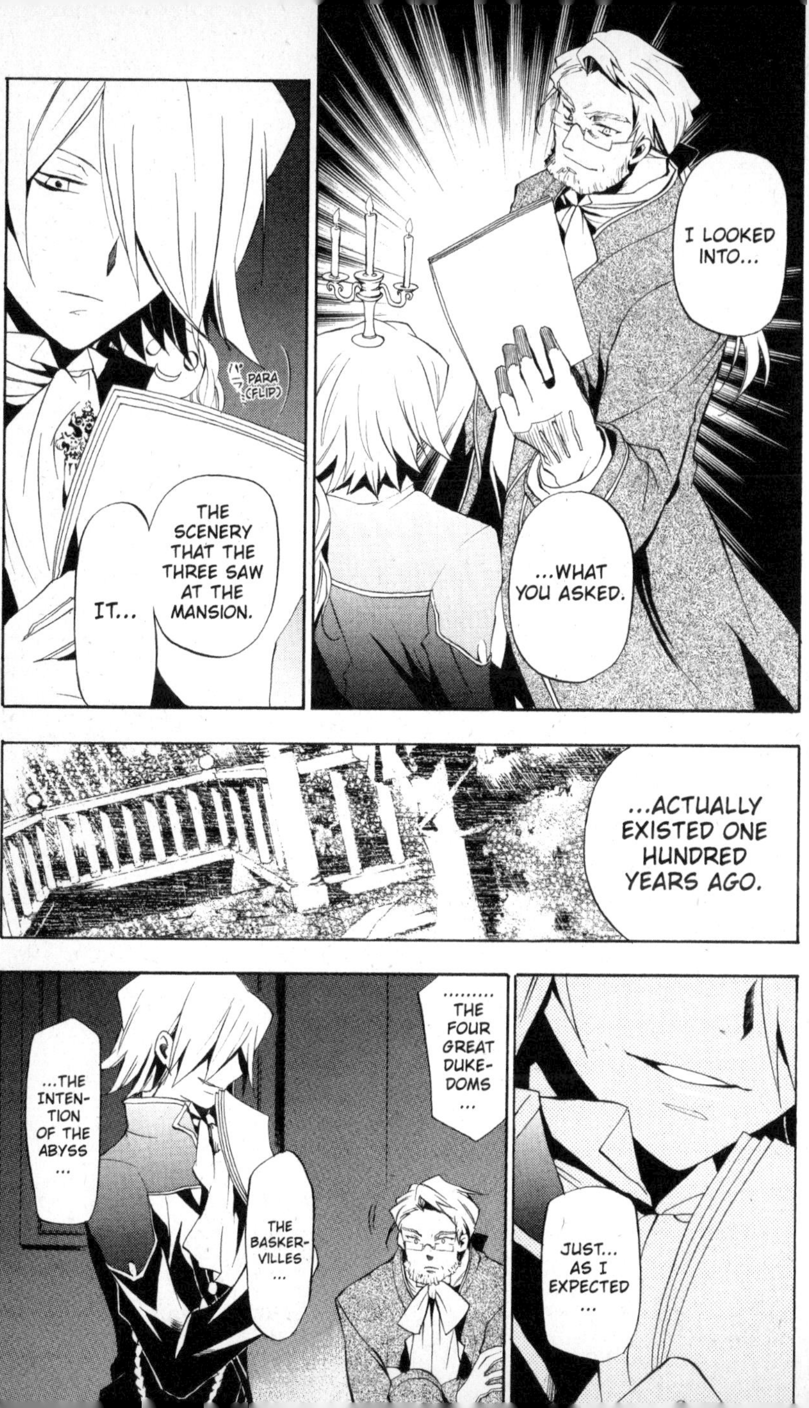
I LOOKED INTO...
...WHAT YOU ASKED.
THE SCENERY THAT THE THREE SAW AT THE MANSION.
IT...
PARA (FLIP)
...ACTUALLY EXISTED ONE HUNDRED YEARS AGO.
JUST... AS I EXPECTED ...
.... THE FOUR GREAT DUKE-DOMS ...
...THE INTEN-TION OF THE ABYSS ...
THE BASKER-VILLES ...

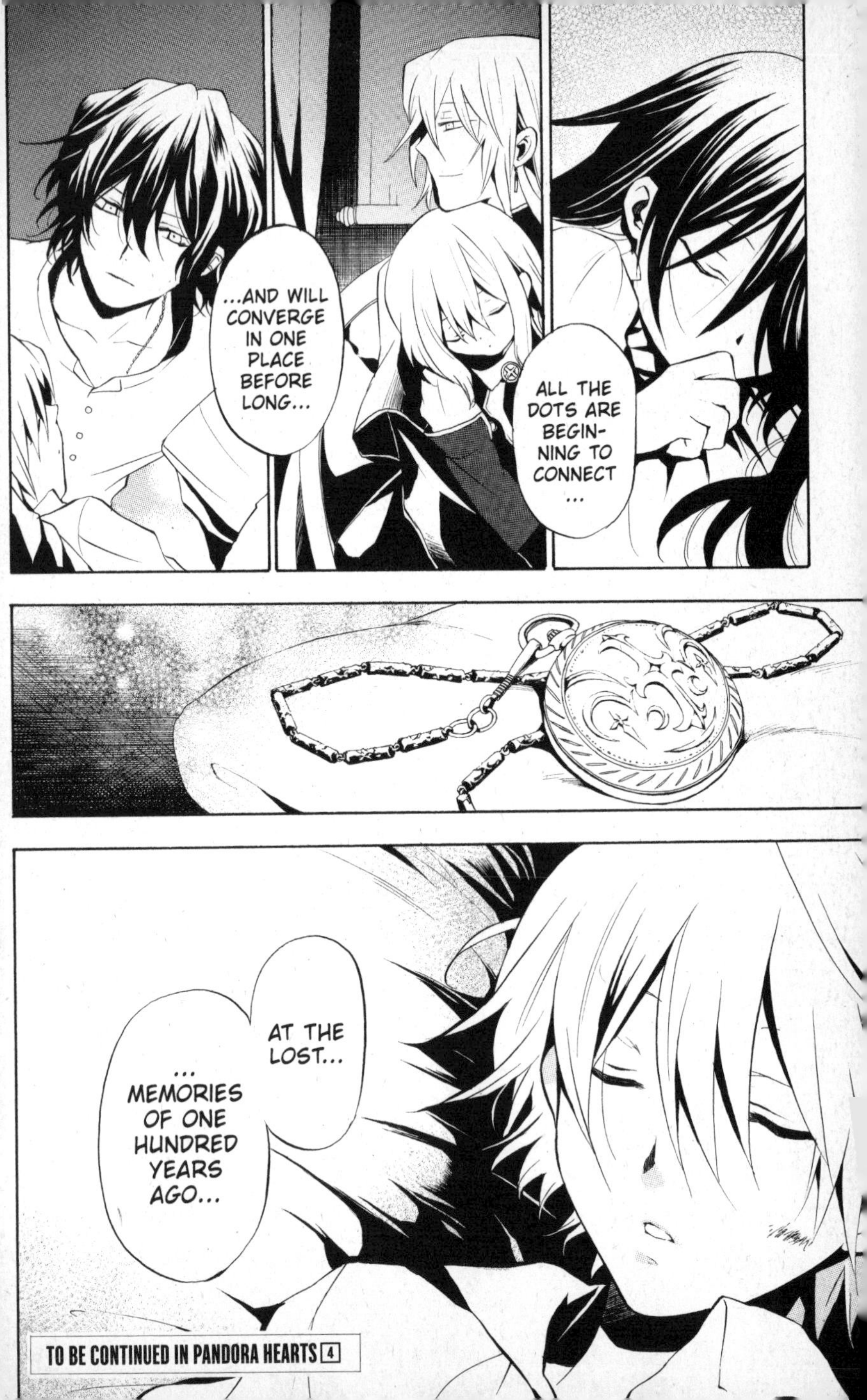
ALL THE DOTS ARE BEGIN-NING TO CONNECT...
...AND WILL CONVERGE IN ONE PLACE BEFORE LONG...
AT THE LOST...
...MEMORIES OF ONE HUNDRED YEARS AGO...
TO BE CONTINUED IN PANDORA HEARTS 4

Special Thanks!

FUMITO YAMAZAKI
SEIRA MINAMI-SAN
SOUICHIROU-SAN
CHIYO AYABA-SAN
BIREN KEIZUKI-SAN
SHINYUU-SAAAAN ☆
K-SAN AND T-SAN

MY EDITOR,
TAKEGASA-SAMA-SAMA-SAMA-SAMA

AND YOU !!!

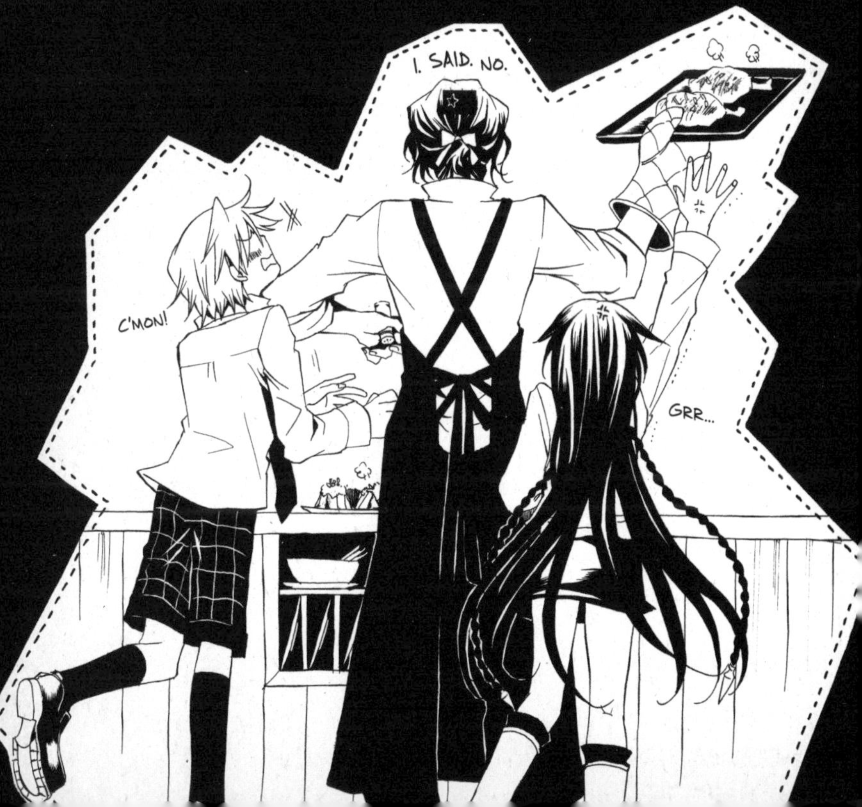
I. SAID. NO.
GRR...
C'MON!

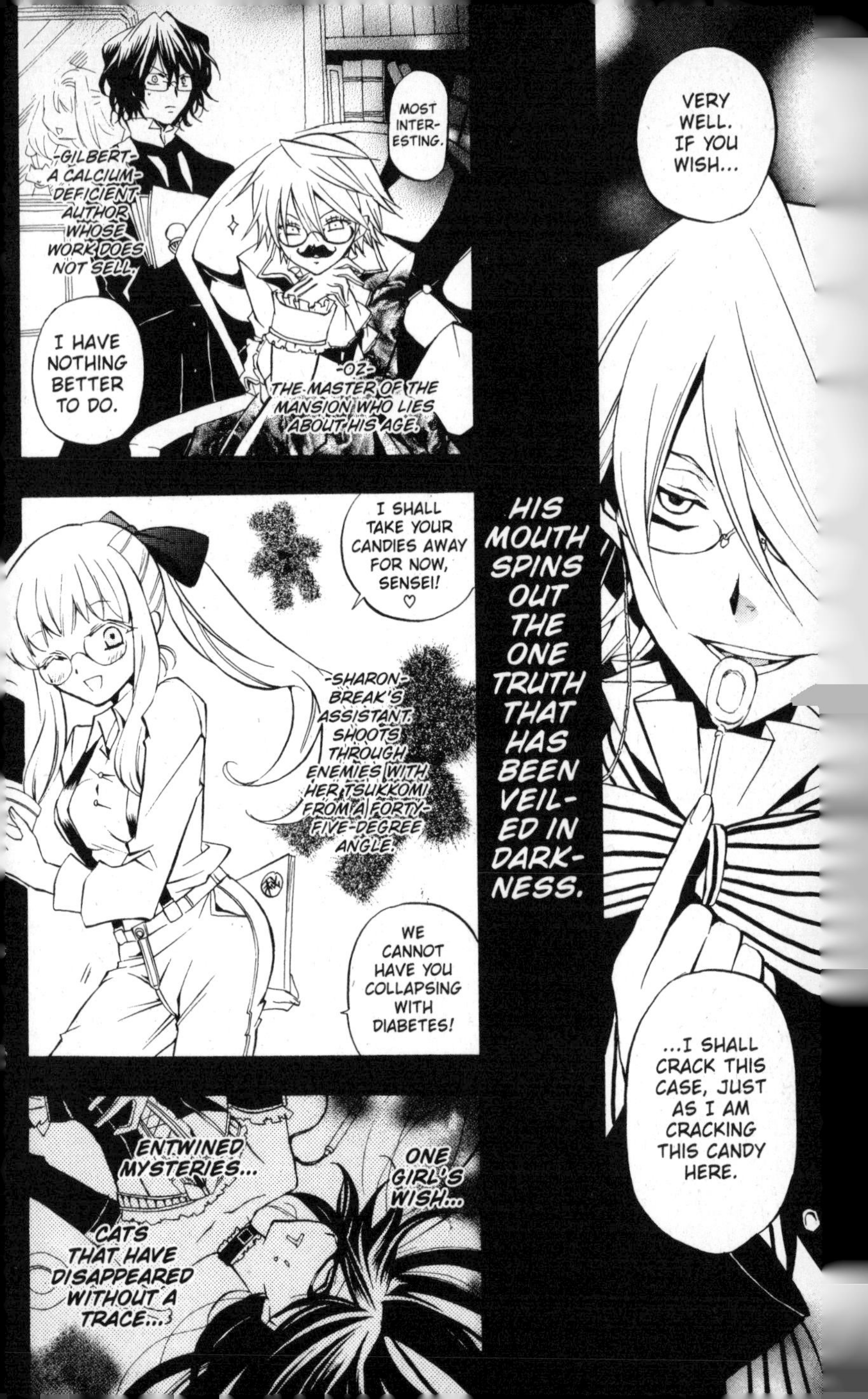
VERY WELL. IF YOU WISH...
HIS MOUTH SPINS OUT THE ONE TRUTH THAT HAS BEEN VEIL-ED IN DARK-NESS.
...I SHALL CRACK THIS CASE, JUST AS I AM CRACKING THIS CANDY HERE.
MOST INTER-ESTING.
-GILBERT- A CALCIUM-DEFICIENT AUTHOR WHOSE WORK DOES NOT SELL.
-OZ- THE MASTER OF THE MANSION WHO LIES ABOUT HIS AGE.
I HAVE NOTHING BETTER TO DO.
I SHALL TAKE YOUR CANDIES AWAY FOR NOW, SENSEI! ♡
-SHARON- BREAK'S ASSISTANT. SHOOTS THROUGH ENEMIES WITH HER TSUKKOMI FROM A FORTY-FIVE-DEGREE ANGLE.
WE CANNOT HAVE YOU COLLAPSING WITH DIABETES!
ONE GIRL'S WISH...
ENTWINED MYSTERIES...
CATS THAT HAVE DISAPPEARED WITHOUT A TRACE...

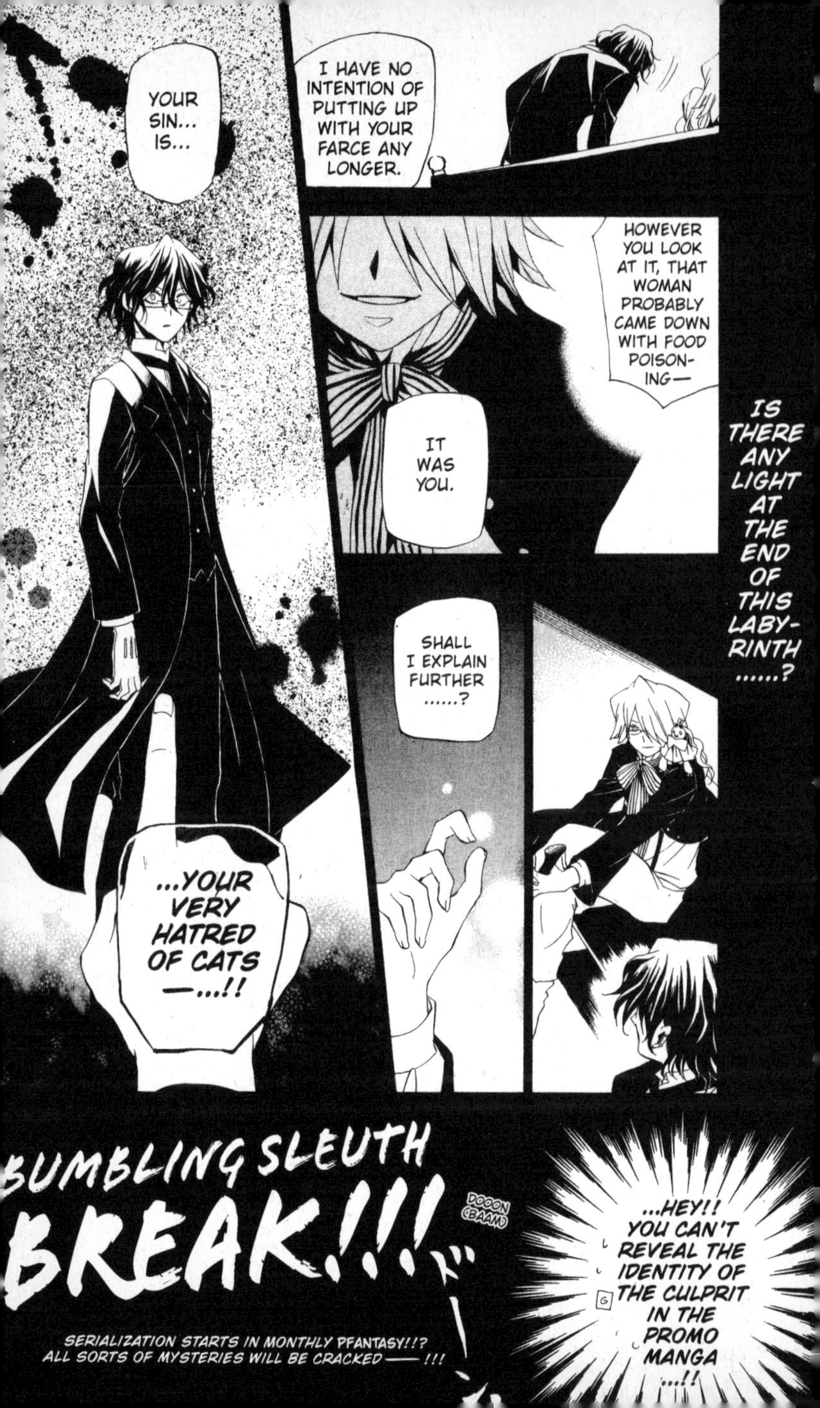

I HAVE NO INTENTION OF PUTTING UP WITH YOUR FARCE ANY LONGER.
HOWEVER YOU LOOK AT IT, THAT WOMAN PROBABLY CAME DOWN WITH FOOD POISONING—
IT WAS YOU.
IS THERE ANY LIGHT AT THE END OF THIS LABYRINTH......?
SHALL I EXPLAIN FURTHER......?
YOUR SIN... IS...
...YOUR VERY HATRED OF CATS—...!!
...HEY!! YOU CAN'T REVEAL THE IDENTITY OF THE CULPRIT IN THE PROMO MANGA...!!
BUMBLING SLEUTH BREAK!!!
DOOON (BAAM)
SERIALIZATION STARTS IN MONTHLY PFANTASY!!?
ALL SORTS OF MYSTERIES WILL BE CRACKED——!!!

COMMON HONORIFICS

no honorific: Indicates familiarity or closeness; if used without permission or reason, addressing someone in this manner would constitute an insult.

-san: The Japanese equivalent of Mr./Mrs./Miss. If a situation calls for politeness, this is the fail-safe honorific.

-sama: Conveys great respect; may also indicate that the social status of the speaker is lower than that of the addressee.

-kun: Used most often when referring to boys (though it can be applied to girls as well), this indicates affection or familiarity. Occasionally used by older men among their peers, but it may also be used by anyone referring to a person of lower standing.

-chan: An affectionate honorific indicating familiarity used mostly in reference to girls; also used in reference to cute persons or animals of either gender.

Echo's bow   page 57

The "forty-five degree bow" is a very polite form of bowing. (The other two forms are the "fifteen degree" and the "thirty degree" bows.)

tsukkomi   page 178

The straight man in Japanese two-person stand-up comedy (*manzai*) who is also prone to hitting his/her partner for being a fool.

Bumbling Sleuth Break   page 179

A play on words, the title of this detective series parody reads *Meitantei Bureiku*, which would normally be "Great Detective Break" in this context. However, because of the kanji used in writing it, the title ends up being homophonous, literally reading "Bumbling Sleuth Insolent Saying."

PandoraHearts

I'm scared about my new cell phone vibrating on its own when it shouldn't be. And I feel it's been happening more often lately......(*shake shake shake*) Is it the grudge of my previous phone, which lost its life after I dropped it into my coffee...!?

MOCHIZUKI'S MUSINGS

VOLUME 3

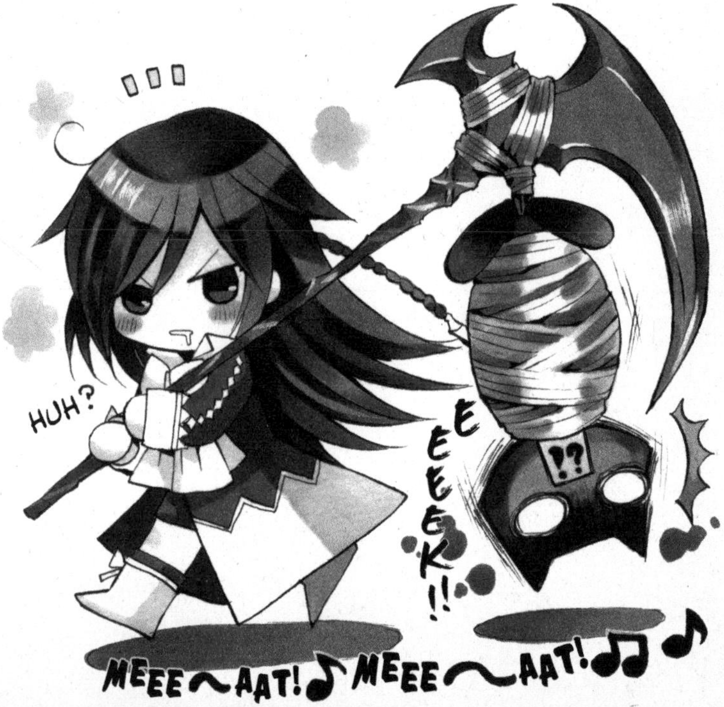
HUH?
EEEEEK!!
!?
MEEE~AAT!♪ MEEE~AAT!♫♪

PandoraHearts

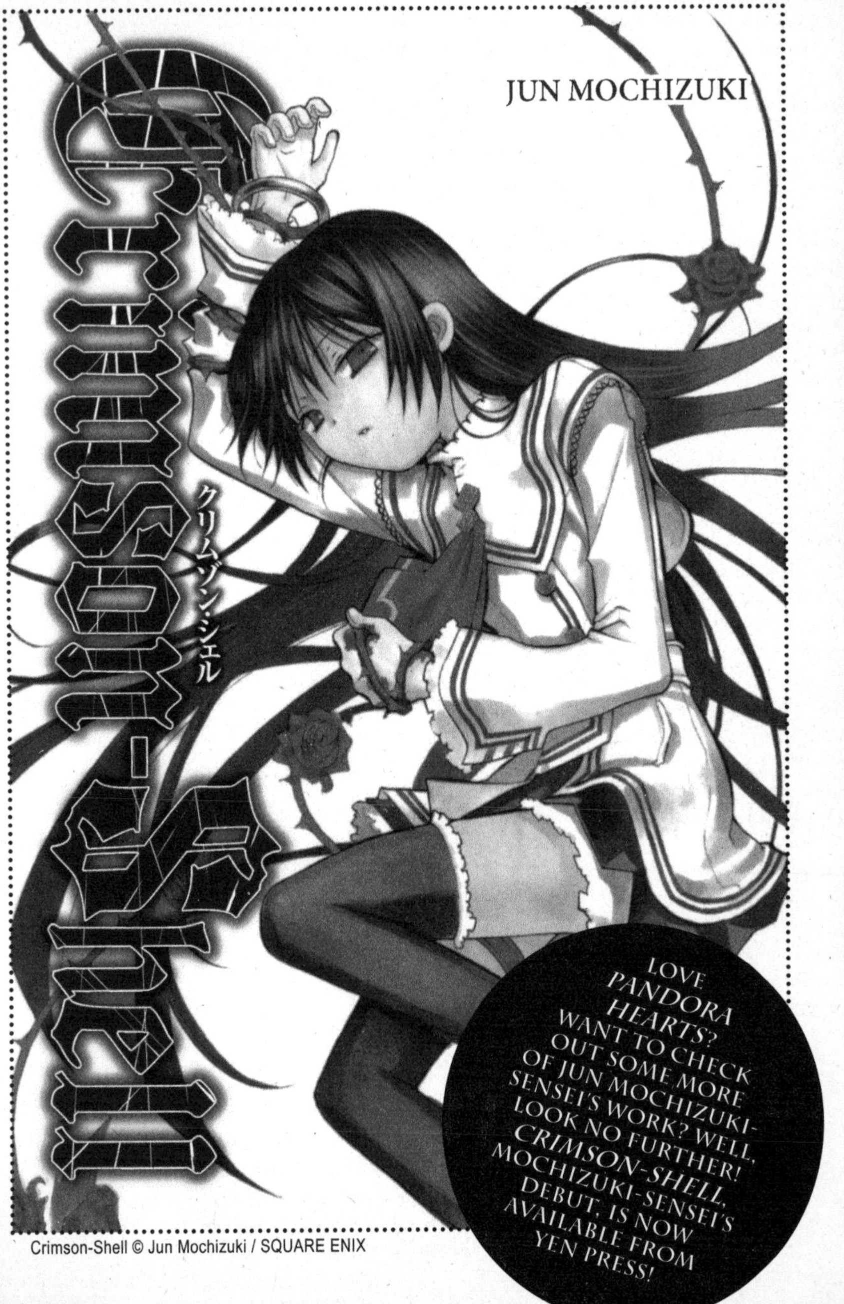
Crimson-Shell
クリムゾン・シェル
JUN MOCHIZUKI
LOVE PANDORA HEARTS? WANT TO CHECK OUT SOME MORE OF JUN MOCHIZUKI-SENSEI'S WORK? WELL, LOOK NO FURTHER! CRIMSON-SHELL, MOCHIZUKI-SENSEI'S DEBUT, IS NOW AVAILABLE FROM YEN PRESS!

PandoraHearts

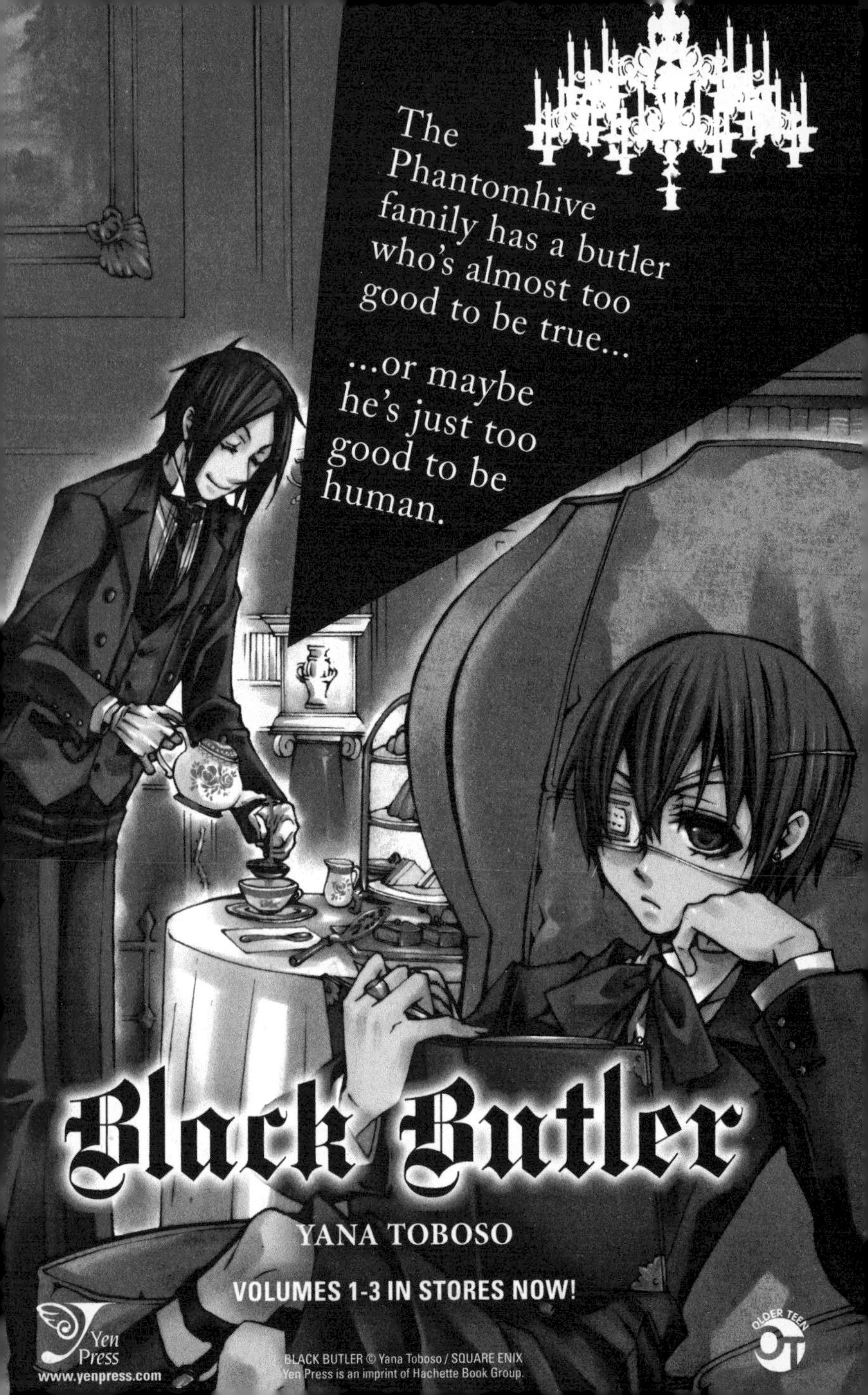
The Phantomhive family has a butler who's almost too good to be true...
...or maybe he's just too good to be human.
Black Butler
YANA TOBOSO
VOLUMES 1-3 IN STORES NOW!
Yen Press
www.yenpress.com
OLDER TEEN
OT
BLACK BUTLER © Yana Toboso / SQUARE ENIX
Yen Press is an imprint of Hachette Book Group.

THE POWER
TO RULE THE
HIDDEN WORLD
OF SHINOBI...

THE POWER
COVETED BY
EVERY NINJA
CLAN...

...LIES WITHIN
THE MOST
APATHETIC,
DISINTERESTED
VESSEL
IMAGINABLE.

Nabari No Ou
Yuhki Kamatani

MANGA VOLUMES 1-4
NOW AVAILABLE

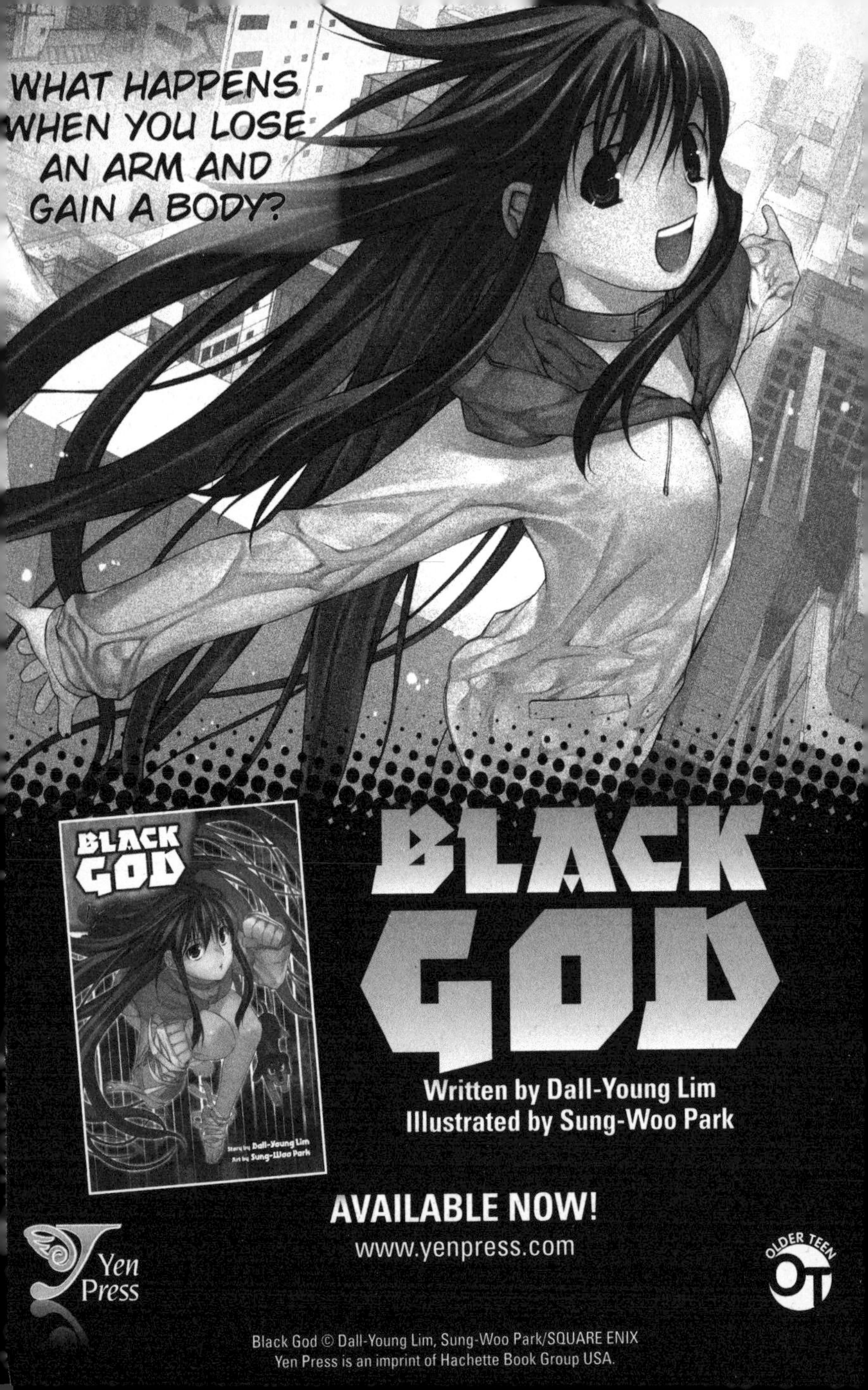
WHAT HAPPENS WHEN YOU LOSE AN ARM AND GAIN A BODY?
BLACK GOD
Story by Dall-Young Lim
Art by Sung-Woo Park
BLACK GOD
Written by Dall-Young Lim
Illustrated by Sung-Woo Park
AVAILABLE NOW!
www.yenpress.com
Yen Press
OLDER TEEN
OT
Black God © Dall-Young Lim, Sung-Woo Park/SQUARE ENIX
Yen Press is an imprint of Hachette Book Group USA.

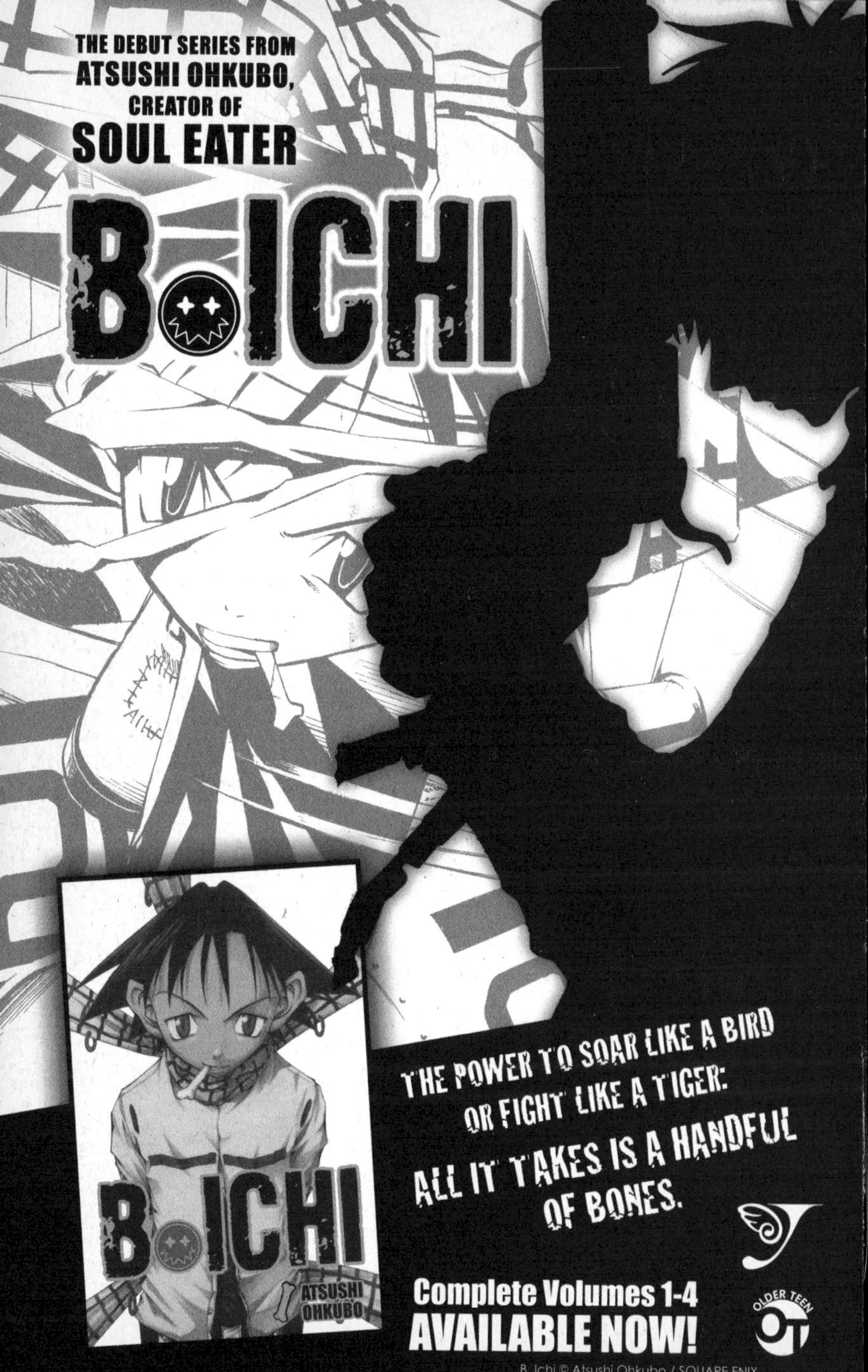
THE DEBUT SERIES FROM
ATSUSHI OHKUBO,
CREATOR OF
SOUL EATER
B. ICHI
THE POWER TO SOAR LIKE A BIRD
OR FIGHT LIKE A TIGER:
ALL IT TAKES IS A HANDFUL
OF BONES.
B. ICHI
ATSUSHI OHKUBO
Complete Volumes 1-4
AVAILABLE NOW!
OLDER TEEN
OT

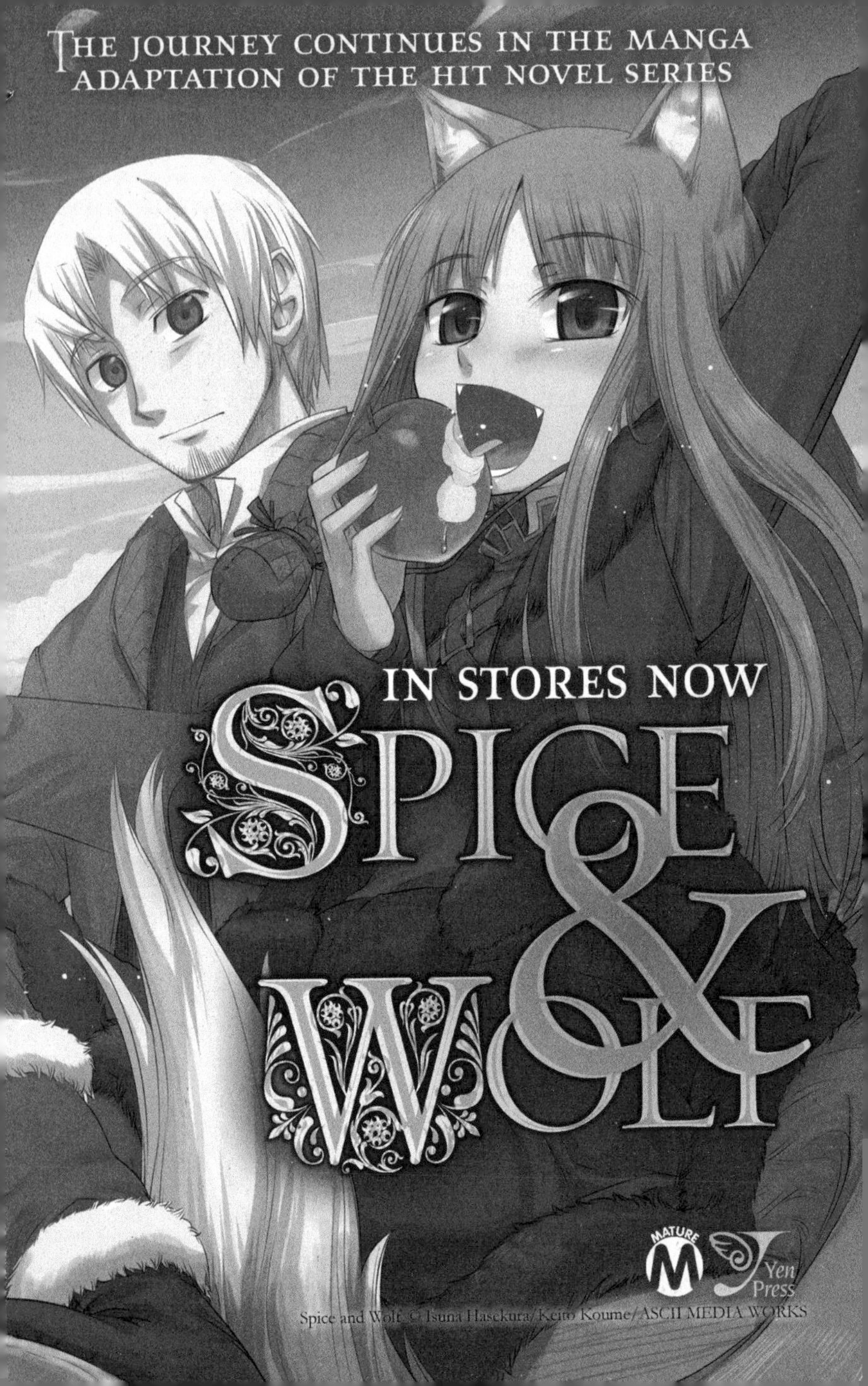
THE JOURNEY CONTINUES IN THE MANGA ADAPTATION OF THE HIT NOVEL SERIES
IN STORES NOW
SPICE & WOLF
MATURE
Yen Press
Spice and Wolf © Isuna Hasekura/Keito Koume/ASCII MEDIA WORKS

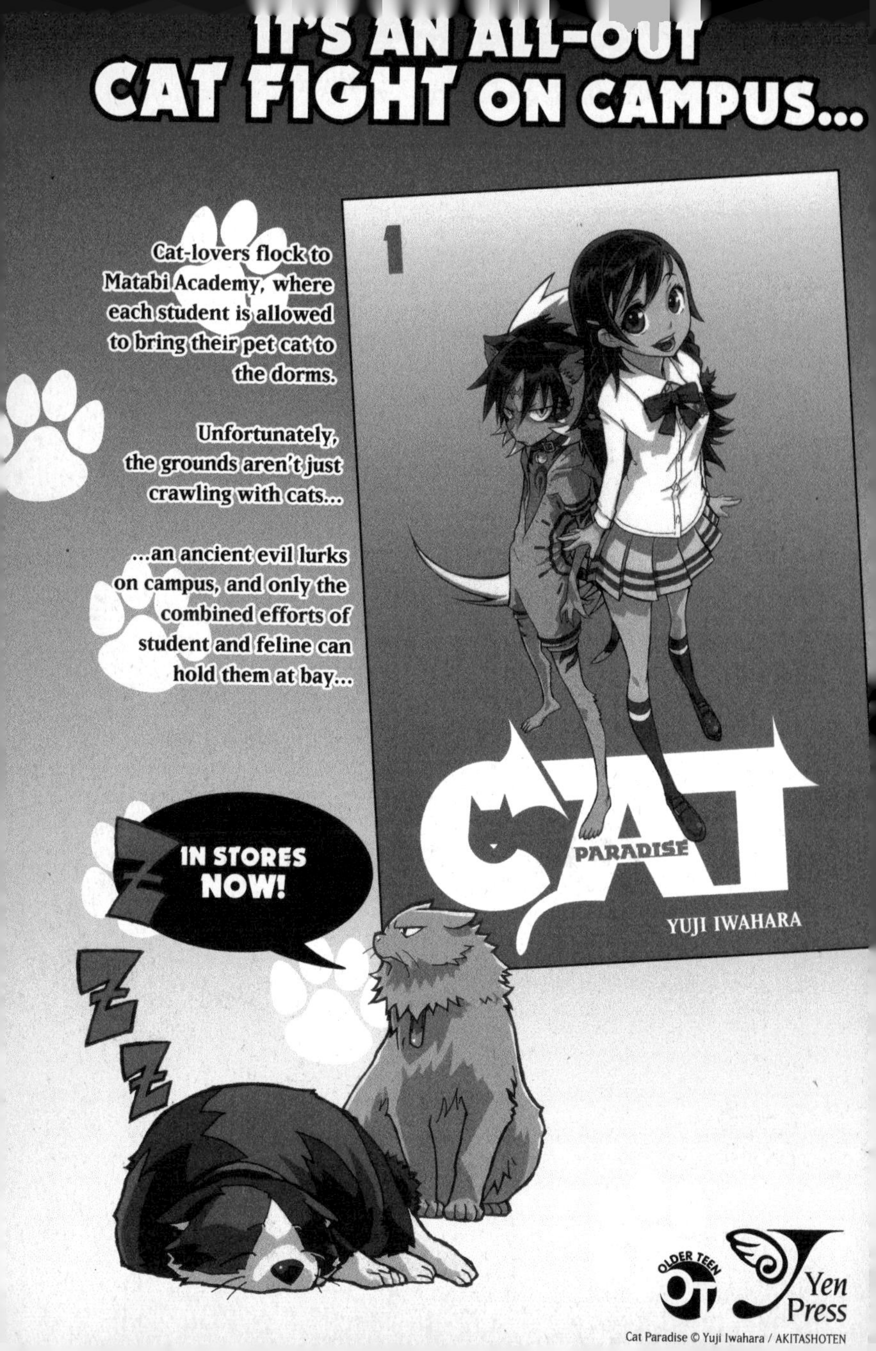
IT'S AN ALL-OUT
CAT FIGHT ON CAMPUS...
Cat-lovers flock to Matabi Academy, where each student is allowed to bring their pet cat to the dorms.
Unfortunately, the grounds aren't just crawling with cats...
...an ancient evil lurks on campus, and only the combined efforts of student and feline can hold them at bay...
1
CAT PARADISE
YUJI IWAHARA
IN STORES NOW!
OLDER TEEN
OT
Yen Press
Cat Paradise © Yuji Iwahara / AKITASHOTEN

PANDORA HEARTS ❸

JUN MOCHIZUKI

Translation: Tomo Kimura • Lettering: Alexis Eckerman

PANDORA HEARTS Vol. 3 © 2007 Jun Mochizuki / **SQUARE ENIX CO.,
LTD.** All rights reserved. First published in Japan in 2007 by **SQUARE
ENIX CO., LTD.** English translation rights arranged with **SQUARE ENIX
CO., LTD.** and Hachette Book Group through Tuttle-Mori Agency, Inc.
Translation © 2010 by SQUARE ENIX CO., LTD.

Yen Press
Hachette Book Group
237 Park Avenue, New York, NY 10017

www.HachetteBookGroup.com
www.YenPress.com

Yen Press is an imprint of Hachette Book Group, Inc. The Yen Press name
and logo are trademarks of Hachette Book Group, Inc.

First Yen Press Edition: October 2010

ISBN: 978-0-316-07610-4

10 9 8 7 6 5 4 3 2 1

BVG

Printed in the United States of America